Media, Democracy and European Culture

Media, Democracy and European Culture

Ib Bondebjerg and Peter Madsen

intellect Bristol, UK / Chicago, USA

First Published in the UK in 2008 by
Intellect Books, The Mill, Parnall Road, Fishponds, Bristol, BS16 3JG, UK

First published in the USA in 2008 by
Intellect Books, The University of Chicago Press, 1427 E. 60th Street, Chicago,
IL 60637, USA

A catalogue record for this book is available from the British Library.

Cover Design: Gabriel Solomons
Copy Editor: Rebecca Vaughan-Williams
Typesetting: Mac Style, Beverley, E. Yorkshire

ISBN 978-1-84150-247-2

Printed and bound by Gutenberg Press, Malta.

CONTENTS

ACKNOWLEDGEMENTS

The starting point for this book was a large international conference at the University of Copenhagen in the fall of 2006. For three days senior researchers and Ph.D scholars from all over Europe discussed topics related to media, democracy, the public sphere and European culture. The conference was sponsored by the research priority area *Europe in Transition* (director, Professor Morten Kelstrup, see http://www.ku.dk/priority/europe/index.asp) and the local host was the research theme *Media, Democracy and European Cultured* (see http://www.medec.ku.dk) coordinated by Ib Bondebjerg and supported by the research priority area. The editors of this book want to thank Morten Kelstrup and the research priority area for supporting the conference and following publication. Also thanks to Rector and Pro-Rector for the University of Copenhagen for establishing this important interdisciplinary research project on Europe.

There is no doubt that research on Europe is on the rise in many new centres for European research globally. In Denmark no less than three new centres for European studies have been formed recently: Centre for European Politics (CEP, http://www.cep.polsci.ku.dk/english), Centre for Modern European Studies (CEMES, http://www.cemes.ku.dk) and Centre for European Constitutionalization (CEC, http://www.jur.ku.dk/cec). The three centres have their focus on political science, humanities and law and specialization in European studies is also of course important and necessary. But we also need interdisciplinary dialogue and collaboration.

This book is a result of such interdisciplinary research as the conference that started it. Political science, humanities, media studies, law and sociology are among the disciplines covered. The editors want to thank all participants in the conference and the eighteen authors from England, Finland, Denmark, Germany, Greece, Italy, the Netherland, Norway, Scotland, Sweden and Turkey for making this a truly interdisciplinary and European volume.

Ib Bondebjerg and Peter Madsen
Copenhagen, May 20 2008

Notes on Contributors

Bek, Mine Gencel is assistant professor since 2004 at Ankara University, Faculty of Communication, Turkey. She has a Ph.D from Loughborough University, UK, with a study of the Turkish press. She has published articles on tabloidization of news, on Turkish media and journalism and on EU coverage in the media. She has recently co-edited *Communication Policies in the European Union and Turkey: Market Regulation, Access and Diversity* (2005).

Bondebjerg, Ib is professor at the Department of Media, Cognition and Communication, Section of Film and Media Studies, University of Copenhagen, and director of the *Centre for Modern European Studies* (CEMES). From 2000 to 2004 he was – together with professor Peter Golding – the co-director of the European research project *Changing Media – Changing Europe* and from 2002–04 director of the national research project *Media and Democracy in the Network Society*. He was chairman of the Danish Research Councils 1994–97, member of the Standing Committee for the Humanities, European Science Foundation and chairman of The Danish Film Institute 1997–2000. He is editor in chief of the international journal *Northern Lights: Film and Media Studies Yearbook*. His most recent books in English are *Moving Images, Culture and the Mind* (2000), *The Danish Directors: Dialogues on a Contemporary National Cinema* (2002, with Mette Hjort) and *European Culture and the Media* (2004, with Peter Golding).

Collins, Richard is professor of Media Studies, Open University, UK. He is author of several books and articles on the media and the EU including *Broadcasting and Audiovisual Policy in the European Single Market* (1994), *From Satellite to Single Market: New Communication Technology and European Public Service Television* (1998) and *Media and Identity in Contemporary Europe: Consequences of Global Convergence* (2002). In 2005–06 he was specialist advisor to the UK Parliament's House of Lords' Select Committee on the BBC Charter Review and in 2006–07 was senior research fellow at the Annenberg Centre for Communication, University of Southern California, Los Angeles.

Golding, Peter is professor of Sociology and pro-vice-chancellor for research, Loughborough University, UK. He was co-director of the research project *Changing Media – Changing Europe* (2000–04) and he is editor of the *European Journal of Communication* and chair of the European Sociological Association Media Research network. He has co-edited *European Media Culture and the Media* (2004) and he has wide international publication on media, political communication and media and Europe.

Gripsrud, Jostein is professor at the Department of Information Science and Media Studies, University of Bergen, Norway. He is an expert on the relations between media, culture and society and has published extensively on the history and social significance of literature, theatre, film, television, journalism and related theoretical and political issues. His most recent book in English, *Understanding Media Culture* (2002) has been translated into several languages. From 2000–04 he was team leader and member of the Core Steering Group in the research project *Changing Media – Changing Europe*, funded by the European Science Foundation. He is presently leader of the internationally networked research group DigiCult which organizes research activities on the digitization of media and its effect on culture and democracy.

Hauswedell, Tessa is a Ph.D scholar at the Institute of European Cultural Identity Studies, University of St Andrews, Scotland. She has a BA in English Literature, Queen Mary University, London and an MA in Comparative Literature, University College London. From 2002–04 she was managing contents editor of the netmagazine and network of European cultural journals *Eurozine* in Vienna.

Hellgren, Zenia is a Ph.D scholar in Sociology at Stockholm University. She specializes in migration, ethnic studies and political theory. Her dissertation *Voices of the Others: Immigrant Struggles over Borders, Boundaries and Social Membership in Multiethnic Europe* focuses on political claims-making among immigrants in Sweden and Spain. She has co-edited a number of anthologies and published several articles related to the project, most recently 'Los límites de la solidaridad: Sin papeles y niños refugiados apáticos en la sociedad de bienestar sueca', in the anthology *La lucha de los 'Sin papeles' y la extensión de la ciudadanía: una perspectiva global*, eds Liliana Suárez Navaz, Raquel Macià and Angela Moreno (2007). She also participated in the EU project CIVGOV (about organized civil society) and wrote the report *Overcoming the Discrepancy between EU Anti-discrimination Directives and Persisting Discrimination at the National Level* (2005).

Hoffmann, Julia studied Communication Science and International Relations (M.Sc., 2005, *cum laude*) at the Institute of Journalism and Communication Science in Hanover (Germany), Hong Kong University (China) and the University of Amsterdam (The Netherlands). She earned her second degree in International and European Law at the Amsterdam Law School (LL.M., 2007, *cum laude*). Since 2003 she has been working as a research and teaching assistant at the Communication Science Department of the University of Amsterdam, which she joined as a lecturer in August 2006 teaching courses on international communication, globalization, conflict and human rights. Currently, she is working on her Ph.D dissertation on the role of communication rights in the democratization process of the European Union.

Kaitatzi-Whitlock, Sophia, is assistant professor at the Department of Journalism and Mass Communication at the Aristotle University of Thessaloniki, Greece. She has a Ph.D in communication from the University of Westminster, UK, and she has written and published extensively in academic journals and publications, on European audiovisual policy-making, political communication, the political economy of the media as well as on new media and technology policy. Her first book, *The Domain of Information*, was published in Greek (2003), while her latest international book publication is: *Europe's Political Communication Deficit* (2005). She was vice-chair (2001–04) of the COST-A20 research programme on: 'The Impact of the Internet on Mass Media in Europe'. She is currently the chair of the Political Communication section of European Communication Research and Education Association (ECREA) and she is also a member of the International Council of IAMCR. Her current research interests include democracy theory, power relations and the media, and the interlocking between communicative and political practices within the new media domains.

Kevin, Deirdre is a media consultant in Germany and conducts media research on political communication, the development of a European public sphere, and media policy and media ownership issues. She previously worked at the European Institute for the Media in Düsseldorf and the Stirling Media Research Institute in Scotland. Clients include the European Cultural Foundation, the German broadcaster WDR, the European Parliament, the European Platform of Regulatory Authorities, the Broadcasting Commission of Ireland, the Broadcasting Regulation and Cultural Diversity Network, the European Audiovisual Observatory and the Media Division of the Council of Europe. She has edited *Trends in Communication*, and was scientific editor of the *AIM* project with the Dortmund based Erich-Brost Institute. Publications include the comparative study on media coverage of the EU: *Europe in the Media: A Comparison of Reporting, Representation and Rhetoric in National Media Systems in Europe* (2003).

Madsen, Peter professor of comparative literature since 1979, Department of Arts and Culture, University of Copenhagen. Has authored or edited about 100 publications covering a wide range of subjects from textual analysis and literary theory to questions bordering on social sciences, among the more recent ones: *The Urban Life World: Formation, Perception, Representation*, ed. with R. Plunz, Introduction (London: Routledge, 2002); 'World Literature and World Thoughts: Brandes/Auerbach', in C. Prendegast (ed.), *Debating World Literatures*, pp. 54–75 (London: Verso, 2004); 'Elsie', in Franco Moretti (ed.): *The Novel 1–2* (Princeton: Princeton University Press, 2006); and 'Totalitarisme – ideologisk eller videnskabeligt begreb', in Mahdi, Schanz, Thorup (eds), *Totalitarisme – venskab/fjendskab* (Arhus: Århus Universitetsforlag, 2007). He is principal investigator in a collective research project supported by the Danish Research Council for the Humanities: Islam in European Literature (2008–10).

Mancini, Paolo is professor at the Department of Sociology at the University of Perugia, Italy. His major publications include: *Videopolitica: Telegiornali in Italia e in USA* (1985), *Come vincere le elezioni* (1988), *Sussurri e grida dalle Camere* (1994), *Politics, Media and Modern Democracy* with David Swanson (1996), *Manuale di comunicazione politica* (1996), *Il sistema fragile* (2000). With Dan Hallin he has published *Comparing Media Systems* (2004). This book got the Goldsmith Award from Harvard University, the 2005 Diamond Anniversary

Book Award from National Association Communication and the 2006 ICA award. His articles have appeared in *Theory and Society, European Journal of Communication, Communication, Journal of Communication* and in a number of English anthologies.

Moe, Hallvard is a Ph.D scholar at the Department of Information Science and Media Studies, University of Bergen, Norway. His doctorial dissertation is a comparative policy study of European public broadcasters facing new media platforms. His research interests include television studies, media, cultural and ICT-policy and democratic theory. For more information, see http://www.uib.no/people/smkhm.

Nieminen, Hannu is professor of media policy and director of the Communication Research Centre, Department of Communication, University of Helsinki, Finland. His research interests include media and democracy and theories of the public sphere. His publications include *Democracy and Communication: Habermas, Williams, and the British Case* (1997), *Hegemony and the Public Sphere* (2000), and *People Stood Apart: the Constitution of the National Public Sphere in Finland 1809–1917* (2006, in Finnish).

Tjernström, Vanni is associate professor, Media and Communication, University of Kalmar, Sweden. She earned her BA in Sociology and her MA in Mass Communications at the University of Stockholm, and her Ph.D. in Media Studies at the University of Umeå, Sweden. Before returning to academic life, she has pursued a career as a press officer/spokesperson in the City of Stockholm, in the Swedish Parliament and the Nordic Council. Her research interests include comparative Nordic research, diversity of Swedish television news and research on the media as sources for political work in the Parliament. She has published several comparative studies of the coverage of EU themes in Scandinavian and European media, among them her dissertation *Europa norrifrån: En nordisk komparativ studie av europeisk politisk kommunikation* ('Europe in a Nordic Perspective: A Nordic, Comparative Study of European Political Communication', 2001).

Trenz, Hans-Jörg is research professor at ARENA, Centre for European Studies, University of Oslo, Norway. He was former researcher at Münchner Projektgruppe für Sozialforschung and at Humboldt University Berlin where he got his Habilitation in 2004. Major publications include: 'The EU's Fledgling Society: From Deafening Silence to Critical Voice in European Constitution Making, *Journal of Civil Society* 3 (together with John Erik Fossum); *Europa in den Medien: Das europaeische Integrationsprojekt im Spiegel nationaler Oeffentlichkeit* (Frankfurt aM: Campus, 2005); 'Media Coverage on European Governance. Testing the Performance of National Newspapers', *European Journal of Communication*, 19: 3, pp. 291–319, 2004.

Vetters, Regina has studied at the Free University Berlin (Germany) and Columbia University in New York (United States). Her Ph.D dissertation *Constitution + Convention = Public Sphere?* analysed the media coverage of the constitutional debate in Germany, France and Great Britain. In 2006/2007 she worked as a scientific assistant at the Humboldt University Berlin in the ESF-project *Building the EU's Social Constituency: Exploring the Dynamics of Public Claims-Making and Collective Representation in Europe.* As part of the Recon-Project she also stayed several months at ARENA, Centre for European Studies, University of Oslo. In addition to her academic interest in media she has also worked for different media outlets, e.g. as freelance foreign news editor at the news agency Reuters. Currently, she is an associate in a management consultancy.

Vreese, Claes H. de is professor and chair of Political Communication and scientific director of the Amsterdam School of Communications Research (ASCoR), Director of NESCoR, the Netherlands School of Communications Research and adjunct professor of Political Science and Journalism at the University of Southern Denmark. His research interests include comparative journalism research, the effects of news, public opinion and European integration, effects of information and campaigning on elections, referendums and direct democracy. He has published more than 35 articles in international peer-reviewed journals, including *Communication Research, Journalism Studies, Political Communication, International Journal of Public Opinion Research, European Journal of Communication, Journalism & Mass Communication Quarterly, Mass Communication & Society*, and *European Journal of Political Research*. For more information, see http://www.claesdevreese.com.

Ørsten, Mark is associate professor, Ph.D Department of Communication, Journalism and Computer Science, Roskilde University. His Ph.D *Transnational Political Journalism* is a study of how the Danish media covered the European Union from 1991–2001. Mark Ørsten has written articles on the media and Europe for the European Commission's newsletter and for a white book on European journalism from the Danish association of journalists. His most recent research also includes a study of the Danish media's coverage of the war against Iraq, the coverage of the 2004 election to the European Parliament and a study of Danish environmental journalism from 1997 to 2003. He is also the author of three crime novels. He is head of studies at *Journalism* and head of the research group 'Communication, Journalism and Social Change'. He has participated in two major research projects: *MODINET – Media and Democracy in the Network Society* (2002–05) and *PRO-MEDIA: Production, Representation and Organisation of Business News* (2005–).

Introduction

Ib Bondebjerg and Peter Madsen

The role of the public sphere has increasingly come to the fore in studies concerning the state of democracy in Europe. Similarly the role of culture in formations and transformations not only of personal but of political identities as well has attracted attention. It is the purpose of this book to bring these areas together in a comprehensive approach to media, culture and democracy with a view of the public sphere as a crucial mediating field. The contributions represent cutting-edge research on Europe from a social, political, and cultural perspective and with equal focus on cultural and political dimensions of democracy. The role of the media, communication policy, the question of the way media construct and report on Europe, and the notion of a European public sphere are unifying themes for these articles. At the more specific level both success and problems of the European integration project and the relations between nation states, Europeanization and globalization in a broader sense are crucial to the book.

It is evident from all the articles that we cannot speak of one European public sphere or a common European culture and identity. Yet the research behind this book and a number of other research publications, for instance *The European Union and the Public Sphere* (Fossum and Schlesinger 2007), point to the fact that a still closer Europeanization does influence the national public spheres and the rich diversity of national, regional and otherwise diverse culture in Europe. The role of the public sphere in democratic processes is not only a question of a European public sphere, but also a question of the character of the public spheres in the national context. Politics concerning media is a controversial, yet crucial democratic issue – at the national level as well as at the level of EU. The development of conglomerates, concentrations of ownership and political control of public media (with Berlusconi's position in the Italian media system as the most conspicuous example) calls for not only thorough research but normative considerations as well.

In the plethora of studies of the development of modern European integration there is too often a lack of focus on media and communication, and even more a strong cultural dimension in European studies is rare. The aim of this volume is to go against these tendencies by an integration of the media dimension and the cultural dimension and a combination of approaches from the humanities and the social sciences. If we want to understand how modern political communication operates and how democracies function there is no way around the media dimension from print to online communication. There is a long tradition for studies of national media, but studies of the role and impact of globalization and Europeanization on the nation states are far less developed and most often in the form of important but restricted empirical comparative studies of EU coverage in print media and occasionally also TV (see for instance Kevin (2003), de Vreese (2003), Ørsten (2005) and Tjernström (2001)).

Comparative studies of the political media coverage of EU matters are on the rise, but research into a broader cultural dimension in European studies is still very limited. The EU was started primarily as an economic project, but has since developed into one of the most ambitious political integration projects in transnational democracy. Since the Maastricht Treaty of 1992 the EU has developed a cultural dimension and a still stronger cultural policy. Culture and cultural policy is thus very much at the centre of the EU project. Both for this reason, but also in a much broader and deeper sense, the cultural dimension is far too important for everyday life and for the integration process in Europe to be left in the periphery of the research agenda. An integration of the dimensions of media and culture should be developed in a systematic way, with a view of the multiple dimensions of culture: not only culture understood as art, literature, movies, ideas, etc., but also culture as everyday life, norms and values, cultural institutions. In this perspective academic oppositions between studies in 'high' culture and 'popular' culture should be left behind.

The field of visual culture can illustrate some of the dimensions. In 2006 the Think Tank on European Film Policy was founded in Copenhagen with the now former CEO of the Danish Film Institute, Henning Camre, as the leading figure. The founding of this transnational think tank is a sign that producers, directors and other film people experience a growing need to think of European film culture as a more integrated phenomenon. But the official report from the conference with empirical data (see http://www.filmthinktank.org) shows how little we seem to care about films from other European countries and the debates at the conference confirmed the stereotype of national representatives of European cinema. They were nationals first, and Europeans – reluctantly – second and they performed completely according to the expected stereotypes. The general will to create a European cinematic space and transnational culture was there, no doubt, but as soon as it came to practical initiatives and policies it was Italians against the French, against the Germans, etc. They could unite in a demonizing of the United States as the suppressing and dominant other and would tend to blame it all on the Americans. But the problems of European culture are the problems of Europe, and we can blame nobody but ourselves.

These examples taken from the cultural sphere underscores the problems with European integration as such, with transnational democracy, a European public sphere and the strong role of the national in both media, culture and politics. But when we think about how important cultural narratives like novels, films and TV series are for the construction of imagined communities in Benedict Anderson's sense (Anderson 1983) the importance of an integration of the cultural dimension in future European studies becomes obvious. Historical TV series possess an incredible power in shaping cultural and social identities, yet in most European countries the production of visual fiction for film and television is still very much a national territory and even the export and distribution of national products between the European nations is much too limited. The *Eurofiction Project* (Buonanno 2000) demonstrated some of the trends in this field by comparative studies of fictional programming on TV and selected genre studies, and the forthcoming *European Television History* (Bignell and Frickers 2008) is an important contribution to comparative European media and cultural studies. Here we do not get a country by country history but a thematic history with comparative examples from different TV cultures.

Media, power, democracy and the public sphere

This first part of the book focuses on the role of media in sustaining and developing democracy, a democratic dialogue and in fulfilling the role of media as the critical watchdog of the political system and other powerful players on the European scene. It offers both theoretical discussions of the political economy of the media and the question of the public sphere in a European perspective and more concrete empirical studies of media and the EU system. The democratic deficit in the European Union is discussed in relation to the political structure and the power structure of the media sector in Sophia Kaitatzi-Whitlock's article. Two articles by Hannu Nieminen and Hans-Jörg Trenz take up both the theoretical and analytical discussion of a European public sphere and both of them present new theories and concepts of how this public sphere is developing not as a unified sphere but as a network of sub-spheres and segmented publics. Hans-Jörg Trenz takes this discussion further by focusing more directly and in a more detailed fashion on the role of media in the formation of a European public sphere and the role media plays in the process of democratization, Europeanization and integration in the EU.

In Deirdre Kevin's article the question of media policy and regulation is taken into the discussion of media pluralism and the democratic function of a European public sphere and the article gives valuable information on EU media policy and legislation. Finally Paolo Mancini illustrates the links between media ownership, political structure and democracy in a case study of the Italian media situation. The Berlusconi case is not just an isolated Italian phenomenon, but illustrates the European dilemma in general and the uneasy balance between commercialism, private control over media and independent journalism and democracy.

Journalism and the europeanization of the public sphere

The second part of the book focuses on case studies of how EU and European themes are reported in national media from several comparative European studies. But these empirical studies of EU media coverage are integrated in a more general and theoretical discussion of democracy, politics and national identity as well as the development of a European public sphere and the different forms of Europeanization of the national public spheres. In his article Peter Golding draws on a number of national and comparative European studies taking them to a higher level of discussion with focus on the political economy of news journalism in different types of media and the role of news for the development of a transnational democracy.

The four following articles present recent comparative, empirical studies and analyse what they tell us about the degree of Europeanization of the media and a common agenda or public sphere. Claes de Vreese's discussion is based on a large scale study of the television coverage of the EU in 25 countries, Mark Ørsten's is based on a study of the development of the Danish EU coverage over time. This study is particularly interesting because Denmark in many other studies stands out as very 'Europeanized' compared to other countries. Regina Vetters reports and discusses the debate on the European constitution in British, German, French, Swiss and American newspapers and demonstrates considerable national differences. Finally Vanni Tjernström bases her article on several comparative studies of EU coverage in Scandinavian Newspapers between 1992 and 2005. In this chapter too the results point to different kinds of national cultures.

Media, culture and democracy

In the third part of the book focus shifts to the often forgotten dimension of democracy and the public sphere: the cultural dimension, understood not only as media fictions, literature, art and music, but as the broader concept of everyday culture as well. Focus on this area is particularly relevant since culture and cultural policy has been an important new policy area of the EU since 1992, and culture in the EU is often linked to questions of a European identity and the need for a deeper integration, at the cultural level too. In his article Jostein Gripsrud underscores the political importance of culture and its function in democracies as a central resource for citizenship. Referring to i.e. the control of culture in authoritarian societies he argues for the inclusion of the cultural sphere in discussions of a European public sphere and democracy. Ib Bondebjerg continues along those lines but focuses more directly on the role of media fictions (film and TV) as narratives creating cultural identities. He looks at the EU film policy and the circulation of films in Europe, not least the relation between national films, European films and American films, and he argues that there is no essential European cultural identity, just as there is not one European public sphere, but that a Europeanization of the audio-visual, European space of different national cultures is beginning to develop.

In Tessa Hauswedell's article a form of media almost never mentioned, the transnational European cultural journals, are analysed. These print based and eletronically distributed journals can be seen as avant-garde in the writing and developing of a new European identity and communicative space, although only for a cosmopolitan elite. The question of identity and European citizenship in a multi-ethnic and multicultural society is discussed in Zenia Hellgren's article. Her arguments are based on a concrete study of how a political and collective identity is being formed by immigrants in Sweden and Spain. Finally, Peter Madsen looks into the important role of intellectuals in the formation of political and cultural visions of the public sphere. In his study he focuses on the European tradition and the way intellectuals have influenced and created media and cultural institutions, from the nineteenth century's newspapers and journals through to modern electronic media. Special attention is given to the creation of quality newpapers during recent decades.

Media and communication policy in Europe

The last part of the book focuses on media policy in a European context. Richard Collins takes a historical turn in his analysis of the media policy in the EU from the early 1980s until today. It is a very critical account that points to inconsistencies and misrecognitions. But Collins also points to more basic problems with the policy and its relation to either a 'communal' or a more 'associative' understanding of European integration. Hallvard Moe likewise deals with public service television, but this time he looks into the emerging and future digital communication environment and its influence on public service television and Internet-based platforms and services, and he also analyses the EU standpoint in this area, which may be seen as a threat to public service broadcasting.

The two last articles take up other aspects of media policy. Mine Gencel Bek systematically analyses the effect of EU membership negotiations on the Turkish media culture. In general this is a story of a positive effect leading to more media pluralism, journalistic freedom and democratic debate. But the article also point to potential dangers in this process. Finally, Julia Hoffmann looks at communication rights and the EU Commission's White Paper on a European Communication Policy in the contexts of the development of further integration and a European citizenship. This far-reaching rhetoric is discussed in relation to the reality of the European democracy.

References

Anderson, Benedict (1983), *Imagined Communities: Reflections on the Origin and Spread of Nationalism*. London: Verso.

Bignell, Jonathan and Andreas Frickers (2008, forthcoming), *European Television History*. London: Blackwell.

Buonanno, Milly (ed.) (2000), *Continuity and Change: Television Fiction in Europe*. Luton: University of Luton Press.

De Vreese, Claes (2003), *Framing Europe: Television News and European Integration*. Amsterdam: Aksant.

Fossum, John Erik and Philip Schlesinger (eds) (2007). *The European Union and the Public Sphere: A Communicative Space in the Making?* London: Routledge.

Kevin, Deirdre (2003), *Europe in the Media: A Comparison of Reporting, Representation and Rhetoric in National Media Systems in Europe*. Mahwah: Lawrence Erlbaum.

Tjernström, Vanni (2001), *Europa norrifrån: En nordisk komparativ studie av europeisk politisk kommunikation* ('Europe in a Nordic Perspective: A Nordic, Comparative Study of European Political Communication'). Ph.D Dissertation, Umeå University.

Ørsten, Mark (2005), *Transnational Politisk Journalistik* ('Transnational Political Journalism'). Ph.D Dissertation, Roskilde Universitetsforlag.

PART ONE: MEDIA, POWER, DEMOCRACY AND THE PUBLIC SPHERE

1

THE POLITICAL ECONOMY OF THE MEDIA AT THE ROOT OF THE EU'S DEMOCRACY DEFICIT

Sophia Kaitatzi-Whitlock

Abstract

This study looks how the EU, by handing over control of the media to business interests, did irreparable damage to its own political communication with its citizens. It looks at the mutual influences and relations between the EU 'Democracy Deficit', politics – both the national and supra-national and the political economy of communications. It holds that both the democracy deficit and the political communications deficit have been created and sustained by a political economy in communications which produces the commodification and disempowerment of citizens, the depoliticization of power relations and the incapacitation of policy processes which have attempted to produce significant changes. The political economy framework of communications which has been put in place offers no redemption from either of these notorious deficits while severely undermining political credibility and a democratic politics.

Keywords

democracy deficit, political communication deficit, citizen commodification, de-politicization, self-regulating media market system, de-commodification

Establishing structures for political and communicative subjugation

'A democracy without democrats is an internal and external danger' Hermann Müller, Chancellor of the Weimar Republic, 1930 (in Mazower 1998).

Since the establishment of EU citizenship by the Treaty of the European Union (TEU, Maastricht, 1992), EU citizens have been afflicted by a *political communication deficit*. In the transition from the national to the supra-national level of politics, citizens of EU member states have been losing out on transparency, accountability and access to political information. The supra-national constellation of the EU now suffers from a systemic crisis of legitimacy, linked directly with the political economy of communications. Nonetheless, the EU can neither confront the crisis nor escape from it. But how long can such a democratic deficit last before corroding the democratic system altogether?

The study investigates why the EC/EU *self-regulating media market system* favours the pathology of concentration of ownership, leading to media baronies and to *de facto* unfair competition. Examined policies, and their impact, reveal a relentless control of policy agendas and outcomes by the most powerful market forces. The malaise of Europe's political communication deficit is the outcome of frustrated policy attempts or obstinate refusals to establish an inclusive, pan-European communications sphere. The long-term consequences of this economically profitable, but politically aberrant EU-style economism result in *de-politicization*, while the deficit in a common civic communication system is the key constitutive vector of the *democratic deficit*.

The 1989 Television without Frontiers Directive (TWFD) was the result of bitter compromises between member states and competing market forces. A critical assessment of the TWFD policy process exposes its catalytic effects on the dual strategic shift: first, from the political to the commercial control of the media and secondly, from the national to the supra-national control of the policy agenda. The foundation of the EC/EU communications policy was the 1984 Green Paper *Television without Frontiers* (GPTWF) which launched structural transmutations in politics and culture. By transforming the role of electronic media, the TWFD dis-embedded politics and the role of citizens who became commodified. Thus, the GPTWF accomplished the crucial objectives of its policy mentors.

Setting up the strategic transmutation – the double shift

The exclusive emphasis of the TWFD on the economic role of communication converted it into a veritable trap. This choice was, legally, grounded on the relevant articles of the Treaty of the European Community (TEC).[1] Under the TEC 'the EC does not have the means to impose a cultural policy. It will, therefore, have to tackle the problem from an economic point of view' (Jacques Delors, quoted in Negrine and Papathanassopoulos 1990: 67). Given the conjuncture of urgent pressures for liberalization and deregulation in communications by global capital forces, the catalytic strategy of the Green Paper consisted in tackling this sector through the circumscribing framework of the EC, rather than through any proactive alternative. The Green Paper provided the discourse and the legal means for an EC-wide intervention in the audio-visual sector, thereby accommodating to extra-institutional global market demands (Venturelli 1998). European Court of Justice (ECJ) jurisprudence on interpreting key TEC Articles was mobilised in conjunction with the evocative power of 'integrationist' rhetoric and the 'pressing need' to develop global audiovisual industries.

The Green Paper bypassed constitutional caveats, notably concerning the imperative need for universally accessed political communication at a pan-European level. Thus, constitutive political prerequisites slipped off the agenda. But, if the EC discarded political communication, what kind of communications policy was it actually pursuing and for whom? The Green Paper (GPTWF) boldly expanded the scope for commodification by deregulating and reinforcing an already prevailing economism. Not accidentally, it was dubbed the 'flagship of the Single Market'.[2] In this vein, member states were asked to make unconditional concessions:

- on sovereignty
- on cultural self-determination
- on prerogatives to frame political spheres.

Conversely, opponent global capital free-marketeers got their gains without having to make concessions to political integration. As a corollary, the normally superordinate objectives of national communications and cultural orders soon became subordinate. The political naïveté of this approach became apparent after the GATS agreement of 1993.[3]

Allegedly, the GPTWF aimed, first, to demonstrate the importance of broadcasting for European integration; 'for the free democratic structure of the European Communities' and secondly to illustrate the significance of the TEC for those producing, broadcasting and re-transmitting audio-visual programmes and for those receiving such programmes (GPTWF 1984: 1)[4]. These objectives are mutually exclusive. The first addresses viewers as citizens, while the second treats them as consumers and as economic agents. But an unresolved tension exists between them. The first objective promoted the ideology of European integration, via broadcasting policy, which commanded enormous rhetorical power, but was legally groundless. Hence, comparatively, it is degraded to a vague *desideratum*.[5] Without constitutionally guaranteed rights at the EC/EU level, freedom of expression is void of any political commitments since the EC/EU could not undertake such responsibilities.

By contrast, the second objective, well grounded in the TEC, was pursued quickly and securely. Besides, the GPTWF conflated civil freedom of expression with that of movement of commercial services. This was arbitrary[6] as it not only blurred distinct categories of civil (human) rights with economic freedoms (of companies), but, further, encompassed mutually exclusive objectives. Commercial 'rights' could thus 'ride' on the vehicle of individual democratic freedom. Such conflicting media roles could only be organized if constitutionally guaranteed and functioning in separate zones, by distinct, strongly regulated, channels. Both advertising-free and advertising-funded channels could operate only under limited competition. The crucial problem is that advertising-funded channels sell packages of viewers, as commodities, to advertised industries (Mills 1956: 304–5; Smythe 1977). In multi-channel environments under intense competition for 'attention', the commodification of viewers constrains their role as citizens and results in de-politicization. But politics presupposes the role of citizens.

The EC failed to legally establish the first objective, or the compatibility between the two objectives in TWFD. Hence, the second objective prevailed. Its imperative and priority goal was to legitimate EC intervention in this, thus far, 'virgin' area and to transfer control of communications sectors to supra-national policy-centres, in order to thereby submit them to the exclusive control of 'self-regulated' markets. This entailed usurping the field of communications from politics and subjugating it to 'big capital' forces. So, the main battle was among economic and democratic political power.

Information was, henceforth, treated exclusively as a commodity, thereby subjecting this socio-politically strategic sector into an entirely different political economy *status*. Here, then, is the turning point for the triple transmutation of 1. the role of communication, 2. the role of individuals as commodities and consumers *versus* citizens, and 3. the role of the Political and of politics.[7] The internal hierarchy between the political and the economic role of communications was reshuffled and so was the balance of power between political and economic stakeholders.[8]

> 'From an economic angle, the establishment of a common market for broadcasting has implications by far transcending mass media. As an advertising medium, broadcasting organisations help to stimulate sales of goods and services in many branches of the economy...[Cross-frontier] broadcasting of advertising promotes cost savings and increases in efficiency. These economic aspects must not be overlooked, if from a cultural and social point of view, the role of broadcasting as a medium providing information, expression of opinion, education and entertainment is to be preserved' (GPTWF 1984: 37).

The circulation of broadcast signals and services shouldn't be impeded (Collins 1994).[9] The huge gains were anticipated by media barons, advertisers and the advertised. Public broadcasting was sacrificed to serve the goals of the economy by boosting consumerism. Thus, behind the ideology of 'transfrontierism' lurked a radical move towards inexorable commercialism. European 'transfrontierism' dawned with commercialisation and the commodification of citizens.[10] So despite the Community's legal incompetence to handle cultural issues, it triumphantly did so.[11] Only, rather than acquiring binding constitutional legitimacy in cultural affairs, Community decision-makers changed the fundamental nature of communications.

This strategic restructuring, called a 'minimum regulation approach', accomplished the 'double shift': the displacement of the field of communications from the national to the supra-national level, and its transferral from the control of political forces to commercial agencies. Ultimate control was thus devolved to the automatic pilot of the *self-regulating media market*: competition. So the Community's lack of legal competence in this area proved extremely expedient.

Commodification: the end of citizens' sovereignty

Up to 1989 the electronic media domains were largely free from the constraints and the corrosive effects of advertising and commercialism. An array of still un-commodified factors were values and ends in themselves. The immediate consequence of the TWFD was that all agents implicated in media and politics became commodified and intensely commercialized: first, individual citizens, secondly, politicians, thirdly, politics and public affairs and, fourthly, audio-visual contents, programming which until then was predominantly based on in-house production; fifthly, airtime on screen. By making advertising-funded channels mandatory, commercial propaganda instantly acquired a pivotal role as power broker and regulator.

In the new political economy of commodified electronic media:

- aggregates of individual viewers are sold by channels to advertised industries
- air-time, notably prime-time, is 'sold' by channels to advertisers
- programming is supplied to viewers by producers via channel rights-holders
- channel performance ratings are sold by ratings companies to advertisers and channels.

Under such premises, 'citizens' sovereignty' is jeopardized (Curran 2002: 205)

In spite of such a tumultuous overturning, not even minimal, counterbalancing 'must carry' rules of any political kind, were set in place. This remarkable omission was perfectly in line with the EC's economism and its conception of the media as a strategic economic instrument for commodification. So, at that conjuncture, the EC was the ideal tool for the onslaught of economistic transnationalization. Social responsibility or a politically proactive media policy (Gurevitch and Blumler 1990: 280; Stepp 1990: 186–201) was inconceivable. Cultural prerogatives were fiercely, yet ineffectively, advocated by nation-centric forces as certain politicians believed, naively, that they could rescue at a national level what was liberalized at the global level.[12]

The entire cycle of commercialized television and its astronomical turnovers are paid for by the end-users of advertised products as a percentage of product-prices. Consequently, in this political economy, the most exploited economic factors are individual viewers. More concretely, viewers are the object of invisible commercial transactions between channels and the advertised/advertisers. Apart from the role of 'commodity', viewers are also

- receivers, at their free will, of transmitted programmes
- viewers are notably, the 'captive audience' of commercial propaganda, but also
- they are the much-coveted consumers of actual products.

Given this multiple economic role, viewers constitute the most sought-after resource of this market; the 'apple of discord' of a fierce competition. On such a battleground, viewers need to be enticed and treated lightly. 'Indigestible' contents are removed; 'attractive', 'popular' programming frantically tries to engage the attention of commodified viewers. Hence, this economic role imposes a totally new division of values. 'Programme quality' becomes obsolete, while 'empowering news' or 'enlightening debates' become undesirable oddities. The goal is to boost the economy via consumerism, and augment channel profits.

Thus, the Directive had a number of regressive effects. In this new division of communication values, citizens' needs appear 'luxuries' since programmes catering for such needs would never become blockbusters. News and current affairs programmes are marginalized, drastically cut down or even removed as 'indigestible'. Along with other valuable cultural forms they fall out of screen visibility. Political programmes are metamorphosed and supplanted by the hybrid genres of 'infotainment' (Gurevitch and Blumler 1990: 276; Stepp 1990: 191; Meyer 2002) to suit profitability requirements.

Consequently, the multi-channel environment that sprung up in the post-1989 era capsized the previous regime and set its own terms for social and leisure life:

- The principle of universal access fell into redundancy.
- The principle of internal pluralism was supplanted by ostensible 'external pluralism'.
- The plethora of new TV channels had to compete for the same zones, which meant that broadcast menus became determined by the automatic pilot of ratings monitors, in line with the *self-regulating media market system*.

In this new configuration, viewers' ratings enterprises rose to strategic prominence. Yet despite their formidable power, holding monopolies in most countries, they remain unchecked. They calculate channel performance incessantly and due to their pivotal role in 'allocating' advertising revenue, they evolve crucially as content arbiters. They became the new censors. Not state, but market censors, holding the power of content agenda setting. Thus, 'programming policy' is eschewed by a blind 'automatic regulation' that eliminates entire genres: documentaries, childrens' programmes, debates, current affairs programmes. Conversely, new genres such as 'reality shows' have come to dominate prime time. A wave of populism has come to dominate television screens. The internal hierarchy of programming has thus been reshuffled on the grounds of market viability.

Lowest-common-denominator programming

The battle had always been fought for the single largest section of viewers to secure economies of scale. Two mutually reinforcing mechanisms operate in this process. The first involves the production of 'mass appeal', eye-catching, inevitably homogenized shows as 'mass-satisfaction' accrues only from bland programming. The superiority of sensationalist programmes in mass appeal defines prevalent blockbuster recipes and supply. Since all channels compete for the largest audiences, homogenized success-recipes are multiplied, jeopardizing 'external pluralism' and diversity.

The second mechanism operates when individual viewers select programmes. From this process, whether random or rational, evolves what media economists call lowest-common-denominator programming. Zappers spend much time searching for their ideal programme. Not finding that, viewers reduce their expectations and accommodate to watching shows of their second, third, etc. preference. Each time a viewer condescends to watch a 'least-bad' type of programme s/he is made, by the self-regulating media market system, to watch partly unacceptable contents. In this way s/he is aggregated to masses of fellow viewers in a similar situation. Paradoxical though it is, all those choosing a programme X, as their 'last choice', collectively raise that programme into a 'mass appealing success', moving it to the top of the ratings. 'Lowest-common-denominator programming' thus prevails, granting economies of scale. The total sum of those watching their second, third, etc. choice, cumulatively adds up to a huge number of viewers. This mechanism is called Hotelling's principle (Cave 1989; Peacock Report 1986).

Hence, in commercial audio-visual markets the most-watched programmes constitute the last, just watchable choices of masses of individual viewers. Conversely, although quality programmes gratify their viewers immediately, the *self-regulating media market system* penalizes them. Bottom of the list, 'minority' programmes are the first to be eliminated. TV-goods are price-marked, and their availability is conditional on the numbers of viewers they can fetch. Consequently, by compromising to watch a 'second-best' or a 'least bad' type of programme, viewers 'collude' with the media market system in deteriorating quality.

Given this subversive bias, the strategic question is: why should one accept that markets are the best mechanism to allocate such values?[13] Ostensibly, people consent to such 'logic' which prioritizes unacceptable or redundant information. If they do, it is only because they remain ignorant of policies and of the implications of these processes. Manipulation, through commercial propaganda and the economic exploitation of receivers (Gurevitch and Blumler 1990: 276; Lukes 2004) suffocate citizens as stakeholders in crucial political processes. How can empowering information ever prevail when it is pushed out by the *self-regulating media market system*?

Media baronies and oligarchy

Frustrated attempts, first, to legislate in defence of pluralism and, secondly, to establish a commonly controlled encoding/decoding encryption system for digital subscription services, belong to notorious policy battles of the 1990s which reveal oligarchic control of policy outcomes in Brussels.[14] As a consequence, policy processes on communications systematically ignore fundamental political *desiderata*. Political and communicative powerlessness is accentuated further by the concentration of ownership in the hands of a small number of media barons. This formidable concentration of power accruing in structural biases corrodes the right of citizens to information and particaption and has a paralyzing effect on independent governance.

The defeat over pluralism

Following the establishment of the 'European Audiovisual Space' (EAS) a wave of mergers and takeovers swept across the Union. From a neo-liberal perspective, these were strategically pursued goals. The TWFD unleashed this wave of mergers and the transnationalization of media ownership which made company conduct inscrutable. The 'growth dimension' of this market contributed to the rate of concentration being 'faster in the media sector than in the rest of the economy' (COM(92)480: 27). Farsighted observers advocated, already in the 1980s, that the TWFD comprise pluralism safeguards against concentration.[15]

Yet the Commission deliberately excluded anti-concentration measures from the GPTWF of 1984. Corporate moves and relations between leading politicians with media moguls, suggest hidden agendas. The GPTWF was drafted by Lord Cockfield, Margaret Thatcher's appointee Commissioner, under the presidency of Gaston Thorn, Luxemburg's ex-premier. Thorn maintained partisan relations both with Compagnie Luxembourgoise de Télédiffusion (CLT) and with ASTRA and was later both chairman of CLT and a founding member of the Association of Commercial Television (ACT) (Kaitatzi-Whitlock 1996).[16] Neo-liberals, such as Silvio Berlusconi, Rupert Murdoch, Margaret Thatcher, Leo Kirche, Martin Bertelsmann and Helmut Kohl, all had enormous stakes at risk, should the TWFD encompass anti-concentration measures right from the start, in 1989:

> L'alliance entre Leo Kirche et Silvio Berlusconi forme 'un réseau international difficilement controlable...Silvio Berlusconi servirait-il de prête-nom à Leo Kirche dans DSF (ex-Telefünf), et Leo Kirche, en échange, servirait-il le prête-nom de Silvio Berlusconi dans Telepiu? En clair, Leo Kirche, ami du chancelier Kohl, et Silvio Berlusconi auraient-ils ainsi contourné les lois contre la concentration audiovisuelle, chacun dans son pays? (Rouard 1994).

United Kingdom, Italian, Luxemburger or German national champions could never have conquered global market shares, unless EC competition provisions were deregulated. Control had to be transferred to commercial forces and information flows be subjugated to their interests.

In view of the seemingly inexorable trend towards concentration, the European Parliament (EP) campaigned for a specific Directive on pluralism and control of concentration, which was strongly endorsed by the great majority of stakeholders.[17] Medium-sized companies and all professional organizations, urged for a media-specific legislation to defend pluralism and diversity and combat concentration.

The implicit conflict of interests concerned the distribution of power (economic and persuasive-political) between those claiming private control over the media and those claiming the field of communications for democratic politics and the public interest. But the controversy raged also between unequal market players, notably medium-sized companies and mega-conglomerates, thereby foregrounding the issue of economic democracy. Nevertheless, the EP's initiative to safeguard pluralism was thwarted. In spite of Article F and Article 128 of the Treaty of the European Union, the Commission, as usual, defined pluralism as falling outside its sphere of competence, thereby restricting the scope of putative intervention to competition and 'freedom of establishment' issues.

The Council Regulation of 1989, on the control of concentrations between undertakings, concerns such practices generally and their impact on competition.[18] Member states cannot apply their relevant legislation to concentrations with a Community dimension (EEC, 4064/89). Putatively, they could protect other values, such as public security, plurality of the media and prudential rules (Druesne and Kremlis 1990: 80). But the Commission's derogation on the Greek Constitution, in 2005, leaves such options as dubious counterfactuals. A grey legal area was created, ostensibly covered by subsidiarity: disaffected 'receiving' countries might a *posteriori* ban infringing transfrontier emissions from other EAS states by taking legal action to protect their rights.

In this way, the EC/EU effaced once again the democratic-political role of the media. As usual, the Commission invited stakeholders to three consecutive consultations, yet eventually, it patently ignored their pro-action verdict. Rather than safeguarding pluralism by a timely regulation, the EC/EU furnished a framework for the *de facto* deregulation of the Political. Consequently, the insuperable problem in the political economy of the EU consists in entrenching this conflict of interests.

This stance was motivated by the allegation that 'by global standards European media companies tend to be small and fragmented'. They, therefore, 'needed' enlargement via take-overs in new markets and wider investment opportunities 'to face up to American and Japanese competition' (Rawlings 1994: 355). Consequently, the twin ideologies of transfrontierism and of company gigantism for global competition legitimated the spectacular mergers.[19] For these players, the fact that, politically, this is a *sui generis* market, indispensable to democratic politics, makes no sense. They seek economic power compounded by political power, as this was crystallized, extremely, in the case of Berlusconi's Italy. Member states with no audio-visual export industries wished to avert media concentration, notably threats to political power, via a policy on pluralism. Yet, they lacked political muscle. The Commission:

- deteriorated pluralism
- disadvantaged small- and medium-sized enterprises, and cultural/linguistic areas
- actively favoured concentration and anti-competitive trends
- refocused the debate in the direction of further deregulation and loss of regional control by prioritizing Internal Market objectives of market access in fields of political/cultural specificity.

Although the need for urgent action against media concentration was established, indisputably, in the triple consultation process, the Commission refused to proceed to a policy proposal and to prevent monopoly control on opinion-forming. Pluralism and freedom of information were sacrificed to 'Eurochampions' for global games. Hence, the EC's weak intergovernmental decision-making structure suits perfectly powerful hegemonic market forces with transcontinental alliances. Such developments vindicate Keohane and Hoffmann's assessment that certain 'governments sought to use Europe to promote deregulation' (1991: 21). The battle for pluralism and against concentration of media ownership was nothing less than a battle to regain political control of communications policy and, thereby, of politics itself. This defeat hampered both political communication and the potential to develop democratic politics in the EU. The extreme phenomenon of 'Berlusconism' in Italy was just the most embarrassing case.[20] Poor statesmanship, but also the supra-national nature of this regime, combined with relentless corporate pressure succeeded in wrecking this policy initiative (Kaitatzi-Whitlock 1996 and 2005; Sarikakis 2004: 154–5).

After five years of policy elaborations the objective of pluralism was frustrated. By shifting the policy terms the Commission buried this crucial issue.[21] Its approach exposed inconsistencies and a problematic 'supra-nationalism' proving the Union, once again, a democratically deficient regime.[22]

Encrypting commodified information

A considerable body of democracy and media theory stresses the need for the independence of the media both from state and corporate control (Gurevitch and Blumler 1990; Stepp 1990; Keane 1991; Dahlgren 1995; Golding and Murdock 1987; Garnham 1990; Venturelli 1998). The dogma of the Commission, however, proves contrary to such theory. The GPTWF expressly praised the importance of independence of information, yet only from state control. Not only did it blatantly ignore market control, but it actually favoured it.

Pay-TV services presuppose economically vigorous viewers. Such services rely on digital ability to encode and decode messages, and on control of destination flows. Encryption systems establish artificial gateways of access at two key points along the supply chain. The first, 'upper gateway', at the sender level, concerns service provision which enables information suppliers to encode and pass on services down to the second passage, and so, to receivers. The second, 'lower gateway', is accessed by paying viewers, via a decoding electronic device (set-top box).

If the interests of all involved stakeholders will be safeguarded, it is imperative that both gateways are regulated. Yet, the EC/EU proved incapable of safeguarding fair play at the 'upper gateway' and the internal relation between competing suppliers. Because of conferring monopoly powers, this impacts negatively also on end-users of the 'lower gate', but crucially also, on the general interest (Kaitatzi-Whitlock 1998). The 'lower gateway' settles only one set of relations. Pay services exist by erecting social divisions between those who can and those who cannot afford them, and it might seem that such policies concern only pay-services 'consumers'. But this is misleading, as such policies impact, culturally and materially, also on all those who can neither afford nor will ever demand pay services.

The fact that a critical mass of audience is indispensable for the financial viability of conventional channels is one aspect of this problem. Similarly, a critical mass of diverse programming is important. So, the fiercest competition is about the scarce resource of 'watching attention'. Thus, buying up copyrights in bulk by monopoly players threatens generalist channels. Moreover, the vertical concentration of Murdoch-owned channels accentuated controversies, as they provided pay-services while Nethold, a company of which he is a shareholder, was the proprietor of the eventually winning encryption system: *SimulCrypt*.

A group of market forces emerged in the early 1990s in a decision-making role on public policy matters. The Digital Video Broadcasting (DVB) Group, a consortium of market forces and the EBU, was invited to propose the standard device-mechanism for encoded TV services: i.e. an encryption system. The objective was to decide within the consortium the digital encryption system that would subsequently be adopted by the EU. Namely, the EU Council 'experimented' by assigning policy mandates to market forces for them to 'self-regulate'. But, this amounted to privatizing public policy-making prerogatives.

As things developed the experiment of 'self-regulation' failed patently due to in-fighting between consortium partners. Conflict erupted notably between the proprietary system owners (Murdoch, Rousselet) and proponents of the open encryption system *Multicrypt* (EBU) (ibid.). This failure brought politicians back to their task of adopting the encryption system. Yet, quite unexpectedly, they rejected the publicly and commonly run *MultiCrypt* for the proprietary system. The Directive on digital subscription television services (1995), thus, allocated control of conditional access services[23] to Murdoch and Rousselet's *SimulCrypt*, granting them significant economic advantages but also power over the supply and the traffic of symbolic goods. The quick collapse of ITV-Digital in the UK is proof of a tremendous anti-competition policy bias, in favour of the same media baron. Moreover, the fact that in many linguistic markets digital subscription TV services form absolute monopolies, further confirms the above assessment. Consequently, this policy advanced 'feudalization' in communications.

Choice and contestability are essential for democracies. Yet, we observe that in controversies between socio-political and leading corporate actors, the latter win unequivocally. Public interest objectives are routinely sacrificed. Comprehensive policy analysis reveals that since the adoption of the TWFD, EU media policy has come under the control of media barons.

Refusing a communications space for European *res publica*
A veil of ignorance hangs over European citizens, particularly as regards the construction of the EU and its objectives. The masses are both ill- and under-informed, and ideals for an expanded and further integrated Europe have been baulked by popular ignorance and indifference (Golding 2005). Such broadly documented ignorance is threatening in terms of democratic prerequisites, but also has real consequences as people become insecure and nationalistic. EU citizens' ignorance is caused by the absence of *ad hoc* pan-European channels, and particularly because incumbent media severely undermediatize EU affairs. Several case, comparative and longitudinal studies establish this practice (*Media Tenor*, 1/2005: 30–35 and 4/2005: 84–87; Kaitatzi-Whitlock 2005) Yet another corpus of opinion surveys establish citizens' ignorance about EU politics (de Clercq 1993: 5; Debony 2001; Kaitatzi-Whitlock 2005; Eurobarometer), while a third type of policy assessment or advocacy (Dacheux 2004; Schlesinger 2004; Kaitatzi-Whitlock, 2005; Vissoll, 2006) focuses on the need for pan-European communications media. The common trait between them is that while the EU and its policies do not constitute a newsworthy topic in incumbent media, and although citizens' 'ignorance is abysmal'[24] EU policies do nothing to remedy these severe shortcomings.

> The spectacular rejection of the draft constitution for the EU by the people in the Netherlands and in France could have triggered a debate about the direction Europe should head for in the future. But just to the contrary, the visibility of European politics has decreased notably in the summer of 2005 – and not only in pre-election Germany.

After the disappointing results of the referenda...TV coverage of EU politics in Germany and the UK dropped to a level below a share of 1% of all news stories. This standstill of discussion reflects rather unfavourably on leading European politicians, who are probably inclined to sit out the crisis. (*Media Tenor*, 4/2005: 84).

As of 1993 the European project entered its Union phase and we were pronounced European citizens. Whatever one chooses to call this supra-national hybrid regime – 'intergovernmental union' or 'con-sociationist institutionalism' (Taylor 1997; Chryssochoou 1997; Sbragia 1992), it constitutes a *quasi-state* whose decisions determine the lives of all EU citizens. Although EU policy-making is comprehensive, even today universally receivable communication channels between this hybrid state and its citizens are lacking. Information dissemination on public affairs, political interpretation of key issues, feedback and debate open to citizens are all indispensable for democratic political communication (Habermas 1989; Dahl 2000: 99, 188; Keane 1991; Dahlgren 1995; Crouch 2004; Lukes 2004).

Ignorance constitutes a democratic pathology, as knowledge is an indispensable prerequisite for democracy's operation. Ignorance is a crucial challenge, as European citizens manifestly express its existence, but also their need to remedy it (de Clercq 1993: 5; Debony 2001; Golding 2006; Kaitatzi-Whitlock 2005). EU citizens are entitled to access such media to cater for their needs. Yet, a proactive policy on unhindered flows of essential information is treated as a 'taboo'. Nevertheless, some serious initiatives have been undertaken, including the attempt to set up the transnational Europa-TV channel, the recommendations of the de Clercq report and Plan-D for Democracy, Dialogue and Debate. Yet, all these efforts were nullified. The global political economy of communications and a new hegemony account for such frustration.

Europa-TV

In 1980s the EP campaigned for a *political communication* channel aiming at Community-building. The rationale was that information is 'perhaps the most decisive factor in European unification' which 'will only be achieved if Europeans want it'. (Hahn Report 1983: 7). According to the EP's assessment a common identity will only develop if 'Europeans are adequately informed' (ibid.). Conventionally, political communication hinged around the national epicentre, however, this has ceased to correspond to prevailing power frames, so, in the context of the EU, exclusive nation-centric media supply is an anachronism.

If tight national control over media were lifted, what should be the appropriate political agency to replace it with? Who could assume the responsibility for pan-European media? How could alternative dissemination of information across borders be supplied? Momentous neo-liberal forces circumvented this pivotal issue by stripping politics away and by foregrounding markets. By contrast, pro-politics agencies lost out, as they lacked effective power to pursue their strategies.

Europa-TV was launched in the momentum of 1980s. The first publicly funded transfrontier channel started broadcasting in October 1985. Five European public service broadcasters from Germany, Italy, Ireland, the Netherlands and Portugal formed a consortium for its creation. The ambition was for it to be genuinely pan-European on several counts: geographical scope, multi-lingual transmissions, blend of output programming and management. 'In many respects Europa-TV lived up to the expectations that had been spelled out' for it by the EP and the Commission (Theiler 2001: 5; Maggiore 1990: 71). News and features had a distinctly 'European perspective' while editorial teams avoided 'the dominance of any single national group'. A non-national 'comparative approach became the essential feature of Europa-TV news portrayal' (Maggiore 1990: 71). However, in November 1986, Europa-TV folded up, under pressure of indebtedness.[25] That experiment demonstrated the difficulty in compiling enticing programmes for diverse audiences. Europe being culturally fragmented, this goal appeared elusive.

However, that experiment did not fail only because of the lack of political support. It was actively sabotaged.[26] 'Many national governments [refused] to secure the Union-wide distribution of its signals and adequate funding' (Theiler 2001: 3). The failure of Europa-TV was blamed on European viewers' disinterestedness. But the medium that aimed to transform the status quo, the vehicle for Europeanizing the public, was anticipating a ready-made Europeanized audience for it. Europeans rather than being helped to change, were expected a priori to have arrived at the intended destination. This is to confuse the means for the ends. Certain myopic governments even expected Europa-TV to be partially self-financing. But, the success of such a channel cannot be predicated either on massive viewerships or financial self-sufficiency.

The De Clercq Report on the communication needs of Europeans

EU citizenship was officially proclaimed in 1993. Citizenship presupposes an array of appropriate political communication mechanisms in support of indispensable attendant civil rights, notably an empowering corpus of knowledge (Habermas 1989; Held 1987; Crouch 2004; Keane 1991). Any policy-making on communications, in the least politically attentive, should normally set in motion a distinct strategic reorientation, so as to put political communication at the epicentre of the EU integration processes, in the service of the polity as a whole. This very omission is at the root of the democracy deficit.

Indeed, the European democracy deficit epitomizes its obstinate refusal to create a 'citizens' Europe' by remedying the crucial communications gap between governments and people. The fundamental problem which dominated the Maastricht process was 'the EU's "democratic deficit", which amounts to the failure to create a "citizens' Europe" and a communications gap between governments and people' (Morgan 1997: 4, n. 10). It highlights especially the alienation of citizens from supra-national political institutions and those elites that run them. Among the fundamental problems which preoccupied the EU at that time (1991–93) was the approval of the Treaty. From its adoption in 1991, and until its eventual ratification in 1993, an acute crisis erupted by its rejection. In the June 1992 referendum[27] Denmark rejected Maastricht outright, while in France it produced a borderline result of 51.04 per cent (Morgan 1997: 10). That rejection revealed mounting popular discontent with the Community which burst out as a crisis.

In view of this crisis an *ad hoc* committee was set up to investigate the manifest civilian disaffection. The group of experts presided by Belgian MEP Willy de Clercq were assigned to diagnose the condition, its symptoms and causes and to come up with recommendations. The brief of the 'committee of wise men' under de Clercq, was to produce a policy draft for the entire College of Commissioners. The Committee examined the 'situation' from the perspective of citizens and submitted its report, in March of 1993. It amounted to a strategy which should enable the EC/EU to face citizens' concerns at a decisive turning point of integration (de Clercq 1993: preamble).

The de Clercq report diagnosed a crystallized *communications deficit*; thereby relocating attention to the need for politicizing both the integration process and communications policy. It highlighted that 'everywhere dissatisfaction with the current community process is nonetheless great' (ibid.: 184). It established that

> the contents and the aims of the Maastricht Treaty are very badly known even in those countries where a debate took place before a referendum and that it was supported or rejected for reasons which had little to do with what it proposed. So, it is the perfect example of the phenomenon of confusion (ibid.: 185).

Contrary to widely held beliefs, it confirmed that only 'a few citizens stated that they were disinterested or indifferent [while] many deplored the lack, inadequacy and inappropriateness of the information within their reach' (ibid.: 205). In fact, it ascertained that 'citizens are open and welcoming to information about Europe, but remain potential passive receivers', but also that 'the absence or weakness of the relayers or mediators of European information is worrying'. (ibid.: 208).

The de Clercq report put on the agenda the issue of addressing European citizens responsibly by informing them fully so as to bring them into European developments. The essence of its recommendations amounted to a remedy of such communications deficit. It went to the heart of the matter, highlighting the need for European political communication. Yet, when it came to implementing such laudable recommendations, nothing happened. They were considered 'too audacious' and were eventually dismissed (Smith 2004). This dismissal was manifest also in the, then just beginning, first revision of the TWFD which patently disregarded all recommendations. Rebuffing the issue of political communication on TV entailed absolute subjugation of audio-visual media to corporate interests. But, if issues cannot be contested or changed, they cease to be political.

So, why had Commissioner J. D. Pinheiro, responsible also for the revision of the TWFD, commissioned the de Clercq Committee? Had the recommendations been acted upon, the TWFD should be shaped quite differently. In fact, the revised TWFD was totally disappointing as it reinforced commercial exploitation of television, rather than the contrary. Thus, notwithstanding calls to cater for such needs, the revised Directive regressed into a deeper commercialization of television, and a tighter control by the advertising-funded barons (Kaitatzi-Whitlock 2005)[28].

Thus, the economistic, but politically amputating original structure of the 1980s proved unshakable.[29]

Significantly, this period coincided with a broader strengthening of neo-liberal trends within the Commission. Communications policy was shaped by Bangemann's Action Plan on Europe's Way to Information Society, as required by industry pressures for expanding liberalization and privatization. In that light, the report's recommendations appeared 'extremely political'. So, in Polanyi's terms, here is an 'attack on political democracy' exerted by a fundamentalist 'liberal doctrine' (1944/2001: 151). A negative reception of the de Clercq report by the press (Tumber 1995: 517; Smith 2004) contributed to its abandonment. But, their burial makes a mockery of European citizenship and of political democracy.[30]

PLAN-D: a plan for European democracy without a *vade mecum*?
Just as with the fervent but ephemeral reaction to the Danish referendum, Community leaders were shocked by the dismissal of the May 2005 referenda, in France and in the Netherlands, on the European Constitutional Convention. The consternation in reaction to this was short-lived. Again, proclaimed remedies got nowhere. In October 2005, Commission Vice-Chair Margot Walström launched an ambitious 'Plan-D for Democracy, Dialogue and Debate' to cure the corrupting malaise of the notorious European *democracy deficit* and, thereby to correct the Union's political-strategic failures: lack of accountability and waning legitimacy.

Plan-D encompassed a long-term plan to 'reinvigorate European democracy and to assist the emergence of a European public sphere, where citizens are given the information and the tools to actively participate in the decision-making process and gain ownership of the European project' (sic) (Commission 2005: 2–3). From a pro-political standpoint it was a most pertinent intervention, as the crisis of legitimacy in Europe was at its worst. The EU lacks community-forming ligaments. Plan-D highlighted the primary elements required for any democratic polity, putting on the agenda the black hole of widespread ignorance afflicting EU citizens, while corroborating evidence on the political communication deficit.

> Faced with declining confidence in political systems, the Commission believes that it is important to ensure that representative democracy continues to maintain the trust and involvement of Europe's citizens. The latest Eurobarometer survey shows that public approval of the EU has steadily decreased over recent months. Whether in terms of trust, image or assessment of EU membership, all the indicators have fallen. A similar decline is seen in the public approval of and trust in the national political process. While membership of the EU is still supported by 54% of EU citizens, the image of the European Union has steadily decreased in citizens' eyes with only 47% of respondents giving a positive response. Trust in the European Union has dropped from 50% of citizens trusting the EU in autumn of 2004 to 44% in spring of 2005. (COM(2005)494 final: 3)

Information deficit became an official issue. In the face of the debacle of the referenda, Françoise le Bail, chief European Commission spokeswoman, admitted: 'There is almost certainly an information deficit[31] and efforts will have to be made to explain things more clearly to citizens' (*Guardian*, 31 May 2005). However, the most crucial question remains mute: through what networks did EU leaders intend to remedy the information gap? European leaders' commitment to Plan-D can best be tested on the basis of this demand. The Plan-D initiative said absolutely nothing about the indispensable means. How would engaging civic roles, competences and the invigoration of democracy materialize?

The relevance of Plan-D for concurrent communications strategies and policies was nil. The second revision of the TWFD coincided with the Grand Project of Plan-D. Yet the DG responsible for the revision, under Viviane Reding, obstinately refused to adopt any measures congruent with and in support of Plan-D's goals. Yet, this badly needed initiative aimed, allegedly, to even start a 'consultation process on the principles behind communication policy' (ibid.). But the Commission blatantly ignored its own declared goals.

The central issues which were set, but not dealt with, by Plan-D concerned fundamental political agency and responsibility: *how, by what media* and most crucially, *under whose aegis* independent flows of information were to materialize? The EC/EU is not prepared to engage in the political task of safeguarding and financing such a public service. 26 years after the Community's first involvement in this domain, information is still grounded at national level, only now it is profitably exploited by global corporate interests. European citizens' alienation could diminish and rights attached to EU citizenship could be enjoyed through interactive pan-European forums,[32] yet today a televised public space has still to be created.

De-politicization: Origins and consequences

> Thus in its most spiritualized form the liberal doctrine hypostasizes the working of some dialectical law in modern society stultifying the endeavors of enlightened reason, while in its crudest version it reduces itself to an attack on political democracy, as the alleged mainspring of interventionism (Polanyi 1944/2001: 151).

De-politicization is organically bound up with ignorance, with communication deficits and with the dynamics of commodifying media capitalism. It derives directly from that political economy of the media which commodifies and neutralizes citizens, afflicting and undermining the main agencies of democratic politics. *Political communication deficits* cause de-politicization. In terms of power and legislative prerogatives, by far the most significant arena of decision-making is that of the supra-state. Today, an estimated 80 per cent of policy areas are decided by EC/EU institutions. Notwithstanding this supremacy in power brokering, the supra-national regime is 'underdeveloped politically'. As a consequence, power brokered at the EU level is neither scrutinized, nor contested, nor accountable, as it is in national institutional frameworks. This hybrid regime still lacks a fundamental political communication framework, corresponding to its role and geopolitical scope. In these crucial political-democratic terms, it diverges from the polity of the nation state in ways which actively produce *de-politicization*.

Questions arising in respect of this politically deficient framework primarily concern the options available to EU citizens individually and collectively, as there is no public space for the activation of civil society agencies in Europolitics, nor pertinent public information. EU citizens do not share information, they ignore power brokerage processes even on issues directly concerning them. They are thus prevented from engaging in the construction of their union. All components which reinforce de-politicization render citizens powerless. The lack of media visibility on key issues only assists the privatizing of decision-making processes and the reign of self-regulating market forces. This is the essence of de-politicization.

In de-politicized regimes citizens are the most vulnerable, but politicians also fall prey to commodification, especially in election periods. This arises from the need of the media to transmit saleable, easily digestible or sensationalist material. The focus is on politicians' own 'personal stories', preferably with hints of scandal. Such media-constructed 'realities' augment ratings and economic profits, but corrupt the essence of politics. Key information is censored out as non-saleable, while scandal-ridden contents cultivate an aversion to politics and defeatism. This process works incessantly to de-legitimate politics, undermining popular confidence that things can actually be changed politically. Both politics itself and politicians are afflicted when publicity about 'issues' is not forthcoming. Covert political matters cannot be open either to contestability or contingent outcomes (Bachrach and Baratz 1962; Lukes 1974/2004). But, when key issues are neutralized and trivialized both politics and political agency become marginalized.

The privatization of the public domain accrues through *de-politicization*: a regression to pre-democratic, feudal regimes. Due to such trends we have reached the condition of *post-democracy* (Crouch 2004). Democracy becomes unviable under de-politicization. The institutional constellation of the EU has, so far, proved the best instrument for promoting de-politicization rapidly and effectively. The liaison of the Commission with powerful lobbies and its relegating decision powers to them is a case in point. The doctrine which would have markets decide for us, serves the most direct form of de-politicization. It is as if markets were the only stakeholders in society.

The control of communications, which itself forms platforms for political dispute, has passed to corporate forces and has thus become excluded from the scrutiny of political agency. This is to suspend actual political power and, therefore, to disempower people and national polities. Such a neo-liberal strategy could only be accomplished by transferring policy prerogatives to supra-national levels. Thus, while politics is becoming divorced form power, (Bauman 2005) media barons increase profits and power, benefiting from de-politicization.

A key contributing element to de-politicization is lack of transparency in public affairs. Mechanisms of commercial censorship, gate-keeping, self-censorship tie in with hidden agendas and the democracy deficit. Thus, 'naturally', key issues are converted into 'non-issues'. In political communication a lack of transparency about public affairs is produced within the confines of inscrutable private corporations. In policy, lobbying and the disposal of inside information become the mode for private-politics, which undermines equality among citizens (Schmitter 1974). Thus Brussels has become the mainstay of corporate power, while depriving appropriate and comprehensible information from its citizens.

Concluding remarks

But while we assert that the application of the absurd notion of a self-regulating market system would have inevitably destroyed society, the liberal accuses the most various elements of having wrecked a great initiative. (Polanyi 1944/2001: 151).

The fundamental premises, immanent in the democratic paradigm, prescribe that people possess empowering political knowledge in order to constitute themselves as citizens. The EU has failed to secure this prerequisite. EU citizens are afflicted by a publicly acknowledged, deep-seated ignorance. Yet, the EU continues to foster this ignorance by keeping individuals at the mercy of the self-regulating media market system: no longer people but commodities. By assessing key moments in EU media policy, prevailing conditions in political communication and the political economy of the media, I have demonstrated that the EU gave away the entire field of communication to private, deregulated, global capital forces. Such a political economy locks citizens and democratic politics out as irrelevant. The *self-regulating media market system* thrives on the de-politicization and the pervasive commodification of all political agency.

All policy attempts to remedy the EU legitimacy crisis and its time-long democracy deficit have failed because they knocked against the unshakable power of leading market forces. EC strategies to commercialize this crucial field seem, thus, irreversible. Media barons and global capital hold this domain under tight control. The de-commodification of the communications media is the only way forward for democracy, yet this is contingent on policy changes. So, the solution is the problem. This is a vicious circle. Will the EU remain for ever a political protectorate of global market forces? This structural regime disempowers both governments and citizens as the essentially political role of communications is not even *recognizable* by the Internal Market framework.

It will never be in the interests of commercial channels to disseminate empowering political information. The only way of escape from this deep structural crisis is the *de-commodification* of the media (Keane 1991: 153). Unless this supra-state assumes such a bold initiative the proclamation of EU citizenship will remain meaningless and the undermining of democracy will remain, embedded in its economistic structure. Commodified and ignorant citizens remain disinterested and politically passive. But there can be no democracies without democrats, nor politics without acknowledged citizens.

Notes
1. The TEC provides for the freedom of movement of services within the Community in Articles 59 §2 and 66. In this framework broadcast programmes are commodities, for remuneration. In conjunction with Articles 66 and 56 certain exceptions regarding public policy, public security and public health are provided for.

2. This attribution belongs to Commissioner Lord Cockfield, Margaret Thatcher's appointee, who drafted the GPTWF in 1984, under the presidency of Gaston Thorn (Kaitatzi-Whitlock 1996).

3. At the Uruguay Round of GATT the EC/EU, in principle, abandoned commitment to cultural specifictiy, leaving cultural industries at the mercy of uneven global competition (Venturelli 1998).

4. According to Commissioner Heinz Narjes, the purpose of the GPTWF was to limit 'the efforts of those lawyers who might try to deny us any powers to act on it' (in Wedell 1985).

5. Only legally grounded objectives are realizable. Legal grounding sets the hierarchy of objectives and determines winners and losers in this crucial battle.

6. Drawing on legal and constitutional jurisprudence Hoffmann-Riem, Hesse and MEP K. Malangre argued against this conflation of dissimilar categories, which unduly dichotomised the role of the media.

7. See Carl Schmitt (1932/1963), *Der Begriff des Politischen*. Berlin: Grunewald.

8. Crouch (2004) elaborates on the condition of 'post-democracy' while Baumann (2005) refers to the 'divorce between power and politics'.

9. Although changes were ground-shaking the GPTWF reassured those fearing commercial domination: '[f]reedom of expression, however, cannot be the prerogative of the higher bidder' (GPTWF 1984: 3).

10. The DG III, the EP and the DG X concurred in pursuing control at the supra-national level, but diverged on the second aim. While the EP envisaged a political role towards European integration via communications policy, the 'agenda-controlling' neo-liberal section of the Commission used it to depoliticize communications altogether. The EP's crucial mistake was to presume a wished 'political will'.

11. "Laissez-faire was not a method to achieve a thing, it was the thing to be achieved" (Polanyi, 1944/2001: 145).

12. The French government applied 'stricter rules at home'. However, in a globally liberalized environment stricter rules can only survive at enormous cost.

13. 'Markets are the best mechanism for value allocation', Kenneth Ducatel, member of Viviane Reding's cabinet, DG Information Society of the Commission, (28 November 2005, interview with the author).

14. In 2005, the Commission launched an attack on the media legislation and constitution of Greece, requiring that media-specific constitutional articles be abolished in line with Community competition policy. This reveals that while the fetish of competition is heedless, the applicability of subsidiarity is questionable.

15. The GPTWF restricted the scope of its proposals allegedly because the TEC adequately covered competition so that it saw no case for further specific harmonization. Among the conspicuously neglected cases were the issues of concentration of ownership and content-development measures in media production.

16. A later example of intermeshing political-economic relations involves ex-Commissioner Martin Bangeman who became a leading executive in Spanish Telefonica, but due to public grievances about incompatibility of holding such a post with his previous position, he was forced to resign. See also footnote 20.

17. These include civil but mainly professional and market players. Significantly, the European Council in their declarations of 1988 and 1989 raised also the importance of pluralism and diversity.

18. The Commission admitted that Community competition law 'in particular Articles 85 and 86 of the Treaty, [cannot] cover all situations in which a threat to pluralism is posed, notably in the case of multimedia ownership'. The same applies to the Regulation on mergers, of 1989, which introduced two parameters for assessing concentration: the geographical area of activity and a quantitative threshold (COM(90)78: 21).

19. These included 1. United International Pictures (UIP), a distribution group comprising such Hollywood majors as Universal, Paramount and MGM, which was granted exemption from competition Article 85 by the DG IV (12 July 1989), although it held a dominant position in EC stock-programming distribution. 2. A 'Eurocartel' of major media companies such as Kirche, CLT, Fininvest, Telepiu, Banque Internationale du Luxembourg (BIL) and Compagnie Internationale de Télécommunication (CIT) which dominated a large part of the EAS. See also footnote 17.

20. Significantly, it was Commissioner Mario Monti, the appointee of Berlusconi, who delivered the *coup de grace* against the policy on pluralism.

21. To circumvent the overwhelming support in favour of this policy the Commission introduced two novel criteria: 'real audience' and 'channel control'. These helped its non-decision-making course.

22. 'The Commission had committed itself politically, but reneged on it, for tabling a worthwhile pluralism regulation proposal in 1992' (Fayot 1994).

23. Conditional Access (CA) services are privately purchasable audio-visual and data contents. Pay-per-view, video on demand (VOD) and subscription television are the usual forms offered by broadcasters.

24. 'There is a considerable, sometimes abysmal, lack of knowledge, in the other [than the Southern and candidate] countries...' (Debony 2001: 9). 'More than 70% of Europe's citizens claim to know very little or practically nothing about the EU, while turnout in elections is on the decline.' (Vissol 2006: 1).

25. Its accumulated debt was £3.7 billion. Financially, Europa-TV depended on the Commission, the Dutch government and the broadcasters involved, but also on anticipated advertising revenue.

26. 'Broadcasters such as the BBC and France's Antenne 2, were made to decide by their respective national authorities – not to participate in the project.' (Theiler 2001: 5, see also EIM 1988).

27. 'Two of the governments which put the question to a referendum – France and Denmark – experienced disagreeable surprises' (Morgan 1997: 4).

28. Advertising time-slots were prolonged, while even interruptions of news programming flows were allowed. Intensifying commercialization was replicated again in the second revision (Kaitatzi-Whitlock 2005).

29. This was another paradox, as the Maastricht Treaty had by 1991 incorporated provisions amplifying its policy scope. Explicit calls for cultural action 'including in the audiovisual sector' exist in Article 151 of the TEC.

30. Irrespective of EU citizens' ignorance about their citizenship, 'EU citizenship' continued to preoccupy elites and its scope was broadened in the revision of the Treaties at Amsterdam in 1997.

31. For data on civil ignorance see http: //europa.eu.int/comm/public opinion/archives/eb/eb63/ eb63 en.htm. For analysis of implications see Kaitatzi-Whitlock 2005, ch. 8.

32. European citizens are entitled to vote for MEPs or stand as candidates in third EU states (TEC, Article 19 (2). This is not realizable without an overarching political communication system.

References

Agence Europe (1995), Mr Monti plans...directive on access to media ownership (September 28), p. 7.

Bachrach, P. and N. S. Baratz (1962), 'The Two Faces of Power', *American Political Science Review*, 56, pp. 947–52.

Bagdikian, B. (1983), *The Media Monopoly*. Boston: Beacon Press.

Baumann, Z. (2005), LSE London, Ralph Miliband Lectures. October 27.

Cave, M. (1989), 'An Introduction to Television Economics', in Hughes and Vines (eds), *Deregulation and the Future of Commercial Television*. David Hume Institute, Paper No 12. Aberdeen: Aberdeen UP, pp. 9–37.

Chryssochoou, D. N. (1997), 'Rethinking Democracy in the European Union: The Case for a Translational Demos', in S. Stavridis et al. (eds), *New Challenges to the European Union*. Aldershot: Dartmouth, pp. 67–83.

Collins, R. (1994), *European Community Audiovisual Policy*. London: John Libbey.

——. 'Unity in Diversity? The European Single Market in Broadcasting and the Audiovisual 1982–1994', in S. Stavridis et al. (eds), *New Challenges to the European Union*. Aldershot: Dartmouth, pp. 329–55.

Commission (1984), Green Paper: *Television without Frontiers*, 8827/84, COM(84)300, 23.05.84, Brussels (GPTWF).

——. (1992), Green Paper: *Pluralism and Media Concentration in the Internal Market (An Assessment of the Need for Community Action)*. COM(92)480.

——. (2005), Communication from the Commission to the Council, the European Parliament, the European Economic and Social Committee and the Committee of the Regions. The Commission's Contribution to the Period of Reflection and Beyond: *Plan D for Democracy, Dialogue and Debate*. COM(2005)494 final, Brussels 13.10.2005.

Council (1989), *Regulation on the Control of Concentrations between Undertakings*, EEC/4064/89, OJ L 395/1-12, 21.12.89.

——. (1995), *Directive of 24.10.1995 on the Use of Standards for the Transmission of Television Signals, Repealing Directive EEC/92/38*. OJ L 281/51-54, 23.11.1995.

Crouch, C. (2004), *Post-Democracy*. Cambridge: Polity.

Curran, J. (2002), *Media and Power*. London: Routledge.

Dacheux, E. (2004), 'Le Visage Actuel de l' Espace Public Européen', *Mediamorphoses*, 12, pp. 26–31.

Dahl, R. A. (2000), *On Democracy*. New Haven: Yale University Press

Dahlgren, P. and Sparks, C. (eds) (1991). *Communication and Citizenship*. London: Routledge.

Dahlgren, P. (1995), *Television and Democracy*. Cambridge: Polity.

Debony, D. [OPTEM- S.A.R.L.] (2001), *Perceptions of the European Union: a Qualitative Study of the Public's Attitude to and Expectations of the EU in the 15 M-S and in 9 Candidate Countries*, Summary Results – EU Commission, June 2001.

De Clercq, W. (1993), *Réflexion Sur La Politique d' Information et de Communication de la Communauté Européenne*, Annexes. Luxembourg : Office for Official Publications.

Ducatel, K. (Commission cabinet member), interviewed by the author, 28 November 2005.

EP (1982), *The Hahn Report and the Resolution of 12.03.82, on Radio and Television Broadcasting in the European Community*, European Communities Official Journal, OJ C 87/109–112, 05.04.1982.

European Communities (2005), *Treaty Establishing a Constitution for Europe*, Luxembourg: Office for Official Publications.

European Institute for the Media (1987), *Towards a European Common Market for Television: Contribution to a Debate*, European Institute for the Media and the European Cultural Foundation, Manchester, Media Monograph no. 8, Manchester University.

—. (1988), *Europe 2000: What Kind of Television?* Television Task Force (president: Valéry Giscard d'Estaing) European Institute for the Media and the European Cultural Foundation, Media Monograph no. 11, Manchester University.

Fayot, B. (rapporteur on pluralism at the EP), interview with the author, 28 August 1994.

Garnham, N. (1990), *Capitalism and Communication: Global Culture and the Economics of Information*. London: Sage.

Golding, P. et al. (eds) (1987), *Communicating Politics*. New York: Holmes and Meier.

Golding, P. (2006), 'Eurocrats, Technocrats, and Democrats: Competing Ideologies in the European Information Society', in *European Societies* Volume 9, Issue 5 December 2007, pages 719–34.

GPTWF (Green Paper), see Commission 1984.

Gurevitch, M. and Blumler, J. G. (1990), 'Political Communication Systems and Democratic Values', in J. Lichtenberg (ed.), *Democracy and the Media*. Cambridge: Cambridge University Press, pp. 269–89.

Habermas, J. (1989), *The Structural Transformation of the Public Sphere*. Cambridge: Polity Press.

Hahn Report (see EP 1982).

Held, D. (1987), *Models of Democracy*. Cambridge: Polity Press.

Hoffmann-Riem, W. (1992), 'Trends in the Development of Broadcasting Law in Western Europe', *European Journal of Communication*, 7, pp. 147–71.

ITC (Independent Television Commission) (1995). *ITC to Draw Up Code on Conditional Access for Subscription Television*. June 18.

Kaitatzi-Whitlock, S. (1996), 'European Audiovisual Policymaking: an Elusive Target'. Doctoral Thesis, CCIS, Westminster University, London.

—. (1998), 'The Privatizing of Conditional Access, Communications and Strategies', *IDATE*, Montpellier.

—. (2003), 'Miserabile Visu: How and Why Lowest Common Denominator Programming Prevails on Television', in L. Vassis (ed.), *Media and Culture* (in Greek). Athens: Entelecheia.

—. (2005), *Europe's Political Communication Deficit*. Bury St Edmunds: Arima.

Keane, J. (1991), *The Media and Democracy*. Cambridge: Polity Press.

Lichtemberg, J. (ed.) (1990), *Democracy and the Media*. Cambridge: Cambridge University Press.

Lukes, S. (2004), *Power: a Radical View*. London: Palgrave. Extended, first published 1974.

Maggiore, M. (1990), *Audiovisual Production in the Single Market*. Brussels: CEC.

—. (1998), *Dark Continent: Europe's Twentieth Century*. London: Penguin.

Media Tenor (2005), 'Business as Usual: the Media image of the EU in Germany and Abroad, 2003–2005', 4/2005, pp. 84–87.

—. 'Europe – a 'quantité négligeable' Long-term Study: Europe in the Media', 1/2005, pp. 30–35.

Meyer, T. with Hinchman, L. (2002), *Media Democracy – How the Media Colonize Politics*. London: Polity Press.

Mills, C. W. (1956/1959), *The Power Elite*. Oxford: Oxford University Press.

Morgan, R. (1997), 'Introduction', in S. Stavridis et al. (eds), *New Challenges to the European Union: Policies and Policy-Making*. Dartmouth: Aldershot.

Murdock, G. (1982), 'Large Corporations and the Control of Communications Industries', in Gurevitch et al. (eds), *Culture, Society and the Media*. London: Routledge, pp. 118–48.

Negrine, R. and Papathanassopoulos, S. (1990), *The Internationalisation of Television*. London: Pinter.

Peacock, A. (1986), *On the Financing of the BBC*. Commission Report. London: HSMO.

Polanyi, K. (2001), *The Great Transformation: The Political and Economic Origins of our Time*. Boston: Beacon Press. First published 1944.

Rawlings (1994), *(PPE) EP Verbatim Report of Session Proceedings*, pp. 345–56, 19/20.01.1994.

Rouard, D. (1994), 'Sur la Piste d'un Eurocartel de la Télévision', *Le Monde*, 25 November.

Sarikakis, K. (2004), *Powers in Media Policy. The Challenge of the European Parlament*. Oxford: Peter Lang.

Sbragia, A. (ed.) (1992), *Euro-politics: Institutions and Politics in the 'New' European Community*. Washington DC: Brookings Institution.

Schlesinger, P. (2004), 'Des Etats-Nations a l' Europe: des Espaces des Communication aux Reseaux', *Mediamorphoses*, 12, pp. 32–38.

Schmitt, C. (1963), *Der Begriff des Politischen*. Berlin: Grunewald. First published 1932.

Schmitter, P. C. (1974), 'Still the Century of Corporatism?', *Review of Political Studies*, 36: 1, pp. 85–131.

Smith, A. (2004), 'Commissioners and the Prospects of a European Public Sphere: Information, Representation and Legitimacy'. Paper presented at the conference *Citizenship and Democratic Legitimacy in Europe*, University of Stirling, 5–6 February 2004.

Smythe, W. D. (1977), 'Communications: Blindspot of Western Marxism', in *Canadian Journal of Political and Social Theory*, 1: 3 (Fall), pp. 1–27.

Stepp, C. S. (1990), 'Access in a Post-Social Responsibility Age', in J. Lichtenberg (ed.), *Democracy and the Media*. Cambridge: Cambridge University Press, pp. 186–201.

Taylor, P. (1997), 'Prospects for the European Union', in S. Stavridis et al. (eds), *New Challenges to the European Union*. Aldershot: Dartmouth, pp. 13–41.

TEC (see European Communities 2005).

Theiler, T. (2001), 'Viewers into Europeans? How the European Union Tried to Europeanize the Audiovisual Sector and Why it Failed', *Canadian Journal of Communication*, 24, pp. 1–29.

Tumber, H. (1995), 'Marketing Maastricht: the EU and News Management', *Media Culture and Society*, 17, pp. 511–19.

Venturelli, S. (1998), *Liberalizing the European Media*. Oxford: Clarendon Press.

Vissoll, T. (2006), 'Is there a Case for an EU Information Television Station?', DG Communication, European Commission.

Wedell, G. (1985), 'Television without Frontiers? (Some Initial Reflections on the G. P. of the EEC Commission)', *EBU Review, Programmes, Administration, Law*, 36: 1 (January).

2

Media: the Unknown Player in European Integration

Hans-Jörg Trenz

Abstract

The debate about the legitimacy of the EU has so far only rarely addressed the question of the role of the media. An instrumental approach prevails towards the media acknowledging that the so-called gap between the EU and its citizens is grounded in a communication deficit and that the EU should therefore strive towards a higher legitimacy in terms of public accountability, openness and participation. The article discusses these technical aspects of 'public-sphere building from above' in relation to the systematic constraints on mediatization that result from the inertia of the existing (national) media spheres. By summing up the main research findings in the field, the article concludes that the assumption of a linear mediatization of the EU that supports the emergence of a European public sphere and democracy cannot be upheld. Media do not straightforwardly promote the democratic legitimacy of the EU. European integration studies should consequently pay closer attention to the selective and interpretative logics of media news-making that put systematic constraints on European decision-making processes and increasingly backlashes on the EU-institutional set-up.

Keywords
European public sphere, democracy, media, public discourse, Europeanization

The illusion of public communication management

A public sphere is most commonly analysed from the input side of political communication and discourse. Political actors and institutions take an active part in public-sphere building. They are the carriers of debates that are promoted strategically within an arena of contention where legitimacy depends on the successful mobilization of attention by the audience. The scope of political discourse is thus determined by strategic and – more often – routine ways of addressing particular audiences, which are seen as relevant for the authorization of political choices.

Such an instrumental perspective does not exclude *a priori* the possibility to transform existing spheres of political discourse, which are mainly bound to the national. The question of a European public sphere rather depends on the capacities of European political actors and institutions to break with existing routines of communication, to introduce European topics into debates and to mobilize new transnational audiences. Accordingly, public-sphere building has been linked to capacity building of those actors and institutions which are said to constitute the European public sphere. Within EU studies, the traditional research focus was thus on the changing quantity and quality of communicative inputs. This included, above all, an analysis of the communicative performance of European actors and institutions as the *initiators* of debates on Europe.

Taking the institutional setting of EU-decision-making processes as a starting point of research, European public-sphere research has mainly analysed the agenda-setting strategies of single actors, the transparency and inclusiveness of procedures and the quality of information provided by European institutions. This includes research on the PR and communication policies of the EU (Gramberger 1997; Mak 2002; Brüggemann 2005), the role of public intellectuals and entrepreneurs (Lacroix 2005), the impact of protest movements (Imig and Tarrow 2001), the contestation within political parties (Eijk and Franklin 2004) or the general contributions of civil society organizations within participatory governance arrangements (Kohler-Koch 2007; Ruzza 2004).

In particular European institutions have internalized this faith in their own constitutive role as a promoter of a European public sphere. It is widely recognized that the EU suffers from a communication deficit, which has widened the gap between the EU and its citizens and that the EU should therefore strive towards a higher legitimacy in terms of public accountability, openness and participation, in other words of democracy (Commission 2006). More recently, the Commission meets with PR specialists and collects insights from managerial knowledge, which should enable it to overcome its legendary communication deficit. This new attitude towards publicness is most visible in the advocacy of 'dialogue' with the citizens as one of the core attributes of 'good governance'. These forms of dialogue are searched through more flexible and dynamic arrangements of participatory democracy, which are relying on the direct inputs of citizens expressed through stakeholder networks and forums. More generally, coalitions with civil society at all levels should be built to involve larger publics in their role as 'active citizens' and to aggregate a European 'common interest' (Kohler-Koch 2007: 18).

This official approach of public-sphere building from above is grounded in what can be called the ideology of public communication management. The remedies to the communication deficit promoted by the EU spin doctors are relying on largely untested assumptions about the disposition of mass media as the general forum to expose their own communicative performance to the larger audience. Public communication management is promoted on the premises that (a) mass media communication should be increased to promote EU legitimacy, (b) that mass media is an impartial transmitter of knowledge, made up of rational arguments and information that enable collective action and participation by European citizens, and (c) that mass media is a fair player that can be committed for the main objectives of European integration and that will support the EU on its way to deeper integration. In short, mass media is seen as a central component of the management of what has been called the EU *auditive democracy* (Brunkhorst 2007). In the auditive democracy, the principal aim of public communication management is to maximize transparency and multiply communicative inputs that allow citizens to listen and to attend to what is going on in the political arena.[1]

Previous efforts of public communication management in the EU (e.g. in the course of Eastern enlargement, the common currency or the process of constitution-making) repeatedly fell short of their aims to broaden public engagement and support (Trenz 2002b; Brüggemann 2005). Such unforeseen failures of public communication management were only inadequately dealt with and exposed the rather limited capacities of institutional adaptation. Even after the implosion of EU legitimacy through popular referenda in France and in the Netherlands the Commission still kept up the illusion of communication management.[2]

Focusing on the media's role as an active player in European integration is one way to make such failures of communication management more predictable. If institutional logics of public communication management are persistent and hard to change it is all the more important to expose the difficulties of adaptation to media logics and its contingent effects on the project of democratic self-determination. Communication with the public through the media becomes much more demanding and also more risky. It is not enough to sell the good arguments and the major achievements of political decision-making. Instead, strategies are required to improve media performance, political marketing, staging and symbolization.

The problem to be addressed after the experience of the popular referenda in France and the Netherlands is rather how to democratize and constitutionalize the EU with or against the media (de Vreese and Boomgaarden 2005). This opens a new perspective on the media not simply as a social technology to democratize the EU but as a cultural and political power that constrains the democratization of the EU (Slaatta 2006). European integration research should consequently pay attention to the performance of the media as an intervening variable that interferes in the course of administrative and intergovernmental action.

Mediatization: a constraining factor to European integration

EU institutions and institutional perspectives on EU governance alike tend to disregard these distorting effects of mediatization. At the best, the effects of mediatization on the political system of the EU are perceived as irritations, as an unwanted and unplanned means of outside intrusion and disturbance, which EU institutions through their internal rules and procedures of decision-making have difficulties coping with. The misconception is that legitimacy is a product that can be advertised and sold by placing particular media messages or images. Media are seen either as an approval mechanism to increase the social acceptance of the EU or as an educational mechanism to enable critical scrutiny and informed debate (Mc Nair 2000). In particular inexperienced EU actors and institutions fail to see the systematic misrepresentation of the logics of political decision-making in the media and tend to attribute instead the responsibilities for their failures of communication strategies to the unfair treatment by the particular journalists involved.

The disregard of media impact in institutional theories of governance and in normative political theory stands out against the alertness within media and communication studies and their fatalistic anticipation of the erosion of the democratic legitimacy of the nation state (Rössler and Krotz 2005). Thomas Meyer (2001) speaks in this regard of a Copernican Revolution of politics in which traditional partisan democracy becomes media democracy. In the media democracy, journalists no longer observe the performance of the political system to enable rational opinion formation of enlightened citizens. Rather political actors observe the media system to learn how to re-present themselves in order to get frequent and positive media coverage.

Most prominently, Jürgen Habermas has also lost his faith in the self-regulatory force of an autonomous media market that sustains and consolidates a well-functioning democratic system (usually in the form of the nation state). In a recent article published in one of Germany's leading quality newspapers[3] he identifies a market failure in the media sector and detects the 'streamlined newspaper business' as one of the most serious threats to democracy. His reminder that 'good news' is either 'cheap news', or news that entertains or distracts the audience, resembles his early critique of the structural transformation of the public sphere. His normative conclusion and political recommendation some 50 years later is strikingly different. Political communication is still seen as a public good that should be protected from market forces. Now, the quality and the informative value of political news are no longer guaranteed by the self-regulatory force of an autonomous public sphere. It is rather the state that assumes the duty of assuring the population's basic supply of political information. For that purpose selected quality newspapers should be granted public legal status and should get financial support to be able to supply the basic public commodity of information and thus to fulfil their democratic function.

The diagnosis of an imminent demolition of democracy is also shared by Colin Crouch, who has proposed the term post-democracy to designate a qualitative change in the development of Western democratic societies (Crouch 2004). His argument is mainly based on a generalized descriptive account that collects rather dispersed empirical indicators:

■ the decline of public authority, private governance, corporate domination and the commercialisation of citizenship

- individualized and fragmented societies and the disappearance of collective actors or stable coalition (e.g. class) that could substantiate the 'rule of the people'
- the replacement of party politics by lobbyism and the rise of new parties as firms and advertisement machines
- the degradation of mass political communication exemplified by the growing personalization of politics, media advertisement and images, which replace rational debates and discourse, the lowering of news quality and the media staging of politics as showbusiness.

If – as it is suggested by these rather loosely collected empirical insights – the effects of mediatization have seriously affected the democratic performance of the nation state, we can expect that mediatization will also have equally strong effects on the viability and legitimacy of European integration. Media are more than a passive infrastructural requirement of political communication in which the legitimacy of political choices is negotiated. Media are frequently an intervening variable that selects among the outputs of the EU-political system to diffuse the relevant information to the general public. They also provide inputs and feedbacks that are used by the EU-administrative apparatus to initiate decision-making processes or to regulate public relations: media play a role as an agenda setter for particular policy initiatives, they lay as a shadow upon the negotiations, they affect the cooperative or conflictive behaviour of the participating actors, they mediate between diverging interests and expectations and they finally evaluate the outcomes of decision-making processes. At certain points, media might also step out of the shadow and take a more active part in European integration. Media become actively involved in promoting particular visions of European integration and strengthening critical or affirmative, pro- or anti-European attitudes (Fossum and Trenz 2006).

Within institutional and normative theory alike, these contingent effects of mediatization and their systematic restrictions on the possibilities of transferring the legitimacy to the EU have only rarely been taken into consideration. A deeper understanding of the autonomy of the media and its particular mode of operation is required to test out the scope of legitimacy of political institutions and decision-making processes. Such a perspective is emphasized by system theory, which analyses the media as a self-regulating and autonomous operational system. Media representations of politics are different and at least partially independent from the institutional order of politics (Luhmann 1996). Bringing in the media as an intervening variable is helpful to expose the inconsistencies of transforming political communication and public communication. Such inconsistencies result from the encounter of specific modes of communication of the political system with the selective and amplificatory logics of the media system. In particular, a focus on the autonomy of media selection and representation challenges the assumption of a uniform opinion and will-formation process that makes political actors and institutions directly accountable to their various constituencies. Instead of the linearity of *mediation*, democratic institutional designs and procedures are faced with the ruptures of *mediatization*.

Mediatization, first of all, refers to the simple fact that EU politics are almost exclusively transmitted through the mass media. The enhancement of public communication through the EU is relying on external organizational capacities and mechanisms of intermediation. Media make political information available and form the knowledge that is used by the 'people' to evaluate the performance of the EU. Media coverage also provides the raw material from which voters form their preferences and become engaged in public-opinion formation. Since only few citizens have the chance to talk directly to EU political actors or make use of their opportunity to visit a European Parliament plenary or make any other direct effort to be informed about the EU, their knowledge is restricted to what the media with irregular frequency report from Brussels.

Mediatization furthermore refers to constraints of adaptation and accommodation of the internal system rules and functional logics of governing institutions to the mechanisms of producing and diffusing public attention through the media (Schulz 2004: 89; Marcinkowski 2005: 341). It is manifested in a confrontation of the EU governing system with the outside environment, which is *not* controlled by the internal system logics. Mediatization thus results in the interpenetration of the political system and the media system which increases contingency on both sides. Of particular relevance for the EU is not simply the question to what extent and in what forms such adaptive processes are initiated through willful design and strategic efforts by institutional actors. The question is rather what conditions such efforts of public communication management in the first place, why European institutions have so far only been able to mobilize very limited capacities of adaptation to media logics and how we can take account of the systematic failures of their communicative efforts.

The contingent effects of mediatization imply that the legitimacy of EU policy-makers is increasingly conveyed through their media performance and through the media framing of their activities. The formal legitimacy derived from compliance with legal procedures and normative criteria is not a sufficient guarantee for social acceptance, which is generated through non-legal attributes such as personal traits of political actors, their mobilizing capacities, their persuasive power, etc. Mediatization thus refers to a two-way process of adaptation in which politics are increasingly made for the mass media and the mass media increasingly shape the image of politics. From this perspective, Meyer (2005) has argued that the mediatization of European integration has slowly undermined the consensus culture of the EU and increased the likelihood of politicization and open-ended conflicts that cannot be settled easily through bargaining or arguing in small elite circles. The concern with the mediatization of the EU is thus that the kind of mainstream media coverage to be found in the member states has affected the erosion of the EU's legitimacy rather than extended its legitimatory basis.

Media and democracy: the case of the EU

From these constraints on the amplification of political communication, the intrinsic difficulties of imposing a democratic design to the EU institutional setup become apparent. It can be expected that mediatization will have a decisive impact on the shape of the emerging EU polity and its possible road to democracy. The question of EU democracy is not simply a question of formalizing procedures of democratic decision-making. It is not simply a question of re-designing institutions according to democratic requirements. The current proposals of re-modelling the EU according to participative, representative or deliberative blueprints have to be faced with the possibility that the EU democracy – in one way or in the other – will also have to be perceived as *media democracy*. Media develop a preference for a certain type of communicative input that the EU political system has difficulties providing, hence the notorious deficits of communication with the general public. Media do further produce a communicative output format that increasingly irritates the political system logics of the EU, hence the insufficient supply of public support and legitimacy through the media that constrains the scope of Communitarian action.

The constraining effects of mediatization are relevant for how we want to conceptualize the European public sphere and how we can conceive the possibilities for its emergence. The article will therefore proceed with a review of normative accounts of the role and function of media in enhancing a European democracy. The main concern of European public-sphere research was to determine the democratic quality of the media measured in the degree of objective knowledge, the degree of fairness and the degree of support of the integration process. This has nurtured a feeling of perplexity when European institutions and their scientific observers had to realize that their expectations could not be met. The strong mediatization thesis therefore is that media – instead of enhancing democracy of a constitutionalized EU – rather put systemic constraints on the widening and deepening of integration beyond the national. In order to test this hypothesis, the article will confront normative expectations of the media's function in democracy with empirical research findings. This will be instructive for re-conceptualizing the role of the media in the project of the democratization of the EU.

Media's contributions to the enhancement of democracy in the EU are discussed controversially. A minimum normative standard is formulated by liberal representatives according to whom the public sphere's main function is linked to safeguarding the transparency and general visibility of the political process. Transparency does notably also include the function of pre-selecting news for the citizens, drawing their attention to particular issues and suggesting what could be of relevance for them. Media administer the restricted budget of citizens to pay attention in public life and guide them on their way through the jungle of politics. The EU ranges low in this hierarchy of relevance, and rightly so, because there are only few occasions that would justify it to bother the average reader of a newspaper with EU politics (Gerhards 2000; Neidhardt 2006).

A more demanding standard of democracy is formulated within the pluralist-participatory model, which attributes a more active and critical role to the media. Political journalism is perceived as a powerful watchdog, revealing abuses of state authority and defending the democratic rights of citizens (McNair 2000). In the EU, the media has stepped forward as the fourth estate on several occasions, e.g. in the corruption scandal of 1999 (Trenz 2000). Research on the EU *corps de presse* has also revealed a change of self-understanding of EU correspondents from primarily representatives of national interests to critical watchdogs of the EU (Meyer 2002). This new autonomy of EU correspondents has helped to break up the small Brussels world and to overcome the confidential relationship between journalists and EU representatives that all too often has obstructed effective controls in the past years.

The most challenging task is formulated by deliberative theory, which conceives the media as the missing link between institutionalized debates and the general-public debate. Media channel the good arguments from the strong publics to the general publics and they sluice diffuse-problem perceptions, opinions and claims expressed within civil society into decision-making processes (Habermas 1992: 435ff). Media thus support the constitution of a democratic sovereign by generally increasing the level of information, reducing the problem of bounded rationality of segmented institutional arenas and forcing all participants to justify their claims and the quality of their choices and preferences (Eriksen 2005: 356). Applied to the EU, this opens a perspective of Europeanization through deliberation, which takes place in transnational networks and issues communities involving people at different places to participate in collective opinion and will-formation.

Public-sphere research has brought in four clarifications to this common normative understanding of the role of media and democracy in Europe. A first clarification refers to the possible scope of political communication that is able to carry a European public sphere. The majority of authors have discarded the possibility for an encompassing European public sphere that is built along the template of the national public sphere (Gerhards 1993, 2000; Schlesinger 1994, 2003). Most importantly, the emergence of a pan-European media system is held to be difficult, if not impossible. Due to the diversity of languages, media cultures and traditions European audiences remain nationally segmented. Political communication in Europe is still mainly channelled through national organizations, parties or elected representatives. This results in a differentiated practice of news production with regard to the EU. European actors and European issues appear, if at all, in domestic debates (Preston and Horgan 2006: 37). The research agenda has thus shifted from an encompassing European media sphere to the *Europeanization* of public and media communication. The 'European public sphere light' is observed by measuring different degrees of Europeanization in existing national media spheres.

A second clarification refers to the possible media formats that are able to carry a European public sphere towards democracy. European public-sphere research has mainly determined the scope of Europeanization in news-making through quality journalism.[4] The selective bias of research mainly follows the internal selective logics of the media system and its parallel differentiation of a highly professionalized sector of European news-making in the member states. Of crucial importance is the performance of EU correspondents and the agenda-setting and control function of the Brussels *corps de presse* (Meyer 2002; Siapera 2004).[5] This shall not exclude the parallel Europeanization of regional news landscapes or the Europeanization of the tabloids, but this will take place in different forms and with a less clear focus on the regular and equilibrated provision of information about the EU or other member states.[6] Political news-making in general, and European political news-making in particular are floating islands in the sea of a dispersed communications that make up the modern public sphere.

A third clarification refers to the functions and malfunctions of the media in enhancing a democratic European Union. Media's concern with rational debate is rather limited and the prime function of most media organs today is to provide the public with entertainment (Wolf 1999; McNair 2000: 42ff; Street 2001: 60ff). Political journalism proceeds through symbolic discourse, drama and infotainment with the main purpose to draw the attention of a broad public (Sarcinelli 1998). As a consequence, the political rationality of the political discourse of the EU is continuously undermined by the media. The Commissioner Wallström even maintains a web page to correct the most unashamed media lies about the EU, which make many people come away with a picture of the EU as a bunch of 'mad eurocrats'.[7]

Seen from this light, journalism puts serious constraints on European institutions to enter a dialogue with European citizens. Media corrodes the exchange of arguments towards a better understanding, they dismantle agreements and they amplify and exaggerate the significance of conflict. Instead of discursive constellations, media communication is determined by monologic situations in which some powerful actors (in the EU usually the national governments) prevail. On the other hand, the entertainment value of the EU is rather low. The kind of un-personalized news about technocratic decision-making that is produced by the political system of the EU does not sell. Also the notorious democratic deficit of the EU and its permanent crisis become rather a commonplace, not classed as exciting news. The general expectations of the public to be surprised and mobilized by news from Brussels are low. This restricts the scope for political news coverage and favours a satirical and polemical view on European politics.

A forth and final clarification refers to the supposed positive relationship between involvement in European political communication and citizens' positive attitudes and support of the European integration project. Numerous studies have pointed to the systematic bias of news media in selecting negative news (for an overview see Cappella and Jamieson 1997: 32). Political journalism is frequently not devoted to fair judgment and substantive critique, but is rather polemical, excessive and overall negative. By and large, media coverage delivers a distorted image of politics as the world of scandals, intrigue, dishonesty and lies. By inflaming public mistrust, anger and frustration, journalism contributes to the erosion of the legitimacy of politics. Content analyses of routine European news coverage revealed the dominance of strategic news framings stressing the power game aspects of politics – winning and losing, self-interest, manoeuvres and tactics, performance and artifice (Cappella and Jamieson 1997: 110; Trenz 2000; Kevin 2003). Experimental designs in audience research indicate that such repeated exposure to strategic news coverage about the EU produces political cynicism and a declined readiness to support the EU (de Vreese 2004).

In the 'spiral of cynicism' the preference of journalism for negative news is seen as corresponding to the preferences of the public and its demand for sensational news (Cappella and Jamieson 1997). In a situation of media market competition this can trigger off a journalistic race for political intrigue and scandals. Cynical publics require ever more negative news. On the other hand, media sensationalism and inaccuracy is also a mechanism of reducing social complexity. From this perspective, the dominant negative news coverage in EU politics is a result of media's own incapacity to deal with complex issues such as the EU. The problem is that political journalists often risk being drawn into the information overflow. Their capacities for selecting relevant information for the fabrication of news are naturally limited and they work under increasing time constraints. Negative news is 'cheap' news, whereas facts, fairness and evaluation require more expensive journalistic investigations. As a result, political news coverage in fields of imbalanced attention and uncertain public preferences becomes less reliable and tends to create easily applicable strategic frames, incoherent stories and political mayflies.

Negative public attitudes and cynicism about politics are seen as causally related to the effects of negative news coverage. Contemporary journalistic culture and their focus on strategy, conflict and motives invite cynicism (Cappella and Jamieson 1997: 31). In the EU, a dominant media negativism has been identified, which leads to systematic misrepresentations of the performance of the EU governance system. EU politicians are portrayed as macchiavellianists unconcerned with the public good. When the head of governments come out of a Council meeting late at night there are national reporters waiting for them who do not want to know whether anything was resolved for the betterment of the EU. They want to know who tricked whom, who was beaten and who got most. In similar terms, strategy coverage produces systematically unfavourable news about the European Commission which is punished by the journalists for its rationalistic, consensual style of policy-making (Meyer 2002). Journalists are not interested in consensus and transparency, they are interested in confusion, controversy and conflict. At the end of this process, the public expects to get only negative news from Brussels and automatically associates the EU with malfunction and corruption.

These findings on the effects of negative news framing on the EU can be qualified with results from attitudinal research of European journalism. Interviews with EU correspondents reveal a generally positive attitude towards European integration and general commitment from journalists to become engaged in normative debates about the democratic and constitutional design of Europe (Meyer 2002; Statham 2006). In the early constitutional process of the EU, journalists were found to display an attitude of 'progressive Europeanism' in commenting on the future of Europe (Trenz 2007). In the ratification period of 2004–05, however, the attitude of newspaper journalists was rather marked by critical distance and laying blame on the technocratic and elitist character of European integration (Trenz et al. 2007).

Conclusion

Media are not automatically the promoter of a European democracy. Their relationship to democracy is much more ambivalent than suggested by normative accounts. Media call for democracy and democratization but they also increasingly restrain democratic procedures and practice. The concern with the 'colonization of politics through the media' (Meyer 2001) is mainly a concern with the 'colonization of democracy through the media', a transformation of Parliamentarian-representative democracy into *media democracy*. The media democracy is conceived critically the extreme point of this relentless development of modern politics in which power is linked almost exclusively to the media competence and performance of political actors. In its preface to Nimmo and Combs (1992), the leading American communication scholar Robert E. Denton argues that 'it is now nearly impossible to distinguish between political talk and political action' (p. xvi). Top politicians do not take decisions, they talk about the taking of decisions in the media. They do not read reports but media outlets. They do not solve problems but stage a talk about problem-solving.

The strong mediatization thesis is thus not simply that the media play somehow a role to be taken into consideration as one of the many factors that shape and constrain political decision-making processes. Media play *the* central role in the staging of democracy; they pervade the democratic procedures and set the rules and standards for the distribution of legitimacy (Kamps 2002: 103).[8] If the European Union is exceptional, this is in the sense that it still excludes its protagonists from the media game. The competent players of the 'playful democracy' (ibid.) have not yet emerged. The 'normal' working day of the EU top politician is still determined by participation in negotiations and deliberations and not by strategic interactions with the media. For those national politicians used to constant media appearances, going to Brussels is therefore often an alienating experience; many may find themselves in need of a media detoxication.

Summing up the main research findings in the field, this article has specified the assumption of a linear mediatization of the EU that supports the emergence of a European public sphere and democracy. Meyer (2005) speaks in this regard of asynchronous and asymmetrical mediatization. Research has demonstrated indeed that only particular types of media pay attention; that issues are still mainly nationally framed and that periods of high media attention are short and usually linked to negative news such as corruption, mismanagement, conflict, but not to regular decision-making processes in the EU. Even the constitutional moment has triggered off only short media debates restricted to the very peculiar condition of national referenda and alarmism in light of the possible 'no' of the electorate.

It has been emphasized that there are different barriers to the mediatization of the EU. One is the prevailing system of news values that hinders the mass media in picking up European issues. The second is the increasing depoliticization of the media, a trend to infotainment which does not support critical debate and deliberation. Commercial pressures on journalism marginalize the EU even further. A common trend to be observed in all EU member states is that the privatization of public broadcasting has restricted dramatically the space of a unified public sphere that speaks to the so-called national public. Audience research points to an increasing diversification of the public. Target specific audiences or specific media-user communities are located within world society and are mostly detached from the nation state.[9]

The diversification and individualization of media use does not necessarily improve the conditions for the emergence of a European public sphere. The disappearance of the unity of the national public sphere restricts also the possibilities for the transmission of European news and ultimately challenges the very idea of the political public sphere as an intermediating and integrating system. A further constraint is that media markets are already saturated, with only small niches left than can be occupied by European political communication. The national public that could become Europeanized in a more or less linear and unitarian way simply does not exist. Processes of Europeanization of public communication lose ground and become increasingly diversified. Ultimately we are faced with what Hannerz (2004: 23) has pointed out as one of the main challenges of cosmopolitanism: the fact that in an era of intense globalization and increased global connectedness, foreign news coverage in many media channels has recently been shrinking and existing communicative spaces become increasingly diversified. In light of the lowering news quality and the demolition of the unified national public sphere, the emergence of a European or Europeanized media sphere should thus be perceived as being even more exceptional.

An open question is to what extent an emerging European public sphere will still have to rely on the capabilities of the mass media. Mediatization through new information technologies presents new opportunities for transnational communication re-approaching the old ideal of direct discursive interaction and communal reasoning. The Internet creates a perfect communicative environment for a deterritorialized public sphere not bound to particular locality (Splichal 2006: 702). In this new interactive virtual space mediatization would thus proceed through active involvement of the media consumer in the production of the mediated political reality. On the other hand, this would imply an inevitable loss of passive visibility and hence a radical transformation of the concept of publicness (ibid.). The interactive virtual public sphere would not only stimulate fragmentation, it would also imply a loss of effectiveness in aggregating public opinion and influencing political decision-making. Democracy is in this last sense still relying on the mediating and aggregating capacities of the mass media. The present lack of effective mediatization and the structural deficits to its creation should therefore become the central issue in the ongoing discussion on the reconstitution of democracy in Europe.

Notes

1. For an evaluation and critique of this technocratic approach of communication management see Trenz (2002a; Trenz and Vetters 2006; Kurpas et al. 2006). See also the EU-funded project 'Adequate Information Management in Europe'. Available at http://www.aim-project.net.
2. Compare, for instance, the recently issued White Paper on an EU communication policy with previous strategic papers of the Commission (e.g. Commission 2001).
3. Jürgen Habermas (2007), 'Keine Demokratie kann sich das leisten', Süddeutsche Zeitung, 16 May.
4. This includes mainly quality newspapers (Trenz 2005a; Peters et al. 2005; Brüggemann et al. 2005; Risse 2004; Koopmans and Statham 2002) and still to a minor extent research on television news formats (Norris 2000; De Vreese 2004).
5. See also the AIM research consortium. Supra, note 1.
6. This has become evident in media surveys which compared the scope of Europeanization of quality newspapers, regional newspapers and tabloids (Koopmans and Erbe 2004; Roose 2006; Vetters 2007). Regional newspapers have only restricted capacities to become engaged in European news coverage and tabloids tend to avoid EU issues altogether.
7. 'Get your facts straight', European Commission, Directorate General Communication, at http://europa.eu.int/comm/dgs/communication/facts/index_en.htm. Accessed 14 August 2007.
8. Media and communication studies critically scrutinize this assumption with rather contradictory findings. In their 2003 annual conference in Germany they spoke about the 'Mythos Mediatisierung' (Rössler and Krotz 2005).
9. For the case of cinema see Trenz 2005b. For the case of ethnic audiences in diaspora see Appadurai 1998; Pries 1998.

References

Appadurai, A. (1998), 'Globale Ethnische Räume: Bemerkungen und Fragen zur Entwicklung einer Transnationalen Anthropologie', in Beck, U. (ed.), Perspektiven der Weltgesellschaft. Frankfurt/Main: Suhrkamp, pp. 11–41.

Brüggemann, M. (2005), 'How the EU Constructs the European Public Sphere: Seven Strategies of Information Policy', Javnost, 12: 2, pp. 5–74.

Brüggemann, M., Sifft, S., Kleinen-von Königslow, K., Peters, B. and Wimmel, A. (2006), 'Segmented Europeanization. The Transnationalisation of Public Spheres in Europe: Trends and Patterns', Transtate Working Papers, 37, University of Bremen.

Brunkhorst, H. (2007), 'Unbezähmbare Öffentlichkeit: Zwischen Transnationaler Klassenherrschaft und Egalitärer Konstitutionalisierung', Leviathan, 35: 1, pp. 12–29.

Cappella, J. N. and Jamieson, K. (1997), Spiral of Cynicism: the Press and the Public Good. Oxford: Oxford University Press.

Commission of the European Union (2001), White Paper on European Governance Work Area No. 1. Report of Working Group on Broadening and Enriching the Public Debate on European Matters (Group 1a). Brussels.

Commission of the European Union (2006). White Paper on a European Communication Policy, COM (2006) 35 final version. Brussels.

Crouch, C. (2004), Post-Democracy. Cambridge: Polity Press.

De Vreese, C. and Boomgaarden, H. (2005), 'Projecting EU Referendums: Fear of Immigration and Support for European Integration', European Union Politics, 6: 1, pp. 59–82.

De Vreese, C. H. (2004), 'The Effects of Strategic News on Political Cynicism, Issue Evaluations and Policy Support: a Two-wave Experiment', Mass Communication & Society, 7: 2, pp. 191–215.

Eijk, van der, C. and Franklin, M. (2004), 'Potential for Contestation on European Matters at National Elections in Europe', in G. Marks and M. Steenbergen (eds), European Integration and Political Conflict. Cambridge: Cambridge University Press, pp. 32–50.

Eriksen, E. O. (2005), 'An Emerging European Public Sphere', Journal of European Social Theory, 8: 3, pp. 341–63.

Fossum, J. E. and Trenz, H. -J. (2006), 'When the People Come in: Constitution Making and the Belated Politicisation of the European Union', European Governance Papers (UROGOV) No. C-06-03. Available at http://www.connex-network.org/eurogov/pdf/egp-connex-C-06-03.pdf. Accessed 12-09-07.

Gerhards, Jürgen (1993), 'Westeuropäische Integration und die Schwierigkeiten der Entstehung einer europäischen Öffentlichkeit', Zeitschrift für Soziologie, 22, pp. 96–110.

Gerhards, Jürgen (2000), 'Europäisierung von Ökonomie und Politik und die Trägheit der Entstehung einer europäischen Öffentlichkeit', in M. Bach (ed.), Die Europäisierung nationaler Gesellschaften: Sonderheft der Kölner Zeitschrift für Soziologie und Sozialpsychologie. Opladen: Westdeutscher Verlag, pp. 277–305.

Gramberger, M. R. (1997), Die Öffentlichkeitsarbeit der Europäischen Kommission 1952–1996: PR zur Legitimation von Integration. Baden-Baden: Nomos.

Habermas, J. (1992), Faktizität und Geltung. Beiträge zur Diskurstheorie des Rechts und des demokratischen Rechtsstaats. Frankfurt/Main: Suhrkamp.

Hannerz, U. (2004), Foreign News: Exploring the World of Foreign Correspondents. Chicago: University of Chicago Press.

Imig, D. and Tarrow, S. (eds) (2001), *Contentious Europeans: Protest and Politics in an Emerging Polity*. Lanham: Rowman and Littlefield.

Kamps, K. (2002), 'Kommunikationsmanagent in der Politik: Anmerkungen zur "zirzensischen" Demokratie', in H. Schatz, P. Rössler and J.-U. Nieland (eds), *Politische Akteure in der Mediendemokratie*. Wiesbaden: Westdeustcher Verlag, pp. 101–110.

Kevin, D. (2003) *Europe in the Media: A Comparison of Reporting, Representation and Rhetoric in National Media Systems in Europe*, Mahwah: Lawrence Erlbaum Associates.

Kohler-Koch, B. (2007), 'The Organization of Interests and Democracy in the European Union', in B. Kohler-Koch and B. Rittberger (eds), *Debating the Democratic Legitimacy of the European Union*. Lanham: Rowman and Littlefield.

Koopmans, R. and Erbe, J. (2004), 'Towards a European Public Sphere?', *Innovation: The European Journal of Social Science Research*, 17: 2, pp. 97–118.

Koopmans, R. and Statham, P. (2002), *The Transformation of Political Mobilisation and Communication in European Public Spheres: A Research Outline*. Proposal submitted to the European Commission. Berlin: WZB. Available at http://europub.wz-berlin.de/Data/reports/Proposal.pdf. Accessed 14-09-07.

Kurpas, S., Brüggemann, M. and Meyer, C. O. (2006), *The Commission's White Paper on Communication: Mapping a Way to a European Public Sphere. CEPS Policy Brief 101*. Brussels: CEPS.

Lacroix, J. (2005), 'Euroscepticism among the Intellectuals (...and how it can help to understand the true nature of the European construct)'. Paper presented at the workshop 'National Identity and Euroscepticism'. University of Oxford, 23 May 2005.

Luhmann, N. (1996), *Die Realität der Massenmedien*. Opladen: Westdeutscher Verlag.

Mak, J. (2002), 'Selling Europe: Communicating Symbols or Symbolic Communication? The Role of the European Commission and the Dutch and German National Governments in Achieving Public Acceptance of the Euro'. Ph.D Dissertation. Florence: European University Institute.

Marcinkowski, F. (2005), 'Die "Medialisierbarkeit" Politischer Institutionen', in P. Rössler and F. Krotz (eds), *The Media Society and its Myths*. Konstanz: UVK, pp. 341–70.

McNair, B. (2000). *Journalism and Democracy: An Evaluation of the Political Public Sphere*. London: Routledge.

Meyer, C. O. (2002), *Europäische Öffentlichkeit als Kontrollsphäre: Die Europäische Kommission, die Medien und Politische Verantwortung*. Berlin: Vistas.

Meyer, C. O. (2005), 'Asymmetric and Asynchronous Mediatisation: How Public Sphere Research Helps to Understand the Erosion of the EU's Consensus Culture'. Paper presented at the workshop 'A European Public Sphere: How Much of it do we Have and How Much do we Need?' State of the art workshop. Amsterdam, 9–10 December 2005.

Meyer, T. (2001), *Media-Democracy*. Cambridge: Polity Press.

Neidhardt, F. (2006), 'Europäische Öffentlichkeit als Prozess: Anmerkungen zum Forschungsstand', in W. R. Langenbucher and M. Latzer (eds), *Europäische Öffentlichkeit und Medialer Wandeln*. Wiesbaden: VS Verlag, pp. 46–61.

Nimmo, D. and Combs, J. E. (1992). *The Political Pundits*. New York: Praeger.

Norris, P. (2000), *A Virtuous Circle: Political Communication in Postindustrial Societies*. Cambridge: Cambridge University Press.

Peters, B., Sifft, S., Wimmel, A., Brüggemann, M. and Kleinen v. Königslöw, K. (2005), 'National and Transnational Public Spheres: The Case of the EU', in S. Leibfried and M. Zürn (eds), *Transformations of the State?* Cambridge: Cambridge University Press, pp. 139–60.

Preston, P. and Horgan, J. (2006), 'Comparative Report on Newsmaking Cultures and Values'. EMEDIATE, work package 3, deliverable 7.

Pries, L. (1998), 'Transnationale Soziale Räume', in U. Beck (ed.), *Perspektiven der Weltgesellschaft.* Frankfurt/Main: Suhrkamp, pp. 55–86.

Risse, T. (2004), 'Auf dem Weg zu einer uropäsichen Kommunikationsgemeinschaft: Theoretische Überlegungen und empirische Evidenz', in C. Franzius and U. Preuss (eds), *Europäische Öffentlichkeit.* Baden-Baden: Nomos, pp. 139–54.

Roose, J. (2006), 'Europäisierte Regionalberichterstattung? Europäische Integration und die Bedeutung von Staatsgrenzen für die Zeitungsberichterstattung'. Berliner Studien zur Soziologie Europas. Working paper no. 4, January.

Rössler, P. and Krotz, F. (2005), *The Media Society and its Myths.* Konstanz: UVK.

Ruzza, C. (2004), *Europe and Civil Society: Movement Coalitions and European Governance.* Manchester: Manchester University Press.

Sarcinelli, U. (ed.) (1998), *Politikvermittlung und Demokratie in der Mediengesellschaft.* Bonn: Bundeszentrale für politische Bildung.

Schlesinger, R. Philip (1994), 'Europe's Contradictory Communicative Space' *Deadalus* 123: 2, pp. 25–52.

Schlesinger, P. (2003), 'The Babel of Europe: An Essay on Networks and Communicative Spaces'. ARENA Working Paper 22/03. University of Oslo.

Schulz, W. (2004), 'Reconstructing Mediatization as an Analytical Concept', *European Journal of Communication,* 19: 1, pp. 87–101.

Siapera, Eugenia (2004), 'EU Correspondents in Brussels: Between Europe and the Nation State', in R. Herrmann, Th. Risse and M. B. Brewer (eds), *Transnational Identities: Becoming European in the EU.* Lanham: Rowman and Littlefield, pp. 129–57.

Slaatta, T. (2006), 'Europeanisation and the News Media: Issues and Research Imperatives', *Javnost* 13: 1, pp. 5–24.

Splichal, Slavko (2006), 'In Search of a Strong European Public Sphere: Some Critical Observations on Conceptualizations of Publicness and the (European) Public Sphere', *Media, Culture and Society,* 28: 5, pp. 695–714.

Statham, P. (2006), 'Political Journalism and Europeanization: Pressing Europe?' *EurPolCom,* Working Paper 13/06, University of Leeds.

Street, J. (2001), *Mass media, Politics and Democracy.* Basingstoke: Palgrave.

Trenz, H. -J. and Vetters, R. (2006), 'No News from Brussels: Comment on the Commission's White Paper on a European Communication Policy', in *European Newsletter,* March/April 2006, The Federal Trust for Education and Research, pp. 3–4.

Trenz, H. -J. (2000), 'Korruption und politischer Skandal in der EU: Auf dem Weg zu einer europäischen politischen Öffentlichkeit?', in M. Bach (ed.), *Die Europäisierung nationaler Gesellschaften* (Kölner Zeitschrift für Soziologie und Sozialpsychologie, Sonderheft 40). Opladen: Westdeutscher Verlag, pp. 332–59.

Trenz, H. -J. (2002a), *Zur Konstitution politischer Öffentlichkeit in Europa. Zivilgesellschaftliche Subpolitik oder schaupolitische Inszenierung?* Baden-Baden: Nomos.

Trenz, H. -J. (2002b), 'Good Governance and Public Communication. An Inquiry into the EU Information Policies and Practices'. Paper prepared for the First Pan European Conference on European Union Politics, Bordeaux, 22–24 September 2002.

Trenz, H. -J. (2005a), *Europa in den Medien: Das europäische Integrationsprojekt im Spiegel nationaler Öffentlichkeit.* Frankfurt/Main: Campus.

Trenz, H. -J. (2005b), 'Das Kino als symbolische Form von Weltgesellschaft', *Berliner Journal für Soziologie,* 15: 3, pp. 401–18.

Trenz, H. -J. (2007), '"Quo vadis Europe?" Quality Newspapers Struggling for European Unity', in J. E. Fossum and P. Schlesinger (eds), *The European Union and the Public Sphere: A Communicative Space in the Making?* London: Routledge.

Trenz, H. -J., Conrad, M. and Rosén, G. (2007), *The Interpretative Moment of European Journalism. The Impact of Media Voice in the Ratification Process.* ARENA Report no3/07. Oslo: ARENA

Vetters, R. (2007), 'Die EU-Berichterstattung von Regionalzeitungen. Ein Vergleich der Berichterstattung zur europäischen Verfassung in deutschen Qualitäts- und Regionalzeitungen', forthcoming in *Medien und Kommunikationswissenschaft* 3/07.

Wolf, M. J. (1999), *The Entertainment Economy: How Mega-media Forces are Transforming our Lives.* London: Penguin Books.

3

SOCIAL NETWORKS AND THE EUROPEAN PUBLIC SPHERE

Hannu Nieminen

Abstract

In this paper I develop an approach to the research of the European Public Sphere (EPS) which I call cultural-diagnostic in contrast to usual normative-prescriptive approaches. I bring into play two central concepts. First, I propose that we should conceive Europe as an intersection of a multiplicity of transnational networks, and the European public sphere respectively as a space of negotiation between these networks. Secondly, I apply freely Charles Taylor's use of the concepts 'background understanding' and 'social imaginary' when discussing the condition of the European Public Sphere. As the paper is a part of a larger research project, it doesn't aim at definite conclusions but it lists a number of issues which will be explored more thoroughly at the later stages of the project.

Keywords
public sphere, Europe, social networks, democracy, media, political communication

Introduction
In the last ten years there has been something like a deluge in academic research on the European Public Sphere. On one hand it tells us much about the European condition. The (political) public sphere is essentially about democratic legitimacy, and this continues to be the sore point in European integration: the more there is discussion on democratic deficit of the European Union, the less there seems to be trust among European citizens for the European

political elite. On the other hand, the expanding research on the European Public Sphere shows the growing concern of social scientists regarding the European predicament. Among scholars there is a widespread normative commitment to democratic ideals, which the recent direction of the EU is increasingly seen to seriously threaten. In this article I propose elements for a new way of seeing the European Public Sphere (EPS): it should better be seen as an intersection of a multiplicity of different European-based networks and their public spheres. In the same manner, national public spheres should be understood as intersections of geographically determined networks and their public spheres.

By social and cultural networks, here is meant the systems of ties and linkages which connect individuals and groups and which create both informal and formal mutual engagements between the network members. Networks have different shapes: informal neighbourhood networks, associations, national organizations, transnational online communities, etc. In order to be functional, each network is supported by a public sphere of its own. These public spheres consist of channels of communication (the media) and their function is regulated by the internal rules of the network – who has access, what topics, whose voice counts, etc. These public spheres serve both the social-communal and will-formation ends of the networks.

As there are several networks which function in the same culturally and geographically designated area and have closely related interests, certain nodal points or intersections necessarily emerge where the networks need either to coordinate their action or start a conflict. It is around these common problems – concerning e.g. security issues, utilization of natural resources, etc. – that the main nodal points develop, connecting different networks. From this point of view, these nodal points can be seen as fields of public contestation between different networks.

Here we can see also the gradual emergence of the extra-network (political) public sphere. On one hand, institutional forms and structures are established which carry the function of negotiation and conflict settlement between different networks and their interests. Thus, these nodal points are the realms where public authorities start to take shape: municipalities, nation states, regional and global structures. On the other hand, these structures reflect always more or less the predicament of the relations between different networks at the moment of their founding: they are always temporally and spatially conditioned answers to specific problems. When these conditions change, also the capability of the structures to solve or settle the original interest-conflicts changes.

The networks always bring about new interest claims which cannot be settled within the frameworks of the old compromises and their institutionalized forms. Here the public sphere emerges as a means for extra-institutional public negotiation space between the networks: the public sphere represents the challenge of the not-yet institutionalized interests against the institutionalized interests. From this point of view, the basic function of European public institutions is to offer institutional framework for European-wide cooperation between these networks. This kind of understanding of the public sphere has several implications which challenge traditional ways of conceptualizing European level democracy and democratic legitimacy.

Background

In recent research literature differing accounts of the European Public Sphere have been offered. At least four ways to understand the concept can be found:

- EPS understood as an agora, as a space of critical debate and opinion formation which is, or which should be, open to all European citizens and has established structures and procedures.
- EPS understood as a special way of organizing relations between an individual and society, historically shaped and matured in Europe.
- EPS understood as distinct from national public spheres, consisting of all public debates and discussions which concern Europe and European issues.
- EPS understood empirically, consisting of all public representations that the European media produce.

Most research seems to have centred on the first approach, although from different standpoints. Where the followers of deliberative democracy have adopted the European public sphere as a positive regulative idea (see e.g. Habermas 2006), the advocates of radical democracy criticize it for forced homogeneity and propose instead a pluralized concept of the public sphere (see e.g. Mouffe 2000).

The second approach, which is perhaps best articulated by Charles Taylor, has been less discussed (Taylor 1992, 2004). Although having a strong affinity to the ideals of deliberative democracy, it takes the debate to a more general level. According to Taylor his approach is based on a 'cultural' theory of modernity, in contrast to an 'acultural' one referring to an empiricist-positivist approach (Taylor 1992).

The third and fourth approaches are less theoretically developed. The definition of the EPS as distinct from national public spheres appears in the documents of the EU (see e.g. Wallström 2005); the EPS as an empirical totality of European media contents is sometimes used in a cultural-critical sense to contrast the dominance of commercial interests in the mainstream media to the participatory-democratic potential of the counter public spheres of activist networks.

For the purposes of this paper, the second or cultural approach will be concentrated on. Some of Charles Taylor's conceptual and theoretical tools will be freely applied in building up the theoretical framework.

Normative-prescriptive vs cultural-diagnostic approach

To begin with the distinction between the first and second approaches will be clarified a further. As mentioned above, the first approach adopts the EPS as a regulative idea. It is an ideal which may never be fully realized but which can act as a normative framework for critical evaluation. The EPS as an ideal would require an institutional framework for the creation of European public opinion and will-formation, inclusive to all European citizens. The EPS would thus give necessary legitimation for European decision-making and governance, which are now in great difficulties (see Habermas 2006). This approach is here called 'normative-prescriptive'.

From this point of view, there are two main obstacles in the way of the realization of the EPS. The first one is the historical anchoring of the public sphere to the narrow and limited frames of European nation states. This is not only a practical problem, concerning the actual functioning of public institutions, but also a theoretical and conceptual problem which concerns critical research as well (see e.g. Fraser 2000; 2007). The task of critical scholarly debate is to bring about the conceptual and theoretical means to realize the potential and establish a transnational European public sphere.

From this point of view, the question is: how best to create conditions and institutional frameworks for as extensive and inclusive formation of European public opinion as realistically possible? To what extent do elements for this exist already, and what is the role of the media? What should or what could be the role of the EU in this? etc.

The second obstacle is the cultural and social heterogeneity of Europe. Many writers refer especially to linguistic and religious diversity but also differences in other societal dimensions are mentioned (see e.g. Schlesinger 2003). Some scholars have presented normative criteria which should be fulfilled before the EPS can be realized. This is reflected also in Peter Dahlgren's notion of civic culture, which includes such elements as civic competence, common values, civic affinity and civic trust, democratic practices, and civic identities (Dahlgren 2004).

Many scholars have aptly criticized the ideal of a (European) Public Sphere for its allegedly naive understanding of power relations (see e.g. Mouffe 2000; Gould 1998). For the purposes of this paper, this discussion is left here for later opportunities. The difference between the first and second approach is not so much in their normative outlooks as in their analytical emphases: if the former is called here 'normative-prescriptive', the latter can perhaps in contrast be characterized as 'cultural-diagnostic' or 'historical-sociological'. The main difference between them can be put in the following way: *in order to make prescriptive judgements, we need better understanding of historical and sociological (pre)conditions of the phenomenon that we call the (European) Public Sphere.*

Thus, we need to ask such questions as:

■ What is our shared understanding of Europe and Europeaness, and from where we have adopted it?
■ How do we speak of Europe and of being Europeans in contrast to other countries and communities?
■ What kind of status do our conceptions of Europe have in our everyday life; how are public discourses on Europe and Europeaness produced? etc.

A key question is naturally, who are 'we':

■ From whose point of view are the questions above articulated?
■ Whom do we include in 'we'? Whom do we exclude?

On the historical background of the public sphere

The starting point here is that our conceptions of Europe and Europeaness form an indistinguishable part of our background knowledge of the world (see Taylor 2004). We think Europe as 'our' continent, Europeaness as 'our' culture in distinction to America, Asia, Africa, which are all 'different', each in their own way. We have adopted our European identity through many institutionalized practices which support each other: childhood socialization, school education, the media and other forms of our symbolic environment.

As historians have emphasized, Europe as an idea, as 'our' Europe, is not a modern invention. We know now that it begun to take shape early in Ancient Greece, when the division between Europe and its 'others', Asia and Africa, was first articulated (see e.g. Pagden 2002; Rietsbergen 2006). This basic distinction was strengthened and institutionalized then, especially by the Catholic Church, and has since then been interwoven in many ways to European mythology.

The public sphere, on the other hand, is clearly a modern phenomenon – although its historical roots have often been placed in Ancient Greece too. The public sphere as a distinct mode of social relationships, as conceptualized e.g. in the works of Jürgen Habermas (1989) and John Dewey (1994), seems to be a phenomenon which is uniquely part of modern European cultural and political history (also in its North American varieties). It is seen as one of the cornerstones of individual moral autonomy, characteristic to Western modernity (see Taylor 2004).

In Habermas' presentation, the concept of an autonomous individual subject developed in the battles of the emerging urban middle classes (or bourgeoisie) against on the one hand the autocratic king and his/her court, and on the other, against the religious conservatism of the church. In these battles the public sphere (Öffentlichkeit, openness, publicity) was effectively used both as a means and as a motto, and the idea of it became embedded in the self-identity of the emerging bourgeois middle classes.

Since then, both as a means of democratic governance and as a regulative idea the concept of the public sphere was adopted as part of the self-understanding of modern liberal democracy. How it has been institutionalized at the European level we can observe e.g. in the European Convention on Human Rights (Council of Europe 1950). An interesting perspective to the historical constitution of the public sphere is offered by a Finnish researcher, Juha Partanen, who has proposed a division between the four borders surrounding the public sphere (1985). In his account, on one side are the things which are thought of private and intimate; on the second are the things which belong to secrecy; on the third side are taboos, the things of which it is forbidden to make public representations; and on the fourth side are the things which are still unknown and as such non-representable and non-conceptualizable.

Secrecy

Intimacy

The public spher

Taboos

The Unknown

Figure 1: The border areas of the public sphere (adapted from Partanen 1985).

The borders between the public sphere and the four surrounding areas are in constant flux. The division between public and private has historically changed greatly, as has the divide between public and secret. Old taboos have become public and new taboos are established, new unknown areas are delineated, etc. Although the borders are flexible, they can yield in both ways, which means that there is no automatic historical expansion of the public sphere. As a concrete example: we have seen lately that in the name of the War on Terror the public sphere has been challenged from all four borders. The question is then, who, why and how controls the borders?

Europe as a public sphere of networks

So far it has been claimed that there is certain historical background knowledge which, at least in a loose cultural sense, is common to all educated Europeans despite their language and nationality. It is embedded first of all in the institutions of socialization, education and the daily media. The question is, however, that as these institutions are mostly firmly national in character, bound by the customs and laws of nation states, how are they supposed to promote common understanding on Europe and Europeanness?

We can seek for an answer in the fact that Europe actually consists – and has always consisted – of numerous transnational networks of cooperation (see Ikegami 2000). Many of them have developed over several centuries and anchored firmly as part of European and global relations. One of the oldest and most powerful networks is the Catholic Church, which in the course of centuries expanded first to all parts of Europe, then to other continents. Other traditional networks are also those functioning in the arts and humanities. Early European universities were established in close contact with each other from the twelfth century onwards; medieval and early modern painters had trans-European connections, and artistic influences travelled across the borders; craftsmen and artisans created their transnational networks; etc. (see Rietbergen 2006). Lately economic and commercial networks – with their ever-expanding arms of financial institutions – have gained a more and more dominating role in defining Europe and Europeanness both on our continent and globally too. (On early developments, see e.g. Abu-Lughold 1989; general descriptions, see Cameron and Neal 2003; Woodruff 2002; McNeill and McNeill 2003.)

These networks have evolved simultaneously with the gradual emergence of the nation states. They have been reined sometimes more strictly and sometimes more loosely by the governments, whose power was originally derived from the networks. Mostly, however, the networks have developed autonomously and have been able to establish their own inner cohesion with the functional logics and criteria of efficiency of their own. Each network has also been able – at least to certain degree – to define its own criteria concerning the above described borders between what is public and what is private, secret, taboo or unknown.

In the general course of the process of differentiation, characteristic to Western modernity (see e.g. Luhmann 1982; Habermas 1989), these networks have specialized, and created their own normative systems, i.e. criteria of judging what is good and bad, right and wrong, etc. Sometimes the normative systems of different networks are close to each other or mutually supportive, as e.g. in the case of many religious movements (see the Ecumenical Movement, WCC 2006) and the supporters of the social welfare state; sometimes they are exclusive, as is the case of the networks in arts and humanities compared to those in the stock market. In the latter case, an attempt to measure the validity and efficiency of the networks in arts and culture using the criteria applied in the stock market would be a violation of the autonomy of the networks in arts and culture.

It is obvious that in their own public spheres these networks have also produced and introduced issues for the consideration of other networks and their public spheres. An example is the environmental movement who has its 'own' public sphere supported by journals and magazines, websites and email lists. At the same time it takes part in the debate in wider public spheres, both national and transnational.

The problem is that there are issues where mere public debate is not enough to solve the problem but coordinated action is needed, as is the case with issues concerning environment, security, employment, etc. In many cases transnational coordination of action can take place through voluntary agreements, as happens with many civil society associations (e.g. environmental organizations, trade unions, etc.). However, when more formally binding mediation is required (e.g. in energy policy, security problems, etc.), the onus of mediation shifts to the level of intergovernmental cooperation, with all its positive and negative aspect, as the experience of the attempts for EU's common energy and security policies have shown us.

The fact that economic and commercial networks have gained a more and more dominating role in defining Europe and Europeanness has brought about an increasing tension between the autonomy of the networks and the urge of the governments to curve this autonomy in the name of better economic efficiency and productivity. The argument is that from the point of view of Europe's global competitiveness, all areas of public activities – including civil society networks – should be brought to support the unity of the EU and its adopted goal, recently paraphrased as: to make the Union 'the most competitive and dynamic knowledge-based economy in the world, capable of sustainable economic growth with more and better jobs and greater social cohesion' (European Council, Lisbon, March 2000; see Euractiv 2006; EPHA 2006). From the point of view of the civil society networks, this would result in 'streamlining' the functional logics of different networks and their normative bases on the basis of economic efficiency. An illuminating example of this is the way the goals of the EU's Seventh Framework Programme for Research have been set (see Cordis 2008).

Against this development several scholars have emphasized the capacity of the networks for self-defence, presented in the form of new social movements and civil society networks. Often cited examples include the recent anti-globalization movement, environmental campaigns, etc. Using the potential of new information and communication technologies (Internet, mobile technology, etc.) the movements have established transnational counter-public-spheres opposing the hegemony of the elite-controlled public spheres. However, as these movements and networks are so diverse and constantly changing, it is not yet clear what their analytical status should be from the point of view of resisting the 'streamlining' tendency described above (see Bennett 2003; Dahlgren 2004).

Differentiation

It has been mentioned above that the processes of differentiation between different areas of social life is characteristic to Western modernity. To sharpen the argument further, it is suggested here that we can make a distinction between three meta-areas of societal life: the social, the political and the economic. The social promotes social cohesion, the political brings about coordination of action and the economic concerns distribution of resources. Together they more or less cover the main activities of modern societies (see Figure 2).

As the goals of the main areas are different, each of them develop and follow their own autonomous functional logics, incommensurable with others. At the same time, however, the need for coordination between the areas increases: if unregulated and uncontrolled, the autonomy of different areas can become self-destructive. This is the case, for example, with unlimited market competition which leads to monopoly and thus to denial of competition; or with the simple majority rule in democracy which leads to the denial of the rights of minorities; or with the ideal of artistic autonomy which leads easily to moral relativism.

For the individual, differentiation poses major challenges. He/she must adopt different rules and competences in order to act in different areas. The roles of an individual, a citizen and a consumer can assume conflicting demands, and there are no simple solutions to solve these conflicts. As a consumer, the choices are supposed to be made on the basis of economic rationality; as a citizen, the choices are supposed to be made on the basis of solidarity and equality; and as an individual, the choices are supposed to be made on the basis of individual ethics and taste as well.

Here we will come back to the notion of networks. In earlier times, the demands were perhaps less and the rules simpler, and there used to be more supporting networks mediating between the meta-areas and individuals: extended family, neighbourhood community, labour union, political organization, etc. We can call these networks micro-networks in contrast to larger nation state or European-level networks, or macro-networks. As with the macro-networks, these micro-networks also used to have public spheres of their own – including basic requirements for a functioning critical public debate. Today most traditional micro-networks seem to have lost much of their earlier competencies: families are smaller and more fragile, neighbourhoods have turned inwards, labour unions have lost much of their clout, political organizations are run by and for smaller elites, etc. Although new networks and new types of social activism have simultaneously developed, this seems not to have benefited those left cold from the older type of networks – the old, the poor, the disadvantaged. There are two developments which are worth of exploring in this respect: the process of mediatization and the expansion of the economic.

Mediatization: At the same time as the influence of traditional networks and their internal public spheres has diminished, the media has gained in importance. Today the media functions as a central mediator between individuals and the main areas of societal life. This means that the media fulfils the role of the mediator in all three realms of the public sphere: cultural, political and economic public spheres (see e.g. Dahlgren 2004; Schulz 2004).

As suggested above, the different societal areas follow their distinct logics. This applies also to the media and the public spheres of different societal areas. When following the media – watching television, reading newspapers, listening to the radio – we apply different criteria of relevance, rightfulness and truthfulness depending on what the media contents in question are: political news, entertainment, market information, etc. This, however, requires that we have access to proper background understanding with which we can make these distinctions meaningful, so that we can read beyond the daily publicness of the media and reflect the media contents critically.

Expansion of the economic: As societal differentiation processes continue, it becomes more and more difficult to coordinate the action between the three meta-areas. The tension between their different functional logics increases. I claimed earlier in this article that economic and

Social area: culture, communality	Political area: state, political activity	Economic area: economy, markets
Cultural public sphere	Political public sphere	Economic public sphere
Individual, intimacy, human relations	Citizen, civic activity	Consumer, household economy

Figure 2: The dilution of the public sphere.

commercial networks have gained a dominating role in defining Europe and Europeanness. The same development can be observed also in the public spheres: there has been a clear expansion of the economic public sphere.

Two simultaneous developments can be observed. On one hand, the political public sphere has narrowed as the economic logic has expanded. This does not, however, mean a change in the formal exposition of political issues in public. Rather, the change has been in the perspective from which political issues are judged and measured. The economization of the political public sphere means that instead of several alternative claims and proposals, supported by different interests, there is more and more often only one, supported by economic arguments. The political public sphere is left void of argumentation and debate which are an elemental part of will-formation. Instead, there are now economic calculations with only one optimal solution (see Louw 2005; Hallin 2000)

On the other hand, this economization of political issues has left a void in the public sphere. Although politics is done more and more outside the public arena, the politicians are still there and in need of the continuous support of voters. Democratic politics requires legitimacy by popular elections: politicians have to be 'sold' to voters by other means than traditional policy proposals and promises of redistributive measures if and when elected. This means that the political void in the public sphere starts to fill with political entertainment: politicians turn out as celebrities and the media reports dutifully of their marriages, babies, divorces, accidents, homes, vacations, etc. Thus, it is not only the economic which dilutes the political public sphere but also the social and cultural.

Problems arise, when these borders are confused and traditionally applied criteria do not appear valid any more. One example is the claimed entertainmentalization of political journalism, allegedly a central feature of the tabloidization process of the media (Sparks and Tulloch 2000). Another example is the recent phenomenon of reality TV which has bemused the audiences and confused traditional notions of the borders between fact and fiction (Hill 2005). These tendencies have raised much public concern, based on the claim that a big part of the public does not have the necessary competence to interpret the new hybrid programme forms in a sense-making way or in a way that the producers have expected.

Distinction between three levels of the public sphere

Above, general conditions of the emergence of the modern European public sphere have been discussed. In the classic accounts of the development of the public sphere it is usually linked with the birth of the press and other forms of mass communication. How should we accommodate the media with the cultural-diagnostic approach outlined above? In order to get a better analytical grip on the role of the media a distinction between three levels of the public sphere is proposed here:

- European social imaginary
- European publicness

■ European Public Sphere in the sense described above – as an intersection of a multiplicity of European-level networks.

European social imaginary is in a sense a reservoir of meanings: it concerns the shared background understandings of most educated Europeans. These consist of both conscious and sub-conscious knowledge of the basics of Christianity, classical humanism, market economy, liberal popular sovereignty, concepts of Europe's 'others', etc. As a result, the European social imaginary consists of certain kinds of understandings of the world – what is possible and real, what is good and virtuous – which are recognized and probably shared by the majority of educated Europeans (see Delanty 2005). This does not mean that they have to agree on the normative basis of these understandings, often the opposite is the case. There are a number of networks which have been established just in order to safeguard certain understandings and values in opposition to other competing conceptions – say, e.g. the opposition between the Catholics and the Protestants in North Ireland. Thus, it is in the core of Europeanness that the basic values, norms and beliefs of what Europeanness is about are hotly debated and contested. However, the conceptual framework is commonly shared, and it is what makes the European social imaginary.

European publicness is referred to here as the conception of Europe and things European that the media brings us daily. Publicness seems somehow to be penetrated by immediacy, and it is presented us as transparent – as if it reflected the world as it is, as real or in its 'realness'. In creating this publicness, i.e. daily interpretations and definitions of actual issues in the world, the media has to refer to the reservoir of meanings that social imaginary presents. Here it must necessarily utilize the common European social imaginary – the values, beliefs, norms that form our understanding of Europe. However, in its transparency the daily publicness does not allow dialogue or critical debate: we cannot ask questions and we cannot challenge the presentations, we can only watch and observe. The media in its publicness establishes in a way an interface between us and the world 'beyond'.

From these premises, the European Public Sphere must always be conceived in plural: it is an intersection of multiple public spheres of European networks. What makes it possible for us to speak of the European Public Sphere are the public institutions, such as the European Union and the European Parliament, whose function it is to forge the range of monological voices and particular interests on European issues into a dialogue, aiming at common will-formation and decision-making.

Differentiation and cultural interpreters

The processes of differentiation between the areas of social action and the problems which concern the establishment of functional coordination between them have been described. As different areas of social action are based on different functional logics, their coordination requires specialized expertise and interpretation. This actualizes, especially at the main intersections of social networks, both on local (municipal) and national levels.

A central feature of democracy is that all public actions must be justifiable on the grounds of common background understanding and shared value basis, i.e. there must be general acceptance of the rationality of public actions. This is why democracy needs *interpreters* who can translate and adjust the specialized functional needs of different areas publicly, and who can also produce respective orientations for mutually coordinated action to society at large.

This interpretative orientation can be seen at work e.g. in the newspapers' editorials as they cover a number of areas of specialized knowledge and present suggestions for coordinated action or policy proposals. An example can be found in the editorials of any major newspaper, whose different topics all include an interpretation from the point of view of the expected readership and also a suggestion for action.

An argument will be put forward here that certainly needs future refinement but which seems helpful for my purposes. In respect of the three levels of the public sphere as sketched above, it can be said that democracy requires two types of interpreters: those who specialize in the matters on the level of background knowledge, and whom we can initially call *ideologues*, and those who specialize mainly in matters of daily publicness and whom we can call *mediators* (see Louw 2005: 198–205).

The task of ideologues is to upgrade and renew (recreate) our background knowledge so that our basic values, norms and beliefs are brought into accordance with our new experiences of the world and that our background knowledge allows us to make sense of the world. Main institutional forums for the ideologues are science (universities, research institutions, etc.), arts and culture. One of the constant tasks of the ideologues is to redefine and renegotiate the borders of the (national, European) public sphere in relation to the areas of secrecy, intimacy, taboos and the unknown (see Figure 1).

The task of the mediators – journalists, teachers, cultural critics, public intellectuals – is to offer answers to daily issues and phenomena, and interpret them with the help of the expert services of the ideologues, i.e. to refresh the daily functional competence of citizens (Louw 2005: 202–3). From the point of view of the European Public Sphere this means that actual issues and daily events must be interpreted with the conceptual tools of local and nationally shared background knowledge. Again, if the members of the public don't share at least a minimum of common conceptual reservoir, only a part of the public is able to make sense of the public sphere. In relation to the borders of the public sphere, the role of the mediators is to follow the interpretations given by the ideologues – they cannot make contradictory definitions e.g. on questions of what is secret or what is intimate.

From the point of view of the European Public Sphere several problems can be seen arising. One is linked with the work of ideologues. They can work only with material that can be critically contested and from which justifiable arguments can be derived. All conclusions should be acceptable under criteria shared by the community.

Thinking of the recent developments in different European countries, including the results of the referenda on the European Constitution in France and the Netherlands in the summer of 2005, the questions concerning Europe and the future of the EU seem to be still too controversial and contested among the different elite networks. All attempts at simple answers are doomed to fail. This can be exemplified by the fate of the White Paper on European Communication, adopted by the European Commission in February 2006. Despite of all the efforts to create European-wide debate and discussion, the White Paper was all but buried by the end of October 2006.

No firm conclusions can be drawn which could be justified through a consensus or at least widely shared majority opinion within the EU ideologues. The concepts of Europe and Europeanness are still in flux, so much that there is not enough shared background understanding to make common definitions possible. This makes the work of the mediators problematic. It is difficult and often even impossible to make sense of the issues and phenomena concerning Europe and Europeanness as long as the common conceptual reservoir is lacking.

Conclusions

What follows from the cultural-diagnostic approach that has been outlined above? Briefly put: our conceptions of Europe and Europeanness are always products of certain situation-bound public discourses and dependent on the networks we are attached to. Although we share historically grounded background knowledge of Europe and Europeanness with most of other educated Europeans, the definitions are not clearly marked. Dominant definitions are always temporary compromises between competing elite networks, both national and transnational. Through their battles and compromises the borders of the European public sphere are delineated again and again – i.e. what can be said in public and what cannot, which issues and which approaches are favoured and which are not, etc.

Dominant definitions cannot however be arbitrary: they must always be anchored to commonly shared background knowledge, to intersubjectively shared social imaginary, recognized at least by the majority of people. If not, the elite discourse of Europe and Europeanness does not make sense and appeals to the popular social imaginary do not find a connection with the lived experience of the European people. It seems obvious that latest attempts to establish the European Public Sphere have suffered from this type of elite bias. The dominant discourse of Europe, managed by the economic elites, includes the notion of Europe primarily as an economic entity, which all Europeans should support and promote. As such, it does not appeal widely to popular background knowledge outside the elite networks, as shown in many recent opinion polls (see e.g. Eurobarometer 251:2006, 255:2006). The result is that the mediators, in producing popular publicness, are not able to lean on the ideologues' expert services, as the required commonly shared background knowledge has not yet been formed.

If we try now to answer the question of the title of this paper, the answer would be: there is a commonly shared background understanding of the relationship between an individual and society that we can call European and Europeanness. When I say 'commonly shared', I mean that this background understanding and the social imaginary arising from it are shared by the networks of educated urban middle classes, and that it includes more or less uniform sensibility of European history, European arts and culture, European humanism and European modernity. In this sense it also forms a kind of a 'proto-public-sphere', a proto-EPS.

This background understanding does not, however, include firm and solid definitions of what Europe and Europeanness mean in each instance and each situation. It is more like a reservoir of possible definitions and significations which actualize in different ways in different social networks and in different circumstances in European daily publicness.

Following from this, there is not a European Public Sphere in the sense that we could imagine the formation of a European public opinion or European common-will-formation. There are neither institutional structures nor democratic procedures to fulfil these functions. Instead, there are a variety of different European and transnational networks, exercising their own public spheres and bringing forward elements for European public discourses which realize in different forms and in different fora. The assessment as to what extent the emergent intersection of these networks fulfils the conditions of a European civic culture is a task of empirical research.

(*This article was written as a part of the research project 'European Public Sphere(s): Uniting and Dividing', funded by the Academy of Finland between 2005 and 2007. The writer wants to thank the Academy.*)

References

Abu-Lughold, Janet L. (1989), *Before European Hegemony: The World System A.D. 1250–1350*. New York: Oxford University Press.

AIM: Adequate Information Management in Europe (2006), http://www.aim-project.net/index. php?id=4. Accessed 24 October 2006.

Bauman, Zygmunt (1987), *Legislators and Interpreters: On Modernity, Postmodernity and Intellectuals*. Cambridge: Polity Press.

BBC (2006), 'Blocks to Openness Law Considered, http://news.bbc.co.uk/1/hi/uk_politics/5228140. stm. Accessed 31 July 2006.

Bennett, W. Lance (2003), 'New Media Power: The Internet and Global Activism', in Nick Couldry and James Curran (eds), *Contesting Media Power*. London: Rowman and Littlefield, http://depts.washington. edu/gcp/pdf/bennettnmpower.pdf. Accessed 8 August 2006.

Cameron, Rondo and Neal, Larry (2003), *A Concise Economic History of the World: From Paleolithic Times to the Present*. Fourth Edition. New York and Oxford: Oxford University Press.

CIDEL: Citizenship and Democratic Legitimacy in Europe (2006), http://www.arena.uio.no/cidel/index. html. Accessed 24 October 2006.

Dahlgren, Peter (2004), 'Civic Cultures and Net Activism: Modest Hopes for the EU Public Sphere'. Conference on 'One EU – Many Publics?' University of Stirling, 5–6 February 2004, http://www. arena.uio.no/cidel/WorkshopStirling/PaperDahlgren.pdf. Accessed 8 August 2006.

Cordis 2008: Understand FP 7, http://cordis.europa.eu/fp7/understand_en.html. Accessed 18 August 2008.

Delanty, Gerard (2005), 'The Idea of Cosmopolitan Europe: On the Cultural Significance of Europeanization', International Review of Sociology – Revue Internationale de Sociologie, 15: 3 (November), pp. 405–21.

Dewey, John (1994), The Public and its Problems. Athens: Swallow Press. First published 1927.

Cordis (2006), 'Towards FP7: Research Themes', http://ec.europa.eu/research/future/themes/index_en.cfm. Accessed 8 August 2006.

Council of Europe (1950), Convention for the Protection of Human Rights and Fundamental Freedoms, http://conventions.coe.int/Treaty/Commun/QueVoulezVous.asp?NT=005&CL=ENG. Accessed 8 August 2006.

EMEDIATE (2006), 'Media and Ethics of a European Public Sphere from the Treaty of Rome to the "War on Terror"', http://www.iue.it/RSCAS/Research/EMEDIATE/Index.shtml. Accessed 24 October 2006.

EPHA (2006), 'An Introduction to the Lisbon Strategy', http://www.epha.org/IMG/pdf/Intro_to_Lisbon_strategy.pdf. Accessed 8 August 2006.

EU COMPOL (2006), White Paper on a European Communication Policy (presented by the Commission). COM(2006) 35 final. 1.2.2006, http://ec.europa.eu/communication_white_paper/doc/white_paper_en.pdf. Accessed 8 August 2006.

Euractive (2006), 'Lisbon agenda', http://www.euractiv.com/en/agenda2004/lisbon-agenda/article-117510. Accessed 8 August 2006.

Eurobarometer 251: The Future of Europe, May 2006, http://ec.europa.eu/public_opinion/futur_en.htm. Accessed 8 August 2006.

Eurobarometer 255: Attitudes towards European Union Enlargement, July 2006, http://ec.europa.eu/public_opinion/archives/ebs/ebs_255_en.pdf. Accessed 8 August 2006.

EUROPUB.COM: The Transformation of Political Mobilisation and Communication in European Public Spheres, http://ec.europa.eu/research/social-sciences/knowledge/projects/article_3479_en.htm. Accessed 24 October 2006.

Feldblum, Miriam (1997), '"Citizenship Matters": Contemporary Trends in Europe and the United States', in Stanford Electronic Humanities Review, 5 February 1997, http://www.stanford.edu/group/SHR/5-2/ferldblum.html. Accessed 8 August 2006.

Fraser, Nancy (2000), 'Transnationalizing the Public Sphere'. Yale University, http://www.yale.edu/polisci/info/conferences/fraser1.doc. Accessed 8 August 2006.

Fraser, Nancy (2007), 'Transnationalising the Public Sphere: On the Legitimacy and Efficacy of Public Opinion in a PostWestphalenian World', in Seyla Benhabib, Ian Shapiro and Danilo Petranovich (eds), Identities, Affiliations, and Allegiances. Cambridge: Cambridge University Press.

Gould, Carol C. (1998), 'Diversity and Democracy: Representing Differences', in Seyla Benhabib (ed.), Democracy and Difference: Contesting the Boundaries of the Political. Princeton: Princeton University Press, pp. 171–86.

Habermas, Jürgen (1989a), The Theory of Communicative Action. Volume Two: The Critique of Functionalis Reason. Cambridge: Polity.

Habermas, Jürgen (1989b), The Structural Transformation of the Public Sphere. Cambridge: Polity. First published in German, 1962.

Habermas, Jürgen (2006), *Time of Transitions*. Cambridge: Polity.

Hallin, Daniel C. (2000), 'Commercialism and Professionalism in the American News Media', in James Curran and Michael Gurevitch (eds), *Mass Media and Society*. Third Edition. London: Arnold, pp. 218–37.

Hill, Annette (2005), *Reality TV: Audiences and Popular Factual Television*. Milton Park: Routledge.

IDNET: Europeanization, Collective Identities, and Public Discourses, http://ec.europa.eu/research/social-sciences/knowledge/projects/article_3501_en.htm. Accessed 24 October 2006.

Ikegami, Eiko (2000), 'A Sociological Theory of Publics: Identity and Culture and Emergent Properties in Networks', *Social Research* (Winter), http://www.findarticles.com/p/articles/mi_m2267/is_4_67/ai_70451657. Accessed 24 October 2006.

Kurpas, Sebastian and Brüggemann, Michael and Meyer, Christopher (2006), *The Commission White Paper on Communication: Mapping a Way to a European Public Sphere*. Centre for European Policy Studies. CEPS Policy Brief No 101/May 2006, http://www.epin.org/pdf/KurpasBruggemannMeyer2006.pdf. Accessed 31 October 2006.

Louw, Eric (2005), *The Media and Political Process*. London: Sage.

Luhmann, Niklas (1982), *The Differentiation of Society*. New York: Columbia University Press.

McNeill, John Robert and McNeill, William (2003), *The Human Web: A Bird's-Eye of World History*. New York and London: W. W. Norton and Co.

Mouffe, Chantal (2000), *Deliberative Democracy or Agonistic Pluralism*. 72 Reihe Politikwissenschaft, Political Science Series. Institut für Höhere Studies (HIS), Wien. Institute for Advanced Studeis, Vienna, http://www.ihs.ac.at/publications/pol/pw_72.pdf. Accessed 8 August 2006.

OpenDemocracy (2006), 'People Flow: Migration in Europe', http://www.opendemocracy.net/people-migrationeurope/debate.jsp. Accessed 8 August 2006.

Pagden, Anthony (ed.) (2002), *The Idea of Europe: From Antiquity to the European Union*. Cambridge: Cambridge University Press.

Partanen, Juha (1985), 'Julkisuutta tutkiessa [Reflecting the Public Sphere]', *Tiedotustutkimus* [Mass Communication Research], 3, pp. 31–37.

RECON: Reconstituting Democracy in Europe, http://www.arena.uio.no/recon. Accessed 24 October 2006.

Rietbergen, Peter (2006), *Europe: A Cultural History*. Second Edition. London: Routledge.

Rose, Nikolas (1996), 'The Death of the Social? Refiguring the Territory of Government', *Economy and Society*, 25: 3, pp. 327–56.

Schlesinger, Philip (2003), 'The Babel of Europe? An Essay on Networks and Communicative Spaces'. ARENA Working Paper 22/03, http://www.arena.uio.no/publications/wp_03_22.pdf. Accessed 31 October 2006.

Schulz, Winfrid (2004), 'Reconstructing Mediatization as Analytical Concept', *European Journal of Communication*, 19: 1, pp. 87–101

Splichal, Slavko (2006), 'In Search of a Strong European Public Sphere: Some Critical Observations on Conceptualizations of Publicness and the (European) Public Sphere', *Media, Culture and Society*, 28: 5, pp. 695–714.

Taylor, Charles (1992), 'Modernity and the Rise of the Public Sphere'. The Tanner Lectures on Human Values. Delivered at Stanford University, February 25 1992.

Taylor, Charles (2004), *Modern Social Imaginaries*. Durham and London: Duke University Press.

Wallström, Margot (2005), 'Bridging the Gap: How to Bring Europe and its Citizens Closer Together?' Speech at the Stakeholders' Forum co-organized by the European Economic and Social Committee and the European Commission, 8 November 2005, http://backupcese.qwentes.be/stakeholders_forum/08_11_2005/speech_Wallstr%C3%B6m_en.pdf. Accessed 8 August 2006.

Woodruff, William (2002), *A Concise History of the Modern World: 1500 to the Present. A Guide to World Affairs.* Fourth Edition. Basingstoke: Palgrave Macmillan.

4

Journalistic Freedom and Media Pluralism in the Public Spheres of Europe: Does the European Union Play a Role?

Deirdre Kevin

Abstract

This chapter provides an overview of regulation of journalism and media markets in the European Union, those markets that form the basis of the European public spheres. It addresses the issue of journalism ethics and independence, its regulation and obstacles to such independence. Many of the constraints on journalism and pluralism of information are related to issues of media ownership. The approach to regulating markets and promoting political and cultural pluralism are outlined in relation to both the national and European levels, indicating what role is played by the European Union. These issues are highly relevant to discussions on the nature of the role of the media in developing democracy at the European Union level.

Keywords

media regulation, media policy, Europe, public sphere, journalism

Introduction

It is generally accepted that a plural media system (in terms of both the 'external' number of outlets, and 'internal' variety of content and sources), accompanied by a strong public service system, and an ethical and independent journalistic culture are fundamental to the functioning of democratic debate. It is also widely argued that democratic debate on a European level, or a unified European public sphere is limited by the lack of a European media system, and the absence of a European audience for those European outlets that do exist, outside of the Brussels policy community and the national elites (Schlesinger and Kevin 2000).

Hence, in approaching the assessment of the role of the media regarding public information concerning the political development and policy-making of the European Union, the focus of much research has logically been on the national media systems in the European Union (for example Siune 1993; Morgan 1995; Anderson and Weymouth 1999; Slaatta 1999; Basnée 2002; Eilders and Voltmer 2003), and often with cross-national comparison (for example Blumler et al. 1983; de Vreese 2003; Kevin 2003; Meyer 2003; AIM Consortium 2006). In terms of content analysis (and in some cases also analysis of journalism practice) such work continues to reveal the influence of national political and journalistic cultures, and above all the importance of national relevance, in the framing of European news. It is frequently the case that similar themes and debates on similar issues occur in national media systems, particularly during moments of heightened interest: elections, enlargement, referenda, or in relation to crisis. Communication between the European Union and the citizen occurs then in a system of 'overlapping public spheres' (Schlesinger 1999) or 'segmented transnational topic-related public spheres' (Eilders and Voltmer 2003). This chapter will outline broadly the regulatory structures relevant to these public spheres at the European and national levels and illustrate the shape of media markets that serve EU citizens.

Journalistic freedom

Of fundamental importance for a strong journalistic culture are the concepts of freedom of expression, freedom of information, journalistic ethics and independence. At the international level this is protected under the following declarations, conventions and charters: Art. 19 of the United Nations' Universal Declaration on Human Rights; The Council of Europe European Convention on Human Rights (Art. 10.1); and The Charter of Fundamental Rights of the European Union (Art. 11) which states that:

> 1. Everyone has the right to freedom of expression. This right shall include freedom to hold opinions and to receive and impart information and ideas without interference by public authority and regardless of frontiers. 2. The freedom and pluralism of the media shall be respected.

The right to *freedom of expression* has been enshrined in the national constitutions of all EU member states (in the United Kingdom through the Human Rights Act of 1998). In all a similar right exists regarding the freedom to have and express opinions, and each is either indirectly or directly, or through case law, related to the role of the media in disseminating information and providing the citizen with a range of opinions. In several countries this freedom dates back to the eighteenth or nineteenth century.[1] Additionally several legislative systems have specific Acts/ Laws relating to freedom of expression, or freedom of the press or the media,[2] or additional or extended constitutional articles relating to media freedom,[3] or within the context of media legislation.[4] In addition most member states have developed a process for ensuring *freedom of information* through the enactment of laws.[5]

While the constitutions of the 'new' democracies already incorporated this freedom at the outset of transition to democracy, leading to Parliamentary Acts to set out how the system will function,[6] some of the older EU member states (United Kingdom, Germany) have taken longer to put such a system in place. The UK Act of 2000 established a system in 2005. In Germany, such a freedom does not exist at the federal level, although several of the *Länder* have a system for access to information. Legislation usually contains certain caveats: regarding public or national interest, which allows authorities to define the way in which information is expressed, and also which information can be accessed. These systems can only be judged in practice, i.e. as the result of judicial decisions, or self-regulatory processes, or through information provided by media professionals regarding their freedom in practice. Hence effective implementation can be affected by exemptions (obligatory or mandatory), restrictive clauses (e.g. as in Italy where 'a personal concrete interest' is required)[7] or with financial charges.

Journalism ethics and practice are generally addressed under a self-regulatory model: there are codes of practice/ethics both at the national and international level.[8] These codes relate to standards in accuracy, fairness, honesty, respect for privacy, and also the obligation to uphold the high standards of the profession by avoiding plagiarism, defamation or the acceptance of bribes, and are generally adjudicated upon by a Press Council, or Ethics Commission. Many media outlets (particularly Public Service Broadcasters, but also some quality newspapers) also have individual editorial policies, systems for standards, or codes of ethics.

The way in which the above context for journalism freedom (constitutional rights, acts relating to freedom of information, and self-regulation of ethics) functions is dependent on several factors: political culture, the economic context of the media and the working environment of journalists. Government, politicians, authorities and companies need the media in order to publicize policies, explain policies, gain support for their parties (or sell their products). The media also needs the cooperation of these groups in order to receive information, and to write stories. In each country a system will have developed over time regarding how this process of information exchange works in both formal and informal ways. The formal approach involves press conferences and press briefings, and the informal processes may involve information being given to one outlet over the others (scoops), or 'off-the-record' information from actors. The development of 'spin-doctor' tactics by political actors and the sophistication of public relation activities of both authorities and commercial companies complicate this process. The work of the AIM project (2006) reveals how such a system of information exchange and news management has developed at the EU level centred on the daily briefings of the European Commission's spokesperson service. In this way a type of European journalism is emerging. The research also shows that there are still significant differences in the cultures of journalism. For example the various national press corps have different expectations regarding openness and transparency of political institutions (from very open cultures in Sweden or Norway to much less transparent systems in Italy).

There are many factors that influence the practice of media ethics and the freedom of journalism. These range from the standards of training and education of journalists, the working conditions of journalists, to the influence of business and political interests on the management of media outlets. Such influence can be exerted via direct or indirect ownership interests, and also the financial investment of advertising. The 'war on terrorism', the fight against crime and the fight against right-wing extremism are issues that have frequently been cited[9] as political developments that serve to place restrictions on investigative journalism. With regard to laws concerns have been expressed[10] in France regarding the outdated defamation legislation and frequent challenges to the principle of confidentiality of sources and in Poland regarding the Penal Code, where journalists often face prison sentences on the grounds of insult or defamation. In addition the former (and now renewed) situation in Italy in the broadcasting sector wherein a unique combination of economic, political and media power in the hands of one man, the premier Minister, Silvio Berlusconi is one of the stronger examples of political influence on a democratic media system.

From a financial perspective, the media, particularly the press industry, has been confronted with an economic crisis in the past few years. Part of the problem is the competition with online media, particularly regarding advertising, which in turn makes it logical for newspapers to have an online presence. A recent OSCE report cited a German Union representative who explained that publishers are lobbying for a relaxation of laws in order to consolidate, they are cutting back on staff and administration which impacts on quality, and they are focusing attention on East European markets where they hope for a higher return on capital than is possible in the national market (OSCE 2003: 99). According to the OSCE less than half of journalists in the UK have works councils. Additionally, where foreign media companies operate, for example, Hungary and Poland, the EFJ (2003) expressed concern regarding foreign publishers creating less favourable working conditions than in their home companies, paying low wages and hence discouraging professionalism.[11] The predominance of freelance and 'payment per piece' practice can lead to journalists being financially insecure and open to becoming spokespeople for companies or politicians. Alongside external pressure, and fear of repercussions from political or business interests, journalists and editors in many of the former soviet states (including several EU member states) frequently practice self-censorship, or avoid certain topics completely (IREX 2007). The European Union plays a very minor role in the protection of journalism ethics or independence (see more detail in the next section). It has been rather the Council of Europe that has addressed journalistic freedom via human rights activities and also the jurisprudence concerning Article 10. However, the EU, in its activities with EU applicants and other countries, funds projects that enhance democracy, which include the development of media systems (see below).

Policy and regulation relevant to media markets in the European Union

European level: European Union
The role of the European Union is quite limited as regards the protection of pluralism in the EU media markets. There are two Directorates General (and to a lesser extent three others) who play

a role in development of European media markets, and hence in shaping European public spheres. The European Commission Directorate General, Information Society and Media (formerly Media Education and Culture), has played some part in the protection of European cultural output since the introduction of the Television without Frontiers Directive in 1989[12] through the development of a quota system requiring broadcasters to broadcast a minimum level of European audio-visual production, and independent production. Assessments of this process reveal that the results of this policy vary widely: implementation varies as regards the strength of policy, the monitoring of output and the ability to impose sanctions (Graham and Associates Ltd 2005). The main purpose of the Directive was to introduce minimum standards in broadcasting concerning: advertising, sponsorship and tele-shopping; protection of minors and the right of reply. The Directive was reviewed in 1998 with the insertion of a provision concerning major events of interest to the public, whereby governments produce a list of events that must remain in free-to-air broadcasts. One widely debated issue is that of jurisdiction: currently television companies are regulated according to the country of origin (or establishment) and not that of reception, an issue that can be problematic when standards are different. A further review has just been completed leading to the Audio-visual Media Services Directive (AVMS) 2007. It has applied certain principles to broadcasting online such as protection of minors and respect for human dignity, and it has also relaxed certain advertising rules. Through the MEDIA programme of the EU, the production and distribution of film in Europe is supported.

The Information Society and Media Directorate also promotes the use of, and access to, the Internet and new communication services. The regulation of telecommunications and new communications services within the Information Society directorate has increasing relevance for broadcasting. The regulatory framework for electronic communications networks and services, the so-called 'Telecoms Package'[13] is currently under review (since December 2007). The proposals will *inter alia* affect the planned use of the radio frequency spectrum after analogue broadcasting ends and broadcast services will no longer have a priority position with regard to access to the spectrum.

The Directorate General for Competition regulates mergers and anti-competitive behaviour, also in the media sector. Unlike in several member states (Germany, Austria, the United Kingdom and Ireland, see below), the competition approach does not distinguish the media industry from other industries as having any particular characteristics (i.e. democratic and cultural roles). The competition *acquis* is based on Article 31 (State monopolies of a commercial character), Articles 81–85 (Rules applicable to undertakings), Article 86 (Public undertakings and undertakings with special or exclusive rights) and Articles 87–89 (Rules applicable to state aid) of the EC Treaty.

Article 87 of the EC Treaty prohibits any state aid granted by a member state or through state resources, which distorts or threatens to distort competition by favouring certain firms or the production of certain goods, for instance: state grants; interest relief; tax relief; state guarantee or holding; provision by the state of goods and services on preferential terms. There are exceptions wherein Article 87 of the EC Treaty allows: aid having a social character, granted to individual consumers; aid to make good the damage caused by natural disasters or exceptional occurrences; aid designed to promote the economic development of underdeveloped areas; or to promote the execution of an important project of common European interest; or to facilitate the development of certain activities or areas; promote culture and heritage conservation.[14]

Additionally, a particular approach to broadcasting was agreed in the Protocol of the Amsterdam Treaty (1997):

> The provisions of the Treaty establishing the European Community shall be without prejudice to the competence of member states to provide for the funding of public service broadcasting insofar as such funding is granted to broadcasting organisations for the fulfilment of the public service remit as conferred, defined and organised by each Member State, and insofar as such funding does not affect trading conditions and competition in the Community to an extent which would be contrary to the common interest, while the realisation of the remit of that public service shall be taken into account.[15]

Furthermore, the European Court of Justice in its ruling of the *Altmark* case (2003) laid down conditions governing the compatibility of public service compensation that constitutes state aid. Certain conditions should be met: that it is a genuine service of general economic interest within the meaning of Article 86 of the EC Treaty; there are clear public service obligations and a method for calculating compensation; the amount of compensation may not exceed what is necessary to cover the costs incurred in discharging the public service obligations; over-compensation must be avoided.[16]

For public service broadcasting organizations a result of the privatization of broadcasting (aside from competition for viewers) has been the increasing tendency of commercial broadcasters to initiate cases questioning the nature of public funding to public service broadcasters. The first cases concerning the financing of public broadcasters began with Spain in 1992 based on complaints from commercial broadcasters Telecinco and Antena 3. Similar complaints were made by the private broadcasters in the 1990s in France, Italy, Portugal and Greece. Here the concern was over the use of dual funding (advertising revenues and state funding). Further investigations were launched concerning the United Kingdom (2001) and digital services, and Denmark (2004) concerning excess compensation to the public service broadcaster. The most recent investigations concern the financing of Dutch, German and Irish public service broadcasters and concern the use of state funding for mobile telephone services, e-commerce services, online programme guides and the acquisition of pay-TV sports rights. The Competition DG, hence, needs to examine and assess both the financing of public service broadcasters and where funds are used for public service or commercial activities, and also, as a necessary context for this examination, they need to examine the public service remits of the broadcasters.

It has been argued, on the one hand, that decisions taken by the EC Competition in the media field have had a positive effect on pluralism in the market for broadcasting (Ward 2005) and film distribution (Herold 2005). However, EU competition policy focuses mainly on the common market, the EU market (and intervention mostly dependent on EU-wide thresholds), and so does not impede companies from having substantial interests (within national ownership boundaries where they exist, see below) in the media sectors of a variety of European Union countries.

The European Commission DGs Enlargement and External Affairs provide funding for research, exchange and seminars supporting governance development in accession and third states. This has included work in the area of media freedom and independence:[17] with the focus on accession states and external countries such as the CIS countries.

The European Commission DG Communication plays an important role in the development of a European public sphere (or spheres). Efforts have been made over the years to increase transparency, including in relation to access to documents, to the launching the 'People First' campaign, campaigns regarding the introduction of the Euro, and enlargement. In the process of improving the communication of Europe due to the 'democratic deficit', the press and spokespersons service have developed a sophisticated news management system,[18] one that resembles the news management processes of national governments. Most recently the launch of a *White Paper on a European Communication Policy* indicates an approach to 'go local', give the EU 'a face', deliver 'stories' to the media about the European Union, and to invest further in communicative structures. The focus appears to be generally more on assuring news coverage, and as far as possible positive news coverage. While this contributes to the information flow necessary for a European public sphere, it is uncertain to what extent it may enhance debates and discussions within such a sphere.

National media law and policy: Media ownership restrictions[19]
The right to freedom of expression is frequently used as an argument against media ownership restrictions as this is seen as a limitation of an individual right to establish a media outlet. Despite this, the regulation of media ownership, with the intent of protecting pluralism, can be seen as creating an environment in which as wide as possible a *range of opinions* can be expressed. The approach to the regulation of media ownership varies widely in the member states of the European Union. Concerning the press, ownership is limited through market share in Italy and France, and through types of publications in Greece. Aside from this, the press is treated by and large in a liberal way. Regarding competition policy in certain countries competition policy includes media specific rules: in Austria and Germany thresholds that provoke investigations in a merger or acquisition are lower than for other industries; in Ireland and the United Kkingdom the Minister may intervene and in the UK a public interest test has been developed.

In other countries various levels of cooperation takes place between broadcasting and competition authorities. In broadcasting, horizontal concentration of media ownership is regulated in a wide variety of ways (see Table 1 below). Several countries have no or few restrictions regarding horizontal concentration in the television sector (Belgium, Denmark, Estonia, Finland, Lithuania, Luxembourg, Netherlands, Sweden and United Kingdom). Regarding cross-media ownership, there are, again, a variety of ways in which this is restricted (see Table 2 below). Of significance is the fact that there exist no restrictions in many of the EU member states that limit the extent to which companies can have an interest in a whole range of media sectors (see Table 5).

A variety of measures are used to assess a company's influence on the market, and to limit the influence of companies: circulation and audience share, number of licenses, capital shares, voting shares, advertising revenue, or involvement in a certain number of media sectors. Given these differences it is difficult to propose any kind of harmonization of rules between the EU member states. The systems have developed alongside and partly in response to the national markets, which in each country have specific characteristics. In several countries, while there may be general legal statements prohibiting media monopolies, and dominant positions, there are no/few provisions to limit ownership: Denmark, Finland, Lithuania, Poland, Portugal, Sweden. The approaches can be grouped in groups of nations.[20]

The Nordic countries Finland, Sweden, Denmark and to a lesser extent Norway have no or very few media ownership restrictions, where media experts, regulators, government and industry are, in general, content with the status quo. In these states emphasis is always placed on the role of government subsidies, which serve to maintain a plural press system. The media sectors in these countries tend to be highly concentrated, and public service broadcasters tend to be very strong (see Table 4). The Nordic states are home to some of the major companies active on a pan-European level: Bonnier, Modern Times Group, Schibsted and Orkla Media (see Table 5).

The Baltic States, in terms of geography, and sometimes language (Estonia and Finland having some common linguistic links) are in many ways linked to their Nordic neighbours. Furthermore, much is made of the take off of new technology in the Baltic States and the high levels of

Table 1: Horizontal concentration control mechanisms.

Ownership control in television broadcasting	Member State
Horizontal concentration	
Limits of ownership shares (capital shares)	Cyprus, Latvia, Portugal, Slovenia
Limits of ownership shares (voting shares)	Hungary, Malta
Limits on market shares (audience/listeners)	Germany, Norway
Capital share and licenses	Austria, Greece
Capital share and voting share	Slovak Republic, Spain
License limit and audience share	Czech Republic
Capital share, audience share, and licensing procedure	Belgium Walloon
Licensing with cross media or media operator restrictions	Ireland
Licenses, share of system and revenue share	Italy
Voting rights, audience reach, capital share and license limit	France

Table 2: Cross-media ownership control mechanisms.

Cross-media ownership control	Countries
License restrictions based on market share (and/or dominant position) in other media sectors in the same market	Austria, Germany, Italy
Radio license restrictions based on interest in other media sectors in the same market	United Kingdom (radio)
License restrictions based on capital shares of applicant in other media types in the same market	Cyprus, Hungary Slovenia, United Kingdom (for ITV and press)
License refusal based on interest in publishing sector in the same market	Slovakia
Limit on interest a company with broad media interests can have in a broadcasting company	Ireland
Limit on types of media a company can have interest in	France 'two out of four' rule Greece 'two out of three' rule
Restrictions concerning radio and television cross-ownership but not press and broadcasting	Malta
Limited restrictions	In Sweden concerning local radio
Vague restrictions	Poland 'No dominant position in mass communications in a given area'
No restrictions	Czech Republic, Denmark, Finland, Latvia. Lithuania, Luxembourg, Portugal, Spain

Internet penetration and use, which also aligns them with their Nordic neighbours. Although a similar liberal approach is taken here to media pluralism, unlike in the Nordic states public service broadcasting is very weak (see Table 4) and foreign companies dominate private broadcasting. Just like in Sweden and Norway, many of the important companies in the Baltic States are Swedish and Norwegian (Bonnier, Schibsted and the Modern Times Group, see Table 5).

Alison Harcourt (2003) examined the way in which models of media regulation developed in *Central and East European states*, outlining the role of Western governments, Western companies, international organizations and Western NGOs in this process. Similar to the Baltic States a rapid transition was needed to separate media and the state, to privatize, to regulate and to incorporate EU legislation. Many media experts[21] have noted the difficulties experienced in trying to regulate for freedom and independence while at the same time regulating market structure, and regulating for the opening of markets for EU membership. The different policy goals and agendas have made the introduction of media legislation rather complicated and controversial in these states. The status of public service television broadcasting in these member states has not been resolved (and they are often quite weak). The experience of these countries also implies that other (related) issues are of concern to media professionals, policy-makers and academics. Journalists and other media organizations are still striving for full independence and professionalism. Ownership of the media whether foreign, political or industrial inhibits many of these developments.

A further group includes *Germany, the United Kingdom, the Netherlands, Belgium, Luxembourg, Austria and Ireland*. Already, one can note that of these countries the United Kingdom, Ireland, Austria and Germany are the only EU member states where competition policy treats the media sector as an industry with special significance for society and hence enacts a different process for regulating mergers and concentrations. The countries each have very strong public service broadcasters (like those of the Nordic states). Of these, Germany and the United Kingdom are two of the core states of the European Union with the largest populations, and the home base of many of the important pan-European media companies. While both have relatively plural media systems, there are uncertainties regarding future development and also the slow process of deregulation. In the Dutch case, where there is a particularly highly concentrated press market, there is pressure to increase regulation in the media field. The new Austrian regime represents a comprehensive approach to regulation of the media sector, (mainly through licensing) but the Austrian media market is already a highly concentrated market. The Belgian law, regulating two communities, regulated by two separate authorities has a rather minimal approach to ownership regulation that also operates mainly through the licensing system in broadcasting. In Ireland the licensing of private broadcasting has also been the prime method of control of media ownership.

Similarities also exist between certain *Mediterranean countries* (France, Italy, Spain, Malta, Cyprus, Greece and Portugal) as regards the range of laws that exist which deal with the issue of media ownership, which are further enhanced by constitutional case law. Spain, Greece and Portugal have experiences in common with many of the new member states, having only in the 1970s become democratic states. Part of the democratization process involved the development of more voices in the media. In most cases large media actors emerged, and there are strong links between media ownership, politics and industry, as is the case in Italy. The links between media companies and large industry is also an issue of concern in France. The ownership of media outlets (radio in Cyprus and radio, television and press in Malta) by political parties has developed partly through the wish to increase pluralism and partly due to lack of capital being available elsewhere. Italy, France and Greece are the only three countries with specific limitations in the field of press ownership. In France and Greece this implies a limitation of share capital, while in Italy this is limited by market share.

Other problems arise in the implementation of these measures, not least the ability of companies to hide their ownership of other companies, to establish subsidiaries and holding companies. The issue of transparency of ownership is of particular relevance in East and South Eastern

Europe, where many West European (and American companies) operate. It is also a problem with regard to the involvement of politics and industry in the ownership of the media in all countries (See SEENPM/Peace Institute 2004 and Kevin et al. 2004).

Role of national regulatory authorities in protecting pluralism and promoting diversity[22]
European media regulatory bodies are many and varied. The membership of the EPRA now totals 51 authorities from 42 European countries, in itself a very broad and diverse network, also in terms of competences and remits. Each national jurisdiction has broadcasting legislation, which as a minimum (for those states in the EU) implements the standards mentioned above of the Television without Frontiers Directive (Audio-visual Media Services Directive) and in the case of Council of Europe states, the Convention on Transfrontier Television (with similar provisions to EU law). Additionally media law include aspects of fairness and accuracy in reporting and rules for media coverage of elections and referenda. Many regulatory authorities have the task to monitor such coverage to ensure fair treatment of candidates and parties according to the law. For the most part, the regulatory authority licenses media outlets, and in general licenses are granted subject to particular criteria, several of which relate to issues of media pluralism and to the promotion of diversity.

Table 3: Examples of criteria for licensing commercial television.

Licensing criteria	Countries
Regulators keep in mind inter alia:	
The promotion of diversity of opinion and pluralism of expression	Austria, France, Slovakia
Diversity of services so no domination of particular company	Ireland, Poland, Slovakia
Applicants agree inter alia:	
To provide a proportion of independent programming	Austria, Portugal
To provide a proportion of in-house production	Portugal, Slovenia
To provide a proportion European production	Czech Republic, Poland
To cover issues of cultural relevance to the nation	Austria, Ireland
To provide programmes in the national language	Belgium Walloon, Ireland
To support the journalistic and creative independence of journalists via terms of employment and collective bargaining	Cyprus
Transparency of ownership	Czech Republic, Slovakia
To provide programmes/content for minority cultures	Czech Republic
To implement journalistic and professional codes of conduct	Greece, Portugal
To ensure correct and unbiased presentation of information	Lithuania, Portugal

Source: Licensing policy documents on the websites of Regulatory Authorities.

Licensing

In terms of the licensing of broadcasters, many European regulatory authorities attach specific criteria to the award of broadcasting licenses (see Table 3), aside from the financial plan, experience and history of the applicant. The examples below relate more specifically to aspects of pluralism, diversity and journalistic freedom and practice.

Monitoring of media ownership

The monitoring of media ownership regarding mergers and acquisitions is dealt with by the competition authorities of the member states. In Germany there is a specific independent regulator responsible for media, the KEK. Regulatory authorities have varying responsibility in this process: either as above through the licensing system or for example through the monitoring of, and provision of reports on, the landscape, as in the Netherlands.

Other aspects of promotion of diversity in programming[23]

Several regulatory authorities have schemes to promote non-commercial local radio and television, community and campus broadcasting (the German authorities, Denmark). Some are involved in award schemes for good journalism (Malta, Bavarian Authority), or for quality programming (Malta, Bavarian Authority, Irish authority). In addition both the BCI in Ireland and the BLM in Bavaria have funding schemes for the production of programming: in Ireland this is funded with a percentage of fees paid by the broadcasters for their licenses and focuses on programmes related to Irish culture, heritage, the Irish language, adult literacy; in Bavaria the programming focuses on programming dealing with cultural economic, social and religious issues. In this way they contribute to the quality of in-house programming in the commercial sector, although very much with reference to the national sphere.

Digital Terrestrial Television

The development of digital broadcasting is ensuring a broader range of channels is available to viewers. Regarding free-to-air DTT (Digital Terrestrial Television), the regulation at the national level tries to ensure that the systems will enhance pluralism and diversity. 'Must carry' rules exist for certain channels and content, as is usually the case also with cable television. In addition, in most countries, the public service broadcasters have been granted at least one Multiplex in order to ensure their presence in the DTT system. The levels of development of DTT vary dramatically throughout the EU. In Finland analogue broadcasting has ceased, while in other states policy and strategy for DTT is only in the development stage.

The shape of the media landscapes in the European public spheres

The media landscapes in the countries of the European Union have in many cases developed over several decades, with the deregulation of the broadcasting industry bringing about major changes in this market during the 1990s. The broadcasting industry has historically been characterized by monopolistic or duopolistic systems due initially to the scarcity of spectrum, and also the monopolies of public service broadcasting, or state broadcasters. For many of the new EU member states, development occurred rapidly after the transition to new democracies, with often a large influx of foreign capital into these markets. As such it should be noted that

Table 4: The position of public service broadcasting in the EU markets (2004)

Combined audience share	of public service channels in EU countries	of top two commercial channels in EU countries*
Very High 60–75%	Denmark 72%	Czech Republic 65% Hungary 61%
High 50–60%	Poland 54% Austria 52%	Portugal 57% Lithuania 55% Finland 52%
Medium to High 40–50%	Italy 49% Finland 44% France 43% Belgium Flanders 41% Germany 41% Ireland 40% Sweden 40%	Netherlands 47% Estonia 44% France 44% Germany 43% Slovenia 42% Italy 41% Latvia 40%
Medium 35–40%	Netherlands 38% United Kingdom 38% Slovenia 35%	Greece 37% Malta 37.5%** Belgium Flanders 36% Poland 36% Sweden 35% United Kingdom 34%***
Low to Medium 25–35%	Malta 33% Czech Republic 31% Spain 30% Portugal 28%	Belgium Walloon 30%
Low 10–20%	Belgium Walloon 19% Latvia 19% Estonia 18% Hungary 18%, Cyprus 17% Greece 15% Lithuania 12%	Austria 10% Denmark 15% Ireland 13%**

Source: Kevin et al. 2004.

*In the case of Italy and Ireland, the share is just one channel.

**In Austria German channels have a 37 per cent share; In Ireland United Kingdom channels have over 40 per cent share; In Malta Italian channels have 19 per cent share; in Belgium Walloon French channels have a 30 per cent share; in Estonia, 40 per cent of the Russian speaking community watch Russian channels.

***Including ITV network, which is considered to have certain PSB obligations. Figures for Austria, Belgium, Cyprus, Denmark, Finland, Greece, Italy, from 2004. Figures for Czech Republic, Estonia, France, Germany, Ireland, Lithuania, Malta, Poland, Slovenia, Sweden, from 2003. Figures for Latvia, Netherlands from 2002. Luxembourg has no PSB (RTL cover some of this remit).

Table 5: Main European companies operating in EU media markets.

Parent company	Interests	Media markets in EU member states
Bertelsmann Germany	*in other companies* RTL Group 52%, Random House, Gruner und Jahr	**Radio:** Belgium, France, Germany, Luxembourg, Netherlands **Television:** Belgium, France, Germany, Hungary, Netherlands, Spain, United Kingdom
Bonnier Sweden	*in other companies* Alma Media (FI) 26.8%	**Press/publishing:** Hungary, Poland, Germany **Radio:** Sweden **Television:** Sweden, Finland **Press/publishing:** Sweden, Latvia, Finland, Poland, Lithuania
CanWest Global Communications Corp (Canada)	*in other companies* SBS Broadcasting: 7%	**Television:** Ireland, United Kingdom
Central European Media Enterprises (Bermuda)	*Ownership structure...* Lauder Family 100% (A) voting	**Television:** Slovenia, Slovakia
Fininvest, Italy	*in other companies* Mediaset 48.36%, Mondadori *Ownership structure...* Berlusconi Family 96%	**Television:** Italy, Spain **Press/publishing:** Italy
Lagardère Media, France	*in other companies* Discovery Communications 50% Discovery Channels 100% AOL Time Warner 4% News Corp 24%, Viacom 1% Vivendi Universal 4% SBS Broadcasting 21% UnitedGlobalCom 51%	**Cable TV** **UPC:** Austria, Belgium, Netherlands, Hungary, Poland, France, Czech Republic **Liberty Media:** Ireland, United Kingdom (Telewest)
Modern Times Group (Swedish owned, UK based)	*Ownership structure...* Invik 9.3%, Kinnevik 7.5% SEB 6.8%, Emesco 5% 4th AP-Fund 4.9%, Robur 4.2%	**Radio:** Latvia, Sweden **Television:** Latvia, Lithuania, Sweden

Parent company	Interests	Media markets in EU member states
News Corporation US	*in other companies* Fox Entertainment, Fox Broadcasting News International *Ownership structure...* Liberty Media 24%	**Satellite Television:** United Kingdom: Ireland, Italy **Press:** United Kingdom, Ireland **Radio:** Netherlands
Orkla Press Norway	*in other companies* Schibsted 3.3%	**Press/Publishing:** Poland, Lithuania, Sweden
Passauer Neue Presse, Germany		**Press/Publishing:** Czech Republic, Poland, Germany
Ringier, Switzerland		**Press/Publishing:** Czech Republic, Hungary, Slovakia
SBS Broadcasting US (Luxembourg)	*Ownership structure...* UnitedGlobalCom 21% Janus Capital 7.3% EnTrust Capital 7.2% CanWest Global Comm Corp 7.1%	**Radio:** Sweden **Television:** Belgium, Hungary, Netherlands, Sweden
Vivendi Universal	*in other companies* Universal Pictures Universal Music Group Universal Studios Canal+ (51%) *Ownership structure...* Canal + (51%) Canal+ owned Canalsatellite 66% Sogecable 16.38%	**Television:** Belgium **Satellite Television:** Netherlands, Spain, France **Cable:** France, Spain
West Allgemeine Deutsche Zeitung Group Germany	*in other companies* 20% share in BWTV a shareholder in RTL Group	**Press/Publishing:** Germany, Poland

Data from Kevin et al. (2004).

while many regulatory systems were put in place *before* market developments (such as the regulatory structure prepared before the launch of commercial broadcasting in, for example, Ireland or Sweden), in other countries the systems are often attempting to deal with a *given status quo* in the market (Poland, Italy). Specific characteristics of media markets need to be borne in mind in terms of size: from populations of less than 0.5m in Malta, Cyprus, Luxembourg to populations of 82m Germany, 60m France and UK, 57m Italy; and also with reference to cross border broadcasting (see below).

In certain countries (according to available figures) there is a very high dominance of public service broadcasting in the market (Denmark, Poland and Austria). Commercial channels are weak in Austria, Denmark and Ireland. Public service broadcasting is significantly weak in Belgium Walloon, Latvia, Estonia, Hungary, Cyprus, Greece and Lithuania; and weak in Spain and Portugal.

As noted earlier, several of these countries have no or few restrictions regarding horizontal concentration in the television sector (Belgium, Estonia, Lithuania). On the other hand Denmark and Finland also have no or few restrictions, which implies that a cultural difference regarding media (Nordic traditions) or a hangover from public perceptions of state television (Baltic States) may come into play. Either way, the Baltic states largely took the Nordic approach to regulating media, one that does not appear to have enhanced pluralism.

In terms of European public sphere issues, such data could be usefully compared with resource allocation in terms of EU correspondents by television channels, and also the levels of coverage of EU issues on these channels. The significance of transnational broadcasting on coverage of the EU is also an issue for further investigation (see for example comments in Corcoran and Fahy 2006 regarding UK media outlets' influence on Irish EU debates).

The logic of concentration of the industry is clear from the perspective of industry actors. Media corporations have expanded their interests vertically in order to control content development, production and distribution, as convergence along the supply chain reduces costs and enhances potential profits. They have also integrated vertically across sectors (cross-media ownership) in order to exploit revenues or promote content e.g. the promotion of films through publications or music through film. With the development of media technologies and the convergence of audio-visual content, IT and telecommunications, media corporations also seek to develop their ownership of, or links to, the variety of distribution platforms now available for content.

Recently, we have witnessed further trends in deregulation of the media industry with an increased loosening or easing of the rules regarding ownership at the national level, with the Federal Communications Commission in the United States planning a relaxation of ownership rules (allowing media corporations to reach 45 per cent rather than just 35 per cent of television viewers), and the Communications Act in the UK (relaxing foreign ownership restrictions, cross-media ownership rules). Both moves were highly controversial and in the case of the United Kingdom a compromise has been reached with the development of a 'public interest test' which is intended to determine the potential share of the 'public voice' which a merged company would have (as mentioned above).

From the perspective of practitioners, the European Federation of Journalists have highlighted their concerns regarding the concentration of ownership in Europe and focused on three major threats to the media landscape: the threat to public service broadcasting, to media pluralism and to emerging markets in Eastern Europe (EFJ 2002). It is clearly an area of concern for civil society, for practitioners and policy-makers.

Concentration and consolidation in the media industries and policy responses of the European Union and the Council of Europe

Concerns regarding the concentration of media industries date back to the 1970s when several countries began implementing regulations to control the development of the market. With the rapid expansion and commercialization of the media sectors in the 1980s these issues again came to the fore, with the push for free trade and deregulation of industries including the media. While in Western Europe the number of media outlets increased, a consolidation of the industry took place through mergers, acquisitions, agreements, etc. This development has been on the international rather than European level and sparked further concern leading to the development of a system for monitoring developments at the Council of Europe.

The Council of Europe has been very active in the field of media concentration/media pluralism and diversity through recommendations and reports. The first recommendation on transparency was adopted in 1994, although work on the issue had already started in 1989,[24] followed by the recommendation on measures to promote media pluralism adopted in 1999.[25] Two reports: *Pluralism in the Multi-channel Market: Suggestions for Regulatory Scrutiny* (1999) and *Media Pluralism in the Digital Environment* (2000) were published by the group of specialists on media pluralism. In 2003, the Advisory Panel to the Council of Europe Steering Committee on the Mass Media (CDMM) on media concentrations, pluralism and diversity questions compiled a report on media diversity in Europe.[26] At the sixth European Ministerial Conference on Mass Media Policy, which was held in Krakow in June 2000, the Ministers of the participating states agreed, *inter alia*, that the 'human and democratic dimension of communication should be at the core' of states' activities in the field, and should focus on four essential axes:

- the balance between freedom of expression and information and other rights and legitimate interests
- pluralism of media services and content
- the promotion of social cohesion
- the adaptation of the regulatory framework for the media in the light of ongoing developments.

In particular, with regard to pluralism, the Ministers agreed that the CDMM should monitor the impact on pluralism of the development of new communication and information services and the trend towards greater media concentrations, and examine the importance for pluralism of preserving the diversity of sources of information. In the context of the European Union, the development of media markets in Europe was considered an important concern in terms of safeguarding European cultural and political identities in the face of US domination of the information and cultural industries. The EU has always been caught between the two, often contradictory, desires to develop strong media organizations on a pan-European level in order to counteract US or Japanese strength in the media sector, while also desiring to retain pluralism at the national level in terms of cultural representation and political opinion.

However, member states have frequently blocked or hindered any pan-European approach to establishing harmonized rules with the argument that the regulation of market structure is more appropriately dealt with at the level of the nation state. One example was the *Green Paper on Pluralism and Media Concentration in the Internal Market* of 1992, which due to political and industry opposition did not result in the adoption of a directive. Therefore, the main legal instruments at EU-level up to now have been the TV Without Frontiers Directive, the 'Telecom' package which entered into force in July 2003 and the competition rules, in particular the Merger Regulation.

However, the European Parliament remained active in the field by adopting a number of resolutions over the years.[27] A resolution on media concentration was adopted in 2002 where the Parliament called upon the Commission and the member states to safeguard media pluralism. It also called on the Commission to launch a broad consultation process assessing the impact of thirteen new technologies on media pluralism and on the right to freedom of expression, aiming at drawing up an updated Green Paper on these issues. A further resolution was adopted by the Committee on Citizens' Freedoms and Rights, Justice and Home Affairs in 2004 concerning risks of violation, in the EU and especially in Italy, of freedom of expression and information, with specific reference to Italy. The resolution contained a number of recommendations for actions at the European level, which to date have not occurred (see European Parliament 2004).[28] It did not recommend an overriding EU Directive on ownership legislation but rather: a change in the approach to competition policy; the provision of data on markets; a directive on transparency of ownership; support for public service broadcasting; and the need to ensure both ethical standards and fair employment terms in journalism. A research project examining methods of measuring and ensuring media pluralism in the member states was launched by the European Commission in 2007.

Conclusion

Journalism practice and ethical standards are largely self-regulated. This practice is influenced by political cultures, and not least by the financial situation of media outlets, and the employment situations of journalists. The EU plays a very minor role in developing these issues in comparison to the work of the Council of Europe. As far as freedom and independence of the media is concerned, this is only addressed by the EU with relation to external countries, or those considered as aspiring to the 'presumed' democratic standards of the EU member states.

The approach of the European Union to media policy has broadly focused on the strengthening of European media companies *vis a vis* those of the United States. The growth of these companies is somewhat controlled via competition policy, although as can be seen from above, major companies have followed a tactic of spreading their interests across a broad range of member states.

The EU also contributes to promoting the development of the information society whereby the regulation of telecommunications and new communication services is becoming more and more relevant to broadcasting. Support is also provided to independent production via the Directive and to the European film industry via the MEDIA programme. On the basis of the Directive TWF/AVMS, new member states were compelled to introduce broadcasting or media laws to incorporate these aspects, which ensured that all member states have broadcasting legislation. As noted above the simultaneous opening of markets, with the attempt to regulate, was not without problems.

The communication policies of the EU, in the sense of how they communicate with their citizens, have been developing, increasing resources and professionalism. The extent that this contributes to spheres of debate rather than news management needs further examination.

National media regulation varies widely in relation to media pluralism with many states having few or no restrictions of ownership. Regulatory authorities play a role in pluralism regarding the licensing process, and in some cases regarding journalism in the promotion of quality programming. The media markets, despite levels of regulation are not without problems. Often this is a matter of structure and characteristics: size, proximity to same language larger states, political cultures. Levels of concentration, concentration and cross media ownership are relatively high, but the effects can only be considered in the broader context of media culture, media use, strength of public service broadcasting, etc. In many states public service broadcasters still have a strong share, or a reasonable share with the top two commercial channels, while in others public service broadcasting is very weak.

To date the main responsibility for regulating media markets remains with the member state, as it is in most cases in the interest of the member state to retain this competence due to the economic, political and cultural specifics of the national markets. While the European Union had previously shown little interest in regulating media pluralism issues in the member states, the more recent developments in the regulation of new communication services and the use of the frequency spectrum will undoubtedly affect the work of national regulators in the future.

Notes
1. For example: Sweden (1766); France (1789); and Austria (1867).
2. Austria, Sweden, Finland, Italy, Luxembourg.
3. Belgium, Portugal, Greece, Hungary, Slovakia.
4. Estonia, Latvia, Lithuania, Poland, Slovenia.
5. This tradition is oldest where transparency of information was addressed in the 1795 Declaration of the Rights of Man in the Netherlands, and in the Freedom of the Press Ordinance of 1766 in Sweden. For a comprehensive overview see Banisar (2003).

6. Estonia 2000, Czech Republic 2000, Hungary 1992, Latvia 1998, Lithuania 2000, Poland 2001, Slovakia 2000, Slovenia 2003.
7. Decree No. 352/92: http://www.governo.it/Presidenza/DICA/documentazione_accesso/normativa/dpr352_1992_eng.html.
8. International Federation of Journalists; European Federation of Journalists.
9. See Kevin et al. (2004), and also the International Freedom of Expression Exchange: http://www.irex.org and Reporters Without Frontiers: http://www.rsf.org.
10. As above.
11. There are a wide range of resources available through international organizations who continually monitor and support media freedom throughout Europe where further information and updates on these issues can be accessed: the Council of Europe, Media Division; the Organization for Security and Cooperation in Europe; the European Federation of Journalists; the International Federation of Journalists; the International Freedom of Expression Exchange; the International Press Institute and Reporters Without Frontiers among others.
12. Revised in 1997, and currently going through a review process as the proposed Audio-visual Media Services Directive.
13. This combines: the European Union: Directive 2002/21/EC on a common regulatory framework for electronic communications networks and services; Directive 2002/19/EC on access to, and interconnection of, electronic communications networks and services; Directive 2002/20/EC on the authorization of electronic communications networks and services; Directive 002/22/EC on universal service and users' rights relating to electronic communications networks; Directive Directive 2002/58/EC concerning the processing of personal data and the protection of privacy in the electronic communications sector; and Regulation (EC) No 2006/2004 on consumer protection cooperation.
14. http://europa.eu.int/comm/competition/state_aid/overview/.
15. Amsterdam Treaty: protocol on the system of public broadcasting in the member states, http://www.europa.eu.int/eur-lex/lex/en/treaties/dat/11997D/htm/11997D.html#0109010012.
16. Directorate-General for Competition DG D (2004): Community Framework for State Aid in the Form of Public Service Compensation, http://europa.eu.int/comm/competition/state_aid/others/public_service_comp/en.pdf.
17. For example the Taiex projects, PHARE project, TACIS funding, and the Bridges of Knowledge programme.
18. See AIM Consortium (2006), report on second field study.
19. Information on media ownership legislation taken from Kevin et al. (2004); and from relevant government and/or regulatory websites.
20. For more detail see Kevin et al. (2004).
21. For example Harcourt (2003), Jakubowicz (1996, 2003, etc.), Hrvatin and Petkovic (2004).
22. Information from: Council of Europe (2003), and from the media legislation available on national government wesites, and media policy available on the Regulatory Authorities' websites, of each country.
23. Information from a review of the online information of the EPRA members.
24. Rec (1994)013 and Explanatory Memorandum, RECOMMENDATION No. R (94) 13 of the Committee of Ministers to member states on measures to promote media transparency.

25. Rec(1999)001 and Explanatory Memorandum, RECOMMENDATION No. R (99) 1 of the Committee of Ministers to member states on measures to promote media pluralism (Adopted by the Committee of Ministers on 19 January 1999 at the 656th meeting of the Ministers' Deputies).
26. All are available at: http://www.coe.int/
27. Resolution in OJEC C 68 of 19.03.90, Resolution in OJEC C 284 of 2.11.92, B4-0262 in the OJEC C323 of 21.11.94, B4-0884 in OJEC C 166 of 3.07.95.
28. The report of the Committee was based on the work provided in Kevin et al. (2004). See also SEENPM/Peace Institute (2004).

References

AIM Consortium (ed.) (2006–2), *Report of the Second Field Study. Adequate Information Management in Europe Working Papers*. Project co-funded by the Sixth Framework Programme of the European Commission. Germany: Projekt verlag.

Anderson, P. J. and Weymouth, A. (1999), *Insulting the Public? The British Press and the European Union*. UK: Longman.

Blumler, J. (ed.) (1983), *Communicating to Voters: Television in the First European Parliamentary Elections*. London: Sage.

Bainsnée, O. (2002), 'Can Political Journalism Exist at the EU level?', in R. Kuhn and E. Neveu (eds), *Political Journalism: New Challenges, New Practices*, pp. 108–27. London: Routledge.

Banisar, D. (2003), *The www.freedominfo.org Global Survey: Freedom of Information and Access to Government Record Laws Around the World*, http://www.freedominfo.org/survey.htm. Accessed: 10.09.07

CEC (1992). Resolution in OJEC C 284 of 2.11.92.

CEC (1994). B4-0262 in the OJEC C323 of 21.11.94.

CEC (1995). B4-0884 in OJEC C 166 of 3.07.95.

Corcoran, F. and Fahy, D. (2006–2, forthcoming), 'Ireland Report', in the *Report of the Second Field Study. Adequate Information Management in Europe Working Papers*. AIM Research Consortium (ed.). Project co-funded by the Sixth Framework Programme of the European Commission. Germany: Projekt verlag.

Council of Europe: Rec(1994)013 and Explanatory Memorandum, RECOMMENDATION No. R (94) 13 of the Committee of Ministers to member states on measures to promote media transparency, http://www.coe.int/t/e/human_rights/media/. Accessed: 05.02.07

Council of Europe: Rec(1999)001 and Explanatory Memorandum, RECOMMENDATION No. R (99) 1 of the Committee of Ministers to member states on measures to promote media pluralism (Adopted by the Committee of Ministers on 19 January 1999 at the 656th meeting of the Ministers' Deputies), http://www.coe.int/t/e/human_rights/media/. Accessed: 01.10.07

Council of Europe (2000), *Report on Media Pluralism in the Digital Environment*. Adopted by the Steering Committee on the Mass Media in October 2000,

Council of Europe (2001), *Case Law Concerning Article 10 of the European Convention on Human Rights*. File Number 18. Council of Europe.

Council of Europe (2002), *Media Diversity in Europe*. Report prepared by the AP-MD (Advisory panel to the CDMM on media concentrations, pluralism and diversity questions). Strasbourg: December 2002.

Council of Europe (2003), *An Overview of the Rules Governing Broadcasting Regulatory Authorities in Europe*. DH-MM(2003)007. Media Division, Directorate General of Human Rights Council of Europe. Strasbourg.

De Vreese, C. (2003), *Framing Europe: Television News and European Integration*. Amsterdam: Aksant.

European Federation of Journalists (2002), *European Media Ownership: Threats on the Landscape. A Survey of Who Owns What in Europe*. Brussels: September 2002, http://www.ifj.org/assets/docs/252/115/714aafc-9039473.pdf. Accessed: 02.03.07

European Federation of Journalists (2003), *Eastern Empires. Foreign Ownership in Central and Eastern European Media: Ownership, Policy Issues and Strategies*. Brussels: June 2003. Retrieved from http://www.ifj.org/en/articles/eastern-empires-. Accessed: 05.04.07

European Parliament (2004), *Report on the Risks of Violation, in the EU and Especially in Italy, of Freedom of Expression and Information (Article 11(2) of the Charter of Fundamental Rights) 2003/2237(INI))* Committee on Citizens' Freedoms and Rights, Justice and Home Affairs. Rapporteur: Johanna L. A. Boogerd-Quaak.

Eilders, C. and Voltmer, K. (2003), 'Zwischen Deutschland und Europa. Eine empirische Untersuchung zum Grad von Europäisierung und Europa-Unterstützung der meinungsführenden deutschen Tageszeitungen. [Between Germany and Europe: An Empirical Examination of the Level of Europeanization of, and of support for Europe in the Influential German Daily Newspapers]', *Medien und Kommunikationswissenschaft*, 51: 2, pp. 250–70.

Gandy, O. (1982), *Beyond Agenda-setting: Information Subsidies and Public Policy*. Norwood: Ablex.

Graham, D. and Associates (2005), *Impact Study of Measures (Community and National) Concerning the Promotion of Distribution and Production of TV Programmes Provided for Under Article 25(a) of the TV Without Frontiers Directive. Final Report*. Prepared for the Audio-visual, Media and Internet Unit, Directorate General Information Society and Media, European Commission.

Harcourt, A. (2003), 'The Regulation of Media Markets in Selected EU Accession States in Central and Eastern Europe', in *European Law Journal*, 9: 3 (July).

Herold, A. (2005), 'European Film Policies and Competition Law: Hostility or Symbiosis?', in M. Gencel-Bek and D. Kevin (eds), Communication Policies in the European Union and Turkey: Market Regulation, Access and Diversity. Ankara: Ankara University, pp. 293–336.

Hrvatin, S. and Kucic, J. (2004), 'Regional Overview', in *Media Ownership and its Impact on Media Independence and Pluralism*. Ljubljana: SEENPM/Peace Institute.

International Research and Exchanges Board (IREX) (2007), *MSI Europe and Eurasia: The Development of Sustainable Media in Europe and Eurasia 2006/2007*. Available online: http://www.irex.org/programs/MSI_EUR/index.asp. Accessed 10.08. 2007.

Jakubowicz, K., Bodhan, J. and Kowalski, T. (eds) (2003), *Green Paper: Premises for the New Law on Electronic Media and Amendments to other Legislation*. A Paper prepared under the PHARE project.

Kevin, D., Ader, T., Fueg, O. C., Pertzinidou, E. and Schoenthal, M. (2004), *Final Report of the Study on 'Media Ownership Regulation and Media Landscapes in the EU 25'*. Prepared on behalf of the European Parliament by the European Institute for the Media. August 2004. Available online at the EPRA website under press information/downloads: http://www.epra.org. Accessed: 03.07.07

Kevin, D. (2003), Europe in the Media: Reporting, Representation and Rhetoric. New Jersey: Lawrence Erlbaum Associates.

Meyer, C. (2003), 'Political Legitimacy and the Invisibility of Politics: Exploring the European Union's Communication Deficit', *Journal of Common Market Studies*, 37: 4, pp. 617–39.

Morgan, D. (1995), 'British Media and European Union News: The Brussels News Beat and its Problems', *European Journal of Communication*, 10: 3, pp. 321–43.

Organization for Security and Cooperation in Europe (OSCE) Representative on Freedom of the Media (2003), *The Impact of Concentration on Professional Journalism*, eds J. v Dohnanyi and C. Möller. Vienna 2003.

SEENPM/Peace Institute (2004), *Media Ownership and its Impact on Media Independence and Pluralism*. Ljubljana: SEENPM/ Peace Institute. Available: http://www.mirovni-institut.si/media_ownership/index.htm. Accessed: 05.04.07

Schlesinger, P. (1999), 'Changing Spaces of Political Communication: The Case of the European Union', *Political Communication*, 16, pp. 263–79.

Schlesinger, P. and Kevin, D. (2000), 'Can the European Union become a Sphere of Publics?, in Erik Oddvar Eriksen and John Erik Fossum (eds), *Democracy in Europe: Integration through Deliberation*. London: UCL Press.

Siune, K. (1993), 'The Danes said No to the Maastricht Treaty: the Danish Referendum of June 1992', *Scandinavian Political Studies*, 16: 1, pp. 93–103.

Slaatta, T. (1999), *Europeanisation and the Norwegian News Media: Political Discourse and News Production in the Transnational Field*. Oslo: University of Oslo.

Ward, D. (2005), 'Television Pluralism and Diversity: an Outline of the European Commission's Competition Policy and the Role of the member states in Maintaining Media Pluralism', in M. Gencel-Bek and D. Kevin (eds), *Communication Policies in the European Union and Turkey: Market Regulation, Access and Diversity*. Ankara: Ankara University, pp. 215–46.

5

The Berlusconi Case: Mass Media and Politics in Italy

Paolo Mancini

Abstract

The paper tries to place the Berlusconi case within the framework of old and new features of Italian politics and mass media. His figure has to be understood in connection with the transformations of the political system which derived from the 'Tangentopoli' (bribery city) scandals and the commercialization of the mass media system of the 1980s. Berlusconi introduced within the old tradition of parallelism between media and politics a completely new way to approach the voters. He has been able to popularize Italian political culture introducing within it new attitudes and new imaginaries. At the same time he has applied to political struggle all those skills, marketing approaches and centralization that he was able to derive from his business experience. All this doesn't diminish the seriousness of the conflict of interest he introduced into the Italian democracy.

Keywords
Italy, Politics, Berlusconi, mass media, popularization

The political environment
I understand that this article could disappoint all those who see Berlusconi as the biggest problem facing media democracy in Italy today is. Many scholars and observers have correctly stressed this point (Ginsborg 2004; Stille 2006). However though this article doesn't support

Berlusconi it will try to show that his figure has to be understood within the framework of Italian democracy, of its past and its shortcomings. It seems to me that there is a sort of Berlusconi common sense that goes more or less like this: Berlusconi has become such an important political figure because he is the owner of a television conglomerate. Many others have stressed his connection with the mafia and his involvement in corruption. Both views are undoubtedly correct, but they are, nevertheless, partial: to understand the 'Berlusconi case' you have to place it within the old and very well-rooted reality of the Italian political and mass-media system, paying less attention to more 'exotic' interpretations which tend to focus only on the exceptionality of his case. One also needs to recognize all the novelties Berlusconi has managed to introduce into the Italian political arena.

Before getting into the discussion of mass media, let us look at the political environment and the changes that it has gone through recently. As a matter of fact the 'Berlusconi case' has to be placed within the vacuum that was created in 1992 with the Tangentopoli (bribery city) scandal. Many important political leaders were arrested; the oldest and most important political parties were all involved in the scandals and, because of their judiciary consequences, all of the major parties that up to then had had the responsibility for the Italian government suddenly disappeared from the political arena. Democrazia Cristiana (DC), Partito Socialista Italiano (PSI), Partito Socialista Democratico (PSDI), Partito Repubblicano Italiano (PRI) and the Partito Liberale Italiano (PLI) were all forced out by the scandals. For almost 50 years this group of parties had together supported the government majority. Between 1992 and 1993 they all vanished as many of their leaders were either arrested or left active political life altogether. A vacuum was created in the middle (between leftist and rightist parties) of the Italian political arena.

When, in 1994, new political elections took place voters, who for years had voted for the same parties, no longer found their old symbols to check off on the ballot. As a matter of fact, up to that moment the Italian political arena was characterized by a consistent and very well-rooted 'affiliation vote' (Parisi and Pasquino 1977): for almost 50 years Italian citizens had always basically voted for the same parties. Suddenly those parties disappeared. This is the point: Berlusconi filled that political vacuum establishing, in the very short period of four months, a new party called Forza Italia, which was able to capture most of the votes that up to then had gone to those parties which had now disappeared (Poli 2001). The question is: how was that possible? How was it possible to establish a brand new party in such a short period of time? And how was it possible to get the allegiance of those voters?

Mass media features

To answer this question we have to look to the field of mass media. As a matter of fact Berlusconi has to be put in the context of the political arena which emerged from the bribery city scandals, and, at the same time, his success was dependent in large part on his use and abuse of the mass media. Here lies the Berlusconi common sense: limiting the reasons for his political success to his ownership of the biggest private television corporation in Italy is just not enough because in some ways Berlusconi really does represent a mixture of the old and new features of the

Italian mass media system. On one side, he has been able to profit from some deeply rooted characteristics of the Italian mass media and, on the other, he introduced a completely new way of behavior and communicating in the field of politics.

Let's start with a look at the past. Since its establishment, the Italian mass media system has been characterized, as many other mass media systems in the Western world, by a very high level of political advocacy and parallelism. The print press was born with a strong tendency toward political advocacy and a self-appointed educational role (Asor Rosa 1981). Because of the elitist dimension linked to cultural (low literacy rates, a professional model very much linked to some sort of enlightened vision of the mission of the journalist) and economic developments (very late development of a market-driven economy, absence of a strong bourgeois class), over the years this particular characterization has remained in place in Italy, and through the recent commercialization transformation of the 80s as well. Television was also born and developed within this tradition of political involvement and educational efforts: political parties, and mostly the government, had been able to dominate and direct broadcasting so as to use it as an instrument to establish and maintain political consensus (Hallin and Mancini 2004).

The tradition of political bias in the print press and TV news has always been linked to a very strong party system and a very high level of political participation, at least since the years of the Resistance. Party membership had been high as had voting turnout, one of the highest in Europe. Areas of strong sub-cultural affiliation had spread out and the mass media had been linked to the existing ideological and cultural areas, thus reinforcing their role as agents of political socialization. In other words, more than a profit-making machine to be placed within a market-driven logic, the entire mass media system in Italy has been structured, and acted as, a political means to support either political or economic interests outside of the mass media field itself. Both large private and public corporations and political organizations have been able to establish very well-rooted connections within the mass media, either through direct ownership of it or other systems of influence so that most, if not all of the news organizations respond to their own particular economic and political interests (Murialdi 1986).

The mass media system (both print press and broadcasting) has therefore been structured as the sort of public sphere similar to that James Curran has defined as 'radical democratic', in which 'the media are a battleground between contending forces' (Curran 1991: 29). Through the mass media the political elite, interest groups and private economic groups can express their ideas, improve their level of consensus and negotiate their interests and goals with the other groups (Mancini 1992).

The high level of political participation is also reflected in news media consumption. On one hand, circulation of the print press has remained very low, third from last position in the Fiej ranking.[1] Newspapers essentially circulate among the political and cultural elite (Forcella 1956). Each newspaper, but also each TV station, has its own following based on political affiliation: communists read communist newspapers (and watch TV news) that are close to communist culture and ideology; Catholics read catholic newspapers (and watch TV news) linked to the Catholic Church, etc. On the other hand, Italians have always shown a great interest in the TV news: the main Rai TV newscasts reach an average audience of 6 million, as do the main Mediaset newscasts. Current affairs programs dealing with politics have always scored very well in terms of audience and the tendency towards infotainment has not limited their number.

The political parallelism between mass media and politics has caused an underdevelopment of professionalism in journalism and a tradition of continuing overlapping between political figures and mass media figures. It has always been easy to shift from one role to the other in Italy and this is also true for all of the political leanings. The long-lasting elitist tradition, and therefore the poor nature of the mass as financial sources, has facilitated, as it has been already said, the ownership of the media by different groups both of a political and economic nature, which have used the media to reach and support their own particular interests.

A tendency towards mass media instrumentalization has therefore taken place: the mass media, and particularly the news media, have been used as a means to reach the goals of the particular groups to which each is linked. This phenomenon is coupled with a traditionally low level of rational legal authority. More than general interest, the particular interests of my 'own group affiliation' have been more important[2] and the rules have always counted little in Italy (Hallin and Mancini 2004). This is also true for the media professionals who, despite a unique experience of institutionalization,[3] have always lacked a strong traditional code of ethics. The rules of professional journalism have often overlapped either with the rules and behavior of political participation and socialization or with the rules of market-driven competition and the need to construct consensus in favour of corporations and interest groups.

The commercialization which took place in Italy in the 80s, as in many other Western European countries, did not destroy this system of influential connections and overlapping. New media organizations were born but maintained this general attitude of partisanship and strong links with different social and economic interests and the mass media. Nevertheless, mass media commercialization has had dramatic consequences which deeply affected Italian culture and the processes of political socialization.

For many reasons, Berlusconi is the result of the mass media commercialization of the 80s. But, again, the commercialization took place within an established set of rules and habits. The already existing tradition of partisan media attitudes, together with the absence of a strong and rooted professional journalism and mass media rules, determining a very sensationalist approach, has facilitated the dramatization, trivialization and personalization of politics essentially in relation to a television audience which is the least educated and has the least access to other media resources. The traditional partisan tradition has survived mixed with a high level of dramatization of political life.

A sort of dichotomized situation has therefore taken place. On one side there is the large mass audience depending on television: trivialization and personalization of politics, together with the already mentioned partisan tradition, has had an easy job with this audience making the Berlusconi success story possible. On the other side, the print press has also maintained its partisan nature, addressing a more educated and socialized readership. In this situation, where the different political voices are still linked to media system even if within a market-driven logic, the main problem seems to be the lack of any effective law on mass media ownership concentration. Because of the very well-rooted attitude towards mass media instrumentalization and, therefore, because of the pressure from either economic or political groups, the Italian Parliament has been unable to approve any serious law ending the present duopoly, making real mass media pluralism impossible. Rai and Mediaset control almost 90 per cent of all advertising resources, thereby blocking pluralistic competition.

With the 1992 Commission *Green Paper on Pluralism and Media Concentration in the Internal Market* the EU has left to member states the duty to approve legislation (Kaitatzi-Whitlock 2005). The Italian legislation on pluralism and media concentration is ineffective and the absence of an anti-concentration law, together with the dubious identity of professional journalism, has facilitated the path towards the already mentioned trivialization of public life which, in turn, has not improved the standards of Italian democracy.

The Berlusconi novelties

It is time to look at the novelties that Berlusconi introduced into the field of political communication when he decided to enter the political arena. As it has already been said, he had given political representation to those interests, of both an economic and social nature, that up to 1992 had been inherent in the disappeared centre-left coalition parties. But he gave a voice to those interests in a completely new way. Berlusconi was able to understand much better and much earlier than his competitors the cultural, but also the social changes, that the mass media commercialization of the 80s had introduced. Of course he was well ahead of his competitors because he came directly from the mass media which had so dramatically changed Italian society.

As the Italian philosopher Norberto Bobbio said in 1994, when Berlusconi ran his first election campaign, he had been able to pick up the fruits of twenty years of his own broadcasting (Bobbio, Bosetti and Vattimo 1994). In other words, the Berlusconi televisions had already created a culture which stressed success in business and sports, inviting Italians to share a life of ease and riches as represented by his transmissions as well as by his own personal lifestyle. Berlusconi himself was the prime example of that culture and it was very easy for him to understand the changes that his own television stations had determined.

The first thing Berlusconi understood seems obvious and banal today: he understood that mass media, essentially television, had replaced the old traditional sources of political socialization. A party structure was no longer needed in order to communicate with the people. All one had to do was buy TV time and attract the attention of the news media. It is not a coincidence that the Forza Italia party Berlusconi founded was named a 'plastic party' in that it was not founded with a base structure of people, but on the TV set, which represents the common denominator between its members, the Party and the citizens (Calise 2000).

It was in attracting media attention that Berlusconi's experience and skills came to good use, qualities he had acquired when he founded and managed his TV networks. He had a better understanding, and he had it before his adversaries, of the fact that television programming responds above all to the logic of commercial competition, and therefore one must pay attention to the logic behind the communication which guides TV programming. His competitors did not have this sensitivity; they were accustomed to interaction with mass communication dealing directly with political logic, instrumentalization and public service. Berlusconi also depended on consolidated habits of instumentalization using at least some of his stations[4] in a completely partisan manner, but at the same time, relying on his own experience of mass media owner, he was able to ensure himself the opening slot in the TV news and first page in the print press (Mazzoleni 1995).

Berlusconi understands, better than his competitors do, that the new competitive logic of mass media requires a high level of dramatization and personalization when it comes to political communication. Only with these two elements can one hope to be seen on TV and be read about in the newspapers. These are the two elements which permit the mass media news organizations to sell more copies and to get a larger audience.

All of Berlusconi's campaigns, beginning with the one in 1994, have been extremely personalized. Berlusconi himself becomes the story, and around him and his vicissitudes news stories are made, around him and his vicissitudes current affairs programmes are constructed. The vicissitudes, symbols and imaginary which surround Berlusconi are a total break with the tradition of Italian political communication (Abruzzese 1994). The old arguments are no longer there, the old issues, even the old dreams and myths of political communication are gone. When the mass media speak of Berlusconi, and they speak a lot about him, his name becomes part of a completely new set of sensations, emotions, dreams which have little to do with the traditional Italian political discourse.

Right after the 1994 campaign Mario Morcellini wrote a book entitled *E-lezioni di TV* (*E-lections of TV*) (Morcellini 1995). The title, and the ambiguities hidden therein, was right on target. On the one hand, it underlined the role of television in the electoral (elezioni) campaign and, and, on the other, it suggested that, from then on there would be much to be learned (lezioni). What could be learned? In the end, I think that both Norberto Bobbio and Alberto Abruzzese were right, though coming from absolutely opposite positions, when they wrote, with the victory of the 1994 elections close at hand, that Berlusconi represented something completely new on the political and communication stage of Italy. The title of the work of Bobbio, in which he dealt with this argument, was in itself illuminating: in *The Left in the Era of Karaoke* Bobbio wanted to show how and how much Berlusconi was intimately identified with that television imaginary to whose creation he had himself contributed with his networks, and which the philosopher from Turin soundly condemned.

Alberto Abruzzese, with his *Elogio del Tempo Nuovo* (*Eulogy to New Times*), underlined the implications of the symbolic and ideological novelties which arrived with the entrance of

Berlusconi on the scene. In his piece, and here all of the dramatic prospective differences become clear, Bobbio decries the abandonment of the usual political debates and personal involvement which, in the era of Karaoke, are suddenly excluded due to the new era of television and its content. Abruzzese, on the other hand, was more interested in using the Berlusconi campaign to bring to light the incongruities and delay on the part of the left in understanding how the world was changing and how Berlusconi, like him or not, was proof of this change. In both essays the authors' attention was focused on television and its fundamental role in determining the shape and mechanisms of modern democracy. Bobbio saw it as a devastating role and as a deterrent to the correct functioning of democracy, whilst Abruzzese's attitude had a more critical/interpretative spirit which derived from the acceptance of the ever growing importance assumed by that which the author called the 'new media'.

Two other essays can be useful in understanding the novelties Berlusconi introduced in the field of Italian political communication. They are brief essays which appeared in different issues of *Micromega*, a magazine read by the intellectual left which, beginning with the 1994 electoral upset, would from that day onwards fight a bitter war against 'il Cavaliere' and his political creation, Forza Italia. Ilvo Diamanti, in his piece, described with great clarity how the forces of marketing had taken over politics and, therefore, how Berlusconi had greatly profited whilst distorting the up-until-then reigning definition of the word 'politics'. Diamanti was, at the same time, among the first to unmask the alliance between Berlusconi own firms and the structure of the newly born political organization, and the subsequent spill over of culture from one to the other.

Two points merit a closer look. Berlusconi, in fact, brings not just his experience and his communicative talent to the field of political communication, but also all of his accumulated knowledge and research ability born from his experiences with market logic. Before entering the arena, he conducted a long series of public opinion polls which confirmed that he, Silvio Berlusconi, was in fact the one person who could inherit all of those votes that usually went to the parties which had made up the centre-left coalitions and governed Italy for almost 50 years. He conducted surveys in a political arena that in exactly those years, for the first time, was beginning to be shaped as a 'market arena' where the voter was no longer tied to his old political party. No political contender in Italy had ever, before him, used such an in-depth survey technique on such a large scale. The strategy, as Diamanti says, is that of marketing: know your voters and their needs and send out the appropriate message to your target audience. In the previous situation of 'affiliation vote' no political force was ever forced to need such knowledge.

It is in the use of marketing strategy that a peculiarity exclusive to the Berlusconi case emerges: he is one of the few politicians in the world to apply corporate culture and logic to politics. He uses surveys as a research instrument and this is done by almost all politicians the world over. But above all he uses the same management strategy, centralization and efficiency techniques for politics as for his business. Berlusconi goes a step further: not only does he use the same techniques he applies in business, but he even transfers the same staff members. Many of his top managers actually end up leaving the company to set up the new party and throw their hats into the ring (many Fininvest managers in fact got elected to Parliament or local administrations in 1994). Gianni Pilo's case is the most exemplary: first marketing manager at Fininvest, he becomes Berlusconi's pollster in 1994, then leaves the company and enters Parliament.

Berlusconi's relationship with the world of business is also symbolic: he presents himself as a guarantor of efficiency. Just as he was able to construct a huge business empire in a few short years, he would be able to give politics a total makeover. He was adept at transferring those concepts and policies of efficiency, which he so well used in determining the success of his business, to his governing of the country. In other words, Berlusconi offers himself as a 'new', as opposed to 'old-style', politician. All of his 1994 campaign was constructed around this identity: new Berlusconi against old-style politics and the efficiency of his company is an integral part of the 'new' which he intends to exploit, and 'new' includes football. Alessandro del Lago, a football loving sociologist, keeping in mind his own love for football and of his latest studies on the phenomenon of sport fans, shows how important the connection was which Berlusconi was able to construct between himself and the world of football by actually buying the Milan football club, which, it just so happened, also won several championships in those years. In this way he created a new image based on values (entrepreneurial and sports success, managerial efficiency) absolutely revolutionary in the Italian political arena (Dal Lago 1994).

Other research (Livolsi and Volli 1995; Mancini and Mazzoleni 1995; Morcellini 1995) contributed to emphasize the novelties associated with Berlusconi's entrance in the political arena. In each instance the absolutely revolutionary role of mass communication and, in particular, television was stressed. Berlusconi's entrance into the political arena, the formation of a new party in just a few months, the electoral campaign and the triumph of Forza Italia pointed out their significance to be absolutely sensational compared to the usual canons of political communication and, in a more general sense, of democracy itself. Certainly today, as then, much of the analysis is still rooted in polemics and an often a priori criticism that does not help us to understand what changed and what is still changing. Abruzzese had seen this risk and attributed it to the blindness of a left unable to see into the future, closed into an a priori and terrorised refusal of the 'new'. The main distortion was, and in part remains, attributing Berlusconi's success only to his ownership of television channels and his illegal behaviour. Certainly these are determining factors beyond which, however, we must look in order to understand the processes of change that Berlusconi identifies. We must go beyond this common sense.

What could help us to better understand the novelties of the Berlusconi case, beyond the common sense? There are several points I think need to be emphasized. The story of Berlusconi and politics, the electoral success of a party set up in a very short period of time and his political communication strategies show us, first and foremost, that the old political communication mechanisms had become obsolete. This is a very generalized observation, by and large taken for granted and, obviously involves the very functions of democracy itself. But what has really changed? In very simple terms I would say that it has been shown that the political parties no longer constitute the main source of information, not just about politics, but about the entire life of the community. They have lost their role as socialization agencies on the general affairs of the community and have been substituted by the mass media.

What are the implications of this taken for granted statement? The first thing that becomes obvious is the diminished importance suffered by the party and the loosening of the close ties which for decades held it to a specific segment of the population. Its organizational structure weakened its ability to reach out to its voter base and involve it in political activity diminished dramatically. In many respects, Berlusconi and Forza Italia are nothing more than the living testimony of the disappearance of mass parties, as predicted by Panebianco in 1982, and their substitution by a 'professional electoral party' (Panebianco 1982). The idea of the 'partito azienda' (party-corporation), as many observers of Forza Italia have noted, is nothing more than the application in its purest form of all of those professional implications and the use of specialized techniques that are implicit in the new sense of an electoral-professional party already seen in the United States and, after the 1994 elections, would be successfully used by both Blair and Schroeder, just to name a couple, and many others. These are the structural and general characteristics of the mutations Berlusconi's political adventure imply.

We cannot ignore the fact that Forza Italia also presents quite a few conflict-of-interest problems. Berlusconi, after all, bold facedly mixed the self-interest of his company, its culture and structure into the very make-up of his newly formed party. Not only that, but this mixing highlights the ethical problem even further, involving the very nature of democracy, which this new party seems to assume: should politics adopt the communication and structural/organizational styles and methods of the corporate world and function in the same manner? Not an issue to be treated lightly.

We can come to a conclusion of this first point by saying that the 1994 experience signified the transformation from 'party logic', with the political party as centrepiece and with its own communication philosophy and style, to a 'media logic', in which the power of mass media and its way of doing things is definitively affirmed as the main protagonist. Media logic brings with it, as we shall see in the next point, the mixing together of elements: in the first place pure politics gets lost in mainstream subjects and advertising. This necessarily implies the need for simplification: not just shorter messages time-wise, but messages reduced to mere slogans, special effects phrases, the search for people and objects as easy and widespread symbols to which to entrust the spreading of ideas and complex projects, and their consequent reduction into more readily understood concepts and images. In other words a 'simplification' of old political discourse has taken place (Corner and Pels 2003).

Politics is not a universe separated from daily life and its imaginary

Let us pick up and develop a point we briefly touched on earlier. With the arrival of Berlusconi, politics and therefore its methods of communication leaves the realm to which it had been relegated up to that point: many people consider this a very grave and negative aspect which deprives politics of its focus and predisposition to that rational debate and discussion which was the very essence of politics in an era of mass party. Others see this same loss as positive, representing a step towards the inclusion of those who, up to then, had been excluded.

The loss of specificity has two main implications: on the one hand political communication gets absorbed into advertising, the most diffuse language of mass media. On the other hand, politics itself tends to get muddled up with passion, facts, symbols, values and daily life. Berlusconi's political adventure is the perfect example of this change. With regards to the first point, there is no doubt that a great part of his success in the 1994 elections came about because of his massive television advertising campaign, at least in the first phase of his campaign. At the same time, as we have already seen, it was the efficient businessman who won, the successful entrepreneur, the owner of the winning football team: all non-politically specific symbolical associations which could be disconcerting but do show how politics became to be increasingly judged with the parameters, values and emotions of daily life (Van Zoonen 2005).

Another proof of this tendency is the personalization process that has characterized Berlusconi's adventure, as it has in the case of many other politicians the world over. Ideas and political projects tend to become intertwined in personal figures: their command of respect, their skill in eliciting credibility and authority and their personal charm count much more than their ability to explain and debate complicated ideological questions. It becomes more important than the image and existence of the party apparatus and organization that furthermore, as we have seen, also loses its importance for a myriad of other reasons. Here again we are dealing with a simplification issue: daily life and all of its complications seem to leave no room for a more complex discussion or in-depth analysis of politics as was once the case (Mazzoleni and Schulz 1999). The expression 'Eulogy to new times' explains very well how Berlusconi was imitated by his adversaries and direct competitors who studied his moves and adopted his methods in their own efforts and who tried, perhaps because they were obliged to in the end, to personalize political encounters as he had done. Not to lavish praise on the man from Arcore, but one must admit that beyond the dramatic and very implicit problems of democratic correctness that he represents, a new era of political communication had dawned: an era of conflict-creating personalization, eliciting different and opposed reactions in line with the new logic of the of mass communication discourse that never had happened before in a country, like Italy, characterized by a very deeply rooted 'affiliation vote'.

Television is more important than the printed word
In 1994 Berlusconi taught us that television was more important than the print media. Several aspects of this must be considered. To begin with, as we have already explained, the question cannot be boiled down to the simple ownership of TV channels. It certainly helped to have three channels during the 1994 elections and beyond, but to say that that is the only reason for his success is to ignore other equally important aspects.

It is an instrumental political interpretation that helps us, up to a certain point, to understand what happened and consequently learn from it. Berlusconi demonstrated that television is the most important means of mass communication, first, because it can reach the largest number of people, and second, because, at least in Italy, it dictates the agenda for the rest of the media. He has presented himself at a man of television, and not just because he owns channels: from television, its language and its methods of expression, the image of Berlusconi has invaded all of the other media as well (Mazzoleni 1995). He has forced them to follow the mirage of TV, its logic and language. Bobbio is certainly right about one point: 'il Cavaliere' is mystique and values personified, at least those values which he propagated on his TV networks for the entire decade leading up to his election.

The predominance of television, the second point of caution to be taken into consideration, is an all-Italian phenomenon to be found to a lesser degree in other countries. In Italy this predominance becomes concrete reality due, above all, to that capacity of television as agenda setter that is not found elsewhere. This supremacy is in large part a result of the characteristics of the structure of the Italian communications market, with its low print-media circulation figures and strong television audience. Whether they like it or not, successful political communication must take this uneven distribution into account, as it must also take into account the average middle-class Italian citizen with his relatively lightweight media consumption. In other words, Berlusconi and Forza Italia seem to have chosen as their privileged target public exactly those people who had been excluded from political participation up to then: the avid low- to medium-class watchers who had abstained from political activity, and if we want to be more precise, mostly female. All of the surveys confirm this (Itanes 2001 and 2007). Here again we are not dealing with an evaluation (is it good or bad to target, even in a banal and simplified manner, those excluded from politics?) but a significant awareness which admits that the supremacy of television also means that we must recognize the change in the main focus of communication and its addressees.

The Berlusconi case, therefore, seems to be a mixture of the old and the new. He has used the old and consolidated tradition of political parallelism between mass media and the party apparatus. But he has also used this mix in a totally new way, understanding before, and better than his adversaries, how the public arena had been profoundly changed by the growth period and transformation spurred on by the media commercialization of the 1980s. His business experience and, above all, his experience with television, deeply influenced his political adventure. None of this could have happened, however, if the political scene had not been so dramatically altered by 'Tangentopoli' and the subsequent disappearance of the old-school political leaders.

Overcoming the 'Berlusconi common sense' means exactly to put his political adventure within the framework of old and new features of Italian politics and media system. His mixture of old and new points out serious problems to a correct democratic life: instrumentalization of the mass media system persist together with a strong tendency towards trivialization and personalization of politics that undermines any possibility of serious political debate.

Notes

1. The circulation of Italian print press is the lowest in Europe with the exception of Greece and Portugal.
2. A very convincing picture of this tradition was drawn by anthropologist Edwards Banfield with his analysis of the a community in Southern Italy (Banfield 1958).
3. In Italy, to be a journalist one needs to pass a professional exam to become a member of the Ordine dei Giornalisti.
4. Rete4 and Italia1, two of his three networks, are completely biased in his favour, whilst Channel 5, his biggest channel, maintains a more balanced approach also due to the larger size of its audience.

References

Abruzzese, A. (1994), *Elogio del Tempo Nuovo: Perchè Berlusconi ha Vinto*. Genova: Costa and Nolan.

Asor Rosa, A. (1981), 'Il Giornalista: Appunti sulla Fisiologia di un Mestiere Difficile', in *Storia d'Italia*. Torino: Einaudi, pp. 1227–1255.

Banfield, E. (1958), *The Moral Basis of a Backward Society*. Chicago: The Free Press.

Bobbio, N., Bosetti, G. and Vattimo, G. (1994), *La Sinistra nell'era del Karaoke*. Milano: Reset.

Calise, M. (2000), *Il Partito Personale*. Bari: Laterza.

Curran, J. (1991), 'Rethinking the Media as a Public Sphere', in P. Dahlgren and C. Sparks (eds), *Communication and Citizenship*. London: Routledge, pp 27–58.

Corner, J. and Pels, D. (2003), *Media and the Restyiling of Politics*. London: Sage.

Dal Lago, A. (1994), 'Il Voto e il Circo', *Micromega*, 1, pp. 138–47.

Diamanti, I. (1994), 'La Politica come Marketing', *Micromega*, 2, pp. 30–48.

Forcella, E. (1956), 'Millecinquecento lettori', *Tempo presente* 6, pp. 37–51.

Ginsborg, P. (2004), *Silvio Berlusconi: Television, Power and Patrimony*. London: Verso.

Hallin, D. and Mancini, P. (2004), *Comparing Media Systems: Three Models of Media and Politics*. Cambridge: Cambridge University Press.

Itanes (ed.) (2001), *Perché ha Vinto il Centro-destra*. Bologna: Il Mulino.

Itanes (ed.) (2006), *Dov'è la Vittoria?* Bologna: Il Mulino.

Kaitatzi-Whitlock, S. (2005), *Europe's Political Communication Deficit*. Suffolk: Arima.

Livolsi, M. and Volli, U. (eds) (1995). *La Comunicazione Politica tra Prima e Seconda Repubblica*. Milano: Angeli.

Mancini, P. (1992), 'Cittadini Informati o Combattenti Organizzati', *Problemi dell'informazione*, 17: 3, pp. 333–51.

Mancini, P. and Mazzoleni, G. (eds) (1995), *I Media Scendono in Campo*. Roma: Eri.

Mazzoleni, G. (1995), 'Towards a Videocracy? Italian Political Communication at a Turning Point', *European Journal of Communication*, 10: 3, pp. 291–321.

Mazzoleni, G. and Schulz, W. (1999), 'Mediatization of Politics: A Challenge for Democracy', *Political Communication*, 16: 3, pp. 247–61.

Morcellini, M. (1995), *Elezioni di TV*. Genova: Costa and Nolan.

Murialdi, P. (1986), *Storia del Giornalismo Italiano*. Torino: Gutenebrg.

Panebianco, A. (1982), *Modelli di Partito*. Bologna: Il Mulino.

Parisi, A. and Pasquino, G. (1977), 'Relazioni Partiti – Elettori e Tipi di Voto', in Parisi (ed.), *Continuità e Mutamento Culturale in Italia*. Bari: Laterza.

Poli, E. (2001), *Forza Italia*. Bologna: Il Mulino.

Stille, A. (2006), *Citizen Berlusconi*. Milano: Garzanti.

Van Zoonen, L. (2005), *Entertaining the Citizen: When Politics and Popular Culture Converge*. Lanham: Rowman and Littlefield.

PART TWO: JOURNALISM AND THE REUOPEANIZATION OF THE PUBLIC SPHERES

6

European Journalism and the European Public Sphere

Peter Golding

Abstract

In this paper I ask to what extent European journalism contributes to the formation of a European public sphere. This question, of course, presupposes several others. What might we mean by European journalism for example? I suggest there remains considerable variability within this rather general notion across the continent. Is there a European public? Clearly without one there can be no European public sphere. I also question the role of technological change in opening new possibilities for the active engagement of a European public, and ask to what extent the construction of new opportunities by exploitation of digital technologies is allowing the EU in particular to reach and command the interest and support of a public otherwise largely disaffected. The paper draws in part on research undertaken as part of the programme of the Adequate Information Management programme (AIM) coordinated by the University of Dortmund.[1]

Keywords
Journalism, Media, public sphere, Europe, Democracy, political communication

The technology of journalism – Blogging is the future?

The technology of both production and reception of news is plainly undergoing massive renewal. It is often argued that this will mean a radical restructuring of the character of both news and journalism. For news production it is not just print technologies that have changed, although this alone has made major changes to the practice and conventions of traditional journalism. It is also argued that changes in the nature of broadcasting and print enable cheaper, swifter, more diverse news production systems. Paradoxically the huge expansion of information production, both in scale and scope, seems to have accompanied a diminishing appetite for its consumption amongst audiences across the world.

These technological changes are also assumed to enable a far more discriminating, and indeed differentiated audience for news, as particular audience segments are able to satisfy their specific and sectoral interests by organizing their consumption of news according to their own tastes and preferences rather than those of producers. As yet there is limited evidence of this, though the decline of readerships for traditional newspapers is palpable, as we shall see.

Far more radically, the new technologies are seen as recasting the traditional nature of mass communications – the few communicating to the anonymous many in a largely one-way mode. By contrast, new technologies, it is suggested, allow interactivity, self-expression, and horizontal communication. Blogging, in which individuals are able to cast their personal thoughts and observations onto the cyber-waters, has become enormously popular, and is growing on a scale which makes any report of it immediately out of date. It is worth pausing, however, to ask if the often romanticized affection for blogging as the new pathway into democratic expression and information dissemination, is all that it seems.

By early 2006 perhaps 25 million bloggers worldwide were to be found (or more likely not found) on the web. A Pew Center survey in the USA in 2005, however, found that 60 per cent of online Americans had never heard of blogs. 73 per cent had never read a blog and many of those who had, had done so once or twice out of curiosity. Only 7 per cent of adult Internet users had created a blog, and fewer than one in ten read political blogs. Blog readers, like Internet enthusiasts generally, tended to be male, young and better off.

The enormous success of some sites is salutary. Craigslist, initially (inevitably) the product of a young computer enthusiast in the Bay area of San Francisco, has cornered what many large American newspaper corporations regard as a terrifyingly large slice of the classified advertising market, with more than 40 million page views per month. Phenomena like the Korean OhMyNews International have created unprecedented inroads into the news consumption sector. But the mainstream news media continue, and enduringly provide the major source of social and political information for most people, while the distinctively interactive and democratically novel features of digital information have yet to become central to their operations.

In the United Kingdom, national newspaper circulations have fallen by about a quarter in the last 40 years, while competition for readers among regional and local papers has been virtually eliminated, with local monopoly having become the norm. Audiences for television news are similarly diminished, reduced by above 10 per cent in the last decade (Hargreaves and Thomas 2002). Current affairs programmes have progressively moved to the margins of television schedules with smaller and more concentrated audiences. Hargreaves and Thomas note also that in the United States 'Audiences to network television peak-time news bulletins in the United States have plummeted, from 90% of the television audience in the 1960s, to 60% in 1993 and 30% by 2000' while 'regular newspaper readership is also down from 58% in 1993 to 46%' in 2002 (ibid.: 11). The 2004 World Newspaper Congress reported circulation increases in only 35 of 208 countries.

Across Europe a similar pattern can be found. Lauf points to a decline in newspaper readership especially among younger readers. 'A rapid decrease of readership can be found in France, Denmark, Luxembourg and the UK. Only in the Netherlands and Italy, is the decline below average and in Germany daily readership even increased marginally' (Lauf 2001). His stark conclusion is that 'the most striking finding is that in all [nine EU member countries the author studied in 1980, 1989 and 1998]...age has become the strongest predictor for the daily use of newspapers as a source of political information: newspaper readers are getting older' (ibid.: 238).

Analysis by the World Newspaper Association argues a more optimistic case (World Association of Newspapers 2005). They find world circulations to be up by 2.1 per cent in 2004, with an increase in titles, though most notably a big increase (by 32 per cent) in audiences for newspaper websites. However, in the EU, newspaper sales dropped by 0.7 per cent in 2004. Indeed, in the fifteen countries of the 'old' EU all but two reported circulation falls throughout the first years of the new century, representing in all a drop of 5.9 per cent in aggregate circulations in these countries over five years. In the 2004 accession countries, circulations fell 2.8 per cent in the five years from 1999.

Whatever the precise calibration of these shifts, we are left with two questions. The most fundamental is 'does journalism have an audience?' In assessing how far journalism may play a part in forging a common consciousness, or in contributing to an informed democracy whether nationally or transnationally bounded, it is first essential that news is itself an object of attention and interest to audiences construed as citizens. Secondly, we need to consider further how far we can see journalism contributing to some form of European forum, or public sphere, in which a rudimentary polis is being constructed around social, political and cultural involvement in a common civil arena transcending the nation state.

Journalism: Theme and European variations

Journalism as a public means of societal surveillance, informing citizens about the remote, the intriguing, the important and the merely diverting, through regular and anonymous report, has emerged as a key feature of the cultural landscape in every European society. From origins in the direct and *ad hominam* reports of commissioned observers reporting directly to patrons in the early years of mercantile capitalism, through to the vast media empires and publishing conglomerates of recent times, there is much in common to observe. Not surprisingly these common features loom large in comparative accounts. Hoyer and Pöttker (Hoyer and Pöttker 2005) describe what they term the 'news paradigm', which over the last century or so has diffused universally. It comprises five elements: an event, criteria for reporting it called news values, the news interview, the inverted pyramid, that classic formulation of accounts which start with essentials and moves on to further detail, and most problematically, journalistic objectivity, and overarching professional commitment to detachment and balance (ibid.: 11).

One of the great fascinations of a historical approach to the analysis of news media is to trace the variation in experience and adoption of these differing elements. The news interview is probably a transatlantic import, while the key commitment to objectivity is seen by many as peculiarly Anglo-American, far removed from either practice or indeed aspiration in many other parts of the globe, whether the 'development journalism' so critical to anti-imperialism movements in mid-twentieth-century Africa and Asia, the party-loyal journalism of Leninist theory and practice, or simply differing traditions even within Europe. Mancini reminds us that we would do well to keep a clear picture of these variations (Mancini 2005). He describes the Anglo-American tradition, with its separation of the press from other power centres, a claim to professional standards, including objectivity and the separation of reporting from comment. This tradition (in which he finds the United Kingdom closer to European than Anglo-American norms) is distinct from the European model, which is very often and in origin much more partisan, and certainly much closer to and entangled with the political party system. Nonetheless he draws attention to variation within Europe, not least between north and south, with the latter more likely to have links to literature and thus to comment and interpretation.

British journalism emancipated itself more early than most from a close embrace with political parties, and through the 'retail revolution' of the late nineteenth century rapidly turned itself into a low price daily adjunct of consumer commerce, with a mass popular press expanding rapidly between 1920 and 1940 (Murdock and Golding 1978). The entertainment core of popular provision, enhanced by the emerging mid-nineteenth-century Sunday press, and not least by circumvention of taxes on newspapers through producing newspapers with no news, found its expanding echoes in the mass entertainment press of a century later, presenting an apparent disregard for the mainstream of politics evident also in the 'Boulevardzeitungen' of central Europe. Italian journalism has been typically highly partisan while less committed, at least traditionally, to a professional autonomy and independence. For some observers from a rather different tradition (ostensibly) this becomes even a matter of some distaste. One American analyst investigating Italian journalism in the 1980s concluded that 'Perhaps the most important thing Italian journalism could learn from the vocation in the United States is a deeper sense of professionalism and a larger reputation for it' (Porter 1983).

French journalism has equally shown a slow and halting emergence from the yoke of politics. Indeed, political activity is often seen as the goal and target of a journalistic career. For much of its history French journalism has been a creature of the state, with media that remain closely entwined with the political apparatus. As Neveu and his collaborators (see footnote 1) explain, in an economy dominated until relatively recently by small entrepreneurs, the conglomeration common elsewhere was late to develop, as was a dependence on advertising, and for press magnates political ambition was the primary purpose of newspaper ownership. Here the prevalence of advocacy journalism endures, and the literary ambitions and style of journalism result in what Neveu and his colleagues describe as 'something like fencing with a pen'.

By contrast, in northern Europe things were often different. In Norway, for example, local news and politics have taken prime position in the press, and journalistic norms have borrowed from the long tradition of public broadcasting, with a commitment, despite close party connections, to impartiality and balance enshrined in statute, and of such severity that in 1997 the national journalists' union decided to exclude public relations and information officers from membership, so different was their task and practice.

Yet we can go only so far in tracing these fascinating variations and traditions before recognizing a common core. The daily and routine reporting of public events, and the finite range of locales, both geographic and institutional, which lend themselves to journalistic observation and report, are sufficiently circumscribed to make comparative analysis possible, and to allow us to speak meaningfully of journalistic norms, conventions and ideologies. The disavowal of 'objectivity' and the refusal to dispense with a journalism of opinion, so tenaciously sustained in some countries, are nonetheless expressed in explicit debate with the more austere and 'professional' norms of the Anglo-Saxon world. The twin evolution of democratic representative political structures and late capitalism necessarily lends a common frame to the mass media systems of all these countries, and in turn the quasi-professional occupations such as journalism which have grown within them.

Journalism: New times and perspectives

If there is indeed a recognizable universal core to journalism, above and beyond national and local variation, is it now undergoing radical change? Three trends detectable in many journalistic cultures would suggest such change is indeed in process. First is the growing importance of holding and attracting audiences. Though never wholly absent from journalism, it is now often argued that news has become so embedded in the entertainment industries that it has become imbued with the same values and styles as other forms of media provision. The term 'infotainment' has been coined to describe this shift, and its worst effects in diluting the information provided by news to citizens, and thus the value of journalism to democracy, have been dubbed 'tabloidisation' (McLachlan and Golding 2000).

The second change we can observe is the globalization of journalism's embrace. While reporting from the far flung corners of empire or the distant horizons of overseas adventure was always part of journalism, modern communications put most of the world within the reach of news media in various ways. The growth of the nineteenth-century news agencies created a structure which has largely survived, if technologically and organizationally far grander and more sophisticated than before. However, news audiences remain stubbornly parochial, and in many countries the increased availability of global news is met by diminishing interest in it.

The third change is technological, with an explosive expansion of communicative possibilities arising from digital media and new forms and systems of telecommunications. Resources for journalism to be found on the Internet as well as the use of digital communications for both reporting and indeed production and distribution of news may well be revolutionizing journalism itself. It must be said, however, that such claims seem premature at present, and, as I have suggested above, the romantic elevation of such practices as 'blogging', as though they presaged a wholesale replacement of existing forms and structures of the news market, are almost certainly exaggerated, if not wholly misguided.

Journalism in Europe: The Brussels beat

For many 'Europe' means the EU. Research into the success of the European journalists' corps undertaken in collaboration with colleagues in a project coordinated by the University of Dortmund (see footnote 1) has thrown doubt on the impact of this work in many countries. The outcome of the 2005 referendums in France and the Netherlands, suggests further evidence of the failure of the European 'grand projet' to secure the affection of European hearts and minds.

In the UK, persistent hostility to the EU among much of the press has prompted the EU Representation in London to produce a regular rebuttals to Euromyths it discovers in national media. Recent examples with which it has had to contend include:

- Condom dimensions to be harmonized (*Independent on Sunday*) but chosen size 'not suitable for British assets'.
- 'Hands off our Barmaid's Boobs'. *Sun*, 4 August 2005.
- Teabags banned from being recycled. *BBC News Online*, 7 January 2005.
- Eurocrats call time on light ale. Bureaucrats in Brussels want to force British brewers to change the name of light ale. *Daily Mail*, 11 May 2005.
- Shake 'n back – EU tells women to hand in worn-out sex toys. *Sun*, 4 February 2005.

For many journalists who work in Brussels this continuing torrent of distortion and caricature is an embarrassment which they stoically accept and work within. Nonetheless, our programme of interviewing with journalists suggests a recurrent number of views that are far from enthusiastic about the European ideal, or indeed the EU specifically. These include:

- Many journalists, though based in Brussels actually cover 'Europe' more generally, and prefer to do so.
- In the period of our interviews some had gone, with great relief, to Rome to cover the Italian elections for example. But even this is seen as at the periphery of interest for United Kingdom audiences.
- Many feel the EU story has gone 'off the boil' since the French and Dutch referendums, the United Kingdom presidency, and, 'good stories' like the Santer commission resignation.
- The Commission is not very interesting, and though people are willing and hard working the journalists are not impressed with the news-sense of Commission spokespersons and communications people – they just get in the way.
- It is rare for the Commission to generate 'real' news stories, and the Parliament is 'just a joke' (a phrase used several times).
- Journalists feel that it would be better if people stopped promoting the 'grand project', European citizenship and so on, and just got on with the business of doing something.

- The story about EU intervention in roaming mobile phone charges got unusually strong and sympathetic coverage in the United Kingdom media, and was several times cited by interviewees as a better example of the proper business of the Commission.
- Journalists draw a distinction, common in journalistic occupational ideology, between pragmatism (a virtue) and ideology (a vice). The former is especially a British characteristic and means, in this context, doing useful and specific policy things like building a bridge or controlling phone charges. Building Europe or developing transnational identity is pointless, meaningless, futile, undesirable, ideological, idealistic and inappropriate in the view of many journalists.
- Journalists go to the midday briefings, but to network with other journalists; it is of no major value as a source of information.
- The EU (as a set of institutions) is just not very newsworthy – all those men in suits at meetings – how dull.
- The United Kingdom is and will remain very uninterested in or hostile to the EU, and it is not the job of journalists to change this, but to recognize it as a limit on what they can do. For them it is about never repeating the Second World War, 'but remember, the UK is the only EU country that won the war', as one correspondent commented.
- The Wahlstrom initiatives (proposed by the EU Commissioner for Institutional Relations and Communication Strategy, and including a possible EU news agency) were derided by journalists as worthless and naive.

News media and a European public sphere

The expectation, or indeed aspiration, that Europe may be the home to an embryonic political culture transcending the national is a necessary dimension to the 'European project'. Schlesinger has argued, as much in hope as expectation, that we may be witnessing the birth of an 'emergent supranational political culture' (Schlesinger 1997), but recognizes that this requires the further development of a number of pre-conditions.

If we are to see the gradual construction of

a range of European publics, typically these would be composed of transnational citizens who have (a) an equal and widespread level of communicative competence, (b) relatively easy access to the full range of the means of communication, and, (c) a generalized communicative competence that embodies sufficient background knowledge, interest, and interpretative skills to make sense of the EU and its policy options and debates.

If there were indeed such a set of European publics, for it would as yet be a plural entity, it would

(a) involve the dissemination of a European news agenda, (b) need to become a significant part of the everyday news-consuming habits of European audiences, and (c) entail that those living within the EU have begun to think of their citizenship, in part at least, as transcending the level of the member nation-states (Schlesinger 1999).

These are serious tests, and we need carefully to assess how far they are being met. Four questions follow. First is there any indication of the growth of a European public, for without a European public plainly there can be no European public sphere. Secondly, are there European media whose audience, rationale and production logic is geared to a European scale? Thirdly is there a common discourse, linguistically or thematically, for a European public? Finally, are there vehicles for citizen interaction that are located and rooted in the European dimension of people's experience?

Following the traumatic rejection of the new EU constitution in the 2005 referendums in France and the Netherlands, it was salutary to read Eurobarometer findings that more than one third of European citizens were in fact unaware of the existence of the constitution. At the end of 2004 people who saw themselves as both European and as a citizen of their country were 7 per cent of those interviewed, while 41 per cent saw themselves only as national citizens. Only 4 per cent foresaw a future as primarily European citizens (European Commission 2005). The percentage of persons interviewed who consider that they know nothing or almost nothing about the European Union (scoring one and two out of ten) is relatively stable (19 per cent). The majority of respondents (51 per cent) rated their level of knowledge between three and five, considering therefore that their knowledge about the European Union is fairly limited.

Of course, such findings would doubtless be replicated similarly at national level, the widespread indifference to or knowledge of mainstream politics being a constant object of distress for more informed, educated, or involved elites. It is also important not to confuse ignorance of the EU with disenchantment with or distance from the broader sense of a European common culture or inheritance that lies behind the 'European project', though this too has its problems as we will see. The evidence as it is, however, does not speak convincingly of a European political public.

Occasional and persistent attempts to develop European media have rarely been successful. Robert Maxwell's *European* newspaper was one of many high-profile honourable failures. Pan-European television has not evolved into any position of prominence or persistence. Indeed in the last decade such channels as do exist have increasingly localized their pan-European material (Chalaby 2002). Chalaby further shows how much pan-European television provision is addressed to other forms of transnational collectivities, especially ethnic and diasporic ones (Chalaby 2005). *Euronews* survives, though with small audiences (Machill 1998). There are of course specialist targeted media: *European Voice* produced by the Economist Group has a circulation of about 16,000; it is distributed free to MEPs and EU officials. The *Economist* itself has some claim to globalized status if not European standing. But it is the former rather than the latter. Of its circulation of just above a million, four out of five are outside Europe.

Other transnational magazines, constructing as much as addressing cosmopolitan financial elites, find much of their market in one country. While increasingly international, this intercontinental clientele is both a highly selective and up-market one, and also significantly based in a few countries. The *Financial Times* has 68 per cent of its readership outside the United Kingdom, but magazines like *Newsweek* and *Time* continue to be largely read in the United States (87 per cent and 82 per cent of their circulations respectively). The *International Herald Tribune* describes itself as the paper for 'the global class', those 'people who move across continents, who bridge sectors and industries, and who are at home in several cultures'. Published in Europe in partnership with the Frankfurter Allgemeine Zeitung Publishing Group it is plainly addressing a niche and cosmopolitan elite.

If we move to television we find ample evidence of the preference of European audiences for domestic and local products, with little traffic between European countries in programmes (except programme formats like *Big Brother*), and the essentially facilitating apparatus of Eurovision, the operational service of the European Broadcasting Union. Eurovision manages the exchange of more than 30,000 news items every year while distributing over 15,000 hours of live sport and cultural events each year. Nonetheless, as Ruß-Mohl concludes, 'Looking at the readership or audience all European publications and programs are simply irrelevant. The field of political information is dominated by national newspapers and magazines, networks and talk-shows.' (Ruß-Mohl 2003)

Even where notable examples of 'European' cultural events can be discovered we should be wary of hasty deductions. The growth or attractiveness of European media events does not, in itself, of course, speak to a transnational cultural formation. Many would indeed argue that such events as the Eurovision Song Contest or European football competitions celebrate the national. What engages the emotions more – the singing of the largely unheard 'European song' (officially the 'UEFA Champions League Music' composed by Tony Britten) prior to European cup football matches, or the team-specific support rolling in frenetic waves from the terraces, albeit for 'local' teams increasingly composed of multi-national squads of sporting mercenaries? In an optimistic reading of what is plainly a contradictory and mixed picture, Martin suggests that 'football may [be] bringing Europeans together...more than any number of EU initiatives to breathe life into the notion of a sense of belonging to Europe' (Martin 2005).

It would be generous, at the very least, to suggest this embryonic supra-nationalistic identification would be found among the crowds at the average UEFA encounter. On the one hand one could argue that a more complex understanding of a European consciousness would see it constituted of a multiple of national consciousnesses, entangled with and articulated to a wider trans-national complex of understanding and awareness. On the other hand, it could be argued that such opportunities for intensified and exaggerated national symbols of identity inhibit rather than advance the potential of a European consciousness. This remains as much a political as a theoretical conundrum.

My third question was the existence or otherwise of a common discourse through which experiences and images could be described and shared? The growing installation of English as the common language of international finance, computing, business, research and tertiary education is a matter of great convenience for the native speaker and great irritation for some, not least the French, for whom this development has cultural as well as linguistic consequences.

But Europe remains a polyglot arena, with English (and primarily its transatlantic form at that) far from universally spoken, and certainly not a vehicle for common experience or utterance.

But language is not the only vehicle for which the claim of an emerging common symbolic terrain is made. As Hall has noted, 'supra-national communities...cannot simply be political, economic, or geographical entities; they also depend on how they are represented and imagined: they exist within, not outside, representation, the imaginary' (Hall 2003). In part this demands a common historical sense. But it may well be that the ideas and mythologies being deployed to advance this sense of common origin and future are themselves gendered, national and indeed even racist. Hall argues that the myths that make and made Europe have their origins in some very specific and increasingly (in the wake of enlargement) contentious, and philosophically partial foundations.

As Dunkerly et al. point out, Europe 'as a term has been inseparable from political developments... To speak of certain core aspects of a European identity, such as Christianity or the Greco-Roman heritage, is to miss the fact that these do not reflect the experiences of *all* Europeans' (Dunkerley et al. 2002). Cronin, examining one such attempt by the Council of Europe notes that it 'has produced a series of policy documents that aim to define Europe through a common "European culture"'. He argues that the ideas of Europe, culture and consumerism that are used in the report 'redefine the terms of European belonging and rights' and he explores 'the gendered and racial interconnections in these definitions and the rhetorical use of cultural heritage' (Cronin 2002).

A European consciousness of terrorism as a threat can be construed as just the kind of common threat and commonly defined problem that fosters unity, shared consciousness and cross-border integration. But it just as easily translates into the simpler and yet more destructive forces of xenophobia, racism and animus which are the very antithesis of a common sense of people and place, and practice seems to exemplify this fear. Thus topic or action provide a foundation for the expression of difference as much as of common identity. Where there may be common ground for identity it is likely to be in residual definition against 'the other' with all the regressive and divisive tendencies such values can mobilize.

Fourthly came the question of a vehicle for interaction, in other words an effective and dynamic set of practices and institutions through which citizens could interact with and be sensitized to a world of action and decision beyond the nation state. Turnouts in EU elections are of course notoriously low – in 2004 the average across the EU was 45.6 per cent, and while just 4 per cent lower than in 1999 this was 15 per cent lower than in 1984, falling to under one in four in Poland and Slovakia. The so-called democratic deficit in the EU can readily and easily be called in evidence for a wholesale rejection of or at least indifference to the EU as a project, and by extension the European programme as a whole. This is too facile, however. Antipathy, or even outright hostility, to the institutions or practices of the EU may be an expression of awareness and political belief as vital and significant as outright enthusiasm and engagement. This case must remain, to date, unproven.

Eurocrats and technocrats

The emergence of the Internet is sometimes proposed as meeting the need for a transnational medium of communication and interchange. At best such interaction may, even allowing for frequent and sometimes romanticized exaggeration, speak to the genesis of emergent interest groups or proto-communities. However these are seldom more than rudimentary in cultural or social structure, and still founder on the obstinate evidence of a 'digital divide' which is as prevalent in Europe as elsewhere. A recent EU report on this issue focuses, like many more recent overviews, on the divides opening up with the widening availability of broadband. The major division assessed is that between availability in rural and urban areas; indeed income inequality and poverty do not feature in the report at all (Commission of the European Communities 2005).

The report nonetheless notes the limited take-up of broadband compared to its availability – on average, by January 2005, only 10 per cent of the EU-15 population had a broadband subscription, when broadband was available to about 88 per cent of them. This figure falls to 8.6 per cent if the enlarged EU is included. Despite the rural-urban split which gives this report its focus, recurrent analyses identify income as the major obstacle to entry into the new communications market place for most consumers. The still high and, more importantly, recurring costs of maintaining information technology currency in the home, mean that lower income households either manage without or, as the emerging picture of broadband demonstrates, manage with lower-level technologies than higher income groups. It is for this reason that simple survey investigations of Internet use or experience often mask major inequities of real availability and advantage. Thus in seeking a vehicle for trans-border community formation, and discovering its potential in the Internet, we need to pay close regard to the continuing and resilient inequities in access to new communication technologies.

These stark facts pose a problem for the recurrent enthusiasm for an 'e-Europe' which is endemic among many in Brussels. There is a problem to be solved. That European citizens are largely ill-informed about the mechanisms and institutions of Europe's embryonic supra-national organization is manifest and familiar. Before the 2005 referendums one-third of European citizens were completely unaware of the existence of an EU constitution, and well over half told the Eurobarometer survey that they had 'little knowledge' of its contents (European Commission 2005). Just a few months after the European elections in June 2004 two thirds of respondents were unaware that the elections had taken place. It would not be difficult to document at length the evidence of widespread ignorance, or more fundamentally, indifference, about the doings and structures of the European Union as a political and institutional edifice. The 2005 referendums, of course, were analysed as a more explicit and aware rejection of much that the Union seemed to be promising or offering people, and I do not here propose to interrogate this analysis. The point is to identify readily a problem as perceived by advocates of the European project, namely their inability to enthuse or even inform much of the putative population of the emerging Europe.

If the Eurocratic imperative is to force-feed the growth of a digital Europe and to drag an unwilling, unskilled and uninformed population into it, the technocratic imperative is the corporate driver, voraciously encouraging whatever is technologically possible to become socially desirable. The visionary home of the future often features in the research laboratories and demonstration pageants of the major companies to whom so much of the EU research budget is devoted. Siemens promise 'switching on the heating at home from somewhere out of town while checking traffic reports and train departure times and downloading the results of lab tests from your last visit to the doctor'. Microsoft CEO Bill Gates expects the twenty-first century to see the 'birth of the PC-Plus era enabling millions of Americans to live the digital lifestyle at home with their families', no doubt helpfully supported by Microsoft software around the house.

The Microsoft Concept Home in Seattle greets visitors by name after checking your retinal scan at the door, plays music of your choice once it's confident it is you coming in, and checks the fridge contents through RFID sensors before filling the wall-filling plasma screens with appropriate mood music and scenes to match your detected temper. A home's heating, ventilation and air conditioning may all be programmed and calibrated to meet pre-determined systems and regimes. Such digital homes are maintained by most major high-tech companies, including Phillips in Eindhoven. One mildly disturbed journalist paused to consider that only after installation do users

> realize that the kitchen's automated inventory management doesn't work with the produce you buy at the farmers' market (and besides this technology is not appreciably easier than just looking in the pantry). Your media server computer will think you're trying to steal a movie when you want to take a copy to a vacation house. When you add some other vendor's hardware or software to the system things start to break. (Pegoraro 2004)

Smart appliances are ever more readily promoted and developed. Microwave ovens connected direct to the Internet for downloadable recipes, a baking mixer that communicates with the microwave, and a refrigerator that does not tolerate food past sell-by dates, have all been demonstrated as examples of technologies whose standards and expectations few, in truth, feel able to meet. From e-Europe to e-everything is a small step. A promotional leaflet for the 'e-court' notes that a 'feeling of disappointment is spread among the European citizens regarding the functioning of the judicial system in their country'. The solution is the e-court, providing multi-media trial recording, '"normalization, standardization, interoperability and global convergence" among public administration' and 'providing added value information... to institutions and experts'.

Once freed by these new judicial logistics it is a short but tempting move to 'My-Grocer' using 'RF-enabled automatic product identification and wireless technologies' for 'automated home replenishment management'. To save finding the right buttons around the house, wearable technology will solve the 'where did I put the shopping list?' problem, and outside the home has the potential to unleash what has been termed 'blue collar computing', incorporating data gloves and ultrasonic transmitters into standard operative dungarees and work-wear.

Such innovations are easily lampooned, and often unfairly so. Many have the potential genuinely to enhance and ease both work and domestic chores. In the wider context, of remote health-care for example, progressive and valuable applications are legion. However, the emphasis in the technocratic imperative is often 'if it can be done it should be done, and if it is done then users need to be made ready and enthusiastic to embrace it'. As a Philips press release notes, 'consumers may reject a new idea because they do not understand it... our research projects are explorations of the future and they help create a familiarity between people and technologies that are yet to come'. The digital age is the age of the producer-educated consumer.

We are left then with uncertain answers to the four questions posed. Without a European public there can be no European public sphere. Vehicles for the transmission and sharing of common symbols, debates or concerns are rudimentary or fragile, and such common language or conceptual apparatuses as do emerge tend to speak to a negative or regressive agenda.

Journalism and the European public sphere

Our question remains that at the heart of the conference reported in this book. How far is it possible to see the news media as a vehicle for the further promotion of a sensitivity to and enthusiasm for Europe, however construed? The increasing sense that nation states remain the primary locus of identity and action for most citizens is an inevitable obstacle to some versions of the 'new citizenship'. Increasingly this has led to a reconstruction of the notion of a European public sphere as an aggregation of national public spheres or an element of all of them, rather than as a novel and displacing form of consciousness which will rapidly supplant the nation state, construed somewhat hopefully as a historical but ephemeral transitional stage in the evolution of a global society.

If global sensitivities are to emerge, whether focused on the notion of 'Europe' or elsewhere, it is increasingly obvious that they will emerge from the fostering of values and beliefs which reach beyond the immediate, the calculated and the self-interested. Notions of the 'other' become generalizable and internationalizable if first made common in the political and social discourses with people commonly engage. Thus it is the role of political rhetoric and of popular culture (if indeed one should imagine they have a teleological role at all) to embed in public discourse and imagination the sense of mutual and global responsibility which underpins any public sphere beyond the nation state. This raises questions and policy challenges well beyond the role of the media, as indeed it should.

Note

1. See the programme website at http://www.aim-project.net/. The paper also draws on material in my article 'European Journalism and the European Public Sphere: Some Thoughts on Practice and Prospects', in Hans Bohrman, Elisabeth Klaus and Marcel Machill (eds), *Media Industry, Journalism Culture and Communication Policies in Europe*. Cologne: Halem, pp. 25–40 and on 'Eurocrats, Technocrats, and Democrats: Competing Ideologies in the European Information Society', *European Societies*, Volume 9, Issue 5 (December 2007), pp. 719–34.

References

Chalaby, J. (2002), 'Transnational Television in Europe: The Role of Pan-European Channels', *European Journal of Communication*, 17: 2, pp. 183–203.

— (2005). 'Deconstructing the Transnational: a Typology of Cross-border Television Channels in Europe', *New Media & Society*, 7: 2, pp. 155–75.

Commission of the European Communities (2005), *Digital Divide Forum Report: Broadband Access and Public Support in Under-Served Areas*. Brussels: European Commission.

Cronin, A. (2002), 'Consumer Rights/Cultural Rights: a New Politics of European Belonging', *European Journal of Cultural Studies*, 5: 3, pp. 307–23.

Dunkerley, D., Hodgson, L., Konopacki, S., Spybey, T. and Thompson, A. (2002), *Changing Europe: Identities, Nations and Citizens*. London: Routledge.

European Commission (2005), *Eurobarometer 62: Public Opinion in the European Union*. Brussels: European Commission Directorate General Press and Communication.

Hall, S. (2003), 'In But Not of Europe – Europe and its Myths', *Soundings*, 22, pp. 57–69.

Hargreaves, I. and Thomas, J. (2002), *New News, Old News*. London: Broadcasting Standards Commission and Independent Television Commission.

Hoyer, S. and Pöttker, H. (eds) (2005), *Diffusion of the News Paradigm 1850–2000*. Göteborg: Göteborg University Press.

Lauf, E. (2001), 'The Vanishing Young Reader: Sociodemographic Determinants of Newspaper Use as a Source of Political Information in Europe, 1980–98', *European Journal of Communication*, 16: 2, pp. 233–43.

Machill, M. (1998), 'Euronews: the First European News Channel as a Case Study for Media Industry Development in Europe', *Media, Culture and Society*, 20: 3, pp. 427–50.

Mancini, P. (2005), 'Is there a European Model of Journalism?', in H. de Burgh (ed.), *Making Journalists*. London: Routledge, pp. 77–93.

Martin, P. (2005), 'The "Europeanization" of Elite Football: Scope, Meanings and Significance', *European Societies*, 7: 2, pp. 349–68.

McLachlan, S. and Golding, P. (2000), 'Tabloidisation in the British Press: a Quantitative Investigation into Changes in British Newspapers, 1952–1997', in C. Sparks and J. Tulloch (eds), *Tabloid Tales: Global Debates over Media Standards*. New York and Oxford: Rowman and Littlefield, pp. 75–89.

Murdock, G. and Golding, P. (1978), 'The Structure, Ownership and Control of the Press 1914–1976', in G. Boyce, J. Curran and P. Wingate (eds), *Newspaper History: From the 17th Century to the Present Day*. London: Sage/Constable, pp. 130–48.

Porter, W. E. (1983), *The Italian Journalist*. Ann Arbor: University of Michigan Press.

Ruß-Mohl, S. (2003), 'Towards a European Journalism? Limits, Opportunities, Challenges', *Studies in Communication Sciences*, 3: 2, pp. 203–16.

Schlesinger, P. (1997), 'From Cultural Defence to Political Culture: Media, Politics and Collective Identity in the European Union', *Media, Culture and Society*, 19: 3, pp. 369–91.

— (1999), 'Changing Spaces of Political Communication: The Case of the European Union', *Political Communication*, 16: 3, pp. 263–79.

World Association of Newspapers (2005), *World Press Trends 2005*. Paris: WAN.

7

Television News Has Not (Yet) Left the Nation State: Reflections on European Integration in the News

Claes de Vreese

Abstract

In research on 'the European public sphere' there is much speculation about transnationalization and Europeanization. Empirical evidence focuses largely on elite newspapers and provides only modest evidence in support of a European public sphere. This article looks systematically and cross-nationally at television news – the most widely used information source for citizens in Europe – and shows that television news is still largely structured along the boundaries of the nation state. That said, trends towards increasing Europeanization are visible, albeit at a modest level.

Keywords

Television, News, European integration, media and the nation state, public sphere

Introduction

The discussion about the EU's democratic deficit is intertwined with a discussion about the EU's 'communicative deficit' (de Vreese 2003). The importance of the media in alleviating or contributing to the democratic deficit focuses on the media's ability to contribute towards a shared framework of reference and a European identity. EU institutions have been unsuccessful in shaping European identity and promoting the connection between citizens and EU institutions via the media (Anderson and Weymouth 1999; Anderson 2004). While the EU and its institutions need to promote, or at least profile, themselves, they are oftentimes confronted with media outlets that are either sceptical or uninterested (Anderson and McLeod 2004; De Vreese 2002; Meyer 1999). Accordingly, negative news and, in general, a lack of news regarding the EU is thought to contribute to a lack of legitimacy and to detract from the formation of a European identity.

The lack of a European public sphere has been referred to as the public communication deficit (Scharpf 1999; Schlesinger 1999). From this perspective, the development of European democracy depends on the existence of a European public sphere which entails a common public debate carried out through a common European news agenda (Schlesinger 1995), ideally in a European media system (Grimm 1995, 2004). Several scholars have formulated less rigid criteria for a European public sphere. The criteria include corresponding media coverage in different countries with shared points of reference in which 'speakers and listeners recognize each other as legitimate participants in a common discourse that frames the particular issues as common European problems' (Risse and van de Steeg 2003: 21). At the very least, a European public sphere could be conceived as national media reporting on the same topic using common sources, including EU sources and sources from other EU countries. Therefore, a discussion of European issues amongst a set of EU actors in the media is important to the development of a European public sphere, or Europeanized national spheres, which will sustain democracy in the European Union and develop it further.

'The media' is a catch all term. In the extant literature there is a strong bias towards investigating newspapers. In this position paper I fully – and deliberately – discard the role of newspapers. While newspapers are part of our studies, I wish to focus on television only, primarily because of the virtual absence of research in this area and secondly because television news is repeatedly identified as the key source of information (about politics in general and the EU in particular) by citizens across Europe (Eurobarometer). I draw on large-scale, comparative content analyses conducted at the Amsterdam School of Communications Research (ASCoR) in the past years. I include evidence from the European elections in 1999 and in 2004 and from a routine period of news in 2000.

Structured knowledge about the media's coverage of European affairs is emerging. Studies of the European public sphere have focused mostly on quality newspapers or magazines and have tended to cover a handful of countries (for example, van de Steeg 2002; Meyer 2005; Peters et al. 2005; and Trenz 2004). I focus first on the visibility and amount of attention devoted to the European Parliamentary elections by national television news. Contributing to a European public sphere, increased visibility of the elections in the news gives citizens an indication of the salience or importance of the election. In addition, visible news coverage is expected to give citizens information about candidates and party positions. Second, addressing both the public sphere and the democratic deficit, I show the extent to which national television news presented the elections as a national or European event. Greater emphasis on EU actors indicates a Europeanized debate while a greater emphasis on national actors may contribute to the democratic deficit.

The 'how much' question?

While some studies have focused on the Europeanization of the media in a single country (e.g. Koopmans and Pfetsch 2003), or the coverage of particular cases by media across countries (e.g. de Vreese et al. 2001; Meyer 2005; Risse and van de Steeg 2003), our knowledge about the way in which EP elections specifically are covered is quite limited. The 1979 campaign was virtually absent from the media agenda until the final weeks before the elections (Blumler 1983; Siune 1983). No systematic and comprehensive cross-national study of media coverage was carried out until the 1999 EP elections. In 1999, a research team at the Amsterdam School of Communications Research conducted an analysis of the most widely watched television news programmes in the then fifteen EU member states in the two weeks leading up to the 1999 European elections. The results showed that the average portion of the programme (based on time) about the election in the main evening news programmes for all EU member states was about 7 per cent. Belgium, Britain, Germany, Ireland, the Netherlands, and Spain devoted even less than 5 per cent of news to the elections. Austria, Denmark, Finland, France, Greece, Italy, and Sweden are somewhat above average, spending 8 to 13 per cent of news time on European elections (de Vreese et al. 2006; Peter et al. 2004).

The visibility of the EP elections matters. Information about key democratic moments such as elections in the news is a prerequisite for enhancing public awareness and possible engagement

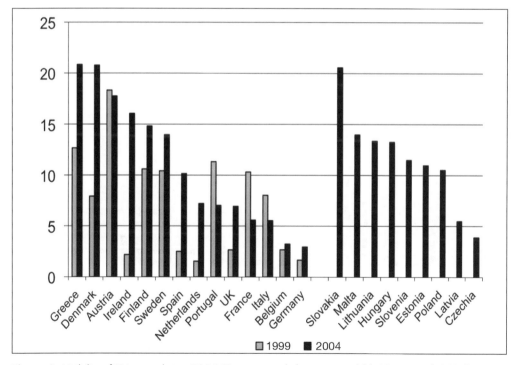

Figure 1: Visibility of EU news during 2004 EP campaign (television news) (de Vreese et al. 2006).

in EU politics. Moreover, the EU, faced with challenges of legitimacy and unclear structures for political accountability, is dependent upon media coverage to reach its citizens.

More news about the elections

Looking at the *visibility* of the 2004 EP elections in national television news, we found (see Figure 1) that EU news took up 9.8 per cent of the news, on average, in the two weeks leading up to election day. The average visibility of EU news in 2004 was higher in the new member states (10.4 per cent) than in the old member states (9.2 per cent). Of the news about the EU, 80 per cent on average was devoted specifically to the EP elections. Figure 1 displays the visibility of news about the EP election and of other EU-related issues in television newscasts during the 1999 and 2004 EP election campaigns. The fifteen old EU countries are displayed on the left-hand side and the new member states, which took part in the EP elections for the first time in 2004, are shown on the right-hand side.

The EU-wide average of 9.8 per cent contains significant cross-national variation. In Greece, for example, the elections took up 21 per cent of the news, whereas in Germany the elections took up only 3 per cent of the news. In addition to Greece, the elections were most visible in Denmark, Slovakia, Austria and Ireland, taking up more than 15 per cent of the news in these countries. In addition to Germany, the elections were least visible in Belgium and the Czech Republic, where less than 5 per cent of the news was devoted to the elections. On average, in the old member states we found an increase in the news devoted to the EP elections from 6.6 per cent in 1999 to 9.2 per cent in 2004, and ten of the fifteen old member states showed an increase in visibility. Among the new member states, seven countries showed more than 10 per cent EU news.

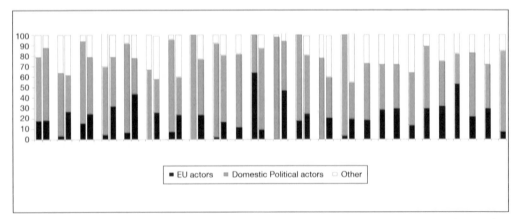

Figure 2: Share EU, domestic political and other (non-political) actors in EU news, 1999 and 2004 (De Vreese et al., 2006).

European elections: Slowly expanding the domestic battlegrounds

Figure 2 shows the proportion of actors featured in stories about the EP election across the 25 EU member states. A comparison is also made with the actors featured in the coverage of the 1999 EP election. Clearly, in both election years, domestic political actors dominated the coverage of the EP elections. In 1999, four countries (Germany, Ireland, Portugal and Sweden) either had no EU actors in EP election stories or they did not exceed 1 per cent. The Netherlands was the only country where EU actors were more frequently featured than domestic actors in EP election news, but in 1999 there were only two stories on national television news about the elections. Some changes are evident in 2004. Although the coverage was still focused on domestic actors, there was an overall increase in the proportion of EU actors. In several countries, the proportion of EU actors reached or exceeded the proportion of domestic political actors (Malta, Portugal and France).

Similar patterns are evident when looking at the other actors in the news stories. Across the member states, countries that had a higher proportion of main protagonists that were EU actors also had a high proportion of other actors that were from the EU. Therefore, although EP election news coverage still predominantly featured domestic political actors, there was an increase since 1999 in attention paid to EU actors. In all member states during the 1999 election, 83 per cent of actors in EU election stories were national political actors, whereas in 2004 a comparatively lower proportion (50 per cent for main actors and 48 per cent for other actors) were national political actors. However, these figures for domestic political actors were still higher than those for EU actors.

We might expect that the new member states would focus more on domestic political actors. This tendency to be less European focused in news coverage may stem from the news media in these countries being less familiar with covering EU issues and therefore placing greater reliance on domestic sources. Also, EU actors in these countries may be more difficult to identify. However, Peter et al. (2004) show that there tend to be more EU representatives in the news in countries that are holding EP elections for the first or second time than in countries that have held several elections. From the analysis of 2004 news coverage, we see little difference between old and new member states in terms of the focus placed on domestic and EU actors. In new member states, 27 per cent of main actors and 21 per cent of other actors in news stories were EU actors. In the old member states, the focus was similar: 25 per cent of main actors and 21 per cent of other actors were EU-level actors. There are also small differences between commercial and public service broadcasters. They tend to feature similar proportions of EU and domestic political actors, with 20 per cent of actors in commercial news stories and 18 per cent in public television news stories being EU-level actors. Given that public broadcasting has an educational mission, we expected that public television news would tend to have a greater EU focus, but this does not appear to be the case.

The 'why' question

A relevant question is of course why we see these cross-national differences. To start answering this question I rely on a study conducted in 2000 (Peter and de Vreese 2004; de Vreese 2002).

Here we found that on television there is generally little EU coverage and that it only peaks around the summits of the EU heads of government. We also found that EU coverage is more prominent during summit periods than during routine periods. EU summits lead to a change of the placement, length and presentation of EU stories. In addition, a crucial qualification has to be made. EU stories were by and large more prominent than their political counterparts. The EU may be invisible, but it is not unimportant. In other words, it is an *invisible importance* that characterizes the coverage of the EU. *If* the EU is covered, it is covered prominently – however, the EU is rarely covered (Peter and de Vreese 2004).

What may influence the amount and prominence of EU coverage? We tested for the impact of broadcasting type (public broadcasters have more political and more EU news), polarized elite opinion (when politicians disagree about Europe, there is more news) and summit periods (high-profile events create more news).

Conclusion

Coverage of European affairs tends to be cyclical in nature with coverage of the EU virtually absent from the news agenda and then peaking around important EU events to vanish off the agenda again (de Vreese et al. 2001; Norris 2000a). This pattern of news coverage has also been found to apply to EU summits, which are pivotal moments for EU decision-making and where news coverage of EU affairs is much more visible than during 'routine periods' (de Vreese and Boomgaarden 2006; Peter and de Vreese 2004; Semetko and Valkenburg 2000). During other key events, such as national referendums on issues of European integration, EU news can take up a substantial part of the news agenda, especially in the final weeks of the campaign (de Vreese and Semetko 2004). During routine periods, i.e. outside the referendum periods and when there are no scheduled events of the magnitude such as European Council meetings for example, EU politics is marginal in national news (Gerhards 2000; Peter and de Vreese 2004; Peter et al. 2003).

The negligible coverage of EU officials may result from the EU's limited external communication (de Vreese 2002). The EU's public information efforts are frequently criticized as rather poorly coordinated and inadequately staffed (Meyer 1999). Political accountability is often obfuscated to circumvent public scrutiny. If the media are provided with information about who advocated what, this information cannot be attributed to politicians, but to diplomatic sources, usually spokesmen of the Directorate Press and Communication. However, as Meyer (1999: 633) argues 'without the personalization of political debate and decisions, political accountability remains invisible' – a conclusion which is mirrored by our findings.

Television news, to a large extent, is oblivious of a large-scale development in Europe. This is far from the conclusion reached by studies of elite, broadsheet newspapers with a limited circulation. While the notion of a European public sphere, or Europeanized national public spheres, is perhaps desirable and theoretically challenging, the data on mainstream television suggest that there is no European public sphere. Television news, it seems, has not (yet) left the nation state.

References

Anderson, Peter J. and McLeod, Aileen (2004), 'The Great Non-Communicator? The Mass Communication Deficit of the European Parliament and its Press Directorate', *Journal of Common Market Studies*, 42: 5, pp. 897–917.

Blumler, Jay G. (ed) (1983), *Communicating to voters: Television in the First European Parliamentary Elections*. Sage: London.

De Vreese, Claes H. (2002), *Framing Europe: Television News and European Integration*. Amsterdam: Aksant Academic Publishers.

De Vreese, Claes H. (2003), *Communicating Europe*. London: The Foreign Policy Centre.

De Vreese, C. H., Banducci, S., Semetko, H. A. and Boomgaarden, H. A. (2006), 'The News Coverage of the 2004 European Parliamentary Election Campaign in 25 Countries', *European Union Politics*, 7: 4, pp. 479–506.

De Vreese, Claes H. and Boomgaarden, Hajo G. (2006), 'Media Effects on Public Opinion about the Enlargement of the European Union', *Journal of Common Market Studies*, 44: 2, pp. 419–36.

De Vreese, Claes H. and Semetko, Holli A. (2004), 'News Matters: Influences on the

Vote in the Danish 2000 Euro Referendum Campaign', *European Journal of Political Research*, 43: 5, pp. 699–722.

De Vreese, Claes H, Lauf, Edmund and Peter, Jochen (2006), 'The Media and European Parliament Elections: Second-rate Coverage of a Second-order Event?', in Wouter van der Brug and Cees van der Eijk (eds), *European Elections and Domestic Politics: Lessons from the Past and Scenarios for the Future*. Paris: University of Notre Dame Press.

De Vreese, Claes H., Peter, Jochen and Semetko, Holli A. (2001), 'Framing Politics at the Launch of the Euro: A Cross-national Comparative Study of Frames in the News, *Political Communication*, 18: 2, pp. 107–22.

Gerhards, Jürgen (2000), 'Europäisierung von Ökonomie und Politik und die Trägheit der Entstehung einer europäischen Öffentlichkeit', in Maurizio Bach (ed.), *Die Europäisierung nationaler Gesellschaften. Sonderheft 40 der Kölner Zeitschrift für Soziologie und Sozialpsychologie*. Wiesbaden: Westdeutscher Verlag, pp. 277–305.

Grimm, Dieter (1995). *Braucht Europa eine Verfassung?* [*Does Europe need a Constitution?*] München: Carl Friedrich von Siemens Stiftung.

Grimm, Dieter (2004), 'Treaty or Constitution? The Legal Basis of the European Union after Maastricht', in Erik O. Eriksen, John E. Fossum and Augustin J. Menéndez (eds), *Developing a Constitution for Europe*. London, Routledge, pp. 69–87.

Koopmans, Ruud and Pfetsch, Barbara (2003), 'Towards a Europeanised Public Sphere? Comparing Political Actors and the Media in Germany'. Paper presented at the international conference 'Europeanization of Public Spheres? Political Mobilization, Public Communication and the European Union'. Berlin, 20–22 June 2003.

Meyer, Christoph O. (1999), 'Political Legitimacy and the Invisibility of Politics: Exploring the European Union's Communication Deficit', *Journal of Common Market Studies*, 37: 4, pp. 617–39.

Meyer, Christoph O. (2005), 'The Europeanization of Media Discourse: A Study of Quality Press Coverage of Economic Policy Co-ordination since Amsterdam', *Journal of Common Market Studies*, 43: 1, pp. 121–48.

Norris, Pippa (2000), 'Blaming the Messenger? Political Communications and Turnout in EU Elections', *Citizen Participation in European Politics*. Demokratiutredningens skrift nr 32. Stockholm: Statens Offentliga Utredningar, pp. 99–116.

Peter, Jochen and de Vreese, Claes H. (2004), 'In Search of Europe – A Cross-national Comparative Study of the European Union in National Television News', *Harvard Journal of Press/Politics*, 9: 4, pp. 3–24.

Peter, Jochen, Lauf, Edmund and Semetko, Holli A. (2004), 'Television Coverage of the 1999 European Parliamentary Elections', *Political Communication*, 21: 4, pp. 415–33.

Peter, Jochen, Semetko, Holli A. and de Vreese, Claes H. (2003), 'EU Politics on Television News: A Cross-national Comparative Study', *European Union Politics*, 4: 3, pp. 305–28.

Peters, Bernhard, Sifft, Stefanie, Wimmel, Andreas, Bruggemann, Michael and Kleinen-Von Konigslow, Katharina (2005), 'Seven National and Transnational Public Spheres: The Case of the EU', *European Review*, 13, pp. 139–60.

Risse, Thomas and van de Steeg, Marianne (2003), 'An Emerging European Public Sphere? Empirical Evidence and Theoretical Clarifications'. Paper presented at the international conference 'Europeanization of Public Spheres? Political Mobilization, Public Communication and the European Union'. Berlin, 20–22 June 2003.

Scharpf, Fritz (1999), *Governing in Europe: Effective and Democratic*. New York: Oxford University Press.

Schlesinger, Philip (1999), 'Changing Spaces of Political Communication: The Case of the European Union', *Political Communication*, 16: 3, pp. 263–79.

Semetko, Holli A. and Valkenburg, Patti M. (2000), 'Framing European Politics: A Content Analysis of Press and Television News', *Journal of Communication*, 50: 2, pp. 93–109.

Siune, Karen (1983), 'The Campaign on Television: What Was Said and Who Said It?, in Jay Blumler (ed.), *Communicating to Voters: Television in the First European Parliamentary Elections*. London: Sage, pp. 223–40.

Trenz, Hans-Jörg (2004), 'Media Coverage of European Governance: Exploring the European Public Sphere in National Quality Newspapers', *European Journal of Communication*, 19: 3, pp. 291–319.

Van de Steeg, Marianne (2002), 'Rethinking the Conditions for a Public Sphere in the European Union', *European Journal of Social Theory*, 5: 4, pp. 499–519.

8

THE EUROPEANIZATION OF THE DANISH NEWS MEDIA – THEORIZING THE NEWS MEDIA AS BOTH NATIONAL AND TRANSNATIONAL POLITICAL INSTITUTION

Mark Ørsten

Abstract

This chapter investigates the European news media's change form being a national to also being a transnational political institution. The chapter will do this through a focus on Danish news media, since several studies of European news media point to Denmark as an especially successful example of Europeanization. Further, by looking at the norms and routines that according to institutional theory constitute the news media as an institution, the chapter will suggest that the reason for the slow changes toward a more Europeanized media content, lies in the fact that many of news media's norms and routines, such as news values and audience orientation are inherently national in their focus. However, this is not the full explanation. The norms and routines of the news media are, according to new institutionalist theory, not just influenced by the news media themselves, but also by the historically structured interaction between the media system and the political system. Within the 27 member states of the European Union at least three different models of media and politics can be found, according to Hallin and Mancini (2004). The chapter closes by discussing how the different models of media and politics may be at the heart of the matter when it comes to the question of what helps or hinders the process of Europeanization in the news media.

Keywords
Europeanization, new institutionalism, journalism, political communication, EU coverage, Denmark

Introduction
Today many scholars view the news media as a political institution (Cook 1998, 2006; Sparrow 1999, 2006; Ørsten 2005; Ryfe 2006). The argument behind this, in origin an American, theoretical approach, is that the news media fulfill a critical role in the communications process between the constitutional branches of government (executive, legislative and judiciary) and the public. But looking at it from a European perspective the focus on the *constitutional* branches of government tends to define the news media as a merely *national* political institution, thereby neglecting the still more important transnational communication between the news media, the political institutions of the EU and the public (de Vreese 2002; Ørsten 2004, 2005, 2006). However, new studies show that the news media in many European countries also *do* fulfill a critical role in the communication between the EU institutions and the public (de Vreese 2002; Ørsten 2004; Baisnée 2002; Maier and Tenschler 2006). Through the slow process of Europeanization of media content EU actors and themes have gained a small, but significant stronghold on the news agenda in many European countries. The studies, however, also show that such institutional change comes at a slow pace and in some EU member states not at all.

The news media as a political institution
Political scholars Aspinwall and Schneider (2001: 2) note that the neo-institutional approach to the study of politics has, since its emergence in the mid-80s, become somewhat of a 'mainstream' theory bridging together some of the earlier gaps between otherwise different schools of political science. Much the same can perhaps be said about the 'institutional turn' in media studies that we have seen since the late 1990s. Building on the many studies of news media and news organizations done in the 1960s and 1970s the books by Cook (1998) and Sparrow (1999), 'by linking the study of news routines and practices to new institutionalist theory' (Ryfe 2006:136) were able to 'capture the essence of what (many different) scholars had learned about the news media over the last three decades' (ibid.). As Ryfe (2006) also notes the 1980s saw the death of theorizing on news production and the current success of new institutionalism in media studies can been as a result of new institutionalism's ability to link itself to the groundbreaking research of the past, while also pointing to new and interesting directions of future research – as this chapter also hopes to illustrate.

New institutionalism in media studies, as well as new institutionalism elsewhere, comes in different shapes and forms. Though Cook (1998) and Sparrow (1999) are often mentioned in the same breath, they do, as they themselves point out, differ greatly on central issues (Cook 2006, Sparrow 2006). These differences aside there is of course a central new institutional argument, or rather several, as many scholars have pointed out (Cook 2006, 2001; Sparrow 2006; Ryfe 2006; Benson 2006; Esser et. al. 2001). One is the focus on the news media's political role. Cook (1998:3) writes:

not only is the news a 'co-production' of the news media and government, but policy today is likewise the result of collaboration and conflict among newspersons, officials, and other political actors...Indeed I will claim that the American news media today are not merely part of politics; they are part of government.

And Sparrow (2006: 150) writes: 'The media are a crucial part of national politics and a full participant in the political process and governmental system.' The other central focus is the understanding of the news routines and practices as institutions and therefore as 'social patterns of behavior identifiable across the organizations that are generally seen within a society to preside over a particular space' (Cook 1998:70).

Turning first to the 'political' question the argument here is that the news media fulfill a critical roll in the communications process between the constitutional branches of government (executive, legislative and judiciary) and the public (Cook 1998, Esser 2001). In the age of 'government by publicity' (Esser 2001) where most if not all political communication is facilitated through different media (Sparrow 2006) the line between news-making and policy-making become all but indistinguishable (Cook 2006). Thus the news media serve to 'structure' the actions of political actors and thereby government (Sparrow 2006). But it is not only the media that influences government. Indeed Ryfe (2006), Cook (2006) and Kaplan (2006) all point to the fact that the state or, more broadly, polities are also the 'major exogenous forces on news production' (Ryfe 2006: 138). This puts the focus on the media-politics relationship as also pointed to by Hallin and Mancini (2004). It does, however, also offer up a rather narrow view of both the state, politics and who the political actors in late modern society really are. New institutionalism's focus on the state, or the constitutional branches of government, tends to ignore that facts stated in governance theory that the field of politics today is made up by an ever-increasing number of political actors both national, international and transnational (Ørsten 2004, 2006). From a European perspective the political institutions of the European Union play almost as large a role in the formation of membership countries national politics as does the national Parliament (Hix 1999; Ørsten 2004; Pedersen 2001). Thus the concept of governance and the existence of political actors outside the nation state are a challenge to the new institutional focus on the politics of the state, and a challenge to the concept of the news media as merely a *national* political institution.

Europeanization and the nature of news rules
The issue here is the question of if and how we can identify a *Europeanization* of political communication at the level of media content, supplementing the Europeanization of political and administrative institutions such as parties, Parliaments, ministries, agencies and private organizations that many newer studies have documented (Esmark 2002). Europeanization of political communication is often translated to mean the extent to which both mediated and non-mediated political communication deals directly or indirectly with the European Union (Machill et al. 2006; Esmark and Ørsten 2006). In this understanding Europeanization of media content refers to two central criteria: (a) an increased focus on European themes and actors, and (b) an evaluation of theses themes and actors from a non-nation state dominated

point of view (Gerhards 2000). According to Gerhards' Europeanization should take place when, 'in the national public's sphere, over time, reporting increasingly focused on the European decisions and the elites taking the decisions'. For Gerhards as for Esmark (2005) the public sphere is here largely understood to mean a mediated public sphere populated by politician's, voters and other political actors. This means that Europeanization as understood here refers to an Europeanization on the level of the national media content in the leading news media.

In other words a change in the way that the news media covers politics is required in order for a Europeanization to take place. A move away from the traditional focus on the constitutional branches of national government and towards a focus on the political actors at the EU level: the Commission, the Council, the Parliament, etc. Change, and most often the lack of, is however also the *second* central focus when viewing the news media through the eyes of new institutionalist theory. In new institutionalist theory the news media is viewed as a *single* institution due to the fact that all news media, according to Cook:

> despite different technologies, deadlines and audiences are structured similarly in their internal organization, the way they interact with sources, the formats they use, and in the content they provide...This transorganizational agreement on news process and content suggest that we should think of the news media not as a set of diverse organizations, or even a batch of individual institutions, but collectively as a single social institution. (Cook 1998: 64)

The book most often referred to as the starting point of the neo-institutional turn in political science is March and Olsen's *Rediscovering Institutions* (1984), the same book which Cook uses as a starting point for his study of the news media as a political institution. The key argument behind March and Olsen's neo-institutional theory can be summed up as follows:

> life is organized by sets of shared meanings and practices that come to be taken for a given for a long time...actors act and organize themselves in accordance with rules and practices which are socially constructed, publicly known, anticipated and accepted (March and Olsen 1994: 4–5).

Because of this actions and outcomes in organizations are affected by institutions (i.e. rules, procedures, norms, etc.), and not solely by rational organizational goals/policies or rational individual action. This also means that rational action alone cannot bring about immediate change in political institutions. As March and Olsen underline, institutions preserve themselves and can be very resistant to change. This is due to the fact that 'routines are sustained by being embedded in a structure of routine, by socialization and by the way they organize attention' (March and Olsen 1994: 55).

To March and Olsen this suggests that action taken by agents is guided by a 'logic of appropriateness', that is to say that agents, when considering an action, will ask themselves 'what kind of situation is this and what are my obligations' (Ryfe 2006: 205). 'Rules that are more familiar are more likely to be evoked, and so recently used or recently revised rules comes to attention' (March and Olson 1994: 25). When applying this definition to journalism, writes Ryfe (2006: 205), 'we might define a journalistic rule as a normative assumption or expectation about appropriate or legitimate modes of behavior – what a journalist's role is, what her or his obligations are, what values and commitments are appropriate – in the context of news production'. Ørsten (2005) expands the argument of understanding news rules as 'logic of appropriateness'. He writes that for March and Olson the logic appropriateness was set within the environment of a relatively closed political institution. An important factor in understanding the nature of news rules as a logic of appropriateness, is, however, to understand that the logic, the rules, is not only influenced by 'one' institution, but by a whole 'institutional setting'. The news media as a political institution is embedded in its relationship with other political institutions, and it is this broader 'institutional setting' that guides and influences the rules of journalism. This is also a point made by Kaplan (2006) who writes that an organization's environment should be 'conceived as a broader societal sector that supplies the pressures and ideals defining the organization and its specific field' (Kaplan 2006: 176). In short this means that the rules of journalisms influence the institutions that journalists interact with, but the practices of journalism, the rules, are also influenced by these institutions. In the case of Europeanization this would mean the rules guiding journalistic coverage of Europe are not only influenced by the rules of journalism, but also by the rules of the European Commission, the Council, the Parliament, as well as the rules guiding the national political process of implementing EU legislation. As Ryfe (2006) also writes, but seems to forget in his discussion of news rules, polities also are the 'major exogenous forces on news production'. This is also the case of the European polity.

Mapping Europeanization on a country level

The news media may indeed be viewed as a political institution in most Western countries, but as Esser et al. (2001) point out in their institutional study of election coverage in Germany, Britain and the United States, the institutional context will of course differ between countries. Not counting the Baltic States, and the Eastern European countries, three different models of media and politics can be found within the EU (Hallin and Mancini 2004). These models are: (1) the Mediterranean or polarized model, which includes France, Greece, Italy, Portugal and Spain; (2) the Northern European or democratic-corporatist model, which includes Austria, Belgium, Denmark, Finland, Germany, the Netherlands, Norway, Sweden and Switzerland and; (3) the North Atlantic or liberal model, which includes Britain, the United States, Canada and Ireland. There are of course many characteristics that make up the different models, but for the purpose of this chapter they may be summed up as follows: 'At the most basic level' write's 'Hallin and Mancini' (2004: 49), 'a distinction can be made between liberal democracies – with the Untied States as the most obvious example – and the welfare state democracies that predominate in Europe, especially on the content'. To this distinction you can add a three-way distinction in the role of the state between 'liberalism in the US and Great Britain, statesim in France and Japan, and historically in Greece, Spain and Portugal, and corporatism in the small European states and to a lesser extent in Germany' (Hallin and Mancini 2004: 50). Three further important basic distinctions between the three models can be made:

1. The level of journalistic professionalism, which is high in both the liberal and corporatist model, and lower in the Mediterranean model.
2. Market dominance in the liberal model and press subsidies and public service broadcasting that dominate the corporate model, and to a lesser extent the Mediterranean model.
3. Journalistic ideals also vary within the three models. In the corporatist model journalists operate under a clear democratic ideal, where it is the media's role to represent all significant interest in society and facilitate their participation in public life (Kirstensen and Østen 2007).

This is most sharply contrasted with the journalistic ideal of the liberal model, where the role of the media is seen as more understood to be a 'neutral' channel of information between citizens and government (ibid.).

Europeanization: Quantitative results

For a long time the question of Europeanization was merely a theoretical question. But as Machill et al. (2006), and Ørsten (2006) have pointed out, both quantitative and qualitative results are now coming in covering a wide range of country studies, as well as several comparative studies, all focusing on the Europeanization of Europe's news media. The following will try to give a small overview of both general and country specific results.

As regards the general results, Peter and de Vreese (2004), based on a large comparative study, give the following characterization of EU reporting. In general daily reporting on the EU is low in many European news media. However during summits, referendums, crisis and scandal the coverage may be intense and remain so for some time. In general, news stories on the EU tend to focus on the national political level and not the transnational political level. In some countries there is a slight tendency to cover the EU in a negative tone. To these general results Ørsten (2004) and Trenz (2005) add that the coverage may vary significantly from media to media, with more coverage in quality morning/broadsheet papers and on public service television, and less coverage in more commercial news media, both print and television. Also the different political institutions get different coverage in the news media, according to Ørsten (2004). The Commission is the preferred source in newspaper coverage, whereas television news prefers the Council as news source. Neither newspapers nor television focus their European news coverage on the action, or members, of the European Parliament.

Based on recently published studies it is also possible to give a more specific understanding of the level of Europeanization in different member states (Machill et al. 2006, Ørsten 2006):

France: Even though France is one of the original membership countries of the EEC several studies of French media coverage suggest that the EU is not a highly prioritized subject in the French news media. In Machill et al. (2006) the French media is judged to have been subject to a moderate level of Europeanization at the level of media content. Peter and de Vreese (2004), in a comparative study of Europeanization in Danish, French, German and Dutch news media, conclude that in so-called routine weeks about 2 per cent of French news media content concerns itself with the EU. However, during summits the level my rise to 11 per cent. Neveu et al. (2005) conclude that French television shows very little interest in covering the EU, and only when a political issue on the EU agenda can be linked very clearly to a political issue on the national French political agenda, will EU stories rise to the top of the French media agenda. Likewise Gerstle et al. (2006) in a study of the French news media's coverage of the 2004 EP election concludes that coverage of the event was extremely marginal and negative, especially television coverage.

Great Britain: The EU coverage in British news media is first and foremost characterized by a sceptical, slightly negative tone that according to Basinee (2003) is more typical of the British tabloids than for the broadsheet papers. However, a report investigating the BBC (Wilson 2005) concludes that on television there was also a tendency to be negative and sceptical when covering the European Union. Machill et al. (2006) characterize the general coverage of the EU in British news media as low, and Peter and de Vreese (2005) conclude that in routine weeks about 2 per cent of the news coverage in British media concerns the EU, whereas during summits the overall coverage may rise to about 10 per cent.

Germany: Like France, Germany is a founding member of the EEC, and Machill et al. (2006) as well as Trenz (2005) both conclude that German news media, especially the broadsheet papers, tend to have a high coverage of European Union affairs. Rosenwerth et al. (2005) is far more sceptical, and concludes that only 3 to 4 per cent of the overall news coverage has the EU as it main focus. In his study of the news coverage of the 2004 EP election Tenscher (2006) concludes that the news coverage was overall limited and mostly focused on national political actors and the national political agenda. Peter and de Vreese (2005) conclude that in routine weeks about 4 per cent of the news stories in German media focus on the EU and that this level may rise during summits to about 10 per cent.

Netherlands: Machill et al. (2006) find the level of Europeanization to be high in the Dutch news media, a conclusion that is supported by Peter and de Vreese (2005) where the coverage of the EU in routine weeks is found to be about 5 per cent, a level that may rise to 10 per cent during summits. However, de Vreese (2006) in his study of the 2004 EP election concludes that the coverage was in general low, although also somewhat better than the coverage of the 1999 EP election, where the entire election went by almost unnoticed by the television news.

Denmark – a 'best case' of Europeanization? According to Machill et al. (2006) the level of Europeanization of Danish news media may be categorized as high. They conclude: 'the public spheres of the Netherlands, Denmark and Germany are the most Europeanized' (Machill et al. 2006: 78). Peter and de Vreese (2005: 15) conclude: 'there is reason to believe that EU affairs are approached differently in Denmark, which materializes, among others ways, in the amount of EU-coverage' (Peter and de Vreese 2005: 15). In a longitude study of the Europeanization of the Danish news media Ørsten (2004) concludes that from 1991 to 2001 a relatively large number of European issues were covered by the Danish media, but more so by the press than by television. In general, 7 to 13 per cent of all news items in the morning papers were connected to the EU; on television the number of EU news stories varied from just 3 per cent to 9 per cent. Ørsten (2004) also found a dominance of national actors in EU coverage, but especially the Commission and the Counsel, also important actors in media coverage.

More important, however, is the change Ørsten (2004) found in the way issues and actors are framed by the media. In 1991 conflict between the Danish government and the EEC was the most prominent news frame. Through a detailed framing analysis Ørsten shows that the conflict frame is the result of a nation-state dominated news discourse that almost exclusively casts the EEC in the role of the 'other'. For this reason almost all European initiatives in 1991 were seen by the media as a threat to the harmony of Denmark as a sovereign nation state. In 1996 and especially in 2001 the conflict frame lost its dominance, and the EU increasingly became accepted as an equal player in the game of politics. In their study of the 2004 EP election Esmark and Ørsten (2006) also find that the election did receive substantial coverage. With substantial coverage in both morning papers and tabloids the 2004 EP election probably received more media attention than any other EP election since the first election in 1979 (ibid.). It is, however, important to note that most of the media coverage is concentrated on the last fourteen days prior to the election, with more than 50 per cent of the coverage appearing only in the last week before the election.

Turning to the themes discussed in the election campaign Esmark and Ørsten (2006) show that television and the tabloids focused more on political strategy than on political substance, whereas the broadsheet papers focused more on substance than on strategy. Under the headline of strategy the specific focus was most commonly on voter turn-out, a subject that has also played a significant role in prior elections. The election campaign itself was also a frequent issue under this headline addressing such topics as campaign financing and the inner-party competition among the candidates. Under the headline of 'political substance' the focus was most commonly on the role of the Parliament, the European Constitution and the enlargement of the EU. Together these issues represent a shift away from the three previous elections (1984, 1989 and 1999) – where other studies indicate a strong focus on national subjects – to a stronger focus on major European issues. Another sign of the media shift in evaluation was the tendency to discuss notions of democracy in a European perspective rather than a strict national perspective, as was commonly done in the findings of Ørsten (2004). Esmark and Ørsten (2006) find in 305 out of a total of 1430 news stories that there were manifest discussions in the texts concerning the nature of democracy as either European or purely national. In 86 per cent of the items a European notion of democracy was evident, indicating that the national discourse found to be dominant by both Ørsten (2004) and Leroy and Siune (1994) is no longer the dominant way European issues are framed in the Danish news media.

Europeanization: Qualitative results – The Brussels beat and the 'national' nature of news rules

Beside the many quantitative studies, an almost equal amount of more qualitative studies have also been done. Theses studies, using mostly observation and interview as the preferred method, have mostly been focused on the journalists working in Brussels, and their experiences in covering the

Brussels beat. There are more than a 1,000 journalists working in Brussels today, but as many of the studies of these journalists show, the news rules governing the daily news production of a Brussels correspondent are remarkably similar across both media type and nationality of the media.

Reporter/editor relation: Negotiating news value

According to de Vreese (2002):

> News organizations operate with a triadic organization with respect to EU coverage. The studio headquarters and central newsroom work together with the political unit and the news's organizations Brussels desk. This set-up is more complex than the traditional set-up for news coverage of domestic coverage where the central headquarters woks together with the Parliamentary unit alone. (de Vreese 2002: 62)

Ørsten (2004) concludes that in *practice* this means that there is very little contact between the Parliamentary unit and the Brussels desk. Instead, the journalists have divided the beats between them, so that they *don't* have to talk to each other on a daily basis. The political unit is happy to cover only the European stories that have immediate and direct influence on domestic politics, and a political reporter in general only spends about a quarter of their time doing this, even when within the political unit the reporter is know as the 'EU reporter'. The central newsroom is in general also far more focused on domestic politics (de Vreese 2002; Ørsten 2004), so that the Brussels reporters are to a large part left with the task of pitching their stories on the phone from Brussels.

This, however, is not an easy task. Slaatta (1999), Palm (1996), de Vreese (2002), Ørsten (2004), Stratham (2004, 2006) and Gleissner and de Vreese (2005) have all interviewed reporters covering the Brussels beat, and in all the studies the reporters state that it is almost always very difficult to pitch stories to their editors since their editors are almost exclusively interested in the domestic political agenda. Almost all the interviewed reporters stated that in order to sell a Brussels story, they had to domesticate it, that is, to focus on the story's importance to the national political agenda or on its importance to a national audience.

Imaging a European reader/viewer

In the studies by Stratham (2004, 2006), Ørsten (2004) and Gleissner and de Vreese (2005) the reporters expand on their thinking about what kind of readers and viewers they communicate their stories to. Here it becomes clear that to the reporters mind there is no such thing as a European identity. To the reporters the viewers and readers of their respective media are all moderately interested in domestic politics; they are however not interested in European politics and their knowledge of the EU is in general small.

Source relations on the Brussels beat

Slaatta (1999), Basnée (2002) and Ørsten (2004) all conclude that there are two major sources for journalists working the Brussels beat. One is the European Commission, the other the national delegations on the embassies of the member states. According to Slaatta (1999) and Ørsten (2004) the most important sources are the Commission and the daily briefing that takes place Monday to Friday at noon. Most reporters find themselves at this briefing a couple a times a week, but apart from it being standard routine, and a chance to meet and talk to colleagues and diplomats, who also attend the briefing in large numbers for exactly this reason, many journalists find the daily briefings close to worthless. The Commission's frequent press releases are often found to be boring and difficult to understand. For this reason many reporters also attend more informal meeting at their national embassy, where the national delegations of diplomats are only to happy to put a national spin on the daily goings-on of the commission. Many reporters are, however, are highly aware of this, and try to attend meetings with a least one other delegation in order not to be 'national' in their coverage of the EU.

Discussion: Media systems, political systems and the question of institutional change

It seems clear that the many studies on Europeanization of news supports the new institutional thesis that news coverage, due to its institutional nature, will tend toward homogeneity even across a wide range of media outlets, and in this case, also across a wide range of countries. But the studies also show that, as Ryfe (2006) states, even though news can be remarkably homogeneous across news outlets, it can also be remarkably variable. This is also Entman's point (2006: 215):

> What institutionalism might help political communication researchers develop further is an explanation of precisely what homogeneity means, how it measure it, when and to what degree news coverage deviates from the baseline assumption of homogeneity, and how a deviation matters to politics.

To this you may add that new institutionalism, in the way suggested in this chapter, may also help to understand how deviations, or in this case change, might be dependent not only on the news outlets/journalists themselves, but also on the whole institutional setting that every news media/journalist is embedded in, in this case and point the three different institutional settings for media and political interaction that Hallin and Mancini suggest.

But starting with the question of homogeneity first. It is fairly clear from the studies mentioned above that the triadic organization of EU news coverage that is characteristic of many major news outlets has a huge influence on the Europeanization of the news. The triadic organization is more complex than the regular organization of political news, and in practice this means that the Brussels correspondents are left to cover the EU 'alone', without much other editorial input than the need to focus on the national agenda. Add to this the fact that there are much fewer correspondents in Brussels than at the national political desk (in Denmark the ratio is 1–2 Brussels correspondents to 3–6 political reporters at Parliament), and it becomes obvious that the news net is not organized in such a way as to optimize EU coverage. The fact the Brussels correspondents are so few may also cause many of them to adhere to strict routines in order to get the often very complex and overwhelming job of covering Europe done in time for the next deadline. This favours the few sources on the Brussels beat who actually make it their job to talk to reporters, the Commission and the national delegations.

Despite the fact that European news organizations also seem to share a 'transorganizational agreement on news process and content', the studies on Europeanization also show some variability, when it comes to the question of the level of Europeanization of media content. In trying to explain the differences in media content in the coverage of the EP election 2004 in almost all 25 member states Adam and Berkel (2006) suggest the need to look at the different media structures in the different memberships countries – much as it has been suggested earlier in this chapter. Adam and Berkel suggest that diversity of media outlets, the degree of commercialization and the media politics relation is central to understanding the differences in the level of Europeanization that studies have found across the 25 member states of the EU. Answering the same question with the help of Hallin and Mancini (2004) supports the thesis that commercialization plays an important part in the process of Europeanization. From the studies of Europeanization is seems fairly clear that public service television and broadsheet papers have the highest level of Europeanization, and tabloids and commercial television the lowest. With regard to the media-politics relation Adam and Berkel suggest that the politicization is to be understood as how much influence the political elite have over media content. In their context the EU is seen a political project of the elite, and the more elite influence over media content the more Europeanization you a likely to see.

Viewing this question through the lens of Hallin and Mancini's work, elite influences are not what springs to mind. Instead what springs to mind is the fact that most Europeanized countries are the countries within the corporate-democratic model. In this model there is both a strong tradition of public service, but also of general press subsidies. The subsidies and public service ensure a low level of commercialization. Due to the high level of journalism professionalism that is also characteristic of the model, press subsidies and public service do not, however, lead to more elite influence on media content. A better explanation of the relatively high level of Europeanization found in the countries within the corporatist model might instead be that the corporatist model of politics, where trade unions, business organizations and other relevant social groups are drawn into political negotiation to a far wider extent then in the liberal model, to a very large extent 'mirror' the political system of the EU. In other words viewed from a country within the corporatist model the vast and complex political system of the EU with its many political actors, its tradition of negotiation and consensus seeking, does not seem such a strange beast, as when viewed from the other political systems. As Esmark and Ørsten (2008, forthcoming) state, when analysing political communication in countries within the corporate model there are two distinct systems of communication: a 'political system' focusing on the Parliamentary actors and a 'corporate system' focusing on business, the unions, etc. In order to understand and cover the politics of the EU, both these systems of political communication have to understood, monitored and contextualized, and perhaps journalists within the corporatist countries simply have a better chance of this, since they are more familiar with this system of politics.

One last factor within the corporatist model worth mentioning is the journalistic ideal of the media serving as a democratic institution and giving voice to all political actors. This ideal is the reason behind both the high level of public service and press subsidies that characterize the model, but perhaps the ideal also serves as an argument in the negotiation of newsworthiness between reporter and editor, because even through Danish editors seem to fear publishing too many EU-stories and Danish correspondents in Brussels also find it hard to pitch their stories to the home desk, EU stories do seem to find their way to the news more often in both Denmark and in the other countries within the corporatist model.

But all of this does not, of course, explain everything you ever wanted to know about Europeanization. Belgium and Austria, both countries within the corporatist model, show only low or moderate signs of Europeanization according to Machill et al. (2006). Combining a new institutionalist approach with the current available data, and the models suggested by Hallin and Mancini does, however, show that the news media does indeed also function as a transnational political institution. The theory presented here also suggests that investigating the rules of journalism, as set within a larger institutional field, may indeed be a prudent way to further investigate similarities and differences found within the subject of Europeanization of the news media.

References

Aspinwall, Mark and Scheider, Gerald (eds., 2001), *The rules of Integration: institutionalist approaches to the study of Europe*. Manchester: Manchester University Press.

Adam, Silke and Berkel, Barbar (2006), 'Media Structures as an Obstacle to the Europeanization of Public Spheres?', in Michaela Maier and Jens Tenscher (eds), *Campaigning in Europe, Campaigning for Europe*. LIT: Berlin, pp. 45–63.

Baisnée, Olivier (2002), 'Can Political Journalism Exist at the EU-level?', in Raymond Kuhn and Erik Neveu (eds), *Political Journalism*. Sage: London, pp. 108–28.

Benson, Rodney (2006), "News Media as a Journalistic Field: What Bourdieu Adds to New Institutionalism, and Vive Versa" in *Political Communication*, vol 23, pp. 187–202.

Cook, Timothy E (1998), 'Governing with the news'. Chicago: Chicago University Press.

Cook, Timothy E (2006), 'The News Media as a Political Institution: Looking Backward and Loiking Forward', *Political Communication*, 23, pp. 159–71.

De Vreese, Claes H. (2002), *Framing Europe*. Amsterdam: Aksant.

De Vreese, Claes H. (2006), 'Continuity and Change', in Michaela Maier and Jens Tenscher (eds), *Campaigning in Europe, Campaigning for Europe*. LIT: Berlin, pp. 207–17.

Esmark, Anders (2002), "At forvalte Europa". Ph.D. Dissertation. Department of Political Science. University of Copenhagen.

Esmark, Anders (2005), 'Europæisk Offentlighed – Politisk Kommunikation i et Komplekst System' *Økonomi & Politik*, 78: 3, pp. 46–59.

Esmark, Anders and Ørsten, Mark (2006), 'Halfway There? The Danish 2004 European Parliament Campaign', in Michaela Maier and Jens Tenscher (eds), *Campaigning in Europe, Campaigning for Europe*. LIT: Berlin, pp. 101–18.

Esmark, Anders and Ørsten, Mark (2008), 'Political Communication in Denmark', in Strömbeck, Ørsten and Aalberg (eds), *Political Communication in the Nordic Countries*. Stockholm: Nordicom.

Esser, Frank et. al. (2001), 'Spin Doctors in the United States, Great Britain and Germany' in *Press/Politics* 6(1), pp. xx

Gerstlé, Jacques, et. al (2006), 'Media Coverage and Voting in the European Parliament Elections in France 2004', in Michaela Maier and Jens Tenscher (eds), *Campaigning in Europe, Campaigning for Europe*. LIT: Berlin, pp. 339–51.

Gerhards, Jürgen (2000), 'Europäisierung von Ökonomie und Politik und die Trägheit der Entstehung einer europäischen Öffentlichkeit', in Maurizio Bach (ed.), *Die Europäisierung nationaler Gesellschaften*. Wiesbaden: Westdeutscher Verlag, pp. 227–305.

Gleissner, Martin and de Vreese, Claes H. (2005), 'News about the EU Constitution', *Journalism*, 6: 2, pp. 221–42.

Golding, Peter, et al. (2005), *The Case of Great Britain*. Erich-Brost-Institute, AIM project.

Hallin, Daniel C. and Mancini, Paolo (2004), *Comparing Media Systems: Three Models of Media and Politics*. Cambridge: Cambridge University Press.

Kaplan, Richard L. (2006), 'The News about New Institutionalism: Journalism's Ethic of Objectivity and its Political Origins', *Political Communication*, 23, pp. 173–85.

Kristensen, Nete & Ørsten, Mark (2003), "Danish Media at war – The Danish media coverage of the invasion of Iraq in 2003, in *Journalism*, vol 8 (3), pp. 233–253.

Leroy, Pascale and Siune, Karen (1994), 'The Role of Televison in European Elections: The Cases of Belgium and Denmark', *European Journal of Communication*, 9, pp. 47–69.

Machill et al. (2006), 'Europe-Topics in Europe's Media', *European Journal of Communication*, 21: 1, pp. 57–88.

March, James G & Olsen, Johan P (1989), *Rediscovering institutions*. London: The Free Press 1989.

Neveu, Erik, et al. (2005), *The Case of France*. Erich-Borst-Institute. AIM project.

Peter, Jochen and de Vreese, Claes H. (2004), 'In Search of Europe', *Press/Politics*, 9: 4, pp. 3–24.

Palm, Göran (1996), *Melleam Idea och Verkelighed – Journalister om EU-journalistik*. Stockholm: Styrelsen för psykologisk försvar, rapport 169–3.

Pedersen et. al (2001) *Europaveje*. København: DJØF

Rosenwerth et al. (2005), *The Case of Germany*. Erich-Borst-Institute. AIM project.

Ryfe, David Michael (2006), 'The Nature of News Rules', *Political Communication*, 23, pp. 203–14.

Simon Hix (1999), *The Political System of the European Union*. London: MacMillan Press LTD.

Slaatta, Tore (1999), *Europeanisation and the Norwegian news media*. Report 36 from Department of Media and Communication, Oslo University.

Sparrow, Bartholomew H. (2006), 'A Research Agenda for an Institutional Media', *Political Communication*, 23, pp. 145–57.

Statham, Paul (2004), *Work Package 6: Interviews with Journalists*. Bristol: Europub.

Statham, Paul (2006), 'Political Journalism and Europeanization: Pressing Europe'. Working Paper 13/06, Centre for European Communications.

Tenscher, Jens (2006), 'Low Heated and Half-Hearted', in Michaela Maier and Jens Tenscher (eds), *Campaigning in Europe, Campaigning for Europe*. LIT: Berlin, pp. 119–39.

Trenz, Hans-Jörg (2004), 'Media Coverage on European Governance', *European Journal of Communication*, 19: 3, pp. 291–319.

Wilson, Lord, et al. (2005), *BBC News Coverage of the European Union – Independent Panel Report*. London: BBC.

Ørsten, Mark (2005), 'Nyhedsinstitutionen: Et ny-Institutionelt Perspektiv på den Medierede Politiske Kommunikation', *Økonomi & Politik*, 78: 3, pp. 13–28.

Ørsten, Mark (2004), 'Transnational Politisk Journalistik'. Ph.D Dissertation, Roskilde University.

9

Just Another Missed Opportunity in the Development of a European Public Sphere: The European Constitutional Debate in German, British and French Broadsheets

Regina Vetters

Abstract

After the rejection of the Treaty establishing a Constitution for Europe through public referenda, the Constitutional process has retrospectively been put into question. Yet, when the debate was launched in early 2002 it was accompanied by high hopes to stimulate open debates and public involvement throughout Europe. A comparison of newspaper coverage on the early Constitutional debate in Germany, the United Kingdom and France shows a definite interest in the topic and a convergence of issue-cycles. Moreover, there was a considerable degree of mutual observation of European neighbour countries. However, the conditions for the development of a European public sphere improved only after the document was hammered out. The old method of intergovernmental bargaining attracted more media attention, corresponded better to the logic of the media and even provoked a more Europeanized coverage. In addition, the qualitative analysis further challenges whether anything like a mediatized European public sphere evolved.

Keywords
European public sphere, constitutional debate, cross-national comparison, quantitative media analysis, frame analysis, mediatization

The European Constitution process
After the rejection of the European Constitution through public referenda in France and the Netherlands and the European Council turning back to a mere 'reform treaty', the constitutional process has been retrospectively put into question. Despite several years of intense preparation and negotiation, most Europeans either rejected the document or were hardly aware that there was a treaty establishing a Constitution for Europe – as it was officially called. They knew even less about how it had been created and were unaware of the document's meaning, importance and consequences. Yet, it was exactly this lack of knowledge, participation and inclusion of the general public that should have been tackled by the Convention on the Future of Europe.

When the Convention started its work in early 2002, high hopes accompanied this newly established body. Its mandate was not only to draft a constitution but also, as stated in the Laeken Declaration, to ensure that the debate would 'be broadly based and involve all citizens' (European Council 2001). Right from the start the convention method has been widely praised for its openness, its transparent mode of working and its ability to enforce practical reasoning amongst its delegates. It was seen as a major improvement compared to the old method of intergovernmental conferences where long hours of negotiations behind closed doors dominated and a gridlock of national interests prohibited lasting results. Not only was the development of a veritable constitution envisaged but the process itself was also seen as a chance to stimulate open debates and public involvement throughout Europe, to create a deepened understanding between Europeans, soften the widely debated democratic deficit and to support the development of a European public sphere.

Half a decade later, the constitutional project has been discharged and the document is now called a 'reform treaty'. With hindsight it is questionable whether the Convention really managed to fulfil its mandate. Was there anything like a European public sphere during the Convention or did it develop during the debates? As this cannot be answered with a simple 'yes' or 'no'. The question needs to be broken down and a European public sphere needs to be operationalized. Were the same topics and actors present throughout Europe during the constitutional debate? Did a common perspective evolve? Was the constitutional process accompanied by a European discourse or did discussions remain national?

In order to answer these questions this study seeks to compare the newspaper coverage of the Convention and the following first Intergovernmental Conference in the period between 2001 and 2003 in Germany, France and the United Kingdom (as well as in Switzerland and the United States as external observers). Building on a short review on hitherto existing research on the European public sphere, the design of and criteria on which this study is based will be outlined before presenting some quantitative and qualitative result that will enhance our understanding of the EU's constitutional endeavour and contribute to the still evolving field of research on the European public sphere.

Different perspectives on the European public sphere

We generally speak about a European or Europeanized public sphere if actors, content and interpretations found in public discussions in European states increasingly reach out beyond the borders of nation states and become transnationalized. As the common realm of reference beyond the nation state is usually the political entity of the European Union, the formation of a European public sphere is often connected to political and above all normative expectations with regard to the development of democracy, consensus and identity within the EU. In this perspective a European public sphere is supposed to inform about the EU, to contribute to the legitimacy of the EU polity and to enhance the acceptance of European politics. It is expected to enable citizens to judge the union according to its authorities and achievements, make European influences in our daily live visible and render a reasoned opinion building possible. In addition, it ought to allow for a common perception of problems and to help embed the European society into the already existing EU institutions.

More controversial than the normative expectations that accompany the European public sphere is the analytical question of how it might develop and how it is structured. While some expect a mere copy of what is already known from the nation state, others assume a public sphere *sui generis*. A standard definition everyone could agree to is still out of sight. Accordingly, different yardsticks are applied to measure the European public sphere. This has led to a remarkable collection of quantitative and qualitative data that has been gathered during the past years guided by a hotch-potch of different operationalizations.

The outposts of the field are marked by two rather extreme positions. For the pessimists there cannot be a common European public sphere as long as there is no common language, no collective identity and no transnational media system (Grimm 2004; Kielmannsegg 2004). A collective identity with some sense of solidarity and perhaps even the idea of belonging to a community of fate is seen as a precondition for a meaningful transnational discourse. The EU however, 'is not a community of communication, hardly a community of memory and only to a very limited degree a community of experience' (Kielmannsegg 2004: 58). Following this logic the EU would need to become a state-like entity and democratize its institution, before anything like a European public sphere could evolve. The optimists, on the other hand, take a European public sphere for granted as long as there is an *acquis communautaire* that binds the member states so that the EU's political decisions are of universal validity for all Europeans (Eder and Kantner 2002; Trenz and Eder 2004). According to their functionalist logic, communication about the European democratic deficit or a possible lack of a European public sphere 'turns out to be self-help therapy that remedies its own negative results'. The rise of claims addressing those deficits is at least partially seen to entail the unfolding of a European public sphere (Trenz and Eder 2004: 7–8).

Between these poles there is a broad spectrum in which the existence of nation-state-oriented as well as Europeanized public spheres are stated. In doing so, a broad range of indicators are used to measure the Europeaness of public spheres, for instance the choice of European topics as a central theme, the mentioning of European actors or the framing, interpretation and evaluation of topics from a European perspective. The majority of studies rely on three criteria: the same topics at the same time in each national public sphere, mutual observation and quotation and finally the same structures of relevance. Some studies also try to analyse the discursive interaction between actors (Brüggemann et al. 2006; Tobler 2002, 2006) or look for indications of a European identity e.g. through the use of a European 'we' (van de Steeg 2006; Risse 2004). Although most authors rely on quite similar sets of criteria, the conclusions reached differ considerably. While some are rather sceptical about the development of a European public sphere and interpretate their data as the glass being at the most half-full (e.g. Eilders and Voltmer, 2003; Gerhards 2001; Groothues 2004; Downey and König 2006; Hubé 2003), others are far more positive and come to some rather confident conclusion about the likelihood of a Europeanization of national public spheres (e.g. Lauf and Peter 2004; Koopmans and Erbe 2003; Diez Medrano 2003; Risse 2004).

For the analysis of the European constitutional debate in this paper the indicators many researchers of the moderate camp rely on will serve as a basis. However, some of the criteria are far more demanding than others: by looking at issue-cycles and the degree of their synchronization across borders it will be investigated whether there was a *topical networking* of the different national public spheres during the debate. Transnational observation and quotation of different media outlets, the presence of foreign speakers and the degree of reporting about other EU member states are taken as signs of the *interconnectedness of arenas*. Similar levels of relevance and common structures of meaning would point to *interdiscursivity*. This can for instance be operationalized through similarities in problem diagnoistization, comparable suggestions on how to deal with the EU's shortcomings, or evaluations of the Constitution that are alike. If there is evidence of Europeanization in all these three realms this already points to the emergence of a European public sphere. Allusions to a common identity, a *collective Europe*, would then be the cherry on the cake that would further confirm and refine the former results. Yet, because the analysis showed that despite a pronounced interest in the topic of 'European identity' there was no agreement on the nature of such an identity and very few indications of common 'we-references', the latter will be skipped here.

Research design

As in the studies mentioned above, the European public sphere will be confined to a sphere of mass media for the purpose of this analysis. Mass media secure communication on a large scale and to many people they are the only contact with political issues. Eurobarometer surveys confirm these findings: asked which sources they use when looking for information about the EU, 70 per cent of all respondents said they watch television, 41 per cent read daily newspapers and 31 per cent listen to the radio. Apart from the media, only discussions with relatives, friends and colleagues are of some importance; all other sources are much less relevant (COM 2007). Thus, information and discussion of European politics are largely transmitted via and shaped by the media. Newspapers play an important role in this, especially where background knowledge and the interpretation of current affairs are concerned.

For the sample, the three big EU countries, Germany, France and the United Kingdom, were chosen. The choice of three comparable countries with regard to size and influence should avoid any potential bias in the degree of media coverage on neighbouring countries due to structural factors. The political and economic weight of all three states makes them the most similar cases with presumably particularly dense flows of communication. At the same time, there are serious differences between these countries with regard to their ideas of a Constitution, of the state, nation, sovereignty and the future of European integration. Identifying common structures of relevance will thus be particularly demanding between these countries.[1]

In order to have a politically balanced view, two nationwide leading quality newspapers were chosen for each country, representing the political right to left spectrum. These are the *Frankfurter Allgemeine Zeitung* (FAZ) and the *Süddeutsche Zeitung* (SZ) for Germany, for France *Le Figaro* and *Le Monde* and the *Daily Telegraph* and the *Guardian* for the United Kingdom. In addition, two external observers were included to contrast the results: the *Neue Zürcher Zeitung* (NZZ) as a non-EU-newspaper and the *New York Times* (NYT) as a non-European one. Despite the importance of the debate, it is not assumed that a topic as advanced and abstract as the drafting of a Constitution will interest everyone. Yet, it is still adequate to show the general tendencies of the discourse. In addition, if there is no European public sphere among the generally better informed and more Europhile elites, one probably does not even have to start looking for one in the broader public.

The analysis starts with the Laeken summit – the decision to establish a Convention – in December 2001 and ends with the failure of the Intergovernmental Conference (IGC) on the Constitution in December 2003. The period is split in two phases: the Convention's drafting of the Constitution and the negotiations between heads of government during the Italian presidency. Articles were collected from the database LexisNexis with the search terms 'europ!' or 'EU' and 'Convention!' or 'constitution!' in the same paragraph with 'europ!' or 'EU'. The final sample for the quantitative analysis contained nearly 2,700 articles, and about 1,900 thereof were also scrutinized for the qualitative part.

The constitutional debate revisited

The presentation of findings follows the above operationalization of the European public sphere. First, the salience of issues illustrated by the amount of reporting will be compared across the different countries. This is followed by an analysis of topics and actors appearing in the articles. Finally, the comparison of common structures of meaning through a frame analysis will be illustrated with two examples. The focus of the results presented will be on the three EU countries, while the NZZ and NYT papers will only be mentioned when they provide some further insights.

Considerable salience and convergence in coverage

The debate on the European Constitution has triggered considerable coverage. All newspapers devoted a number of column inches to report on the Convention's plenary sessions and the debates on the Constitution. Despite some substantial difference in the general amount of

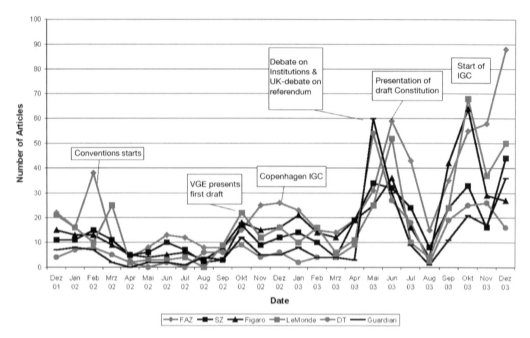

Figure 1: Press coverage during the Convention and the IGC. *Source:* Own illustration.

reporting, there was a clear convergence of issue-cycles.[2] All newspapers reported about the decision to establish the Convention and its inauguration. Further peaks occurred when Valéry Giscard d'Estaing presented the skeleton of the Constitution in October 2002, when the Convention agreed on the final draft and handed it over to the heads of government (summer 2003), and when the Intergovernmental Conference later started its negotiations.

During the first six months of listening and getting to know each other in the Convention, coverage was generally on a fairly low level. The rather technical nature of the issues debated, the missing connection to readers' everyday life and the lack of European 'faces' probably hampered the coverage. The latter problem was eased when more prominent politicians like the German Foreign Minister Joschka Fischer and his French counterpart Dominique de Villepin entered the fray in late 2002 and delivered the demanded soundbites. From that point onwards the German as well as the French newspapers paid increasing attention to the Convention. This might also be due to the increasing seriousness of the discussion in the assembly, but it coincides remarkably well with the arrival of these well-known figures.

Despite the considerable number of articles on the Convention, it is rather low in comparison to the IGC coverage. During the twenty month period from December 2001 to July 2003 about 1,700 articles were published, while the following five months contributed almost 1,000 articles. This confirms earlier findings that coverage of the European Union is highly event-oriented (de Vreese 2001). The latter was also the phase in which the involvement of governments became crucial. The widely praised Convention method, its openness and transparency, the ability to follow the arguments and understand the rationality behind them (e.g. Maurer 2003; Magnette and Nicolaidis, 2004) was seemingly less successful in attracting media attention than the quarrels between the heads of government, bilateral negotiations and coalition building, the setting of conditions for the final outcome and demarcations of 'red lines'.

FAZ and Le Monde on the one hand, and SZ and Le Figaro on the other were sometimes more similar in their reactions than their respective national partners. Pronounced or moderate interest in the European Union seems more important here than national influences. Generally, newspapers across different countries reacted quite similarly in terms of coverage and issue cycles. This does not necessarily mean that the people in these countries were informed about the same things. Although a high degree of overlap can be discerned, there are also cross-national differences. For instance the peak in reporting in British newspapers in May 2003, although triggered by the approaching end of the Convention, was mainly due to a polarized domestic debate on whether or not to hold a national referendum on the Constitution. The other four EU newspapers reported on these British particularities but their own peak in coverage with all sorts of information about the Constitution set in about a month later. By and large, there were enormous differences between the countries with regard to how and by whom topics were put on the agenda: whereas German papers concentrated almost exclusively on the EU level, French papers allowed some room for national voices and the British papers had as many articles on Europe's constitution that emanated from national uproar as from European events.

Europe's topics are equal, national topics are more equal

The Laeken declaration asked the Convention to discuss a wide range of topics and the Convention even expanded this mandate soon after starting its work. This is reflected in the newspaper coverage: several areas were mentioned, but most subjects were merely raised and few were discussed in depth. The newspapers reported on discussions on the EU institutions and procedures as well as on different policy issues. Moreover, the process itself was discussed intensively, for instance the composition of the Convention, assessments of how Giscard d'Estaing fulfilled his role, as well as speculations about whether a compromise would be found or if the process was likely to fail. Splitting the results in two agendas, one for the Convention and one for the IGC, it is obvious that the debate became more focused during the Intergovernmental Conference.

The Convention elaborated on a variety of topics, and the media distributed its attention fairly equally. By contrast, the IGC mainly concentrated on four problems: (1) the voting system in the Council, (2) the Common Foreign and Security Policy (CFSP) and the question whether the EU should build up its own defence capacities, (3) plans to downsize the Commission, and (4) which issues should be decided under qualified majority voting and which should still be subject to national vetoes. For the average reader this consolidation made the issues more tangible. Earlier, topics had only been touched upon but never stayed on the agenda for a longer time. Thus they remained volatile and were not suited to raise awareness or arouse

Convention Top Ten   **IGC Top Ten**

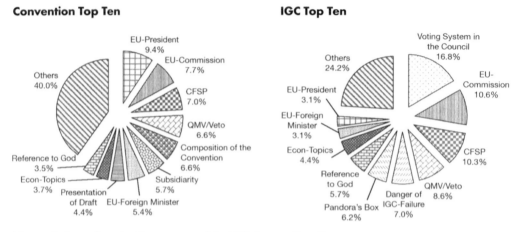

Figure 2: Topics from the Convention and the IGC. *Source:* Own illustration.

contention. If the issue attention cycle is short and new topics are frequently introduced, it is difficult for the audience to attach meaning to an issue. In this respect the Convention's ability to raise public awareness was limited, or at least the IGC structure was more in line with the logic of the media.

In order to go beyond a mere description of tendencies of convergence and divergence an index of thematic similarity provides a more systematic comparison of the different newspapers. For the whole period of analysis each newspaper's main topics were compared on a monthly basis.[3] For each newspaper and topic the categories 'main topic', 'existing topic' or 'no topic' were identified, which made the agendas of all newspapers comparable and quantifiable. If the same importance was assigned to a topic within the same month the newspapers compared were given two points, in case of smaller deviations they received one point. If however, the FAZ made 'subsidiarity' a main topic in March 2002, whereas it was not even mentioned in the *Guardian*, both newspapers would receive zero points. Divided by the number of topics and months this results in an index of similarities between zero and two. The degree of similarity can then be calculated between newspapers to show which newspapers are close to each other. Moreover, it can also be expressed on a monthly basis for all newspapers to detect phases of high and low topical entanglement.

The index shows considerable differences in the relationship between the newspapers. The values range from 0.79 for the most disparate couple (*Frankfurter Allgemeine Zeitung* and *New York Times*) and 1.52 for the two newspaper that are the most alike (*Le Figaro* and *Le Monde*). Thus, the two French newspapers are most similar – and the other national pairs are also among the most similar ones. Although values between 1.41 and 1.52 point to an identical choice of topic, they show that French, German or British national agendas are still more equal than cross-national ones. Thus, national factors seem to be generally most important for the daily selection process within the newspaper's editorial offices. The *New York Times* confirms its role of an outsider by mainly occupying the lower part of the continuum. The *Neue Zürcher Zeitung* on the contrary turns out to be a rather cosmopolitan newspaper that harmonizes with all other outlets.

Figure 3: Index of topical similarity between newspapers on a scale of 0–2.[4]

Relation between newspapers	Index	Same country of origin	Political alike	D–FR	FR–GB	GB–D	with NZZ	with NYT
LF–LM	1.52	French						
SZ–LF	1.51			X				
SZ–NZZ	1.45						X	
GUA–NZZ	1.44						X	
FAZ–SZ	1.43	German						
SZ–LM	1.43		left	X				
DT–GUA	1.41	British						
LF–NZZ	1.39						X	
NZZ–NYT	1.37	non-EU					X	X
FAZ–LF	1.36		right	X				
DT–NZZ	1.33						X	
LM–NZZ	1.29						X	
GUA–NYT	1.29							X
LF–GUA	1.26				X			
FAZ–NZZ	1.26						X	
FAZ–LM	1.26			X				
SZ–GUA	1.23		left			X		
LM–GUA	1.22		left		X			
DT–NYT	1.21		right					X
LF–DT	1.21				X			
SZ–DT	1.19					X		
LM–DT	1.18				X			
FAZ–GUA	1.17					X		
LF–NYT	1.04							X
SZ–NYT	0.98							X
LM–NYT	0.96							X
FAZ–DT	0.95		right			X		
FAZ–NYT	0.79							X

Source: Own illustration.

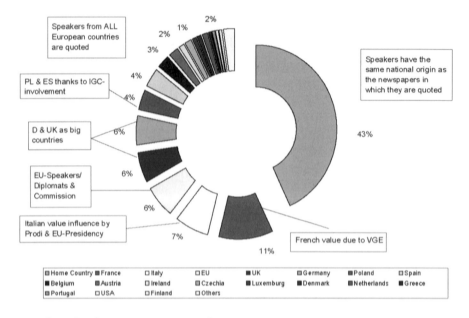

Figure 4: All speakers by origin. *Source: Own illustration.*

Political alignments, on the other hand, do not influence the European agenda: values dither between 0.95 and 1.43 without a visible pattern. The tight Franco-German relationship on the other hand, is mirrored by the newspapers of both countries being relatively close. The more leftist SZ and the more conservative *Figaro* even happen to be the second most similar team. French and British newspapers take a midfield position whereas British and German newspapers bear the least resemblances.

The aggregated value for all newspaper for the whole constitutional debate is 1.26. The Convention's agenda with 1.24 is slightly less focused than the IGC with 1.29. Although smaller than the values of the national newspapers, this is clearly above the value for medium similarity. In addition, there are considerable differences between the 25 months under investigation. During the Convention's listening phase in spring and summer 2002, the months after the presentation of the constitutional skeleton, as well as the summer slump in August 2003, values are lower. It is only during the decisive moments like the decision to set up the Convention, the first presentation of the Constitution, the final sessions of the Convention and the failure of the IGC negotiations that the index reaches values around 1.5. Thus, whenever things become important, the agenda of all newspapers with regard to European news reaches a level of similarity that usually is only found in the everyday reporting within the same country.

All countries debate, some dominate
In order to find out who was heard during the constitutional debate and whether different viewpoints were equally represented, quotations from all articles were counted.[5] On the whole,

each country of the enlarged European Union, including the candidate countries Bulgaria and Rumania, as well as Turkey, had their say at least once in the constitutional debate. Yet within the approximately 4,500 quotations, speakers from Bulgaria, Rumania and Latvia were only mentioned once; Cyprus, Malta and Lithuania appeared twice and Slovaks, Slovenes and Estonians were not much better off either. Except for Poland and the Czech Republic the new Central and Eastern European countries were hardly audible. The same holds true for smaller EU countries such as Sweden, Finland, Portugal, the Netherlands, Greece and Denmark which all remained below 1 per cent.

In fact, actors from a few countries dominated the debate. With regard to actors' origin, the newspapers home countries together with France, Germany, the United Kingdom, Italy and the EU already account for more than three-quarters.[6] This expresses the importance of the bigger countries but it is also a hint to the main actors in the debate. Figure 4 shows the distribution of actors' nationality from all newspapers.

As expected, the biggest share of all speakers came from the same country as the newspaper in which they were quoted. Those actors are usually better known, in reach for the journalists, easier to identify in their position and for all questions of national interest the logical first choice. Even a massive increase in Europeanization of politics is unlikely to change these factors. Thus, mutual observation and transnational quotation does not result in complete similarity, but diversity. This is given with 57 per cent of speakers coming from other countries. All in all, there was a great openness towards foreign actors from Europe in the constitutional debate.

France's high visibility in the foreign press (11 per cent) was mainly due to Valéry Giscard d'Estaing's role as Convention chairman but also to the importance of Jacques Chirac, the Franco-German alliance and partially to other French members of the Convention. The large share of Italians also goes back to a mix of EU and national actors, mainly Commission President Romano Prodi and the Italian Prime Minister Silvio Berlusconi together with his foreign minister, Franco Frattini. The latter two were in charge of the negotiations during the IGC under the Italian Presidency. The share of EU actors (6 per cent) points to a general characteristic of EU reporting.

As information is often not officially available, rumours and gossip are important sources of information for journalists. Most of this unofficial background information comes from diplomats, spokespersons or observers commenting from the sidelines. None of them can be quoted with names or origins and they are thus just called 'EU diplomats' or 'EU civil servants'. Most 'European speakers' can be attributed to this practice. Finally, the other nations with distinguishable shares are Germany, the United Kingdom, Poland, Spain and Austria. Those are exactly the countries that expressed the biggest worries about the Constitution and wanted either further discussion on certain issues, or on the contrary, to block such discussions.

Some additional insight can be gained by running a separate analysis for the Convention and the IGC with regard to the share of national actors. In order to control for the different

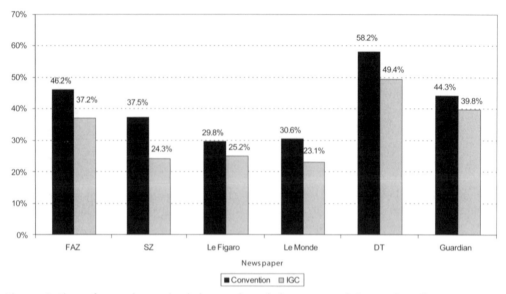

Figure 5: Share of national actors (excluding articles with domestic topics). *Source:* Own illustration.

degrees of domestic contestation around the Constitution only those articles that dealt with European topics alone were taken into consideration. In that way, national characteristics remain but are made comparable. Keeping in mind the criticism of the traditional IGC method with regard to its lack of transparency and the predominance of national interest – negotiations behind closed doors and press-conferences at the end of each summit in which national governments declare victory in front of their national press corps – it would be reasonable to assume that the quantity of national voices increased during the second phase.

Yet, despite the considerable difference in the openness of different broadsheets towards European voices, the share of national speakers decreased during the Intergovernmental Conference in all six papers. The general quota of foreign actors per article rose from 1.05 during the Convention to 1.61 during the IGC. Although vital national interests were at stake, the position of Polish, British, Spanish and even Czech and Austrian neighbours were taken seriously and these were all offered a chance to explain their views. Heads of government and ministers from all over Europe were quoted. In contrast, the members of the Convention that made it into the papers during the negotiation in the first phase usually belonged to the paper's home country. From the bulk of unknown Convention delegates most journalists preferred national representatives who had at least a hint of recognition potential. During the IGC, famous personalities throughout Europe had their say and were given opportunities to explain their point of view. This calls into question whether the Convention method really contributed to truly European public debates.

Common frames but national emphasis

Concerning the issue of common frames that indicate common or different structures of relevance and meaning only two examples will be given: a diagnostic frame that defines the Union's problems and explains why the Convention was necessary and the different reactions and justifications to the question whether to hold a referendum on the Constitution. Both cases demonstrate features that are present in the other indicators of the frame analysis conducted and are hence appropriate in drawing some general conclusions.

Why was a Convention necessary?

Enlargement and the failure of the Nice summit are the two most frequent explanations why the heads of government inaugurated a Convention with the mandate to reform the EU's institutions. Ranking third is the motive 'for the citizens'. Most other lines of reasoning can be assigned to one of these three groups. All categories are described in roughly the same manner by all countries and newspapers: the inherent necessity of the integration process, lessons drawn from the past, or democratic values are described as the main motives.

- *Enlargement*: Facing the enlargement of more than ten new member states, the existing institutions – originally created for six countries – are no longer sufficient. In order to prevent institutional gridlock and paralysis, and to be able to work efficiently with 25 member states, it becomes a necessity to adapt the institutions to the new situation.
- *Result from Nice – Method and treaties*: The catchword Nice alludes to two problems at the same time; the old IGC method in which reforms are negotiated in marathon horse-trading sessions behind closed doors, and the deficiency of the existing treaties. The disappointing Nice summit and its predecessors are accused of undemocratic and intransparent procedures and secret wheeler-dealings supporting the pursuit of national interests. The treaties that came out of these negotiations are considered insufficient, overly complex and incomprehensible. Consequently, a new approach is as much needed as a new treaty.
- *For the citizens – Transparency, legitimacy, democracy*: The disenchanted and disconnected European citizens and their lack of interest in EU affairs are discussed under this headline. The gap between citizens and elites, intransparent procedures of decision-making, the democratic deficit of the institutional system and the lack of efficiency in EU politics in general are lamented upon. The Convention is asked to overcome the gulf of misunderstanding, to ask for trust and to halt Brussels' bureaucratic routine so that it can pay more attention to the people's needs instead.

All newspapers, including the outsiders, are actively engaged in explaining the Convention's existence. However, as in many other realms, the weighting follows mainly national patterns. In Germany and France, the failure of the Nice summit is most frequently mentioned. FAZ and SZ rank enlargement second, the citizens third. *Le Figaro* and *Le Monde* see enlargement and citizens' needs as equally significant. In the United Kingdom the latter category is more important than the problems of method and treaties.[7] As with many other indicators, the *Daily Telegraph* has its very own profile and the *Guardian* presents a mixture of British and continental influences. For the NZZ and NYT enlargement was the main force behind the Convention's

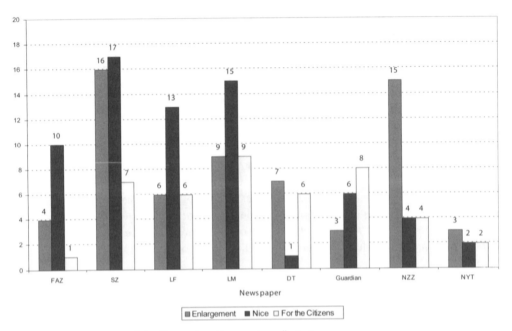

Figure 6: Reasons to install the Convention. *Source:* Own illustration.

inauguration. Regarding the total number of entries it turns out that the Swiss paper is almost more concerned about the enlargement and its possible consequences for the EU than any other paper. Furthermore, the NYT's involvement in this matter points out that the mere existence of a similar frame is not sufficient for the identification of a European public sphere.

To vote or not to vote – Arguments on constitutional referenda

Although the intensity of the debate differed substantially, the question of whether to hold a national referendum on the Constitution popped up in all three countries. In the end, only France gave its people the opportunity to express their opinion, Britain cancelled its envisaged referendum and in Germany the Constitutional Treaty was adopted by a huge Parliamentary majority. However, in 2002 and 2003 none of this was clear. The number of justifications given in the papers on why one should or should not hold a referendum gives an indication of the different degrees of contention in the respective public spheres.

Looking at the figures, the issue was obviously far more contested in France and Britain than in Germany, where the combination of a legal situation that prohibits referenda and politicians that did everything to avoid dispute over EU integration hampered discussion from the start. In France and Britain, claims to hold a referendum and to give the people a voice were far more frequently raised. Yet, the determination to block a national referendum was almost equally strong in all countries. A closer examination of the reasons given further underlines national differences.

In Germany, the proponents of a referendum mainly argued with democratic principles and the right of the people to decide about their future. Although there were also some Euro-reluctant conservative politicians that supported the idea (before being called back by their party leaders), the idea was mainly connected with a broader initiative for more citizens' participation from the Liberal Democrats and some Greens. On the contra-side the legal argument that referenda are not foreseen in the German constitution due to historical reasons was used from time to time. However, the strongest argument against a referendum was the fear that it could be used for anti-European propaganda and populist appeals. An example of this is the CDU spokesman on European affairs, Peter Hinze, who said that a referendum would offer 'a huge stage for all sectarian forces that want to overthrow Europe' (SZ, 11 July 2003).

In France, democracy was also an issue on the pro-side, but equally important was the Europhile idea that a referendum would strengthen the Constitution. Prime Minister Jean-Pierre Raffarin even said that 'a real European cannot not want such as referendum' (LM, 11 October 2003). Thus, one part of the pro-referendum camp was guided by positive views on Europe and the wish to fortify the Constitution through a clear public approval of the document. Moreover, it was hoped that a referendum would evoke a larger public debate in which information on the Constitutional Treaty could be disseminated. At the same time, there were also Eurosceptic voices that called for a referendum in order to get an opportunity to reject the Constitution. Although the left was also partially divided at that time, those fears and worries were mainly uttered from the right. It was predominantly the conservative Le Figaro in which politicians such as 'Mouvement pour la France' – leader Philippe de Villiers – pictured the possible risks of the Constitution and called for a referendum. The opponents of a national referendum mostly replied that the French, whenever asked to give their vote, tended to answer to all sorts of

Figure 7: Number of justifications for and against a national referendum.

Newspaper	Pro-Referendum			Contra-Referendum		
	Domestic Justifications	Justfications from other EU countries	Total (N)	Domestic Justifications	Justfications from other EU countries	Total (N)
FAZ	17	4	21	13	2	15
SZ	5	10	15	7	2	9
Le Figaro	36	4	40	10	2	12
Le Monde	36	4	40	8	5	13
Daily Telegraph	54	4	58	23	0	23
Guardian	29	6	35	10	2	12

Source: Own illustration.

different question and to misuse their vote to punish the current government. In this context, although less explicit, the danger of a possible failure was mentioned a few times.

The British calls for a referendum were mainly put forward by the Tories and conservative newspapers which seemingly acted in a joint campaign against the government and which were both concerned about the nation's independence. For instance, the conservative Convention delegate David Heathcoat-Amory argued that British sovereignty was so deeply threatened, that it was imperative to hold a referendum (*Daily Telegraph*, 21 January 2003). Moreover, the Constitution was described as a 'huge change to the way in which the British people will be governed' (Ian Duncan Smith in the *Guardian*, 26 May 2003). Only in the rather Euro-friendly *Guardian* another spin on the issue could be found. There, several authors suggested using a referendum to pose a final question on whether to join Europe or not and put an end to the endless debate about Britain's role in the Union (*Guardian*, 27 May 2003; 29 May 2003). The government's answer to all arguments was always the same. It described the Constitution as being mainly 'a tidying-up exercise' of current treaties, which would not alter the fundamental relationship between the United Kingdom and the EU. Accordingly, a referendum was not needed and Parliament was the proper institution to decide.

In a nutshell, each country had its very own discourse on the referendum question. Although other nations were observed, their arguments sometimes finding their way into the different public spheres, the national dispute remained detached from their neighbours' discussions and was based on solely national ways of thinking. Thus, the reasons Germans and French used to justify their own pro- and contra-claims were familiar in the United Kingom, but they were not adopted in the British debates. The same holds true for the other two countries. On the other hand, in France and Britain the interest for each other increased as their own national disputes gained importance and this might be interpreted as a general awareness of the wider community. Moreover, all governments were obviously sensitive to the fact that their decision on a referendum could influence other governments. In Germany the idea of being a good role model for others and setting a good example was even used to turn down domestic appeals for a referendum and to argue for a quick Parliamentary vote in favour of the Constitution – which was later scheduled few days ahead of the French referendum.

Conclusion
When the Convention on the Future of Europe was established in order to draft a constitutional treaty for the European Union it was greeted with high hopes and enthusiastic expectations. The Laeken Declaration demanded more democracy, legitimacy and transparency – and the Convention not only accepted this mandate but was also seen as a means to bring the Union closer to its citizens. Taking these claims seriously, this paper has explored whether a pan-European public debate developed around the Convention. It made clear that such a European public sphere does not mean one common set of media, languages and opinions, but rather the existence of mutual understanding and an interconnectedness of topics, actors and viewpoints. In the end, the analysis does neither confirm the pessimistic nor the optimistic view

on the emergence of a European public sphere, but scepticism slightly prevails over confidence. Indeed, there were many hints to tendencies of Europeanization, but at least as many indications for national persistencies.

There was a clear interest in the Convention's proposals and a convergence of issue-cycles between the newspapers of different countries. Europe obviously has its firm place on the agenda of newspapers across member states. On the other hand, earlier findings that reporting on EU-news is highly event-oriented were confirmed: there were visible peaks during a few significant events and far less reporting during the usual work of the Convention. Besides, the IGC was generally more successful in attracting media attention than the Convention and in this respect the new method did not fulfill the hopes that were placed on it. Moreover, the debate got far more focussed during the IGC and potentially easier to follow. In addition, it was only in these phases of heightened importance and political decision-making that the media's agendas converged across national boundaries. In the everyday life of EU reporting, French, German and British national agendas respectively were more similar than transnational ones. The index also shows that Europeanization is no uniform process that develops everywhere in the same patterns. French and German agendas were comparatively similar, French and British newspapers were still quite alike, whereas British and German coverage of the constitutional process bore the least resemblances. Hence, some national public spheres are relatively closely interlinked while others are not.

The examination of actors showed that national actors dominated and had an average of 43 per cent out of all speakers quoted (ranging from 36 per cent to 69 per cent in the newspapers of this study). Still, a considerable share of European actors had their say. Each nation managed at least once to take a hand in the debate. Comparing the two bodies involved, there were even more quotations from non-national actors during the IGC than during the Convention. Power and a prominent position, rather than well-thought-out arguments, were decisive for an appearance in the newspaper. In contrast to heads of state and government, Convention delegates sent by their national Parliaments or the members of the European Parliament did not meet these criteria. Generally speaking, the IGC design corresponded better to the inherent logic of the media. There was greater news value attached to the power struggles between governments and less complexity because visible positions could be connected to well-known politicians, and the debate came with some clear catchphrases.

Finally, the results of the frame analysis point to differences between the national debates concerning the interpretations of the problems at stake and the reasoning that were applied in discussions. Although there was an agreement in principle in such a way that all frames were present in all newspapers, the weighting followed national patterns. In sum, there was a considerable degree of mutual observation but very little participation and responsiveness between the countries under investigation. Interest in their neighbours' affairs increased when there were national points of contact. Yet, as national lines of reasoning remained largely untouched it seems that even this did not led to a merger of debates. Only the idea that national decisions might have influences on other countries and that this European dimension had to be taken into consideration when thinking about them seems to go beyond this. Unfortunately, it is hard to tell whether this was more rhetorical spin to cut off the debate or real concern indicating an awareness of interlinked European political communication.

Notes

1. Whereas Germany is among the most integrationist member states, the United Kingdom is rather Eurosceptical and promotes a more intergovernmental approach. France takes a middle position favouring a strong Europe that still leaves room for national governments (Jachtenfuchs 2002). These views are merged in the expression of a Europe as a 'federation of nation states'.
2. The FAZ had 661 articles in total, the SZ 381, Le Figaro 439, Le Monde 455, the Daily Telegraph 265, the Guardian 262, the NZZ 153 and the NYT 42 articles.
3. To qualify as a main topic, a theme had to occur in at least three articles, be among the five most frequently mentioned topics and (if possible) account for more than 10 per cent of all topics. In the following, it was checked if and to what extent the other newspapers had reported on this topic.
4. Zero meaning no similarities at all with regard to thematically focal points, one expresses a weak degree of similarly and two reflects a strong convergence of agendas.
5. All citations as well as comments that were not put in quotations marks but in which an obvious statement was made were reckoned. For all speakers their position (e.g. head of government, minister, Parliamentarian, opposition, commissioner, Convention member) and their national origin were recorded.
6. Germany, France and the United Kingdom count as 'home country' in their own newspapers. Their other values are derived from their mentioning in the other newspapers. All EU entries are due to European actors without further specification such as EU Commision, EU spokesman or EU diplomat.
7. Frames are not easily quantifiable as the same frame can occur several times in one article but one frame can also be elaborated on in depth. Thus, entries instead of percentages are provided in the following. However, keep in mind that the initial number of articles differs considerably between the papers.

References

Brüggemann, M., Sifft, S., Kleinen-von Königslöw, K., Peters, B. and Wimmel, A. (2006), 'Segmentierte Europäisierung: Trends und Muster der Transnationalisierung von Öffentlichkeit in Europa', in W. R. Langenbucher and M. Latzer (eds), Europäische Öffentlichkeit und medialer Wandel: Eine transdisziplinäre Perspektive. Wiesbaden: Verlag für Sozialwissenschaften (VS), pp. 214–31.

de Vreese, C. H. (2001), 'Europe in the News: A Cross-National Comparative Study of the News Coverage of Key EU Events', European Union Politics, 2: 3, pp. 283–307.

Diez Medrano, J. (2003), 'Qualitätspresse und europäische Integration', in A. Klein, R. Koopmans, H. -J. Trenz, L. Klein, C. Lahusen and D. Rucht (eds), Bürgerschaft, Öffentlichkeit und Demokratie in Europa. Opladen: Leske and Buderich, pp. 191–212.

Downey, J. and König, T. (2006), 'Is there a European Public Sphere?', European Journal of Communication, 21 : 2, pp. 165–87.

Eder, K. and Kantner, C. (2002), 'Interdiskursivität in der europäischen Öffentlichkeit', Berliner Debatte Initial, 13: 5/6, pp. 79–88.

Eilders, C. and Voltmer, K. (2003), 'Zwischen Deutschland und Europa: Eine empirische Untersuchung zum Grad von Europäisierung und Europa-Unterstützung der meinungsführenden deutschen Tageszeitungen', Medien und Kommunikationswissenschaft (M&K), 51: 2, pp. 250–70.

EU Commission (2007). Eurobarometer 65. Public Opinion in the European Union. Fieldwork: March–May 2006, Publication: January 2007.

Gerhards, J. (2001), 'Missing a European Public Sphere', in M. Kohli and M. Novak (eds), *Will Europe Work? Integration, Employment and the Social Order*. London and New York: Routledge, pp. 145–58.

Grimm, D, (2004), 'Treaty or Constitution? The Legal Basis of the European Union after Maastricht', in E.O. Eriksen, J.E. Fossum and A.J. Menéndez (eds), *Developing a Constitution for Europe*. London: Routledge, pp. 69–87.

Groothues, F. (2004), 'Television News and the European Public Sphere: A Preliminary Invetigation', EurPolCom – Centre for European Political Communication, Working Papers Series no. 06/04.

Hubé, N. (2003), 'L'Union Européenne à la « Une »: Un Cadrage Difficile d'une Actualité peu Visible. Regard Comparé sur la Presse Française et Allemande', in G. Garcia G. and V. le Torrec (eds), *L'Union Européenne et les Médias: Regards Croisés sur l'information Européenne*. Pris: L'Harmattan, pp. 67–89.

Jachtenfuchs, M. (2002), *Die Konstruktion Europas: Verfassungsideen und institutionelle Entwicklung*. Baden-Baden: Nomos Verlagsgesellschaft.

Kielmansegg, P. Graf (2004), 'Integration und Demokratie', in M. Jachtenfuchs and B. Kohler-Koch, *Europäische Integration*. Opladen: Leske and Budrich, pp. 49–83.

Koopmans, R. amd Erbe, J. (2003), 'Towards a European Public Sphere? Vertical and Horizontal Dimensions of Europeanised Political Communication', *Wissenschaftszentrum Berlin für Sozialforschung* (WZB), Discussion Paper SP IV 2003–403.

Lauf, E. and Peter, J. (2004), 'EU-Repräsentanten in Fernsehnachrichten: Eine Analyse ihrer Präsenz in 13 EU-Mitgliedstaaten vor der Europawahl 1999', in L. Hagen (ed.), *Europäische Union und mediale Öffentlichkeit: Theoretische Perspektiven und empirische Befunde zur Rolle der Medien im europäischen Einigungsprozess*. Köln: Herbert von Halem, pp. 162–77.

Magnette, P. and Kalypso, N. (2004), 'The European Convention: Bargaining in the Shadow of Rhetoric', *West European Politics*, 27: 3, pp. 381–404.

Maurer, A. (2003), 'Less Bargaining – More Deliberation: The Convention Method for Enhancing EU Democracy', *Internationale Politik und Gesellschaft*, 1, pp. 167–90.

Risse, T. (2004). 'Auf dem Weg zu einer europäischen Kommunikationsgemeinschaft: Theoretische Überlegung und empirische Evidenz', in C. Franzius and U.K. Preuß (eds.), *Europäische Öffentlichkeit*. Baden-Baden: Nomos, pp. 139–53.

Tobler, S. (2002), 'Zur Emergenz transnationaler Öffentlichkeiten. Konfliktinduzierter Kampf um Definitionsmacht und transnationale Kommunikationsverdichtungen im Politikprozess "Internationale Steuerpolitik im EU- und OECD-Raum"', in K. Imhof, O. Jarren and R. Blum (eds), *Integration und Medien*. Wiesbaden: Westdeutscher Verlag, pp. 260–84.

Tobler, S. (2006), 'Konfliktinduzierte Transnationalisierung nationaler und supranationaler Öffentlichkeitsarenen: Indikatoren einer europäischen Öffentlichkeit', in W.R. Langenbucher and M. Latzer (eds), *Europäische Öffentlichkeit und medialer Wandel: Eine transdisziplinäre Perspektive*. Wiesbaden: Verlag für Sozialwissenschaften (VS), pp. 107–30.

Trenz, H -J. and Eder, K. (2004), 'The Democratizing Dynamics of a European Public Sphere: Towards a Theory of Democratic Functionalism', *European Journal of Social Theory*, 7: 1, pp. 5–25.

Van de Steeg, M. (2006), 'Does a Public Sphere Exist in the European Union? An Analysis of the Content of the Debate on the Haider-Case', *European Journal of Political Research*, 45: 4, pp. 609–34.

10

Rare Birds: The 'Why' in Comparative Media Studies. Nordic Ideal Types of Good European Journalism

Vanni Tjernström

Abstract

This chapter reports on four comparative studies that were carried out by the author on media coverage of the European Union (EU) between 1992 and 2005. All these studies indicate the influence of 'macro-social factors' on media content. Properties of the social systems in which media operate seem to explain differences between media content in different countries. Three of these studies concerned Nordic newspapers covering European issues. The Nordic newspapers contributed in differing degrees to a European perspective, i.e. in debating European issues more or less intensively. One macro-social factor accounting for these differences seemed to be the observed difference in national political culture. The Danish newspaper covered EU issues in a superior manner; the other papers seemed, in comparison, limited in scope and presented events with a distinctly national outlook. The article also reports a fourth comparative study where an attempt was made to find content categories that would help define the nature of European political communication or 'good' media coverage of European issues. The method applied was influenced by Grounded Theory. The resulting categories were rearranged into two levels, where 'participation' was the core category, based on the Gemeinschaft and Gesellschaft figure of thought, and the three other categories – legitimacy, identity and mondialization – were defined as supporting categories in the analysis of media coverage of the European Union.

Keywords

comparative research, European Union, European political communication, grounded theory, political culture, journalism, Gemeinschaft/Gesellschaft, Nordic newspapers

Introduction

Several researchers have looked into the issue of mediated communication on the European Union (Gerhards 1993; Anderson and Weymouth 1999; Slaatta 1999; deVreese et al. 2001; Tjernström 2001; Palm 2002; Kevin 2003; AIM Research Consortium 2006). Has European economic and political integration brought changes in the organization of the public sphere where informed deliberation and discussions on common European issues take place? Some argue that there is no need to look for one such sphere; several public spheres will develop which will match the structure of European societies (Schlesinger and Kevin 2000). Most studies find the flow of news and information about the European Union very nationalistic, meaning that political communication on the EU is rooted in the nation state and in national agendas. The EU disseminates directives and pronouncements but up until now hardly initiates broadly based dialogue. For the European economic and political elite, there is a restricted communicative space to be found in the *Financial Times*, the *Economist* and a few other international newspapers and journals, plus the TV channel Arte. Schlesinger and Kevin (2000) conclude that for a broader, common European frame of reference to evolve, one needs to find an audience that recognizes media to offer something distinct from national forms of reporting, with a different agenda and a different institutional focus (ibid.: 229).

The national media are expected to provide information about EU affairs relevant to national and European political decision-making and involvement by citizens, to provide a platform for debate on European political and other issues and to serve as watchdogs on actors in the democratic processes in the EU (Kevin 2003: 7). The national news media, however, have no obligation to promote European integration or identification with Europe, nor are they likely to cover the EU from a transnational perspective (Heikkilä and Kunelius 2006). The need for a European political communication, therefore, has to be stated in normative terms, derived from the assumption of interdependency between politics, media and citizens also in a transnational democratic political system. Central here is public debate on political decision-making, where the role of the media is crucial (Zelizer 2004).

The two 'positions' taken in this article are motivated by the need for increased 'theorizing' in the field of comparative cross-national research. One position is based on Gurevitch' and Blumler's (1990) pioneering work on macro-social factors in comparative studies. Analyses based on such explanatory factors are rare birds in most comparative media research. The majority of comparative studies operate with media-centric understandings rather than societal differences, such as national political culture. Another position is based on my own research into the conceptual nature of 'good' national media coverage of the EU – forming a foundation for a deeper insight into European political communication.

Macro-social factors in comparative studies of media coverage of the EU

Comparative studies have gained importance within the field of media and journalism studies. The approach adopted by comparativists was slow to develop, judging from the calls made by two of its missionaries in the late 70s/early 80s (Gurevitch and Blumler 1990). Especially in European media research, this development has manifestly been stimulated by the development of European political integration in terms of what we now know as the European Union.

Comparative research and macro-social factors

Gurevitch and Blumler defined comparative work in political communication in 1990: 'It is...a matter of trying to take account of potentially varying macro-social-system-level characteristic and influences on significant political communication phenomena' (Gurevitch and Blumler 1990: 306). In their efforts to distinguish comparative work as more specialized activity, they were quite specific: 'It is not, or should not be, just a matter of fielding common instruments in as many societies as possible and seeing what emerges' (ibid.: 306). They went on in their criticism of presented comparative research and of studies to come: 'Nor is it even a matter of simply trying to ascertain how selected phenomena compare and contrast in different countries' (ibid.: 306). My own interpretation of Gurevitch and Blumler's positions: they wanted to emphasize not only the *what*, differences between countries in terms of media coverage in a particular field, or the *how*, how particular phenomena differ that may affect such media coverage, but the *why*, accounting for differences found in terms of macro-social factors in the political systems in which the media operate instead of recurring explanations in terms of media-centric factors.

Specifically, for the purpose of this chapter, they pinpoint the *why* in comparative studies on Europe. Why does the EU coverage in the media differ between countries? Gurevitch and Blumler seem to focus on explanations that include parameters of political systems that promote or constrain political communication roles and behavior. They favour explanatory factors like structures, norms and values of political systems, relations between political systems and media systems, all in all factors that bear upon the question of power in society but also include cultural components. The conclusion is: comparative studies on media coverage of the EU should seek the macro-level factors that may explain differences between different countries in EU media coverage.

An important recent example of this kind of macro-social analysis – although not directly trying to explain media content – is Hallin and Mancini's analysis of media systems in Europe and North America (2004). Not only do they describe *how* media systems vary in Western Europe, but they also attempt to account for variations, e g by the political and economic context of media systems, i. e. answering the question *why* in comparative studies. Hallin and Mancini avoid a too simplistic approach; they are not prepared to identify 'political system variables' as independent variables, and prefer to see the relation between media and political systems more in terms of 'coevoulution' than of strict causal ordering.

The comparative studies on media coverage of the EU in different countries, mainly Nordic, reported in the following were all carried out by the author and guided by similar research questions:

1. To what extent are there differences in the media coverage of the EU between different countries?
2. What factors seem to account for these differences?

Coverage of the French Maastricht Referendum

My own experience in the area of comparative studies of EU media coverage started with a comparative study between Belgium and Sweden (Tjernstrom 1993). I compared the coverage of the referendum in France on the Maastricht Treaty in 1992 in the Belgian *LeSoir* and the Swedish *Dagens Nyheter*. Both papers had declared that they were giving high editorial priority to what at the time seemed to be a crucial step in the development of the EU. The Swedish paper was by far more resourceful (media and editorial factors), but, judging from the content analysis, the Belgian paper was on all counts far superior in its coverage. Why?

It may seem obvious, but French-speaking Belgium must have been culturally much closer to events in France than Sweden (a macro-social factor). Also, the Belgian paper was more 'international' in its coverage, maybe because of its position in the centre of Europe, as compared to the Swedish paper working on the relative periphery of Europe and at that time in a country that was not a member of the community (another macro-social factor, the relationship of the respective country to the EU). In the final analysis, it thus seemed natural to ascribe some of the observed differences in the coverage of the respective newspaper to aspects of the societies they were a part of.

EU coverage in Nordic newspapers, 1993 and 1996

Next, I ventured a study on the EU coverage in leading newspapers of four Nordic countries in 1993, when only Denmark was a member of the EU and the other three countries (Finland, Norway and Sweden) had applied for membership (Tjernstrom 2001). I say venture because many researchers suggested that the Nordic countries are too similar to be suited for a macro-social approach to comparative studies. The results clearly show a sort of superiority on the part of the Danish paper: more European actors, issues, arenas, debate and more of a European perspective, etc. were to be found in the content analysis.

Other differences were also interesting, indicating links between media content and aspects of the specific historical experience in the four countries: more on the EU's role in defence and security issues in the Finnish paper, more coverage of European directives on natural resources (fish and petroleum), regional policy and international peace-keeping efforts in the Norwegian paper, whereas more on EU engagement in industrial and financial issues were covered in the Swedish paper, perhaps mirroring the historic role of Sweden as the major industrial power in the region. The analysis seems straightforward enough. The superiority of the Danish paper seemed at the time to be due to Danish membership in the European Union – again a macro-social analysis of factors influencing content.

A similar study was carried out in 1996 (also reported in Tjernstrom 2001), when Sweden and Finland had been members of the EU for a couple of years. Norway, following the results of a referendum, had chosen to stay outside, and Denmark had considerably reduced the scope of her EU membership – the so-called Edinburgh National Compromise. This developed into a 'natural experiment' that social scientists eagerly look for.

The simple factor 'membership', at first glance, seemed to have some bearing on results (see Slaatta 1999). The Norwegian paper reduced its coverage to half the 1993 level. The Swedish and Finnish papers, from the new EU member countries, on the other hand, both increased their levels of coverage. Following this line of thought – the influence of 'membership' on media coverage – one would expect the Danish paper to reduce the intensity of its coverage, since Denmark was no longer a full member. But in the overall evaluation of the EU coverage of the Nordic papers, the Danish newspaper was still outstanding.

An alternative hypothesis was formulated, the Maturity Hypothesis, suggesting that it takes a number of years for the national press to learn the ins and out of Brussels bureaucracy, to new political channels and for a country's national political discourse to include a European dimension, etc. According to this alternative hypothesis, EU membership would influence content on Europe, but the full effects would not be felt until a few years have passed.

Yet another alternative hypothesis introduced the idea of a different Danish political culture, i. e. in comparison with the other Nordic countries, involving more debate in general, and more experience in discussing EU issues in connection with the many referenda that the country had experienced. Some support in this direction was given in Inglehart (1990) whose data suggest among other things that Danes more often engage in discussing politics, more so than people in neighboring Nordic countries. Siune (1991) also makes the observation that repeated referenda have heated the debate on Europe in Denmark, and put it higher up on the national political agenda.

EU coverage in Nordic newspapers revisited

Finally, a recent study served as revisiting the EU coverage in Nordic newspapers ten years later (Tjernström 2008). The time period chosen was around the much-observed French and Dutch referenda on the EU Constitution mid-2005. The content analysis is summarized in the following, to further support the idea of the influence of macro-social factors on media content.

For the Danish *Politiken* and Finnish *Hufvudstadsbladet*, large-sized articles dominated the coverage. In the two other newspapers, articles were fairly evenly distributed over size categories. Paris and the Hague were very frequent news locations (and Brussels less dominant than would normally be the case). The Parliament was not in session during this period, which is why Strasbourg was rare as a news location. Very often, the capital of the newspaper in question was the venue. Other European capitals were also frequent news locations. In terms of genres, the Danish *Politiken* had a large section for debate and letters to the editor, often dealing with EU matters and often with prominent intellectuals participating. The Finnish *Hufvudstadsbladet* also offered considerable space to external commentaries on EU matters.

Striking was the share of debate in the Swedish *Dagens Nyheter* taken up by the editorial staff of the paper, and the limited external contributions.

The French and Dutch referenda, naturally, dominated the list of themes in all the Nordic newspapers. The Finnish *Hufvudstadsbladet* featured several articles on Finland's dependence on EU security arrangement and on NATO and some on EU's external affairs but relatively few on financial matters. The Norwegian *Aftenposten* also reported extensively on Norwegian participation in various EU projects, although the nation is still outside the Union. In the Swedish *Dagens Nyheter*, some emphasis was given the ongoing processes in EU institutions regarding Swedish state monopolies for alcohol, medicine and gambling.

The Danish *Politiken* featured many articles with comments and analysis of the referendum as an institution and on the consequences of primarily the French referendum for the planned Danish referendum in September on the Constitution. This meant linking events in France and Holland to political processes in Denmark. Many articles were also devoted to the European Constitution as such. The Finnish decision on the Constitution (planned to take place in Parliament) was touched upon relatively seldom in the Finnish *Hufvudstadsbladet*, on the same level as in the Swedish paper. The Norwegian *Aftenposten* created a strong link to events in Europe affecting the situation in Norway and future European development, but did not bring up the issue of another Norwegian referendum on EU membership. The Swedish *Dagens Nyheter* had a fairly even distribution over these themes.

Among institutional actors, French and Dutch actors dominated. These actors were most frequent in the Danish *Politiken*. National governments, Parliaments, political parties, pressure groups and other national institutional actors appeared distinctly in all the Nordic newspapers in the study. The EU institutional actors appeared most frequently in the Danish *Politiken*, especially the Council and Council of Ministers, but also the Commission.

Summing up the content analysis, it is apparent that the Nordic newspapers contributed in differing degrees to a European political communication. The Danish *Politiken* stands out, debating European issues – especially the proposed Constitution – more intensively, and relating the French and Dutch referenda to decision processes in Denmark and to a more sophisticated debate around the national referendum as a democratic institution.

The relative position of the Nordic newspapers is remarkably unchanged from 1993 and 1996, with the Danish *Politiken* representing the cosmopolitan gaze (to borrow a concept from Beck 2006), and the other newspapers in varying degrees representing a national, materialistic and distant approach to Europe. Thereby these other Nordic media communicate to the reader a sense of periphery, of not entirely belonging. Often decisions by EU institutions are mediated as causing domestic problems, or as insufficient help where assistance is needed, e. g. to fight state monopolies. The exception in 2005 is, surprisingly, the Norwegian *Aftenposten* with a rich coverage accounting for relations between Norway and the EU in many political fields (although the formal linkage is only economic).

The analysis of the macro-social factors that may explain these differences in the EU coverage of the Nordic papers will have to remain similar to the previous studies. 'Country membership in the EU' has little or no explanatory value: Denmark's membership in the EU is considerably reduced, yet the contribution of the Danish paper was outstanding; Norway is not a member, yet the Norwegian paper had impressive coverage on several counts. One will have to refer back to differences in 'political culture'. Danes are more eager to discuss politics in general, and the many referenda on European treaties have kept dialogue on a high level. In Norway, the possibility of another referendum on EU membership – as more and more countries are included – is looming high above Norwegian political and media discourse. And in Finland, the EU is forever regarded as part of the new twist in her eastern relationship. Finally, in Swedish politics and the media, the monetary costs and benefits of EU membership overrides ideas of any intrinsic values of cooperation.

Reflecting on the permanence, the stable pattern of coverage of EU affairs, shown in this study, contrary to what is often referred to as media and politics in a constant state of flux, an early groundbreaking comparative study in political communication comes to mind. Summarizing the comparative study of the first direct and simultaneous election to the European Parliament, in 1979, Blumler (1983) emphasized the lesson that communication takes place within (relatively stable) systems, systems of interdependencies between political establishment, media institutions and users/public/voters.

The conceptual nature of European political communication

Position number two in this article concerns the more precise meaning of a European approach in the national media, the contribution to a European public space that we can discuss in terms of European political communication. What is good media coverage of European affairs? Several attempts have been made at answering this question, and the national media usually do not meet the demands thus defined (Palm 2002). My position is: defining good media coverage is most fruitfully arrived at by comparing actual media coverage in different countries and suggesting that whatever media coverage is empirically 'best' in the group of countries studied may be assumed to be 'adequate' EU media coverage suitable as landmarks of comparison. This is superior to normative models of media coverage arrived at theoretically, most of the time demanding unrealistic levels.

A comparative approach

The comparative approach makes it possible to define 'adequate EU coverage' in terms of an empirically existing coverage. Still, it is difficult to define analytically meaningful dimensions of such adequate coverage. In a recent study, I tried to abstract such dimensions based on an analysis of the material in four Nordic newspapers in the summer of 2005. The study was inspired by Grounded Theory, a controversial method in social science. Some of the instructions of the grounded theory approach have been followed, inductive generation of categories from data that have been systematically obtained and analysed, theoretical memos have been written to interpret the empirical data (Glaser and Strauss 1967; Glaser 1978, 1992).

The research questions guiding the inductive study were phrased:

1. What analytical dimensions seem to be determining whether media coverage of the EU is excellent or inadequate?
2. Are any of these dimensions to be regarded as a 'core category of 'European political communication'?
3. How can the respective contributions of the Nordic newspapers be defined in terms of such analytical dimensions of European political communication?

Methodology

Grounded theory as a method provided a program where qualitative research was carried out with analytic procedures, conceptual development and assumptions of the existence of an external world. The original authors seemed to draw upon objectivist assumptions, whereas later writers have moved grounded theory into a more constructionist approach (Charmaz 2000).

The process prescribed by Brytting (1991) was followed fairly closely in my study. First, categories on two empirically close levels were identified, with the ambition to extract categories on a third and more abstract level. The first level of some 100 categories was discovered in the selected texts in the four previously selected Nordic newspapers and consisted of *manifest observations* in the empirical material, more or less in each article, hopefully both analytical and meaningful. The 30 categories identified on the next level were called *empirical theoretical*; the idea was that these should contribute to the emerging theory or *final categories*. In the analysis, intensive work was carried out with the latter type of categories trying to analyse whether there was any e. g. causal relation between them, whether they could meaningfully be assigned to groups. Such groups were linked to a theoretical idea closely associated with that particular category. It seemed natural to try to seek assistance from previous attempts at creating cognitive maps. This stage of the process was roughly equivalent to the *theoretical memos* prescribed by Glaser and Strauss.

The data in this study were selected from the coverage of the European Union in four leading Nordic newspapers (*Politiken* of Denmark, *Hufvudstadsbladet* of Finland, *Aftenposten* of Norway, *Dagens Nyheter* of Sweden). Data were collected during a decisive time period (the spring of 2005, before and after the French and Dutch referenda on the new Constitution). All articles on the EU from May 23 to June 5 2005, a week before and after the first referendum, were identified and classified as to size category, news location, journalistic genre, theme and institutional actors. All editorial content was searched, manually, except for sports, family, local entertainment and special supplements. Articles only mentioning the EU in passing or as one of several international bodies listed were excluded.

From the total material collected, 459 articles, some 40 articles from the four Nordic newspapers, ten from each paper, across different genres and themes, were selected that would hopefully contribute to a deeper analysis and theoretical inspection of the nature of the media coverage of the European Union during the period. In the first stage, articles in the four newspapers from the days around the Sunday following the two referenda (June 5) were analysed, selecting news and comments on the new political situation.[1] Other articles that seemed promising in terms of the theoretical inspection and analysis of media coverage were then added. Theoretical memos, a key step in the grounded theory process, were edited, beginning with a memo on the *Gemeinschaft* and *Gesellschaft* figure of thought. Brief versions of these memos follow, distilling out some fundamental categories of thought which might help identify a deep structure of a normative model of transnational journalism.

Participation – Gemeinschaft and Gesellschaft

Among previously established theories that arrived early in analysing the nature of good media coverage of European affairs were theories of *Gemeinschaft/Gesellschaft*, referring to intrinsical and instrumental motives for participation in a community like the European, theories first developed by German philosopher and sociologist Tönnies in the latter part of the nineteenth century. This analysis produced the first category on the third level of analysis – *participation*.

Asplund (1991) provided an explanation of the *Gemeinschaft/Gesellschaft* dimension. He quotes a number of interpretations by classic sociologists. Merton used the terms 'cosmopolitan society' and 'localistic society' as a translation of Tönnies' concepts. Comte spoke of 'altruism' and 'egotism'. Durkheim's corresponding concepts were 'organic solidarity' and 'mechanical solidarity'. Finally, Weber identified the distinction between 'value- rational' and 'goal-rational' patterns of action.

Olsen and Sverdrup (1997) discussed 'communities based on identity', and 'communities based on calculated interest'. In the former, participants share a subjective feeling of togetherness and share views on what is acceptable or unacceptable behavior. They express a collective identity and a shared sense of belonging and will consider leaving the community only under exceptional circumstances. In the latter calculated interest community, participants find they can achieve more by acting together and choose cooperation after a cost-benefit analysis that results in individual net benefits. Participants are supposed to be opportunistic and prepared to leave the cooperation whenever it no longer meets their demands.

Legitimacy – Status conferral

The second theory that could be usefully leaned on was 'status conferral' which produced the second category – *legitimacy*. To what extent did the Nordic newspapers select the European Union as a topic for coverage (Entman 1993)? To a content analyst, this is the key to other qualities in the text. Selection: there can be no European political communication if the complex European political processes are not visible in the media often enough to make them appear as ongoing work rather than episodes. Salience: to what extent was the idea that there are problems that can be solved only on the levels above the national level, through transnational or intergovernmental cooperation, emphasized in the news or as a subject for debate? Media coverage and dialogue around such issues and alternative solutions would seem to lend legitimacy to a political problem – silence would not.

Another aspect of legitimacy is the extent to which already established observers and commentators are given an opportunity to contribute to media publicity and opinion formation on an issue. Grundmann et al. (2000) make the observation that two of the elite media in their study on the coverage of the Kosovo events hade extensive contributions by what they called 'key intellectuals' such as Gabriel Garcia Marquez, Susan Sontag, Varga Llosa, Norman Mailer and Seamus Heaney, and politicians like Rudolf Scharping and Felipe Gonzalez . All such contributions would lead to media increasing the credibility and legitimacy of the issue in question.

Media content can be seen as a social construction where values are linked to the events and actors related in the media. 'In conferring status, media embed social objects within multiform webs of value' (Simonsen 1999: 113).

Identity – Building on diversity

Many researchers (Bondebjerg 2006; Delanty 1995; Østergaard 1995) have tried to answer what a European identity – if at all possible or even desirable – is supposed to be constructed of. We are talking about some vague feeling of being 'European', of feeling some sort of belonging to Europe – not just to one's own nation – and consequently experience an imaginary bond, a kind of kinship with other Europeans (Daun 1992). Most researchers seem to agree that there is no simple common denominator, but a multitude of peoples, regions, nations and ideas in the European fellowship. Yet, numerous attempts have been made at defining what is European, what is the common denominator for this part of the world and the people inhabiting it (Gerholm 1991; Åberg and Åkerman 1989; Gidlund and Sörlin 1993; Bergquist et al. 1991; Zetterberg 1991).

Important contributions to the discussion of a European identity have been made by Delanty (1995) and Østergaard (1998). They are both critical of the idea of Europe as an ideal linked to freedom, democracy or autonomy or any other European 'spirit'. The ideas of European roots in Christianity, humanism and liberal democracy are unfounded or mystifying; critical reflection is needed around these issues.

Delanty considers Europe an invention, a historically fabricated reality, changing form and content continually. He tries to demonstrate how Europe as an idea is a historic projection, an idea that has emerged under the pressure of fragmentation. It is a cultural theme in contrast to a name on a geographical region, a metaphor for a split civilization. Europe resembles the national projects, with identity-creating processes, the creation of 'imagined communities', Delanty argues. The problem is that Europe is on a higher level of abstraction than the national ideal. For this very reason, the idea of Europe must include diversity. In the future, the triangular process of the national, the European and the global will be even more important both for political and cultural domains of the European public sphere (Bondebjerg 2006).

Mondialization – Dealing with globalization

Finally, observations in the media texts together with guidance from theories about globalization and transnational politics carried the text analyses in the previous study more or less directly towards the category *mondialization*, the idea that the media may also cover European institutions as an active partner in wider international cooperation in fields of interest also to citizens in the Union.[2] There are a variety of EU institutional activities like political and economic cooperation with the United States, Canada and Japan, EU participation in world trade negotiations, EU assistance cooperation with developing nations, EU regional attempts at climate change measures, EU involvement with security matters, human rights, democracy and development.[3]

Giddens (1998) claims the EU is a significant step towards a cosmopolitan democracy, a development of the national resource base in efforts to check global market forces and the harmful sides of nationalism. Many problems remain to resolve, but Giddens evaluates the EU as a step ahead of the rest of the world and as a pioneering effort, testing forms of governance that go outside traditional stereotypes (Giddens 1998: 141–64).

Habermas (2000) analyses the need for the political sector to catch up with the globalization of markets to influence the limits for the transnational economy. The challenge lies in increasing the competitive power without sacrificing cohesion and solidarity and to work within the framework of a democratic society. Habermas proposes a 'global welfare regime' and sees the EU as an important actor. The political measures on a global level require growing 'cosmopolitan solidarity' in the civil society. He finds hope in growing transnational movements with international solidarity on their agenda rather than international elites. Key processes are those that move from international relations to a domestic policy at the world level.

'European political communication' defined

A close inspection of the many linkages between the four categories – participation, legitimacy, identity and mondialization – leads to the conclusion that the core category in the study of mediated European political communication is 'participation', ideas based on intrinsic or instrumental motives for participation or *Gemeinschaft* and *Gesellschaft*. Obviously, participation can be thought of as a continuum, with values from pure *Gemeinschaft* ideas at one end and pure *Gesellschaft* values at the other. The same applies to the other categories. In the following, the desired, from a normative standpoint, identifying assets are rehearsed. With each variable, there are undesired values at the other end of the continuum and the reader has to imagine or define the opposite pole.

Given the preponderance of this participation motive for membership, the other three categories are to some extent consequences: the EU will be regarded with a degree of legitimacy, the idea of European identity based on diversity is easier to imagine, and common goals that require EU activity in the world beyond European borders become more natural. The extent to which the media seem to recognize these intrinsic motives for participation in the Union and accept shared values in turn defines the nature of the political communication they offer.

The three supportive categories proposed thus seem to revolve around the core concept of participation. Figure 1 illustrates, adding final second-level categories for each category which at the same time function as 'definitions' of the often multi-layered categories/concepts.

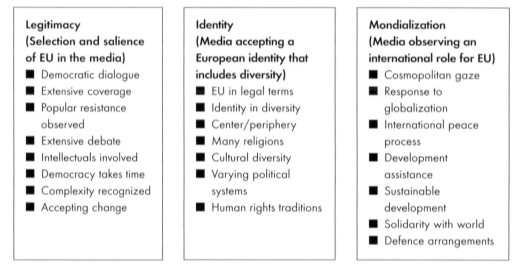

Figure 1: One core category (particpation) and three supporting categories determining the concept 'European political journalism'. With additional empirical and theoretical sub-categories.

Expanding on the key concept in the study, the *Gemeinschaft/Gesellschaft* figure of thought, it is often taken for granted in media texts what assumptions are made in this context. Discussions about the national contribution to the EU budget and whether one's country in a cost/benefit analysis gets enough back in monetary terms is a typical example of *Gesellschaft* thinking. Promoting the EU as an obstacle to national efforts e. g. in the area of alcohol taxes or reduction of chemical substances (to take Swedish examples) is also basically *Gesellschaft* thinking.

The keyword is often 'we', meaning our own country exclusively. Texts seem to understand that there exists a joint effort in e. g. the environmental protection area or peace efforts in the Middle East are examples of *Gemeinschaft* thinking. The keyword is again a 'we', but this time indicating our own country in an effort together with other member states. It is suggested here that this sometimes subtle, most of the time very obvious dividing line, is central to defining good/adequate or deficient media coverage of the EU.

The contribution to European political communication by Nordic newspapers

The results, in terms of the four Nordic dailies and their relative proximity to the normative idea of European political communication, as defined in the present study may be summed up as shown in Figure 2. Obviously, such a summary is a gross over-simplification of the richness of the media coverage analysed in the study and should primarily be thought of as one daring conclusion of the differences brought out in a comparative, cross-national exercise.

When the Danish *Politiken*, and in some aspects, the Norwegian *Aftenposten*, are given the 'highest grades' in this comparison, it does not mean the papers are complete or perfect in terms of European political communication. It means, however, that they may serve as landmarks in a normative comparison with other media. These landmarks are then not theoretically derived normative criteria for what is adequate, but empirically grounded in actual media performance, attainable only through comparative cross-national comparisons. Again, the reader will have to imagine the respective dimensions as covering a wide continuum.

Discussion

First, a few methodological reflections: the conceptual categories might simply be a restatement of the researcher's initial understanding of the research area, making the empirical work redundant (Brytting 1991: 205). One may arrive at normative concepts such as these through a purely theoretical process. Legitimacy has often been proposed as the key concept in discussing normative criteria for a functioning European public sphere. The strength of my analysis is the strong link to actually published editorial material in the four Nordic newspapers, thus is in a sense 'real'.

Secondly, the danger of 'empiricism' in grounded theory work is often exaggerated, since theoretical ideas are present during the whole process, consciously or unconsciously. Previous theoretical knowledge does influence the analysis, as in all other kinds of research, one might add, but not always as consciously and well documented. Glaser (1978: 56) describes how

Figure 2: EU in Nordic newspapers 2005. The contribution to positive framing of the Union (*** is closest to the ideal of a European political journalism).

Dimensions	Politiken	Huvudstadsbladet	Aftenposten	Dagens Nyheter
Participation	* * *	* *	* * *	* *
Legitimacy	* * *	* * *	* *	*
Mondialization	* * *	* *	* * *	* *
Identity	* * *	* *	*	* *

the researcher, after the empirical phase, through integration of ideas, approaches the literature and relates emerging categories to the literature. If the grounded theory approach is only 'grounded', it has severe limitations. At some stage, the analysis must also include 'theory' (Brytting 1991: 212).

The reader may find it odd that the proposed central category defining European political communication, participation, is based on the very old distinction between intrinsical and instrumental motives for joining a community or an organization – Gemeinschaft and Gesellschaft – concepts that have been tossed around by the classic sociologists for many decades. These concepts, however, seem to have a remarkable inherent strength, which may be the reason so many researchers have ended up finding them meaningful in their different fields. This study is no exception; how the media, directly or indirectly, describe the typical motives for a country's participation in the EU, determines the kind of European political communication that will be offered readers or citizens.

In a discursive map of EU journalism, journalists in one position aim at covering the EU from a transnational perspective and address questions of legitimacy of EU institutions and EU policies without reducing them to an exclusively national context (Heikkilä and Kunelius 2006: 45). Some journalists actively look for political identities that cut across national borders. The authors consider such a discursive position among journalists unrealistic and unlikely.

This study, however, suggests that there are examples of excellent European political communication among Nordic newspapers, examples that deserve to be studied as ideal types for conceptual development of European political communication.

Notes

1. A full description of the grounded theory exercise can be obtained by contacting the author (the report is in the Swedish language).
2. Mondialization is a French term, defined as 'considération des problèmes politiques dans une optique mondiale, (Le Petit Larousse illustré 1992, 649).
3. The category 'mondialization' was preferred to globalization as the former obviously included a political field, whereas the latter seemed to be limited to the technological and economic spheres. The category mondialization seemed to include both a political response to globalization and a component in the external orientation of the European Union that can be present in media coverage (Bauman 1997).

References

AIM Research Consortium (ed.) (2006), Understanding the Logic of EU Reporting in Mass Media: Analysis of EU Media Coverage and Interviews in Editorial Offices in Europe. Dortmund: Projektverlag.

Anderson, P. J. and Weymouth, A. (1999), Insulting the Public? The British Press and the European Union. London: Longman.

Asplund, J. (1991), Om Undran inför Samhället [Wondering about Society]. Lund: Argos.

Bauman, Z. (1997), Le Cout Humain de la Mondialization [The Human Cost of Globalization]. Paris: Hachette.

Bergquist, L. (1991), 'Guds Finger: Katolicism och den Världsliga Makten' ['God's Finger: European Catholicism and Worldly Power'], in K. Bergquist, T. R. Blomqvist, G. Gerholm, I. Hägg, H. Karlsson and I. Zetterberg (1991), Det Europeiska Huset [The European House]. Halmstad: Timbro.

Beck, U. (2006), The Cosmopolitan Vision. Cambridge: Polity Press.

Bergquist, K. Blomqvist, T. R. Gerholm, G. Hägg, I. Karlsson, H., Zetterberg, I. (1991), Det Europeiska Huset [The European House]. Halmstad: Timbro.

Blumler, J. G. (1983a), 'Election Communication: A Comparative Perspective', in J. G. Blumler (ed.), Communicating to Voters: Television in the First European Parliamentary Elections. London: Sage, pp. 275–80.

Blumler, J. G. (ed.) (1983b). Communicating to Voters: Television in the First European Parliamentary Elections. London: Sage.

Bondebjerg, I. (2006), 'The European Imaginary: Media Fictions, Democracy and Cultural Identities', paper presented at the international conference 'Media, Democracy and European Culture'. University of Copenhagen, 4–6 October 2006.

Brytting, T. (1991), Organizing the Small Growing Firm: A Grounded Theory Approach. Stockholm: Stockholm School of Economics.

Charmaz, K. (2000), 'Ethics and Politics in Qualitative Research', in N. K. Denzin and U. S. Lincoln (eds), The Sage Handbook of Qualitative Research, 2nd Edition. Thousand Oaks: Sage, pp. 509–35.

Charmaz, K. (2005), 'Grounded Theory in the 21st Century: Applications for Advancing Social Justice Studies', in N. K. Denzin and U. S. Lincoln (eds), The Sage Handbook of Qualitative Research, 2nd Edition. Thousand Oaks: Sage, pp. 507–35.

Daun, Å. (1992), Den Europeiska Identiteten: Bidrag till Samtal om Sveriges Framtid [The European Identity: Speaking of the Future of Sweden]. Stockholm: Rabén and Sjögren.

De Vreese, Claes H., Peter, J. and Semetko, D. A. (2001), 'Framing Politics at the Launch of the Euro: A Cross-National Comparative Study of Frames in the News', Political Communication, 18: 2, pp. 107–22.

Delanty, G. (1995), Inventing Europe: Idea, Identity, Reality. London: MacMillan.

Denzin, N. K. and Lincoln, U. S. (eds) (2000), The Sage Handbook of Qualitative Research, 2nd Edition. Thousand Oaks: Sage.

Denzin, N. K. and Lincoln, U. S. (eds) (2005), The Sage Handbook of Qualitative Research, 3rd Edition. Thousand Oaks: Sage.

Entman, R. M. (1993), 'Framing: Towards Clarification of a Fractured Paradigm', Journal of Communication, 43: 4, pp. 51–58.

Eriksen, O. and Fossum, J. E. (eds) (2000), Democracy in the European Union: Integration through Deliberation? London: Routledge.

Gerhards, J. (1993), 'Westeuropäische Integration und die Schwierigkeiten der Entstehung einer europäischen Öffentlichkeit', in Zeitschrift für Soziologie Jg. 22, Heft 2. Stuttgart: Enke Verlag, pp. 90–102.

Gerholm, T. R. (1991), 'År 2222 – Hur Har Det Gått med Europas Identitet?' ['In 2222 – What Has Happened to Europe's identity?'], in K. Bergquist, T. R. Blomqvist, G. Gerholm, I. Hägg, H. Karlsson and I. Zetterberg (1991), Det Europeiska Huset [The European House]. Halmstad: Timbro, pp. 66–82.

Giddens, A. (1998), Tredje Vägen: Om Socialdemokratins Förnyelse [The Third Way: On the Renewal of Social Democracy]. Lund: Atlas.

Gidlund, J. and Sörlin, S. (1993), *Det Europeiska Kaleidoskopet: Regionerna, Nationerna och den Europeiska Identitetet* [*The European Kaleidoscope: Regions, Nations and the European Identity*]. Stockholm: SNS.

Glaser, B. G. (1978), *Advances in the Methodology of Grounded Theory: Theoretical Sensitivity*. Mill Valley: Sociology Press.

Glaser, B. G. (1992), *Basics of Grounded Theory Analysis*. Mill Valley: Sociology Press.

Glaser, B. G. and Strauss, A. -L. (1967), *The Discovery of Grounded Theory*. Chicago: Aldine.

Graber, D. (1988), *Processing the News: How People Tame the Information Tide*. Lanham: University Press of America.

Grundmann, R., Smith, D. and Wright, S. (2000), 'National Elites and Transnational Discourses in the Balkan War', *European Journal of Communication*, 15: 3 (September), pp. 299–320.

Gurevitch, M. and Blumler, J. G. (1990), 'Comparative Research: The Extending Frontier', in D. I. Swanson and D. Nimmo (eds) (1990), *New Directions in Political Communication: A Resource Book*. Newbury Park: Sage, pp. 305–25.

Habermas, J. (2000), 'Beyond the Nation-state? On Some Consequences of Economic Globalization', in O. Eriksen and J. E. Fossum (eds) (2000), *Democracy in the European Union: Integration through Deliberation?* London: Routledge, pp. 29–41.

Hallin, D. and Mancini, P. (2004), *Comparing Media Systems: Three Models of Media and Politics*. Cambridge: Cambridge University Press.

Heikkilä, H. and Kunelius, R. (2006), 'The Case of Finland', in AIM Research Consortium (ed.) (2006), *Understanding the Logic of EU Reporting in Mass Media, Analysis of EU Media Coverage and Interviews in Editorial Offices in Europe*. Bochum: Projekt Verlag, pp. 33–48.

Hansen, A. (1993), *Mass Media and Environmental Issues*. London: Leicester University Press.

Inglehart, R. (1990), *Culture Shift in Advanced Industrial Society*. Cambridge: Princeton University Press.

Kevin, D. (2003), *Europe in the Media: A Comparison of Reporting, Representation, and Rhetoric in National Media Systems in Europe*. Mahwah: Lawrence Erlbaum Associates.

Olsen, J -P. and Sverdrup, B. O. (1997), 'Samarbejd og Integrasjon i Norden og Europa' ['Cooperation and Integration in the Nordic Countries and in Europe'], *Nordisk Administrativ Tidskrift*, 78: 4, pp. 341–67. Reprinted in ARENA 98: 2.

Palm, G. (2002), *I Nationens och Marknadens Intresse: Journalister, nyhetskällor och EU-journalistik* [*In the Interest of the Nation and the Market: Journalists, Sources and EU Journalism*]. Gothenburg: University of Gothenburg.

Schlesinger, P. (1991), *Media, State and Nation: Political Violence and Collective Identities*. London: Sage.

Schlesinger, P. and Kevin, D. (2000), 'Can the European Union Become a Sphere of Publics?', in O. Eriksen and J. E. Fossum (eds) (2000), *Democracy in the European Union: Integration through deliberation?* London: Routledge, pp. 206–29.

Simonsen, P. (1999), 'Mediated Sources of Public Confidence: Lazarsfeld and Merton Revisited', *Journal of Communication*, 49: 2, pp. 109–22.

Siune, K. (1991), *EF på Dagsordenen* [*EU on the Agenda*]. Århus: Politica.

Slaatta, T. (1999), *Europeanisation and the Norwegian News Media: Political Discourse and News Production in the Transnational Field*. Oslo: University of Oslo. Department of Media and Communication, Report series no. 36.

Strauss, A. and Corbin, J. (1998), *Basics of Qualitative Research: Grounded Theory Procedures and Techniques.* 2nd edition. Thousand Oaks: Sage.

Swanson, D. I. and Nimmo, D. (eds) (1990), *New Directions in Political Communication: A Resource Book.* Newbury Park: Sage.

Tjernström, V. (1993), '*OUI OU NON – en Studie av hur Dagens Nyheter och Le Soir Bevakade den Franska Folkomröstningen om Maastricht-avtalet' [Yes or No – a Study of the Coverage by the Dagens Nyheter and LeSoir of the French Referendum on the Maastricht Treaty]*', Brussels: seminar paper.

Tjernström, V. (2001), *Europa Norrifrån: En Nordisk Komparativ Studie av Europeisk Politisk Kommunikation* [*Europe as Seen from the North: A Nordic Cross-national, Comparative Study of European Political Communication*]. Umeå: Umeå Universitet.

Tjernström, V (2008), 'Nordic Newspapers on the EU: European Political Communication after NON and NEE'. *Journalism. Theory, practice and criticism,* Vol. 9(4), 516–536.

Zelizer, B. (2004), *Taking Journalism Seriously: News and the Academy.* London: Sage.

Zetterberg, H. (1991), 'Det Unika Europa' ['The Unique Europe'], in K. Bergquist, T. R. Blomqvist, G. Gerholm, I. Hägg, H. Karlsson, and I. Zetterberg (1991), *Det Europeiska Huset* [*The European House*]. Halmstad: Timbro, pp. 9–25.

Åberg, A. and Åkerman, S. (1989), *Europas Historia i Fickformat* [*A Pocket Edition of European History*]. Stockholm: Swedish Broadcasting Corporation.

Østergaard, U. (1995), *Europa: Identitet och Identitetspolitik.* Copenhagen: Munksgaard.

PART THREE: MEDIA, CULTURE AND DEMOCRACY

11

THE CULTURAL DIMENSION OF DEMOCRACY

Jostein Gripsrud

Abstract
Political theorists tend to leave out culture and the arts. Similarly, theory as well as empirical research on deliberative democracy tends to bracket out almost all of what goes on in the mediated public sphere. The article discusses ways in which culture in general and the arts – high as well as low – are important to 'democracy as lived experience' as well as to the processes of opinion formation. Music, the most abstract of arts is used as an example.

Keywords
culture, democracy, music, deliberative democracy, public sphere, public opinion

A lack of knowledge

A particular dimension of democracy has been lacking attention in both theoretical and empirical work on democracy, in all relevant disciplines: Neither famous theoreticians nor empirical researchers in political science have cared much about *culture*. This is particularly the case if 'culture' is taken to mean 'the arts and popular culture'. The lacuna is all the more striking to a media and communication scholar since propaganda, film and radio research in early political science is one of the main 'roots' of today's media and communication studies. What we could call expressive culture is evidently of vital importance in the processes of globalization, and political projects such as the European Union or the construction of post apartheid South Africa obviously in addition also depend on culture in a broader sense – that of anthropology and ethnography. Sir Edward B. Tylor in 1871 provided a classic definition of culture here, as 'that complex whole which includes knowledge, belief, art, morals, law, custom, and any other capabilities and habits acquired by man as a member of society' (quoted from Eriksen 1994:15). Raymond Williams was referring to such an understanding when he in *Culture and Society* (1963) said that culture is 'a whole way of life'. It is not only the arts, but the arts are central constituents of 'the complex whole'. Interestingly, the same holistic definition lives on in, for instance, UNESCO's 2002 declaration on cultural diversity, where it is said that 'culture should be regarded as the set of distinctive spiritual, material, intellectual and emotional features of society or a social group' which 'encompasses, in addition to art and literature, lifestyles, ways of living together, value systems, traditions and beliefs'. This phrasing also indirectly maintains that 'art and literature' are central ingredients in a whole which is truly far-reaching and complex.

The UNESCO declaration also says that 'culture is at the heart of contemporary debates about identity, social cohesion, and the development of a knowledge-based economy'. Consequently, if this is accepted and taken seriously, there is a lot of work that needs to be done on the interface between culture and politics. This paper is to argue the importance of culture for democracy in a general way, providing various examples of how the nexus between the cultural and the political is important for the functioning of democratic politics and, moreover, democratic societies. I will be discussing both how democracy relates to the concept of culture in the widest, anthropological sense and how, more specifically, the arts and popular culture are important.

The role of music will be particularly central as an example. If an 'a-thematic' art form such as music is relevant to the workings of democracy, it should be all the more evident that all the other art forms, in the whole spectrum of media, are of considerable importance. Finally, the paper addresses the question of how the arts or 'expressive culture' can be positioned and integrated within Jürgen Habermas' theories of the public sphere and deliberative democracy.

Democracy as lived experience

Taking the political role of culture seriously will not only affect our notion of the cultural and the political, it may also alter our understanding of society in general. Studying how cultural artefacts and activities influence the forming of public opinion and governance will thus not only elucidate the political system as such. It may also yield a better understanding of the ways in which political democracy is tied to certain social and cultural conditions. It will reveal that there is not only a relationship between culture and democracy, *democracy is in itself a cultural form*.

One way to start thinking about this is to look at decidedly non-democratic societies and their characteristics. Censorship and strict control with the mass media, the arts and public life in general are among the most striking of these. Citizens of such societies will as a result tend to feel monitored, mistrusted and fenced in. The regimes in question will, unless they succeed with a brain-washing operation, tend to lose over time any legitimacy they might have had. The governing of a democratic society will, on the other hand, normally rely fully on its legitimacy in the eyes of citizens, i.e. their overall support of the system. The strength and attraction of democracy therefore lies not only in the advantages of its form of government but also in people's daily sense of self-determination and meaning. Remembering Edward Tylor's and Raymond Williams' definitions of culture, one might thus say that democracy is also 'a whole way of life'.

The overall support for the general social and political system in democracies is not least based on a widespread experience of qualities of life associated for instance with cultural pluralism and cultural activities. These phenomena produce a sense of communality and involvement both for individuals and groups that is likely to promote political participation. Consequently, a pluralistic and dynamic musical, literary, theatrical and cinematic life should be seen as an important feature of democracy. A lively, many-sided cultural life, where all sorts of social experiences and opinions are represented and worked through – charming as well as disgusting, harmonious as well as conflicting, liberal as well as authoritarian – makes democracy something noticeable in daily life, in the very air we breathe.

It is not very difficult to understand why theatre, literature, film, television and most visual arts are heavily censored or otherwise monitored in non-democratic regimes. These arts can and often do carry openly political or ideological 'messages', and so a government that fears uncontrolled debate will have to monitor these. It is considerably less obvious that music should be controlled in the same way. Still, a strict political regulation also of musical life was among the common characteristics of the Soviet-dominated bloc. Western-style popular music was for the most part banned and forced into a 'subterranean' existence, and, in most of these countries, jazz was also expelled from public arenas.

Such cultural repression in the Soviet bloc had direct historical ties to the 1930s ban on the rhythmic popular music of those days, jazz, in both Stalin's Soviet Union and Hitler's Germany. The right-wing dictatorships in Spain, Portugal and Greece, two of which were also established in the 1930s and all of which lasted until the mid-70s, likewise tried to regulate music on the basis of their political and moral principles. Some of the ideological basis for this sort of practice has been widespread also in countries with stable democracies, especially before the Second World War. It appeared for instance in the Norwegian labour movement in the mid-30s, when a battle against jazz in general and syncopation in particular was called for (Gripsrud 1981). The idea of fighting syncopation on ideological and moral grounds was certainly related to sexual anxieties. But these anxieties were also closely related to more diffuse anxieties over modernisation's dissolution of borderlines, order and discipline.

This example is telling of music's importance for fundamental social conditions, in particular the formation of identities and social groups, ranging from working class teenagers to fascists and Italian *Mafiosi*. The sociality of music may of course also appear in directly political forms, as in political songs on the left or right or in whole operas where the political is mostly supplied by the lyrics and the libretto. But music *as such* functions primarily in areas we first and foremost experience as existentially important. And this is precisely where we find the most important and overlooked aspect of music's sociality; in this lies its enormous attractiveness and power.

A life lived totally without music would to most people appear both joyless and meaningless. As mentioned above, modern democracy is wholly dependent on more or less active support from the people, and so it has to have a pluralistic and dynamic musical life. The sociality of music is consequently of great interest not only in its directly political forms but also in its primarily existentially significant expressions. Historically, there have been circumstances where one might say the politically relevant and the existentially significant merge. This was arguably the case in the period known as 'the 60s'. But it has more generally also been the case in every major social movement, whether political or religious, that aim for a different society and a different way of life. Music is always part of and supportive of such projects, while it to outsiders also communicates some of their folksy, authoritarian, aggressive, emotional, etc. character.

As far as I know, nobody has yet explicitly tried to investigate and theorize *the culture that characterizes democratic societies* – i.e. democracy as 'lived experience'. I think a reasonable hypothesis for such work would be that a sense of freedom in the production and reception of music and other arts is of great importance here.

The dynamics of deliberative democracy

Having established that democracy is a cultural form with certain qualities in itself, characterizing the everyday lives of citizens, it is time to ask whether culture in the sense of the arts – including popular culture – really is of importance to political democracy. Clearly, its imaginable functions will vary with different conceptions or models of democracy, and there are indeed different opinions on how to understand liberal democracy and its history.

As Jon Elster ([1986]1997) has demonstrated, it is a useful simplification to differentiate between academic approaches within the field that accentuate public discourse, argumentation and the formation of critical public opinion, and perceptions of democratic processes as clashes or tug-of-wars between pre-established social interests that try to influence voters performing the essential democratic act of voting or more generally persuade 'the masses' to support their cause.

The first of these conceptions may be labelled deliberative democracy, while the second, which turns the public sphere into an arena for marketing only, is called the 'social choice' model by Elster. He points out the following main features of social choice theories of democracy:

1. They regard the political process as purely instrumental.
2. The decisive political act is private (secret voting).
3. The goal of politics is the optimal compromise between opposed and actually antagonistic private interests. In line with this it is also supposed that (4) both the preferences of the actors and the alternatives they are faced with are *given*, not dynamic and changeable entities.

Politics is in this way understood as analogous with market mechanisms and the choices of consumers on the basis of their private interests and desires.

This has consequences for how the role of the arts, popular culture and mass media in general is conceived. In a deliberative understanding of democracy, in particular that of Habermas, the media have a central role not least as arenas for the formation of public opinion, for real debates resulting in revised views among participants. In light of a 'social choice' type of understanding, on the other hand, the mass media primarily become manipulative instruments for the production of certain preferences among members of the audience. Such a view was for instance expressed directly by the economist and political scientist Schumpeter, who once said that the will of the people is the outcome of the political process, not its 'motive power' (quoted from Elster ibid.: 27). As Elster points out, this view is fully in line with how Schumpeter regarded the market: to him the preferences of consumers were also largely open to manipulation.

One could say that the market-analogous 'social choice' understanding of democracy makes virtues out of the tendencies Jürgen Habermas has deplored and condemned. A more pragmatic and in a sense more realistic view might be that the deliberative and the 'social choice' versions point to two different, co-existing dimensions of political processes in Western democracies. It is evidently correct that political decisions and measures often will take the form of compromise between different social interests. It is also correct that voters ultimately make their choice between alternatives in the privacy of the voting booth, and that these choices are often made on the basis of private interests rather than concerns for the well-being of society as a whole. But at the same time the 'social choice' perspective appears inadequate in relation to very central aspects of real political processes, not least in a longer historical perspective.

It is for instance possible to point out a number of obvious, more or less consensual changes over time in political preferences and priorities. The role of ecological questions and the views on women's roles in society are two examples, the perception of the apartheid regime in South Africa and the understanding of the situation for Palestinians are two more. Over two or three decades we have seen major shifts in the dominant views on these issues in most Western countries. The 'social choice' perspective cannot really grasp the dynamics of democratic processes that must be ascribed to the existence of a public discourse and a complex public life, including a number of struggles for various 'causes', in which the mass media also play other roles than purely manipulative ones.

The arts, popular culture and mass media are, as pointed out above, both actors and arenas in these processes. They do of course influence the formation of opinion in both capacities, but this influence is hardly adequately described by the term 'manipulation'. The influence is moreover nowadays not normally exercised on behalf of political parties, the entities voters choose between in elections. The view that media audiences are quite easily manipulated on serious issues is also contradicted by modern media theory and empirical research. This is not to say that the media are without a power to influence people in various ways and on various planes. But ideas about stimulus-response relations in serious political matters, involving fundamental social values, were discarded long ago. However cynically realistic one wishes to be in an analysis of modern liberal democracy, there is no getting around the crucial element of deliberation, of public debate and opinion formation.

Whether one regards the individual member of society as a consumer in the political marketplace or as a citizen actively participating in public deliberation, it should be possible to agree that the ideal of a well-informed individual, one who has a basis of knowledge and information for her or his opinions and actions, is of key importance. This is so, even if Immanuel Kant in his classic letter to the editor 'What is enlightenment?' (1784) actually emphasized the courage to think independently of traditional authorities more than knowledge, and even if 'the knowledgeable citizen' ideal has been criticised in very different ways by writers as diverse as Walter Lippman (1922) and Michael Schudson (1998). It is not least the idea that citizens should be knowledgeable that makes the freedom of information, understood as the right to a varied, truly pluralistic menu of cultural products and substantial information and knowledge, absolutely fundamental to any conception of democracy. One could similarly argue that the freedom of expression must be regarded as fundamental to democracy in any understanding of the term.

These two fundamental rights are each other's preconditions. There are still reasons to argue that the former in a sense is primary: it is the prerequisite for well-informed participation of any kind, be it public utterances or voting. One indication of this is that the United States Supreme Court found, in a ruling of great principal significance for media regulation (*Red Lion Broadcasting Co.* v *FCC, 395 U.S. 367* (1969)), that 'the right of viewers and listeners and not the right of broadcasters is paramount', and that the public's right 'to receive suitable access to social, political, aesthetic, moral and other ideas and experiences' is more important than broadcasters' First Amendment (freedom of expression) rights when the two are in conflict. The Supreme Court's formulation is about cultural diversity as a democratic right and it is well worth noting in the context of this paper that it explicitly includes the access to 'aesthetic...ideas and experiences'.

The strength of a deliberative, normative conception of democracy, like the one Jürgen Habermas represents, is not least that it invites evaluations of the *quality* of the information offered in the public sphere, while it also focuses the economic and organizational basis of public communication. It does not reduce democracy to majority votes and 'market shares' for political parties. Consequently, it also points to the possibility and necessity of discussing cultural artefacts and activities from a normative point of view: bad, good, better. Contrary to other conceptions, this one *in principle* grants importance to the practices of criticism.

There are, however, certain limitations to the conception of deliberation in what one might call the Habermasian tradition. One highly relevant example can be taken from the solid and even impressive project Transformations of the State, based at the University of Bremen and the International University Bremen. The Public Sphere Research Group within this project states the following on its website:

> In our understanding, public discourse is a debate accessible to the general public in which statements are backed by justification. We focus on public discourse as an important mechanism for the development of public knowledge and self-understandings. The mass media are the prime carriers of public discourse. We are analyzing national

quality newspapers since they reach a considerable audience and they are widely regarded as the primary medium of continuous discussion of political questions based on justification and arguments. (http://www.sfb597.uni-bremen.de/publicsphere/ Accessed 18 September 2006)

This choice of material for the study of certain debates and certain types of debates is in many ways not only defensible but also sensible and productive. But it is, on the other hand, a severe limitation on the understanding of opinion formation in today's world. It means that the meaning of 'deliberation' as in 'deliberative democracy' is limited to the so to speak explicitly deliberating, properly argued discourses of elite media such as the *Frankfurter Allgemeine Zeitung*. This could be taken to mean that about 99 per cent of what actually goes on in the public sphere of modern democracies are irrelevant to the processes of democratic deliberation. Such a view appears inadequate, to say the least. A key point of this paper is precisely that democratic deliberation must be seen as a constantly ongoing, dynamic process involving multitudes of unjustified statements, badly justified statements and a wide variety of other sorts of inputs. Popular songs and Nobel Prize winning literature, Hollywood movies and contemporary visual art – all of this and much more can and should be thought of in this way. In the following, I will look at some possible perspectives on the roles such phenomena play in the formation of public opinion.

The complex public sphere

It seems useful for further exploration of expressive culture's relation to democratic political processes to think spatially, i.e. to ask *where* e.g. music is located in relation to politics in a spatial model of society. The theory of the public sphere is a logical companion to a deliberative understanding of democracy. And it does indeed provide a space for culture.

In Habermas' classic representation of the historical development of the public sphere in Western Europe from the mid-1700s onwards, he points out that this new social arena is first conceived as a 'literary' public sphere. It should rather be referred to as a 'cultural' public sphere, as it also comprised activities of a theatrical, musical, etc. nature, which within the sphere of intimacy (the family and the home) in different ways treated existential, moral and political issues. Habermas maintains that the subjectivity created within the sphere of intimacy arrives at an understanding of itself in the literary (or cultural) public sphere (1989: 51). And music was an important element both in the sphere of intimacy and in the public domain, then as it is now.

Habermas has however maintained that the highly diverse literary or cultural public sphere's impact on the subsequent development of a political public sphere 'lay more with its organizational forms than with its manifest functions' (1992: 423). He claims that what was most important for the development of democracy was the free, rational and egalitarian discussions, the majority decisions, etc. that were transferred from various cultural forums and organizations to political contexts, not the topics. This implies a borderline in content between culture and politics that is not immediately convincing. Some would say his view here is actually an example of Habermas' tendency to 'impoverish his own theory', in the words of Craig Calhoun (1992: 35).

Calhoun refers to the fact that one in Habermas' original public sphere theory may get the impression that identity and interests are created not in the public sphere but only in the sphere of intimacy, the subject consequently entering the public sphere in completed form. The boundaries between the private and the public are thus drawn too firmly to allow for a comprehension of the exchange between the two fields, as well as an understanding of the historical variations as to where exactly the line has been drawn. Similar points can be made regarding the borders between the cultural and the political public spheres. Public reflection on what it entails to be a woman or an immigrant and how new laws could improve their situation might well be inspired for instance by the experience of a Bollywood movie or a rap concert, and if so, it would be difficult to place in relation to sharp distinctions between the two parts of the public sphere.

It is, however, a striking feature of most of the extensive literature concerning deliberative democracy that the cultural sphere is either completely ignored, or, at best, briefly said to be addressed some time in the future. This pertains to both important and comprehensive contributions to the field, such as James Bohman's *Public Deliberation: Pluralism, Complexity, and Democracy* (1996), and, for instance, solid feminist contributions critical of sharp and ahistorical boundaries between that which is political and that which is not – such as Nancy Fraser's *Unruly Practices* (1989) and *Justice Interruptus* (1997). And you would be wrong to assume that Seyla Benhabib's anthology *Democracy and Difference: Contesting the Boundaries of the Political* (1996) also addresses the problem concerning the boundaries between the political and cultural public spheres. As I have already argued in a slightly different context above, it is, in light of how much of the public forum that is actually filled with so-called expressive culture and the discourses that accompany it, rather striking how thoroughly one avoids phenomena such as art, music, dance, TV drama, novels, comics, computer games, poetry, theatre, movies, advertising, romances, comedy, satire and so on – but also media, journalism, talk shows, reporting, realism, photography and the like.

Craig Calhoun claims that the most lasting value of Habermas' *Strukturwandel der Öffentlichkeit* probably is its ability to constantly generate new scholarly studies – simply because it offers 'the richest, best developed conceptualization available of the social nature and foundations of public life' (ibid.: 41). As demonstrated, Habermas was already at the outset concerned with the social function of art and he has in fact, contrasting most theorists in the field of political theory, kept his interest all along. His famous article regarding modernity as an incomplete project (1983) is but one example.

On the other hand, Pieter Duvenage (2003) has argued that Habermas in his early works considered art a considerable contribution to the enlightenment of the public, but that he, in conjunction with his 'linguistic turn' in the 1970s, came to devote less attention to the role of rationality in aesthetic experience than before. Instead he treated it as a sub-category under communicative rationality, tied to a one-sided comprehension of art as subjective expression. Duvenage's view can, however, appear as a questionable simplification when one considers how Habermas' whole oeuvre on sociology and communication theory offers many possibilities for theorising art in general and music in particular. For instance, the presentation of the concept of a lifeworld in volume two of *The Theory of Communicative Action* provides much room for art and artistic experiences in processes leading to the reproduction of the 'structural components' of the lifeworld, to which the public sphere belongs: culture, society and personality.

Personalities consequently do not enter the public sphere in a completed form; rather, they are created and confirmed as social entities also within the public sphere, not least its cultural part. One may here also refer to points made by, among others, Anders Johansen (2003: 22ff), about Hannah Arendt's (1958) view of civil society or the public sphere: she saw it as not least a sphere for realization of the self – as part of a community – and for the creation of some shared perception of reality. While Arendt's views on the public sphere might generally appear aristocratic rather than democratic today, her underlining of public life as an arena for socialization could well be worth considering both for political theorists and for any participant in, say, *Pop Idol*.

In *Between Facts and Norms* (English edition 1996) Habermas describes the public sphere as a structure situated between the political system, the economic system (the market) and the private sections of the lifeworld. This structure is a complex network that 'branches out into a multitude of overlapping international, national, regional, local, and subcultural arenas' (373). In accordance with the universal processes of differentiation inherent in modernity, the public sphere is differentiated in several specialized sub-spheres pertaining to a variety of themes which are nonetheless accessible to non-specialist citizens. Habermas exemplifies this by referring to public spheres within popular sciences, religion, art and literature, feminism and other 'alternative' political orientations.

The public sphere is also differentiated into different levels based on the 'density' of communication, and the complexity and scope of organization:

> from the episodic publics found in taverns, coffee houses, or on the streets; through the occasional 'arranged' publics of particular presentations and events, such as theatre performances, rock concerts, party assemblies, or church congresses; up to the abstract public sphere of isolated readers, listeners, and viewers scattered across large geographic areas, or even around the globe, and brought together only through the mass media. (374).

Habermas' point is that these undifferentiated and partial public spheres, all constructed by ordinary language, remain 'porous' in their relation to one another.

> The one text of 'the' public sphere, a text continually extrapolated and extending radially in all directions, is divided by internal boundaries into arbitrarily small texts for which

verything else is context; yet one can always build hermeneutical bridges from one text to the next (ibid.).

In this way, products and audiences ranging from the smallest and most temporary of musical sub-spheres to hundreds of millions of television viewers witnessing global media events such as *Live 8*, may be connected not only to each other and a variety of musical spheres, but also to other elements, aspects and parts of the public sphere in a modern democracy.

The sociality of music

It should not come as a surprise that music and social events it gives rise to can acquire the sorts of political relevance I have discussed so far. Music not only accompanies human life from lullabies to funeral hymns, it has also for thousands of years been an important ingredient in just about any part of public life, regardless of how this otherwise may have been defined or manifested. As put by the music anthropologist Steven Feld, music has 'a fundamentally social life' (1994: 77). In modern times music has been a significant element in the internal and external lives of social and political movements, on either side of the political spectrum, and a central feature of religious communities. Music has thus, especially with the addition of lyrics, been used regularly and effectively in the communication of various opinions and ideas.

Importantly, however, music has also always been present in social settings that are not thought of as being about the communication of specific ideas or values. In football stadiums and inside cars, in dance clubs and concert halls, people are offered more or less intense musical experiences in types of 'sub' or 'micro' public spheres that are clearly distinguishable from the political sphere. In relation to democracy, the first question here is whether the music played has been chosen freely, and whether people recognize and appreciate this freedom. But if different sorts of music in themselves can be perceived as having political significance, it means one may also ask whether the distinction between the political and the non-political becomes less clear: can people be involved in 'politics' in some sense just about anywhere?

Music is traditionally perceived as the most abstract of art forms despite familiar 'programme music' such as for instance Smetana's attempt at describing the Moldau and Grieg's attempt at representing Norwegian spring. And it is true that it is mostly very difficult to express verbally what a particular piece of music without lyrics 'is about', especially if it also comes without a verbally meaningful title. Based on earlier theories of musical communication and meaning (e.g. Meyer 1956; Boilès 1982), Stephen Feld maintains that a musical encounter is always a process of communication in which immediate experience and interpretation occur on the basis of previous collective as well as individual experience. Listeners are members of one or more cultural communities and yet also inextricably tied to their specific biographies as individual listeners. Musical communication is thus a very complex process that always is about an encounter between an individual and a number of social and cultural markers present in any specific musical expression or style: 'All musical sound structures are socially structured in two senses: they exist through social construction, and they acquire meaning through social interpretation' (Feld 1994: 85).

Musical structures do, however, not directly reflect social structures (in accordance with a so-called homology model, cf. Frith 1996). Even so, musical acts and experiences constitute a form of communication that, like any other, may be capable of telling us something about cultural and social conditions. In complex societies as well as in more homogenous and egalitarian ones, music and the participation in musical acts are sources of collective experiences important for, in Paul Connerton's (1989) words, 'how societies remember' (ibid.: 41). Encounters with music, in the form of public events, concerts, listening to phonograms (privately and via the media) and, not least, stories told among people about musical experiences, contribute to the constitution of collective structures of experience in society. But musical communication is not necessarily limited by existing linguistic or national communities. This is why it is so central in the establishment of a global public sphere. George Lipsitz (1990) has studied how music contributes to new forms of collective memory in global society and, in particular, in the huge metropolises of post-colonial societies that are characterised by high degrees of cultural complexity.[1] Pertinent to the question of democracy is then to place these issues in relation to public sphere theory and the anatomy of democracy suggested in theories of deliberative democracy. In such a context it is crucial that the main focus remains on what can be termed popular music in an inclusive sense (comprising for instance jazz and folk music). The reasons for this are many.

Habermas has argued (in Chapter 8 of *Theory of Communicative Action*, Vol. II) that there is a process of 'cultural impoverishment' at work in the lifeworld through the establishment of 'elitist expert cultures' in the sphere of art and aesthetics that are cut off from ordinary everyday life (Habermas [1981] 1988: 488). These institutionalized expert cultures may entail constraints and disempowerment for the general public. In a democratic perspective it is worth considering that the initially rather weakly institutionalized popular music renders possible a freedom and power for its enormous, international audience which is far greater than that which firmly institutionalized and expert-dominated art music would allow. The differences between the two fields are visible also in the sharper contradictions, the more frequent parricides and the less stable canon of popular music.[2] Since there is necessarily a degree of overlap (although not identity) between, on the one hand, a human being that has aesthetic experiences in the sphere of intimacy and in the cultural sphere and, on the other, the same human being participating in the political public sphere – one might ask what the consequences might be for democracy of the fact that popular music, in a broad sense, now is the primary frame of reference and source of experience in terms of music for most people – including the members of almost all social elites.

To one of Habermas' most important sources of theoretical inspiration, Theodor W. Adorno, the present cultural dominance of popular music would probably have signified a massive standardization and 'totalization' of public consciousness. This at least appears so if one considers his writings on the popular music of his day and age, i.e. jazz, and the culture industry in general (Adorno [1944]1972; 2002: 288–317,437–500). Habermas has acknowledged his indebtedness to Adorno's sombre perspectives on 'mass culture' and 'mass media' in his earlier works, not least in *Strukturwandel der Öffentlichkeit*. More recently, however, he has reflected critically on this perspective. In the epilogue of a new edition of *Strukturwandel* Habermas refers to the fact that the revolution in higher education had not yet commenced at the time he first wrote the book, and he furthermore acknowledges having acquired new insights into the matter after reading works by Raymond Williams and Mikhail Bakhtin. Habermas concludes that his initial assertion concerning the straightforward development from a politically active audience to an audience 'withdrawn into a bad privacy' – from reasoning to a consuming public – was too simple. 'At the time, I was too pessimistic about the resisting power and above all the critical potential of a pluralistic, internally much differentiated mass public whose cultural usages have begun to shake off the constraints of class' (1992: 438). He continues: 'In conjunction with the ambivalent relaxation of the distinction between high and low culture, and the no less ambiguous "new intimacy between culture and politics", which is more complex than a mere assimilation of information to entertainment, the standards of evaluation have also changed'. This open yet not uncritical attitude to popular culture is a productive starting point for studies of expressive culture in general and not least music's role within and in relation to the political public sphere.

Expressive culture and deliberative democracy
Looking back at the post the Second World War period in the Western world, the period between the mid-60s and the mid-70s seems particularly ripe with interesting evidence of music's intricate involvement in processes of socio-cultural and political change. These were the years of the United States civil rights movement and African American liberation, of student and general youth rebellion, of a new feminist movement capable of winning struggles that had been going on for generations, of anti-imperialist movements capable of swinging public opinion on the war in Vietnam and other issues, of ecological movements capable of altering the agendas of all political parties (at least in Western Europe) within less than the first ten years after the publication of Rachel Carson's *Silent Spring* in 1963.

In all of this, music was an integrated force. From the singing of 'We shall overcome' in the marches of the civil rights movement to the festival at Woodstock, from Miriam Makeba to Bob Marley, from John Lennon to Miles Davis and so on and so forth. The variation is considerable and important to understand, but the main impression is still an overwhelming contribution to a redefinition of cultural, social and political ideas and agendas which can only be adequately assessed if one compares the overall social and political situation in 1955 to that of 1965 and 1975. What would the 'new left' in the Western world have been without Bob Dylan and his generation of non-conformist artists in a transformed field of popular music?

More specific to the issue of democracy and the functions of the public sphere is the question of how music works in the context of public discourse and the norms for rational discussions where the best argument is supposed to prevail, no matter who presents it. Is music basically an irrational phenomenon, or can it actually so to speak enhance rationality? Again, this is partly an empirical question. But it is evidently also a question of what is meant by 'rational' and 'discussion'. In fact, the concept of 'rationality' is, in and by itself, deeply problematic. It covers too much: It obscures the difference between the more or less cynical instrumental rationality characteristic of techno- and bureaucracies and a self-reflexive, hermeneutic practice based also in a sensitivity to, not least, nature inside and outside of human beings. If anything affective or emotional is supposed to be alien to rationality, then music is out, and if anything argumentative, anything related to *logos* in the sense of rhetorical theory, is left out of our understanding of music, then music is irrelevant to public discourse. But there are in fact affective and even emotional dimensions to any sustainable concept of rationality, and there are likewise logos-elements in music.

Even so, this has consequences for where music as a form of expression is located in the public sphere. In his presentation at the seminar organized in his honour as recipient of the 2005 Holberg Prize at the University of Bergen, Habermas introduced a distinction between a 'wild' and a 'serious' part of the public sphere (cf. his 'Religion in the Public Sphere', to be downloaded at http://www.holbergprize.no). His point was that the real existing public sphere is a space where anyone can speak in whichever way they like, using for instance religious imagery and religious motivations for this or that political measure. More or less complete openness to any rhetorical ploy is necessary here so that all sorts of experiences can be heard and taken account of by those who actually make political decisions. In Parliamentary assemblies, in courts and government offices, however, argumentation must be secular in order to achieve the necessary neutrality in relation to the different religious faiths and the opinions on religious matters held by atheists and agnostics.

Music and the other arts belongs almost exclusively in the 'wild' part of the public sphere, i.e. in the phases of political processes that come before the issues end up in Parliamentary decisions, courts and government offices. Music conveys ideas as well as feelings with political relevance. Even if it is often difficult to tell what it more precisely says, military marches and bebop jazz, even if played on the same instruments, carry very different sets of connotations. Music is, moreover, a part of so many composite texts (radio programmes, movies, TV talk shows and even news programmes, etc.) it may well illustrate how difficult and maybe impossible it has become to point out clear borderlines between the 'cultural' and the 'political' public sphere.

At the ICA conference in Dresden in June, 2006, Habermas talked about the ways in which democratic deliberation can be said to take place in today's 'media society', i.e. the relations between normative theories of democracy and the real existing democracies (the transcript is available at http://www.icahdq.org/Speech_by_Habermas.pdf). He underlined that 'the deliberative model of democracy is more interested in the epistemic function of discourse and negotiation than in rational choice or political ethos' (4), the latter two referring to social choice and republican models respectively. 'Here, the cooperative search of deliberating citizens for solutions to political problems takes the place of the preference-aggregation of private citizens or the collective self-determination of an ethically integrated nation' (ibid.). Deliberation is, in Habermas' view, a 'demanding form of communication', but it actually 'grows out of inconspicuous daily routines of asking for and giving reasons'.

The overall function of deliberation is to ensure that political decisions and actions are rationally motivated, i.e. properly based in tried-out reasons that are accepted by at least significant parts of the public. Public deliberation is also to enhance the formation of what Habermas calls 'considered political opinion' as opposed to spontaneous, not-properly thought through ones that may be registered in opinion polls. Political deliberation has, as shown in many experimental studies, a particular cognitive potential in that it leads to changes of opinion based in higher levels of information and broader perspectives and so changes tend to be unidirectional rather than polarized (cf. e.g. Fishkin 1995).

Public deliberation in today's media constituted public sphere has several shortcomings compared to the defining features of (ideal) deliberation. It lacks face-to-face interaction between participants in a shared practice of collective decision-making; it lacks reciprocity between speakers and addressees; its dynamics are driven by the power of media to select and shape the presentation of messages; and social and political power is used strategically to influence agendas as well as the triggering and and framing of issues (Habermas 2006: 9). But Habermas immediately adds that neither the detachment of opinions from decisions nor the asymmetric relations between actors and audiences in mediated communication hinders that the model of deliberative politics is applicable:

> Mediated political communication need not fit the pattern of fully fledged deliberation. Political communication, circulating from the bottom up and the top down throughout a multilevel system (from everyday talk in civil society, through public discourse and mediated communication in weak publics, to the institutionalised discourses at the center of the political system) takes on quite different forms in different arenas. The public sphere forms the periphery of a political system and can easily facilitate deliberative legitimation processes by 'laundering' flows of political communication through a division of labor with other parts of the system (ibid.: 10).

One should not make too much out of the 'laundering' metaphor here. Habermas also underlines that the outcome is not one single, 'correct' public opinion. The main point is that public opinions are formed in a complex set of processes on several levels and in different arenas, whereby they become better informed and more clearly formulated and argued – what he calls considered public opinions (cf. Figure 1 overleaf, taken from Habermas' PowerPoint presentation).

It is again striking how Habermas manages to say so much about the public sphere without ever directly commenting on the role of television documentaries, lifestyle magazines, popular music, movies, soap operas, sit-coms, novels, musicals and stand-up comedy. In his text there are only two gestures in the direction of what I have called expressive culture – he once uses the term 'entertainment' for media content that is totally apolitical, and he once says that the late eighteenth-century establishment of an institution of art tied to a new art market was an example of how considerable institutional independence was possible in spite of the economic reliance on a market.

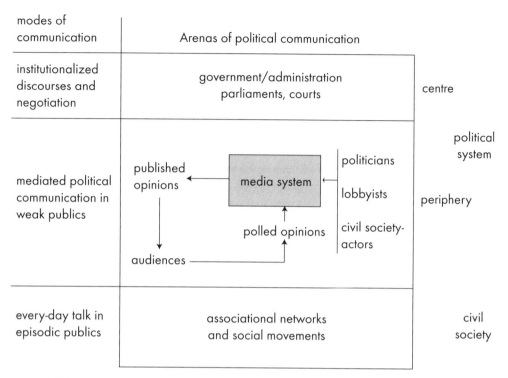

Figure 1: Public opinion model from Habermas 2006.

Still, I think Habermas here contributes to a framework for a clarification of the roles of music and other arts – whether 'serious' or 'popular' – in deliberative democracy. Art of all kinds belongs to what he in his talk about religion (cf. above) called the 'wild' part of the public sphere. In the above diagram it must be located in the lower part(s). But it is also striking that the diagram in the left-hand list of 'modes of communication' has no box/level/area where it is evident that one is supposed to locate even the most straightforwardly political of cultural products. Artworks that have Guantanamo or Abu Ghraib as their theme or a theatre play or film that critically examines corrupt practices in a political elite are most probably not what is meant by 'mediated political communication in weak publics'.

The less directly political forms of art and popular culture will still be without a place in the system of deliberative democracy. This is so in spite of the ways in which African popular music is relevant for the forming of an informed opinion in Europe on the general social situation south of the Sahara, in spite of the ways in which a play by Ibsen may inspire new thoughts about individualism and the status of women when performed in China, just as dozens and dozens of novels sustained and further developed women's rights movements all over the Western world in the 60s and 70s. A new box is clearly needed.

What the diagram and Habermas' argument otherwise demonstrate, is that there are many ways in which art can function within an overall deliberative process even if it is not about explicit and properly sustained arguments. Music as well as literature, movies, soap operas and all the rest may well contribute to the 'laundering' of 'every-day talk in episodic publics'. A further development of the theory of deliberative democracy is clearly needed in this area. It would no doubt benefit from innovative empirical studies, both of historical circumstances and developments and of contemporary situations. There is a lot of work waiting for us.

Notes

1. I am grateful to Hans Weisethaunet for referring me to these studies in the anthropology of music.
2. I am indebted to Leif Johan Larsen for this argument.

References

Adorno, Theodor W. and Horkheimer, Max ([1944]1972), *Upplysningens Dialiktikk* [*The Dialectic of Enlightenment*]. Gothenburg: Röda Bokförlaget.

Adorno, Theodor W. (2002), *Essays on Music*. Berkeley, Los Angeles, London: University of California Press.

Arendt, Hannah (1958), *The Human Condition* Chicago: University of Chicago Press.

Benhabib, Seyla (ed.) (1996), *Democracy and Difference: Contesting the Boundaries of the Political*. Princeton: Princeton University Press.

Bohman, James (1996), *Public Deliberation: Pluralism, Complexity, and Democracy*. Cambridge and London: MIT Press.

Boilès, Charles (1982), 'Processes of Musical Semiosis', *Yearbook for Traditional Music*, 14, pp. 24–44.

Calhoun, Craig (ed.) (1992), *Habermas and the Public Sphere*, Cambridge and London: MIT Press.

Connerton, Paul (1989), *How Societies Remember*. New York: Cambridge University Press.

Duvenage, Pieter (2003), *Habermas and Aesthetics: The Limits of Communicative Reason*. Cambridge: Polity Press.

Elster, Jon ([1986]1997), 'The Market and the Forum: Three Varieties of Political Theory', in J.Bohman and W. Rehg (eds), *Deliberative Democracy: Essays on Reason and Politics*. Cambridge and London: MIT Press, pp. 3–34.

Eriksen, Thomas Hylland (1994), *Små Steder – Store Spørsmål. Innføring i Sosialantropologi*. Oslo: Universitetsforlaget.

Feld, Steven and Keil, Charles (1994), *Music Grooves: Essays and Dialogues*. Chicago: The University of Chicago Press.

Fishkin, James S. (1995), *The Voice of the People: Public Opinion and Democracy*. New Haven: Yale University Press.

Fraser, Nancy (1989), *Unruly Practices*. Cambridge: Polity Press.

Fraser, Nancy (1997), *Justice Interruptus*. New York and London: Routledge.

Frith, Simon (1996), *Performing Rites*. Oxford and New York: Oxford University Press.

Gripsrud, Jostein (1981), 'La Denne vår Scene bli Flammen...' *Perspektiv og Praksis i Sosialdemokratiets Arbeiderteater 1890–1940*. Oslo: Universitetsforlaget.

Habermas, Jürgen ([1962]1989), *The Structural Transformation of the Public Sphere*. Cambridge: MIT Press.

Habermas, Jürgen (1992), 'Further Reflections on the Public Sphere', in Craig Calhoun (ed.), *Habermas and the Public Sphere*. Cambridge: MIT Press, pp. 421–60.

Habermas, Jürgen (1984), *The Theory of Communicative Action*, vols 1–2. Boston: Beacon Press.

Habermas, Jürgen (1999), *Between Facts and Norms*. Cambridge: MIT Press (3rd printing).

Habermas, Jürgen (2005), 'Religion in the Public Sphere'. Lecture presented at the Holberg Prize seminar, 29 November 2005; downloaded at http://www.holbergprisen.no/downloads/diverse/hp/hp_2005/ 2005_hp_jurgenhabermas_religioninthepublicsphere.pdf. Accessed: 10.09.06

Habermas, Jürgen (2006), 'Political Communication in Media Society – Does Democracy Still Enjoy an Epistemic Dimension? The Impact of Normative Theory on Empirical Research'. Lecture presented at the ICA annual convention at Dresden, 20 June 2006. Downloaded from http://www. exmatrikulationsamt.de/thema_14346.html. Accessed: 10.09.06

Johansen, Anders (2003), *Samtalens Tynne Tråd*. Oslo: Spartacus.

Lippman, Walter ([1922]1997)m *Public Opinion*. New York: Free Press.

Lipsitz, George (1990), *Time Passages: Collective Memory and American Popular Culture*. Minneapolis: University of Minneapolis Press.

Meyer, Leonard B. (1956), *Emotion and Meaning in Music*. Chicago: University of Chicago Press.

Schudson, Michael (1998), *The Good Citizen*. Cambridge: Harvard University Press.

Tylor, Edward B. ([1871]1974), *Primitive Culture: Researches into the Development of Mythology, Philosophy, Religion, Art, and Custom*. London: Gordon Press.

12

The European Imaginary: Media Fictions, Democracy and Cultural Identities

Ib Bondebjerg

Abstract

In his seminal book The Undeclared War (1997) David Putnam, one of the key figures behind the European film and media policy, said: 'Stories and images are among the principal means by which the human society has always transmitted values and beliefs from generation to generation and community to community [...they] are at the heart of the way we run our economies and live our lives'. This paper will analyse the 'imaginary Europe' from this perspective and look at what characterizes European television fictions and films and what the structure of the national and the European fictional space is. The European fictional space as a whole is strongly dominated by American culture. But it is a fact that just as national fictional products have formed and influenced our national and cultural identity, our understanding of European culture is also strongly linked to European fictions crossing national borders – just like the American fictions. Our Imaginary Europe is therefore a strong and sometimes forgotten cultural dimension in the European integration project and a dimension with important social, political and democratic implications for the construction of a European public sphere.

Keywords

media fiction, european film culture, media policy, national identity, cultural identity, globalization

Introduction

'Culture and social organization are universal and perennial. States and nationalisms are not' (Ernest Gellner 1997: 4).

'From the standpoint of economics there is but one viable, national cinema – Hollywood – and the world is its nation.' (Dudley Andrews 1995: 54)

What is most important for democracy, politics or culture? The answer this chapter will argue for is basically that they are of equal importance and heavily intertwined in all societies. Stories, narratives, fictions, systems of belief and the structure of everyday life are the structures cultural identities are made of, and cultural identities strongly influence the way politics and democracy work. Nations are formed by both politics and culture, and it is very difficult to imagine any living nation and democracy without the power of images and stories to hold them together. Culture is the form, the knitwear and network of both the banal culture of everyday life and the 'banal nationalism' (Billig 1995), and it is the more aggressive forms of flagged nationalism and symbolic rituals. But the chapter will go beyond this basic assumption of interconnectedness in any historically defined society between culture, politics and democracy. 'The imagined community,' Benedict Anderson (1983) talks about in his seminal book, and which he primarily connects with the print culture has now become fundamentally transnationalized both from the inside and from the outside through electronic media and migration.

In this article, the primary focus will be on the modern audio-visual media and the culture and stories they carry. But it is important to spell out from the beginning that many of the problems identified here, concerning the existence of a European imaginary and the distribution of images and narratives are not the same if we focus on other aspects of European art and culture. Europe has an ancient and well-known literary tradition and European art and architecture, just to mention two areas, are probably much more imbedded in that feeling of being European, which – despite many problems in European integration and feeling of a European common space – is there through education and individual personal experience of being a tourist in Europe. But the new world order of global communication has its own problems and logic far away from the ancient European cultural tradition.

Culture between institutions, media and everyday life

In his groundbreaking book *Modernity at Large: Cultural Dimensions of Globalization* (1996) Arjun Appadurai defines a number of concepts in globalization that contribute more clearly to a differentiated concept of globalization than the often crude denunciation of globalization as multi-national world power and homogenization. Arjun Appadurai's book is also a major inspiration if you want to understand the role of imagination in modern societies. Appadurai's argument is that the global reach of electronic media has changed the traditional local role of myths, legends and stories as rituals outside everyday life to stories and images that pervade and interact with everyday life in a much more direct way. The imaginative work of the media has developed into phenomena that enter into and potentially transform 'everyday discourse' and produce both fictional and factual stories that act as 'scripts for possible lives' (Appadurai 1996: 3).

Appadurai's notion of culture and imagination here is in line with Raymond Williams very early definition of culture as 'a whole way of life' (Williams 1988), a kind of anthropological notion of culture, stressing that the deepest layers of culture has to do with that result of cultural influence which is transformed into living experience and everyday culture and consciousness. Now culture is of course much more that this vary basic definition of culture as received, transformed and lived culture. Culture is also production and creativity, institutions and politics and in that sense culture is tied directly to both that part of the public sphere that Habermas in his first seminal work called 'the cultural sphere' (Habermas 1971) and which was related more to the private sphere and to literary forms in early eighteenth century Europe. But the cultural sphere in modern societies has developed into much a much more mediatized and public space, where cultural diversity is maintained by means of cultural policy, media policy and – particularly in Western European countries – also by public funding for cultural production.

The aim for this cultural policy and support for cultural production is normally to support and sustain the existence of a national culture, to regulate market forces for cultural diversity purposes and to regulate transnational cultural collaboration. Both levels of culture have toady been strongly integrated in the European media and cultural policy and the rising amount of money and programmes aimed at creating a European imaginary space through cinema and television. The purpose of these programmes is of course to Europeanize the three levels of culture indicated here: cultural institutions, the culture of symbolic and aesthetic forms of communication and the culture of everyday life. It is no secret that this endeavour is met with heavy resistance, not necessarily by the active elite of cultural policy and cultural production, but by the sheer existence of heavy national, cultural traditions and institutions making real transnational European collaboration difficult. The lack of a very strong link between the products and everyday culture dominating each of the European nations and the European tradition as such makes it hard to reach a pan-European audience. European audiences are in fact more national and American that they are European.

In his book on cultural globalization, Appadurai doesn't address the European dilemma in particular, but he does point to general tendencies and structures in a new global order, where the relations between centre-periphery are shifting on a global and a national level. All societies gravitate around a centre and in public sphere terms a centre is necessary for the understanding of democracy and cultural identity. The existence of global and national centres are not just products of 'evil' dominance and power-based homogenization. Defining a centre and common framework is a necessary social function of culture and democracy. But Appadurai's point is that 'the building blocks of...imagined worlds' (Appadurai 1996: 33) anchored in different national cultures are by now spreading more efficiently and faster round the globe creating a more complex relation between centre and periphery. What he aims at is a stronger tension between cultural homogenization and cultural heterogenization:

> The globalization of culture is not the same as homogenization, but globalization involves the use of a variety of instruments…that are absorbed into local political and cultural economies, only to be repatriated as heterogeneous dialogues of national sovereignty, free enterprise and fundamentalism in which the state plays an increasingly delicate role (Appadurai 1996: 42).

Appadurais notion of culture is close to the classical definition by Anderson. He sees culture as a pervasive part of human discourse which deals with the distinction between difference and group identity. He also makes a useful distinction between culture in a more low-key sense and as an ongoing social phenomenon in everyday life and what he calls 'culturalism' (Appadurai 1996: 15). Culturalism is a concept used to describe a more deliberate and organized effort to mobilize cultural differences in order to promote a specific cultural or national identity, usually on a state level or at least on a high institutional level. If we take the initiative by the present Danish government and its supporting nationalist party (Dansk Folkeparti) to create a national, cultural canon of literature, film, music, architecture, etc. and the associated reforms of the curriculum for schools in the same direction then we have a clear example of culturalism with a very specific 'ethnic' anchoring. It is furthermore directly and often aggressively aimed at a cleansing of the invasion of global, multicultural elements in Danish national culture.

Also some of the elements of the EU cultural policy to create a 'European, cultural identity' could be called culturalism, even though the very foundation of EU cultural politics is defined as aiming towards 'cultural diversity'. The aim of a transnational cultural policy in the era of globalization and multicultural developments must be to avoid a too narrow and ethnic understanding of European culture. Just as Appadurai wants to install a more complex understanding of culture and the imaginary in a global world, Habermas has actually, in one of his later works, *Between Facts and Norms: Contributions to a Discourse Theory of Law and Democracy* (1996, original version 1992), indicated an understanding of the public sphere as a more complex network of public spheres. The more simple model from 1962, historically situated in a still very national and rather non-mediated society, is replaced by a model where sub-spheres link up to different sectors of society and to national, local and global levels of the public. The public sphere is no longer just situated and defined in a rather homogeneous sense, but differentiated along axes of time, place, culture, the private, politics, etc. – just as audiences today exist both in relation to a main centre and to other sub-centres. Turks living in Denmark for instance are both linked up to the Danish public sphere and media system and to their own original homeland by satellite, just as they most likely belong to different local cultures. Appadurai's way of addressing the same changes in modern, mediatized societies is to define the building blocks in this centre-periphery, local-national-global nexus of the cultural and imaginary. Although he is not dismissing the national and global centre forces in both politics, media and culture he does nevertheless foresee a 'post-national imaginary' and the development of a more 'diasporic public sphere' (Appadurai 1996: 21).

The simple fact that electronic media today allows much more free exchange of culture across national borders is the first indication of a potentially more strong and diverse globalization of the imaginary. But as we already know, these global flows favour certain expressions and cultures over other. However whereas film and television were imbedded in media systems and technologies that were not available for all then the Internet has a much stronger potential for creating a global public sphere with different national and local levels and sub-spheres. In a European context it could be said that national cultures and media are clearly integrated in both a national system, a European system and a global system and in each of these overlapping systems the imaginary is produced and distributed as an ongoing negotiation with audiences over culture and identity and as part of a political, democratic project. Culture cannot be separated from the political, democratic project.

Appadurai defines the structure of this new 'imagination as social practice' (Appadurai 1996: 31) as a combination of *ethnoscapes, technoscapes, financescapes, mediascapes* and *ideoscapes*. Technoscapes and financescapes of course refer to the global network for communication and financescape to the ever more global market for economy. Ethnoscapes on the other hand refer to the global migration landscape of travellers, tourists, refugees, exiles, guest workers, etc. (Appadurai 1996: 33) and points towards the extremely visible change in otherwise ethnically and culturally very homogenous societies of most European countries. No matter what the attitude and reactions in these countries are to these multicultural developments, and no matter what official policies have been adopted to deal with the 'problem', it is a fact that the ethnoscape of the European Union has changed dramatically over the last decades.

The same can be said about the mediascapes and ideoscapes, which Appadurai defines as both the media-distribution facilities in a given area, the world of images and information created, by these media and the relation between media and audiences:

> What is important about these mediascapes is that they provide...large and complex repertoires of images, narratives and ethnoscapes to viewers throughout the world, in which the world of commodities and the world of news and politics are profoundly mixed. (Appadurai 1996: 35)

Just how and to what a degree these global or national images and narratives influence the imagination and hence the imagined communities of the world is a complicated matter to determine. But it is pretty obvious that migrations from the underdeveloped to developed countries have been influenced by the global transmission of Western images and lifestyles imbedded to a large degree in American and European film and television fiction.

We know narrative fictions have played an important role in the building of imagined, national communities, and of course they also play an important role in the transformed ethnoscapes of a more globalized world. They act, as Appadurai points out in many places in his book, as potential scripts that can be transformed into imagined other lives and can fuel national and global images of a more multicultural world. As we shall see later on, even the traditional national space of European nations with a strong national homogeneity and a clear public sphere centre, has been clearly transformed as a symptom of changes and conflicts in what used to be the self-evident and imagined national community. As Appadurai expresses it: 'there is a battle of the imagination' (Appadurai 1996: 39).

A cosmopolitan Europe?

Culture Matters, is the title of a recent anthology edited by Lawrence Harrison and Samuel P. Huntington (Harrison and Huntington 2000) and the underlying assumption behind the book is that values and culture play an important role in human progress. In the book they look at, for instance, the role of culture in economic development and for political development and democracy. The argument behind the book is not just the by now almost trivial fact that Western societies and democracies live in an experience economy (Pine and Gilmore 1999), and that the creative class (Florida 2002) is the new economic elite. A look at economics for information, media and entertainment certainly underlines the fact that culture and information are key economic factors in the global information economy. Mergings and takeovers in the media and communication sector and fights between global multimedia companies over both national markets, the European and the global market happen all the time – and European based global firms play an important role, although Japanese-American firms are dominant. In that sense media politics and cultural politics on a national level – and more importantly on a European level – really matters and makes a difference. The battle over information, media and culture is at the centre of both economy and politics – two forces that largely set the framework for democracy, and for the cultural dimension and cultural diversity.

The understanding of culture in Harrisons and Huntingtons book is largely anthropological in a very basic and broad sense; it is about religion vs secularism, family values and firm authority values vs individualism, the role of national pride and nationalistic outlook vs cosmopolitanism and globalism, etc. The thesis is that democracy is more developed in modern than in traditional societies (Ingelhart 2000: 80ff). In that sense the deep-rooted anthropological concept of culture plays an important role in evaluating how democracy is developed and how strong the cultural basis is for a transnational democracy and a cosmopolitan attitude towards globalization. Huntington's thesis of 'the clash of civilizations' (Huntington 1996) is controversial and much too simplistic for the understanding of a mediatized and globalized culture.

However, Huntingdon and Ingelhart's observations of the distribution of value systems (based on data from World Value Survey (Ingelhart 2000: 82)) are thought-provoking. From a European perspective he divides Europe into three zones based on the distribution of traditional and modern values: Catholic Europe, Protestant Europe and English-speaking Europe. I am sure that these fault lines still play a role in European culture in general and also for media culture.

We know that in the debate about the new constitution, traditional vs modern and religious vs secular cultural values played an important role, and that the debate about how Europe as a whole should tackle these fundamental questions is at the heart of what constitutes a European culture. But to follow Ulrich Beck in _Cosmopolitan Vision_ (2006) a European Union or European Federal State based on traditional and religious values and a narrow cultural understanding of a European culture would be a grave mistake in a mediated, globalized world. Beck talks of the already existing cultural reality of Europe as a 'Europe of diversity' and of a 'cosmopolitan state' (Beck 2006: 176). Perhaps in accordance with not least Castells' theories of the network society (Castells 1996) it would be more appropiate to talk of the political Europe as a kind of network state and to talk about a European culture and public sphere not in the singular but as a 'unity of diversity' and a network of Europeanized national public spheres.

This certainly doesn't point in the direction of Europe as a traditionally organized super-nation-state or a Europe of sharply divided national cultures. No areas of culture, economy, media, politics, etc. today are untouched by ongoing and ever deeper European integration. Europe is already in our heads and our everyday culture, though many citizens may not accept it or see it. The right-wing, nationalistic radicalism in many European countries is the proof that Europeanization and globalization has taken place and is creating a counter-reaction. So in fact we have a contradictory development with deep European integration of more than 50 per cent of all important political and cultural areas, and at the same time deep sceptical attitudes and ideological separation from the EU project. But more than ever it is also time to remember that culture matters. As Beck points out, a United States of America cannot be seen as a viable model for a 'United States of Europe'.

Europe can never be constructed from above and from scratch, because Europe is not just the home of many national and ethnic cultures like the United States, but also a continent with a very long and violent history of fighting between nations, religions and cultures. A European culture and transnational state can only be established through a framework that allows a slow Europeanization among these different nations and cultures:

> Europe can be realized only as the cosmopolitan unity of the recognition and reconciliation of many national and regional histories, or not at all. Cosmopolitan Europe does not mean the extinction or dissolution of nations...On the contrary, it means that the principles of national, cultural, ethnic and religious toleration are institutionally anchored, preserved and guaranteed. (Beck 2006: 176)

Concerning the question of national cultures it is important to note what Gellner said in 1997 (quoted at the beginning of this article), namely that culture and social organization is perennial, nations are not. This of course means that national cultures in their splendid isolation in the minds of the most nationally oriented often seem to be very specific to the nation in question, whereas in reality all cultures address more or less the same universal human themes and are also heavily influenced by other cultures with which they come in contact. Globalization has always been around, today it is only a lot faster because of global networks of communication and the enormous flow of information and culture. As a consequence of globalization and Europeanization the tendencies towards cosmopolitan visions in culture and politics are met with strong nationalistic and traditionalistic counter attacks.

The power of images and stories: Cinema and TV as nation building
It is characteristic for researchers like Huntington and Ingelhart that both the question of democracy and the question of culture are treated with reference to quantitative survey data

only and therefore without regard to the role of media for culture and democracy. Culture is isolated from one of the most powerful dimensions of cultural integration and cultural production: the world of mediated stories and fiction. But it is a fact worth noting that last year the EU and the individual member states in the film industry alone put 1.5 billion Euros into 700 European films, a production almost twice as big as the total Hollywood production (Putnam 2006). And yet, the polemic Dudley Andrew quotation at the beginning of this article is more true than ever: economically there is only one film nation, the United States, and the world is its nation. For almost 75 years, since the beginning of sound film, American films have dominated Europe with about 70 per cent of films originating there.

In the silent era the opposite was true, as David Puttnam, one of EU's most high-rainged advisors, has recently reminded us (Puttnam 2006: 16): in those days European films were seen not just in their national home base, but they also had a huge audience all over Europe, and European films counted for no less than 60 per cent of the American market. But today, with small differences in the individual European nations national films have around 20–30 per cent of the market, 2–5 per cent come from other European nations and American films take up 65–70 per cent (Focus 2000: 24). If we look at television fiction, a similar picture emerges, although here we often see a much stronger dominance of national productions in prime time. According to the latest Eurofiction report (Buonanno 2000: 23) prime-time fiction in the five big countries (United Kingdom, France, Germany, Spain and Italy) showed a strong American dominance in Italy and a 50/50 situation in Spain between national and American programmes, whereas American programmes in Germany and France take up 31–35 per cent. National dominance is very strong on the other hand in United Kingdom (80 per cent) and Germany (69 per cent). But the striking fact is that in the United Kingdom, Germany and Spain there was no euro-fiction, whereas in France euro-fictions represented 18–19 per cent of the total prime-time fiction output.

The consistent pattern over many years in both areas of media fictions is thus that we seem to identify with our own national fiction, that American fiction is trans-nationally extremely popular and that fiction from other European nations very rarely reaches prime time and big audiences – with British fictions as the occasional exception. When we talk about mediated audio-visual fictions it is therefore pretty much a fact that American fiction is the franca lingua of the European Imaginary. Or to put it more precisely and provocatively: European film and TV imaginary is clearly divided into the national and the American. This is the imaginary mediated world that holds us together, whereas the European as a dominant imaginary is roughly non-existent outside the art cinema distribution and consumption system.

Why is this interesting and why bother at all studying patterns of fiction production and fiction use in a European context? The already mentioned British film producer David Puttnam has used a large part of his life developing the EU film and media policy, and he has done it based on the following hypothesis:

> Stories and images are among the principal means by which the human society has
> always transmitted values and beliefs from generation to generation and community to

community. Movies, along with all the other activities driven by stories and the images and characters that flow with them, are now at the very heart of the way we run our economies and live our lives (Puttnam 1997).

Sociological and political studies of the national and the global all too often forget the power of stories and images, of those sides of media belonging to the fictional genres. In fact all too often media as such are forgotten or underestimated. But if the media is taken into consideration in sociology and political science, it is journalism and the genres of news and factual reporting that are analysed, not fiction. But a number of studies do in fact sustain theories taking fictions seriously in the building of nations and national and cultural identities. In the book *Försvenskningen av Sverige – Det Nationellas Förvandlingar* ('The swedification of Sweden', 1993, Ehn et. al), Orvar Löfgren has argued that both Swedish Radio with its daily news broadcasts and the development of a national public service television system has helped create a Swedish national imaginary community. News and fictional programmes opened the nation to the outside, but also very strongly created a sense of national identity, a hegemonization of culture and news through national programmes that were available to and heard and seen by a large majority. The creation of the modern post-war Scandinavian welfare state had the media and not least the national fiction as an important, integrated part.

In his study of English Broadcasting history, *Radio Television and Modern Life* (1996) and *A Social History of Broadcasting* (1991) Paddy Scannell takes the same ethnographic cultural approach in his understanding of how British broadcast media helped create not just a politically oriented public sphere, but also through long-running fictional television serials created a mediated, national cultural space, a space of Britishness that reflected everyday life and national history. Scannell's work emphasizes the importance of the anthropological aspects of culture, the focus on how the imaginary world of fiction and the more factual world of news and documentaries actually influence the mentality of a nation. Scannell's work has a strong focus on the national imaginary and the construction of the modern nation state. But it is equally important to be aware of the phenomenology and everyday culture aspects of the images of globalization and multiculturalism through the media.

The imaginary and mediated Dane

We have two very famous Danish examples of how national media fictions have helped shape Danish cultural identity, everyday life and have also given a sense of historical development and a common background – in fact a mediated form of nation building. From 1978–81 a 24-part long serial called *Matador* kept almost all Danes in front of television for the first time – the highest rating ever measured for a national fiction program. The story is a tale of Danish history seen from the perspective of a provincial town from 1930–47 and with all classes and types of people represented. It is a story of new classes rising and the modernization and democratization of Denmark. It has been broadcast five times (last in 2006) still with a huge audience from all generations. And since the first broadcast it has also been a huge selling success on video and DVD. By now all Danes must know this piece of historical television fiction by heart; it has simply developed into an imaginary signifier of Danish national and cultural identity (Bondebjerg 1993). The strength of the narrative is the precise way in which a provincial micro-cosmos manages to reflect national history and the way in which a comic tone is combined with a social and realist vision of history in both everyday life and the larger-scale political, social and economic history. It is a powerful imaginative piece of media fiction illustrating what Benedict Anderson means by nation as an imagined community (Anderson 1991) and also illustrating what Michael Billig conceptualizes as banal nationalism. It is not a nationalistic story and narrative in any sense, it is just permeated with signs of Danishness in manners, language, scenery and mentality.

In his book on *Nations and Nationalism* (1983) Gellner defines the concept of nation as two men sharing the same culture, the same meaning system of ideas and the same signs and associations and ways of behaving and communicating. He adds to this that these two men must of course recognize each other as belonging to the same nation (Gellner 1983: 7, quoted from Hjort 2000: 104f). It would be easy to point out that persons living in Denmark do not belong to the same nation in accordance with this definition of nations. For many years Denmark, like other European nations, has been a multicultural and multi-ethnic society. The time when one fiction serial could capture the whole population is over, and in fact Danes are living in many different media cultures. But still the national fictions capture a majority of Danes and represent a kind of safe place against globalization and Europeanization – otherwise another broadcast of a serial like *Matador* would not take place. It is also an indication of the both symbolic and real desire for national narratives that a sequel to *Matador* called *Krøniken* ('The Chronicle') was broadcast from 2004–05 with a story about the continued history of Danish culture and society from the 1950s into the modern welfare society, only barely visible in *Matador*. Despite the very different and more fragmented media culture today *Krøniken* still managed to gather the nation in front of the small screen.

In Danish film culture there is a clear national match in a series of thirteen films about *Olsen-Banden* ('The Olsen Gang') from 1968–81. Every year since 1970 the new Olsen-Banden film was the most watched film in Danish cinemas and a tremendous and repeated success on national television and on video and DVD. We are talking about films that through a comic, ironic celebration of Danishness actually manage to save a sense of national megalomania – we are a small nation, but actually the best – but at the same time making fun of national stereotypes and national symbols. The films represent a kind of Danish national identity-building in an age of Europeanization and globalization, and the little gang constantly develop grandiose plans that almost always have do to with foreign crime syndicates, the EU bureaucracy or big multi-national corporations. The narrative for a time allows the Danish audience to feel that the small nation is superior and can rule the world and teach the big ones a lesson – and do it with simple technology and ingenuity. But in the end, the brain and leader of the gang, Egon Olsen, is always back in jail. They are films about national culture and identity under pressure in a global world, and they support the Danish feeling of being superior to the rest of the world, but at the same time the films are loaded with self-irony and a loving display of national symbols as kitsch.

In one of the most lucid of these films, seen in the perspective of national, cultural identities in a Europeanizeed and globalized world, *Olsen-Banden ser Rødt* (1976), the gang literally dynamite historical, national symbols like the Royal Theatre and one of the Danish national plays, as they blow their way through the theatre to the sound of the national musical drama *Elverhøj*. The filmic trick is, of course, that by doing so they ironically undermine the national culture, but at the same time support it, as the dynamite detonations are carefully planned as an underlining of the most powerful peaks of the music. It is worth noting that in no less than two of the thirteen films the EU represents the enemy and is portrayed like a bureaucratic monster of control, technology and faceless, inhuman society. In *Olsen-Banden Deruda* (1977) the theme is the EU butter surplus and corruption and collaboration between the EU system and international money speculators, which the Olsen Gang is of course trying to clean up. In *Olsen-Banden Overgiver sig Aldrig* (1979) the critical attitude towards the EU is even more underlined as Denmark is excluded from the EU as a consequence of foul play involving both international speculators and corrupt EU bureaucrats – our national identity and integrity is above this transnational system, we are actually better off without the others!

In his book *Waving the Flag: Constructing a National Cinema in Britain* (1995)

Andrew Higson talks about the constructed national film cultures as:

> imaginary bonds which work to hold the peoples of a nation together as a community by dramatising their current fears, anxieties, conceits, pleasures and aspiration. A diverse and often antagonistic group of peoples are thus invited to recognize themselves as a singular body with a common culture, and to oppose themselves to other cultures and communities. (Higson 1995: 7)

The two cases of Danish high-profile national constructions of a cultural identity on television and in the cinema are clear examples of this, and it is also clear how this can be achieved by combining a comic and ironic discourse with a strong underlining of an enclosed, national space with a number of both direct and indirect group-signals, signals of both banal and highlighted national identity. In the case of *Olsen-Banden* it is clearly conceptualized as the underdog national identity under pressure in a Europeanized and globalized society hitting back, but done with a self-ironic twist that makes it go down more easily. One aspect of these films as national, cultural signifiers is however that they are clearly formatted in relation to both the British James Bond films and the American crime films and with numerous intertextual references to the global film culture. Both as an imaginary national signifier and in relation to the audience reception patterns in Danish film culture – and for that matter most other European film cultures – a hybridization of national, European and American cultural identities is already pretty advanced. Film and media cultures have never lived in splendid, national isolation and this fact has certainly not diminished during the last couple of decades.

In his interesting study of this phenomenom in recent British film culture, Andrew Higson (2000) notes the almost contradictory, but certainly very complex nature of the cinema experience of the average British viewer. They may certainly be defined as an English audience when watching *The Full Monty*, and as such they are clearly experiencing a 'Britishness'. But they also go together every month to see the latest American blockbuster, and in that sense American, national culture is clearly an important part of European and national cultural identities. If again we think in terms of Benedict Anderson's imagined communities, globalization since the Second World War has clearly meant the creation of a transnational cultural experience and identity on top of national and local identities.

Just like Danish film and TV culture, English film and TV culture is saturated with contradicting cultural identity signifiers. On the one hand we have a whole historical tradition of televized 'Britishness', not least through carefully culturally and socially designed long-running TV serials like *Coronation Street* and *EastEnders*. They are national responses to American serials like *Dallas* and *Dynasty* which can almost be said to function like a weekly historical barometer of British culture and everyday life, the fictional equivalent to the national news. Serials like this interpret national history in an everyday perspective and reinforce the feeling of belonging to an imagined community, and they are certainly filled with a solid underlining of all those everyday signs of 'banal nationalism' that Billig points out in his book (Billig 1995). And in the same way British films like *Four Weddings and a Funeral* (1994) or *Shakespeare in Love* (1998) symbolically express both the present time and historical notion of British culture. But as their international and European success shows, they can function both as expression and part of one specific European sub-culture and as European films. The national imaginary and the transnational and European imaginary are in fact in the last couple of decades beginning to link up in such a way that the political, social and economic network of nations and national cultures is beginning to show.

The transnational and multicultural turn of the cultural public sphere

The transnationalization of modern cinema and media culture is clearly visible as a process of internal multiculturalization in each of the European nations and as the integration into a global transnational network of media cultures of which the specific European network of nations and cultures are but one sphere of interaction. As Mette Hjort has pointed out (Hjort 2000 and 2005) the Danish cinema culture already in the early 1980s came to a significant point in which the official cultural support policy for films through the Danish Film Institute had to change its definition of a Danish film.

When one of the most international and controversial directors of modern Danish cinema, Lars von Trier, started his career in 1984 with the English language and very cosmopolitan film *Element of Crime*, the Danish Film Institute had to ask the Minister for Cultural Affairs to change the definition of a Danish film, so that it was no longer necessary for the film to be in Danish, with Danish actors and shot in Denmark, by a Danish director and a Danish main producer. By now a Danish film is just a film, which in some way can be said to benefit Danish culture, although the conflict between nationalism and cosmopolitanism still lingers on. In the recent government-initiated project defining a canonical Danishness in culture (arts, literature, design, film, etc.) the film committee decided to exclude films that were not Danish-language films and not shot in Denmark. The official discourse is thus out of tune with the actual transnational character of national cinema.

This discussion about 'home', understood as national cinema in the conservative sense of the word, and a new cosmopolitan reality of mediated cultures, can be seen in almost all European countries, although it is almost always assumed that a cosmopolitan attitude is a phenomenon linked to the global elite of business, education, the information sector and the creative industries. Nevertheless it is more and more integrated into the national media culture products – but often in a complex and internally also conflicting and contradictory form. In his discussion of national and transnational cultural identities in modern British cinema, Andrew Higson explains it in the following way:

> One the one hand, modern nations exist primarily as imagined communities. On the other, those communities actually consist of highly fragmented and widely dispersed groups of people with as many differences as similarities and with little in the sense of real physical contact with each other…The public sphere of a nation and the discourses of patriotism are thus bound up in a constant struggle to transform the facts of dispersal, variegation and homelessness into the experience of rooted community. (Higson 2000: 64)

National cinema in our Europeanized and globalized world is based on both internal and external incoherence: the global once thought to be outside the national home territory is actually already inside in both economic, political, social and cultural terms. Lars von Triers films in Denmark are examples of films already belonging to an existing, transnational European and indeed also global culture. But other films reflecting the new and more multicultural national agenda and culture could be Nicolas Winding Refns' trilogy *Pusher I–III* (1996–2005) an aggressive portrait of immigrant cultures in Copenhagen or Ole Christian Madsen's *Pizza King* (1998), which takes exactly the same perspective.

In her analysis of the development from a completely non-ethnically reflected Danish cinema to a clearly reflected and transformed multicultural cinema Mette Hjort (2005: 234ff) talks about the Pusher trilogy as the decisive cinematic move that changed the public mode of dealing with ethnicity and multiculturalism in the cultural public sphere in Denmark:

> *Pusher* and its effective history transformed the landscape of Danish cinema. It made the ethnic other salient as a source of narrative inspiration, thereby effectively giving rise to an ethnic turn in Danish filmmaking. Although stereotyping played a key role during the early moments of this ethnic turn, ultimately its role cannot be deemed insidious…At this point the cinema is one of the single most important forums in Danish society for discussions of citizenships and ethnicity. (Hjort 2005: 269)

Another model of a new transnational cinema is Susanne Bier's widely recognized films *Brødre* (2004) and *Efter Brylluppet* (2006). Rooted in a national story and milieu these films link into global conflicts and social problems that deeply question a traditional national, cultural identity. In the first film the conflict in Afghanistan is brought directly into an ordinary Danish family culture changing it forever and throwing a sharp light on the relation between nation and the global. In the second film the hopeless situation among orphans in Indian rural areas is contrasted with the rich luxury of the Danish upper class. But in a very unexpected turn of the narrative, home and abroad are connected in a surprising way. These new Danish films clearly bear witness to the cosmopolitan visions and problems now entering the national space, and as the Hjort quotation states: films can actually be extremely important claims-making art forms showing how a cultural public sphere can step in at a crucial time in national and European history, where democracy and politics seem to take an extreme right and nationalistic turn.

The cultural dimension in fact is important for a new democracy stepping out of the national boundaries. Cultural products can be both more cognitively and emotionally convincing than political debates, and in that sense culture and the cultural dimension of media are important parts of our everyday life. Culture and mediated fictions can influence and form our attitudes and norms over time, by offering imaginary scripts for our everyday life and the transformation of our once restricted national imaginary.

In her article 'Themes of Nation' (Hjort 2000) and her book *Small Nation, Global Cinema* (Hjort 2005) Mette Hjort makes some useful distinctions between two types of themes (Hjort 2000: 106): *perennial* themes which cut across historical and cultural boundaries, and *topical* themes which are highly specific to a particular historical and cultural formation. Themes of nation are most likely topical themes, but imbedded in the topical themes one might of course find perennial themes. Mette Hjort (2000: 111) furthermore talks about *mono-cultural thematization* (hyper-saturation), which means strong and systematic foregrounding of national cultural elements within a culture portrayed, and *intercultural thematization* which means national thematization through comparative national focus between two different national cultures.

The point here is that national European media cultures before 1980 were much more likely to make films with topical, national themes and with mono-cultural thematization, whereas the new European film and media culture is both much more networked on a European level and much more perennial and intercultural in its themes and forms of cultural identity. Triers, Biers and Refns films are good examples of the latter and they are all on terms with globalization in the form of globalization as an interpretation into a national context of a global and European theme. Maybe one might also point to the international breakthrough of new Danish cinema after 1995 through the Dogme95 movement and manifesto (see Hjort 2005: 34ff). The manifesto was deliberately launched as a European, political film manifesto in Paris, the home of the French New Wave cinema in the 1960s. The whole event was a symbolic attack on American blockbuster films and the traditional national and European mainstream cinema. It was global counter-attack expressed with great symbolic power from the inside of a European cultural public sphere. These developments in Danish cinema are typical for the whole of European cinemas and open up a much more complex and differentiated understanding of globalization, inside this of course the ongoing European integration and Europeanization of the individual national spaces in Europe.

Television fiction as a transnational, cultural platform

We know that American films and also TV series very often become transnational media events, either in the European national mainstream culture (for instance *Dallas*) or as cult phenomena (like David Lynch's *Twin Peaks*). These series become global formats that enter the European everyday culture where they are interpreted nationally (Katz 1986; Gripsrud 1995). But from the perspective of national and global imaginary communities, the large historical serial is perhaps a very strong and important phenomenon as we have already seen with the Danish historical serial par excellence, *Matador*. The history of the historical TV serial is actually a history of European influence on American television culture. The BBC series *The Forsyte Saga* (26 episodes, 1969–70) was originally launched on PBS channels in United States, and was hailed by mainstream producers and TV critics as a previously unseen combination of melodrama and historical narrative that filled out a gap between highbrow and lowbrow culture (Bondebjerg 1993: 287). During the late 1970s and early 1980s this lead to a whole series of 'novels for television' as the phenomenon was called. *Rich Man, Poor Man* (1976) was one of the first.

But the real media event was the broadcasting of *Roots* (eight episodes, 1977) based on Alex Haley's novel on the history of the African-American. Almost 80 per cent of all Americans watched, and they not only watched, but participated in an unprecedented form of collective renegotiation of American history. The number of articles, talk-shows and other media programs related to *Roots* is enormous, and the influence on the national imaginary of the American audience can hardly be overestimated. Following the difficult years of racial dispute in United States, during the 1960s, *Roots* has probably contributed very strongly to the gradual transformation of racial prejudice. Furthermore the serial has given the African-American population a historical identity. A very important aspect of this serial is its subsequent global success. Global success for an American TV serial is not unusual, but the unusual thing is the nature of this product.

Roots was followed by a long series of historical serials, but none with the same impact. The most influential of these is perhaps the historical portrayal of the Jewish holocaust in Marvin Chomsky's *Holocaust* (four parts, 1978). Despite numerous documentary films, history books, news articles and other factual material since 1945, it was clearly this TV serial that sent a shockwave through European audiences, and especially in Germany started a whole collective reworking of the traumas of Second World War (Bondebjerg 1993: 309ff). What the serial demonstrates is the power of fictional narratives as fuel for a global, cultural and political public sphere, the power of the imaginary in transforming both national and global agendas. Especially the impact on the German, national imaginary is interesting. On the first night of the German transmission (January 22 1979) ARD received more than 5,000 phone calls with very strong emotional reactions from the audience. The following weeks and months saw reactions from a huge audience and from all the established media commentators, and the reactions and debates clearly show that the fictional TV serial, despite criticism for being too melodramatic and too emotional, did what loads of historical and political information had not been able to do: 'it opened the locked door to memory, consciousness and personal history' (Elsaesser 1979: 272).

Commentators have described the reaction as an expression of collective psychotherapy for the German people, and the numerous live debates following each episode, extending into talk shows and programmes long after the shows, demonstrate that we are in fact dealing with a piece of transnational fiction with a tremendous power and influence on the national imaginary around the globe. Reactions in Israel and other countries were also quite strong. The German media researcher Dieter Prokop (Prokop 1981, see also Bondebjerg 1993: 311) has made a large qualitative reception study of the serial and reactions to it in Germany, and his results show a strong emotional impact on the audience.

Prokop is very critical towards the serial because of this emotional, melodramatic influence on the viewers, which he claims blocks a real cognitive change. But his study is clearly biased and underestimates the importance of emotions for cognitive reasoning (Johnson 1990). But perhaps the most important and interesting result of *Holocaust* was the German counter-narrative made by Edgar Reitz in 1984 called *Heimat*, an impressive achievement with both strong historical and documentary qualities and at the same time symbolic and artistic qualities that were directly aimed at changing the image of German history *Holocaust* had left (Bondebjerg 1993: 323ff and 2006). The serial follows the history of a small German village, Schabbach in Hunsrück, and the family Simon in three generations from 1919–82. The central feature and perspective of the serial is to look at large-scale historical events and structures through an everyday cultural perspective: to see macro-cosmos in micro-cosmos. This means that Reitz' story of German history does not focus in any detailed way on the atrocities of the Nazi years, nor does he in any detail deal with the industrialization and modernization of post-war Germany seen from a macro-historical perspective. Instead he lets us experience how these major historical events and social historical transformations influence and change everyday life in sometimes direct and sometimes very indirect ways. The point Reitz wants to make is that coming to terms with history and with even very painful events and a kind of collective feeling of guilt cannot be achieved only by a fictional top-down and mainstream kind of way. It involves a more cultural and symbolic working through of these things related to people's perhaps repressed memories:

> If we are to come to terms with the Third Reich and the crimes committed in our country, it has to be by the same means we use every day to take stock of the world we live in. We suffer from a hopeless lack of meaningfully communicated experience. One should put an end to thinking in categories in this respect, even where this terrible part of our history is concerned. As far as possible, we must work on our memories. (Reitz 1979, quoted in Elsaesser 1989: 272)

Following this strategy, which is a strategy aimed at finding a specific European aesthetic and narrative strategy, he recognizes the power of the American mainstream narrative and the global quality in combining a family case-story with a 'history from above' perspective (Bondebjerg 2006). But at the same time he argues forcefully for the need for an alternative strategy, and in doing so argues for the cultural need for narratives and stories that can express and form a European imaginary. Experience and historical imagination together with the activation of collective memory therefore seem to be the keywords in Reitz' *Heimat* project:

The difference between a scene that rings true and a scene written by commercial scriptwriters, as in *Holocaust*, is similar to that between 'experience' and 'opinion'. Opinions about events can be circulated separately, manipulated, pushed across desks, bought and sold. Experiences on the other hand, are tied to human beings and their faculty of memory, they become false or falsified when living details are replaced in effort to eliminate subjectivity and uniqueness...Authors all over the world are trying to take possession of their history, but very often find that it is torn out of their hands. The most serious act of expropriation occurs when people are deprived of their history. With *Holocaust*, the Americans have taken away our history. (Reitz 1979, quoted in Elsaesser 1989: 272)

Reitz' important point is that Europeans have to tell their own stories, and that we need to move into the everyday culture of Europeans in a modern and historical context. That Reitz' strategy for a European fiction dealing in a new way with our European imaginary was successful can be seen from the huge viewing figures it had, not only in Germany but also in other European countries. The serial gave German history a new human face and helped understand that terrible, national atrocities must also always be understood in relation to the way everyday life was experienced and developed. Reitz' serial succeeds in combining a European art cinema-television aesthetic and a mainstream narrative. In Denmark the serial was seen by 1.4 million viewers in average, the American prime-time soap *Dallas* in that same period had 1.8 million viewers. In Germany more than 54 per cent of the population watched the serial, and at the same time it raised a huge public debate on the interpretation of German history. Like the Danish *Matador*, Reitz' *Heimat* can be seen as a strong example of how European fictions to a large degree can influence the European imaginary and how culture definitely influences historical and political consciousness. At least for *Heimat* a nationally defined and produced fiction also managed to become a transnational and European media event.

The way in which *Heimat* addresses the European collective memory and history seems in line with a strategy in which regional and national forms of fiction try to counterbalance American dominance. In the early period of European co-financing of film and TV the films were often supposed to reflect a pan-European culture. The tendency is now to allow national film and TV programmes to maintain their cultural identity, and simply co-finance and improve distribution within Europe. In this way, the strength of cultural diversity in Europe is combined with improved co-financing and co-distribution. That was the way *Heimat* was produced and distributed, and co- produced European art television is at least one important model for European fiction.

Another model is of course the creation of more popular narratives, narratives that can supplement American fiction, which will, no doubt, continue to be dominant. But though American dominance will still be strong, there is no doubt that in the long run new European formats and programmes will develop as the integration of Europe continues and it gradually becomes more natural to involve the cultural dimension.

Europeanization and EU cultural policy

In an article on the early pre-EU collaboration between European countries in film-making, Tim Bergfelder (2000) stresses the importance of recognizing that European films for many years have been working from a transnational perspective, although this may not be as economically powerful as the transnational work of American cinema. This transnational cooperation, known as *Film Europe*, in the years between 1930 and 1960, focused on creating popular European film genres. Between 1949 and 1964 alone more that 1,000 European co-productions were made. But critics often ridiculed the group and saw the films as imitations of Hollywood formulas. These films were not entirely successful with a European audience. Nevertheless the historical examples of European collaboration on mainstream genre level are interesting, because both the mainstream narratives and the art cinema narratives of national European film cultures in recent decades have not travelled very well across the borders in Europe. National European films are popular in their own national territory, and together with American films they are the major players on the domestic market. But at least one film series based on European collaboration has proved successful, namely the James Bond films.

In the film culture domain, Bergfelder also points to the very early contradiction between two fundamentally different European approaches to transnational cooperation: OECC in 1960 stated that 'it was necessary to preserve national film production as a significant expression of national cultures', whereas a European Council Directive in 1961 demanded 'the abolition of all quota regulations in the member states of EEC' (Bergfelder 2000: 142). But despite the problems with pan-European collaboration and the contradictory cultural policy signals, Bergfelder sees this strategy as a 'both culturally and economically viable strategy' in the creation of a more developed European imaginary.

If we move from cinema to a more general media and cultural policy level, it is obvious that the EU already for several decades now, and increasingly so after the Maastricht Treaty of 1993, have focused on matters of culture as part of ongoing European integration. Policies to strengthen both the European film sector and the TV sector have played an increasing role. EU policy in these areas of course reflects political divisions between the European centre-left arguing for cultural support to preserve a film culture not just run by free market forces, and a non-commercial public service sector and a liberal Europe wanting to tear down national walls to create an open market. The questions concerning a European cultural space is – just like the question of a political- democratic space or a European public sphere – not just related to national oppositions, but also a question of political ideology cutting across national differences. But in cultural matters, just as in politics, national interests in EU should *not* come ahead of transnational political interests.

The cultural and media policy has clearly developed from a very instrumental, market-oriented and technological ideology up until 1987. This reflected the fact that the original Treaty of Rome defined the European project primarily as an economic project. The first official cultural program of the EU, *A Fresh Boost for Culture in the European Community* (1987) was still very instrumental in its definition of cultural policy, and in the same way the purpose of the first cultural programme for film and television, MEDIA 92, was defined as a way to secure the competitiveness of the European audio-visual industry and the need for technological innovation (Duelund 1995: 317). But after the Maastricht Treaty and the cultural article (Article 128) and especially after the programme, Culture for the European Citizen of the Year 2000, which was for the first time written with support from European artists, culture, media and art, became important in their own right, and as an important cultural dimension behind European integration, cultural diversity and national and regional cultures were suddenly a keystone of culture in Europe. The more market-oriented and instrumental concept of culture and the top-down policy for the creation of pan-European institutions and a pan-European culture were abolished in favour of a more network-oriented concept of European culture and a more bottom-up approach to European collaboration. But despite this, the budget for culture and media is still small, compared to the astronomic figures for an area like agriculture.

Attempts to create pan-European channels and media platforms have so far not been very successful either. The EBU collaboration between European public service radio and TV stations is maybe one of the most successful and long-running collaborations for not just news exchange, but also cultural events like sports, ceremonies and the European Song Contest (Hjarvard 1995). But even though channels like Euronews and Eurosport are in operation, they do not to any large degree function as signifiers and forums for a European public sphere or as symbols of a common European culture. On the other hand, one should not underestimate a success like the Champions League in creating a European culture in a specific area. The media and film programmes of the EU do not represent massive, cultural ambitions, but can mostly be summarized as 'little investment, few results' (Casado 2006). But on the other hand, if we want to expand European collaboration in the audio-visual sector, there is no alternative to transnational framework programmes that can boost both a pan-European art cinema and mainstream cinema.

The rise of the new digital media culture may create new possibilities to set up platforms for a European public sphere. Brussels clearly wants to create frameworks for a more pervasive European cultural space and media culture and also a digitalized political space. The ambition is to create a sort of interactive, democratic space or European public sphere. In 2002 the EU launched the website for the European citizen (http://ec.europa.eu/youreurope). The website has very practical content on working, studying and living in Europe and as such can be seen as the EU equivalent to the national interactive portals in the individual, European nations. In July 2006, the e-magazine *EUobserver.com* could report that the EU Parliament had decided to start a web TV channel in 2007 mainly for factual reporting and EU news (*EUobserver.com*, 12 July 2006). Just a month earlier the same magazine could report on another initiative towards a common cultural, digital European space, *European Film Online*. The Commission has signed an agreement 'with major EU and US film, internet and telecom players to create a legal' (quoted from *EUobserver.com*, 26 May 2006) online film download system, not least to boost European films to a broader audience, not just in Europe, but through the transnational nature of the Internet, globally.

The question of a European public sphere cannot be debated and analysed without taking culture and the world of mediated fictions that form the European imaginary into consideration. Communication and culture in the broadest sense of the word is a key element in any construction and development of cultural and national/transnational identities. According to Deutsch:

> Social communication is, very broadly understood: it is akin to an all-embracing anthropological notion of culture as a way of life, an interactively sustained mode of being that integrates a given people and provides it with singularity. (Deutsch (1953/66): 96–98, quoted in Schlesinger 2000).

As Schlesinger concludes: 'Communicative integration has a key significance because it produces social closure…Nationality therefore becomes an objective function of communicative competence and belonging' (Schlesinger 2000: 20). Gellner's (Gellner 1983) *Nations and Nationalism* notion of culture also points in this direction: 'culture is "the distinctive style and communication of a given community"' (Gellner 1983: 37–38).

But the argument behind this presentation and discussion is that a European public sphere and a European cultural identity and imaginary cannot be seen as a recreation at a higher level of the national cultures and national public spheres, as a singular pan-European culture. A European public sphere in the political and democratic sense of the word must be developed by a gradual Europeanization of the national public spheres in Europe and some stronger and more trans-European institutions on top of that. And a European imaginary, the collection of mediated fictions in Europe, must benefit from the rich diversity of regional cultures in Europe. But there has to be a stronger transnational framework for this European imaginary to boost the spreading of European stories in European countries. At the same time it must be realized that Europe is not a unified culture, not even just a network of national cultures: it is also a culture that has to be open to global transformations and a multicultural world, coming both from the inside and the outside of the European space. Our 'national' cinema and television culture is already deeply globalized and Europeanized, but the consequence of this is not yet fully recognized. In our post-industrial, global information society, the media are just beginning to grasp and adapt to this situation. The forces of digitalization and the spread of the Internet will probably boost this process of the formation of transnational public spheres even more. Nationalism was a modernist-elitist project historically (Smith 2000: 47) just as the concept of a European Union and a European public sphere is often considered to be an intellectual political elite construction without popular support. But the social and cultural reality of globalization and Europeanization is beginning to transform what we have so far understood as our national cultures. In the future the triangular process of the national, the European and the global will be even more important both for political and cultural domains of the European public sphere.

References

Anderson, Benedict (1983), *Imagined Communities: Reflections on the Origin and Spread of Nationalism*. London: Verso.

Andrews, Dudley (1995), *Mist of regret: culture and sensibility in classical French film*. Princeton N.J.: University of Princeton Press.

Appadurai, Arjun (1996), *Modernity at Large: Cultural Dimensions of Globalization*. Minneapolis: University of Minneapolis Press.

Beck, Ulrich (2006), *The Cosmopolitan Vision*. Cambridge: Polity.

Bergfelder, Tim (2000), 'The Nation Vanishes: European Co-productions and Popular Genre Formulae in the 1950s and 1960s', in Mette Hjort and Scott Mackenzie (eds), *Cinema and Nation*. London: Routledge pp. 139–153

Billig, Michael (1995), *Banal Nationalism*. London: Sage.

Bondebjerg, Ib (1993), *Elektroniske Fiktioner: TV som FortællendeMmedie* [*Electronic Fictions: Television as a Narrative Medium*]. København: Borgens forlag.

Bondebjerg, Ib (2006), 'European Art Television and the American Challenge', in Højbjerg and Søndergaard (eds), *European Film and Media Culture*. Northern Lights. Film and Media Studies Yearbook, vol. 4. Copenhagen: Museum Tusculanum Press, pp. 205–237

Buonanno, Milly (ed.) (1998), *Imaginary Dreamscapes: Television Fiction in Europe*. Luton: University of Luton Press.

Buonanno, Milly (ed.) (1999). *Shifting Landscapes: Television Fiction in Europe*. Luton: University of Luton Press.

Buonanno, Milly (ed.) (2000), *Continuity and Change: Television Fiction in Europe*. Luton: University of Luton Press.

Casado, Miguel Angel (2006), 'EU Media Programmes: Little Investment – Few Results', in Højbjerg and Søndergaard (eds), *European Film and Media Culture*. Northern Lights. Film and Media Studies Yearbook, vol. 4. Copenhagen: Museum Tusculanum Press, pp. 37–61.

Castells, Manuel (1996), *The Network Society*. Vol. 1–3. Oxford: Blackwell.

Collins, Richard (2002), *Media and Identity in Contemporary Europe: Consequences of Global Convergence*. Bristol: Intellect Books.

Deutsch, K. W. (1953), *Nationalism and Social Communication: An Inquiry into the Foundations of Nationalism*. Cambridge: MIT Press.

Duelund, Peter (1995), *Den Danske Kulturmodel*. København: Forlaget Klim.

Dyer, Richard and Vincendeau, Ginette (eds) (1992), *Popular European Cinema*. London: Routledge.

Ehn, Billy, et. al. (1993), *Försvenskningen av Sverige – det Nationellas Förvandlingar*. Stockholm: Natur och Kultur.

Elsaesser, Thomas (1989), *New German Cinema: A history*. London: Macmillan.

Everett, Wendy (ed.) (2005), *European Identity in Cinema*. Bristol: Intellect Books.

Finney, Angus (1996), *The State of European Cinema*. London: Cassell.

Florida, Richard (2002), *The Rise of the Creative Class*. New York: Basic Books.

Focus 2000: World Film Market Trends. Cannes: European Audiovisual Observatory.

Gellner, Ernst (1983), *Nations and Nationalism*. Oxford: Blackwell.

Gripsrud, Jostein (1995), *Dynasty Years: Hollywood Television and Critical Studies*. London: Routledge.

Habermas, Jürgen (1996), *Between Facts and Norms: Contributions to a Discourse Theory of Law and Democracy*. London: Polity Press.

Habermas, Jürgen (1971), *Borgerlig Offentlighet*. Oslo: Gyldendal.

Harrison, Lawrence E. and Huntington, Samuel P. (eds) (2000), *Culture Matters: How Values Shape Human Progress*. New York: Basic Books.

Hedetoft, Ulf (2000), 'Contemporary Cinema: Between Cultural Globalisation and National Interpretation', in Mette Hjort and Scott Mackenzie (eds), *Cinema and Nation*. London: Routledge, pp. 278–298

Higson, Andrew (1995), *Waving the Flag: Constructing a National Cinema*. Oxford: Clarendon Press.

Higson, Andrew (2000), 'The Limiting Imagination of National Cinema', in Mette Hjort and Scott Mackenzie (eds), *Cinema and Nation*. London: Routledge, pp. 63–75

Hjarvard, Stig (1995), *Internationale tv-nyheder*. København: Akademisk forlag.

Hjort, Mette (2005), *Small Nation, Global Cinema. The New Danish Cinema*. Minneapolis: University of Minneapolis Press.

Hjort, Mette (2000), 'Themes of Nation', in Mette Hjort and Scott Mackenzie (eds), *Cinema and Nation*. London: Routledge, pp. 103–119

Hjort, Mette and Mackenzie, Scott (eds) (2000): *Cinema and Nation*. London: Routledge.

Huntington, Samuel P. (1996), *The Clash of Civilizations and the Remaking of World Order*. New York: Touchstone, Simon and Schuster.

Ingelhart, Ronald (2000), 'Culture and Democracy', in Lawrence E. Harrison and Samuel P. Huntington (eds), *Culture Matters: How Values Shape Human Progress*. New York: Basic Books.

Johnson, Mark (1990), *The Body in the Mind: The Bodily Basis of Meaning, Imagination and Reason*. Chicago: University of Chicago Press.

Katz, Elihu and Liebes, Tamar (1986), 'Patterns of Involvement in Television Fiction', *European Journal of Communication*, 2, pp. 151–171.

Kelly, Mary, Mazzoleni, Gianpietro and McQuail, Dennis (eds) (2004), *The Media in Europe*. London: Sage.

Media with a Purpose: Public Service Broadcasting in the Digital Era. Report from the EBU Digital Strategy Group (2003).

Nowell-Smith, Geoffrey and Ricci, Steven (eds) (1998), *Hollywood & Europe: Economics, Culture, National Identity 1945–95*. London: BFI.

Pine, Joseph B. and Gilmore, James H. (1999), *The Experience Economy: Work is Theatre & Every Business a Stage*. Cambridge: Harvard Business School Press.

Prokop, Dieter (1981), *Medien-Wirkungen*. Frankfurt: Suhrkamp.

Puttnam, David (1997), *Undeclared War: The Struggle for Control over the World's Film Industry*. London: Harper Collins.

Scannell, Paddy (1991), *A Social History of British Broadcasting: 1922–39 – Serving the Nation*. London: Blackwell.

Scannell, Paddy (1996), *Radio, TV and Modern Life*. London: Blackwell.

Schlesinger, Philip (2000), 'The Sociological Scope of "National Cinema"', in Mette Hjort and Scott Mackenzie (eds): *Cinema and Nation*. London: Routledge, pp. 19–32

Smith, Anthony (2000), 'Images of the Nation: Cinema, Art and National Identity', in Mette Hjort and Scott Mackenzie (eds), *Cinema and Nation*. London: Routledge, pp. 45–61

Wayne, Mike (2002), *The Politics of Contemporary European Cinema*. Bristol: Intellect Books.

Williams, Raymond (1988), *Keywords*. London: Fontana Press.

13

Writing the New European identities? The Case of the European Cultural Journal *Eurozine*

Tessa Hauswedell

Abstract

The discursive formation of European identity is supposed to take place within the context of the European public sphere through the exchange of arguments, debates and ideas on a transnational scale. The gradual convergence and deepening of the public sphere, it is alleged, will also serve to deepen the still undefined sense of European identity. This article investigates the theoretical assumptions on which the link between identity formation and the public sphere is based, and argues that in current approaches to European identity, civic and political aspects of identity formation have been unduly emphasized. The article introduces European cultural journals as an under-recognized area of research, specifically here the example of the internet journal Eurozine. It is argued that publications such as Eurozine can acknowledge and incorporate issues of European history and memory, which are pertinent vectors in the shaping of the emerging European identity.

Keywords

European identity, cultural journals, European public sphere, memory

Introduction

The concept of European identity has especially since the end of the Cold War emerged as a dominant explanatory idiom for social, cultural and political developments in the European landscape. What exactly this identity is meant to connote, however, can not be satisfactorily pinpointed. Rather, it has in numerous discussions been declared as an essentially empty and ideological construct, and consequently as irrelevant to a real understanding of European integration processes. Nonetheless, debates about it have proved surprisingly abundant and resilient, even where these discussions time and again conclude that in fact 'European identity doesn't really exist'.

Invariably, the question of European identity is tied also to discussions about the European public sphere. Although the public sphere is today an extremely pervasive framework that is being utilized to account for ongoing media developments and democratization processes in countries stretching as far as China, Iraq and Iran (Lynch 2003; Eickelman 2003; Secor 2005), it is in Europe that the concept has been most extensively employed in order to illuminate and highlight problems of European integration. Disagreement exists as to whether the European public sphere is merely a normative construct, or whether it can be used to accurately describe ongoing processes of convergence in the European media sphere. What the actual purpose of this European public sphere is, and which functions it could or should fulfil, is also contested. Several academic debates link the European public sphere to questions of political legitimacy in the European Union. In this article however, the link between the European public sphere and its role in European identity formation will be further explored. This theoretical framework will then be applied to cultural journals as a possible object of further research on discursive identity formation within the public sphere.

The article is structured in three parts. First, European cultural journals will be introduced as an object of research on articulations about 'European identity' within the framework of the European public sphere. The second part will endeavour to explain why the European public sphere has become such a popular and dominant framework for discussing European identity. The reasons behind this, this paper will argue, lie in an existing hesitancy to debate matters as tricky and potentially problematic as identity outside the 'safe' context of critical and rational debate that the European public sphere provides. One bone of contention, which will be discussed in this chapter, is whether European identity should only encompass the formulation of civic rights and duties, akin to Habermas's concept of 'constitutional patriotism', or whether it should relate also to questions of European norms and values. As I will argue, those types of identity expression which stress civic, politically progressive norms are considered more valid than historical and cultural vectors, for reasons which I discuss. The final part will contend that a resonant sense of European identity depends on an affective narrativization that includes aspects of European history and memory. What this entails will be exemplified through the example of the current discussions relating to these topics in the internet journal *Eurozine*.

Situating cultural journals

What follows is a cursory discussion that aims to situate journals in their current context: what is the role of these journals, what are the obstacles under which they operate; what aspects diminishes their efficacy within the public sphere, and what kind of possibilities do they harbour in spite of them? First, a short historical digression is expedient at this point in order to explain the initial connection between journals and the public sphere. Habermas, in his account of the rise of the 'original' public sphere in France, Germany and Britain of the eighteenth century, has referred to the role of these periodicals and journals as one of the pivotal mediums for the formation of the public sphere (Habermas 1989). As a vital part of the emerging print media in the eighteenth century, they are depicted as the 'medium *par excellence* of the Enlightenment' (Bödeker 1990: 435), and as being at the forefront of the development of the criticism and the lofty pursuit of knowledge. They are said to have pursued the notion of an 'impartial' truth based on rational critique that extended slowly into the political sphere in the eighteenth century.

In this context, journals are described as the 'nerve centres' for the transmission and spread of debate and new intellectual trends by developing a discursive style that valued the exchange and circulation of ideas and debates. They incorporated the reader by publishing for example letters to the editor, and in doing so enlivened a germinating debating culture. In terms of their intellectual legacy the editors of these journals are seen as furthering the so-named 'enlightened humanism' and 'liberal cosmopolitanism' that encompassed at least to certain European countries and that was 'open to ideas from everywhere' as Roger Darnton suggests (Darnton 2003: 19). Aspects of nation and religion – it is alleged – were disregarded in favour of providing information and news of discoveries, of book publications, art and theatre reviews, and quite simply of new ideas 'from across the map of Europe', Ann Goldgar points out (Goldgar 1995: 65).

Cultural journals and the European public sphere today

This evidently presents the ideal case scenario of journals in their role at the forefront of rational debate, of discursive interaction and exchange and of providing a progressive, 'enlightened' education to its readers. It is of course a retrospectively applied, idealized version of their role. Evidently the picture that is being drawn here bears little resemblance to the role that cultural journals inhabit within the vast media sphere of today. So how do these publications fit into the wider realm of the contemporary *European* public sphere? It is suggested here that cultural journals present an area of interest because they publish a wide range of themes which potentially touch upon a European dimension. They feature reflexive essays and articles on a broad range of cultural, literary, political or philosophical themes in which Europe can figure as a frame of reference. The publications provide a valid area of research in as far as the articles generally adopt a more long-term and reflexive view on their subject matter. This in turn makes them well-suited to take on, amongst other themes of course, developments of European integration and its impact on our sense of European identity, which will develop, if at all, only over a long stretch of time.

The extent to how pronounced the 'European' dimension in individual journals is differs of course. Some journals carry the European dimension in their title, for example the German *Merkur: Deutsche Zeitschrift für europäisches Denken* ('German Journal for European Thought', or the German edition of *Lettre internationale: Europas Kulturzeitung* ('Europe's Cultural Journal'). Others are simply entitled *Le Débat: Histoire, Politique, Société* ('The Debate: History, Politics, Society'), or *Prospect Magazine: Political and Cultural Essay and Arguments*. Noteworthy about the 'established' print journals however is that they are at once steeped in the intellectual traditions and the social and cultural conventions of their respective countries, while at the some time aspiring – in theory at least – to a 'cosmopolitan' or at least 'internationally minded' agenda, which provides an interesting field of tension in the discourse of these journals.

Journals are suited to probe the question of what kind of identity Europe can project : they address the question how or if Europe can be defined by drawing on the tools traditionally available to intellectuals: the 'invention' of a shared history and common culture, or more concretely by drawing on 'a reservoir of meanings, arguments and symbols' (Cerutti 2006: 12) that history, culture and memory provide. At the same time, they are engaged in a constant exercise of revision, self-reflection, and renegotiation of these European identities rather – rather than fixating or pinpointing them to one singular agenda, which is relevant in the context of European identities, as will be outlined further below.

These considerations aside, their weaknesses, shortcomings and the question of their diminished role must also be mentioned. The print run of even the most well known and biggest journals is a fraction of daily broadsheet and tabloid newspapers and their readership hardly consists of a cross-section of European society, but only a small, segmented part. Harder to pin down is the problematic role of the status of such 'high brow' publications, which these journals and the intellectuals who write in them represent. Here it is alleged that 'high culture' has lost its privileged position within the wider cultural realm as the regulator, or arbitrator of meaning. These reasons would explain why cultural journals do not tend to feature in empirical research on the European public sphere which by and large investigates European quality dailies or weeklies as representative of the print media.

Yet the role of the journals and of the intellectuals who write in them is not negligible. The influence of these journals on political and cultural thought is for example evident in the edited collection of essays, entitled *New French Thought: Political Philosophy* (Lilla 1994). Out of eighteen essays in this volume – which were selected as being representative of current French thought – five contributions alone are translated and reprinted from the journal *Esprit*, and a further three from *Le Débat*. Admittedly, not all journals bear such influence that the essays are being considered as representative of a country's intellectual output. Their likely potential in setting agendas and influencing debates however has been even recognized oddly enough by the American CIA, which considered cultural journals important enough to employ them as tools in the 'culture wars' (Tony Judt's term) between the United States and the Soviet Union in the late 50s and early 60s. In order to counter what was seen as dangerously prevalent communist and Stalinist affinities amongst Western intellectuals in Europe, the cultural journals *Encounter* in Britain, *Preuves* in France, *Tempo Presente* in Italy and *Der Monat* in Germany for example were secretly financed and underwritten by the North American CIA in order to generate an output of pro-Western intellectual debate.[1]

Furthermore, the late political scientist Bernhard Peters has noted that what the cultural journals lack in mass readership, they make up for in influence in debates. He concedes that initially, cultural journals 'come in with very small readerships, a questionable influence on everyday opinion, as it were, on the current public agenda, but with high respect among the educated classes and possibly a long-term influence on wider cultural developments that is very hard to assess empirically' (Peters 2004: 2). In spite of the empirical difficulties however, Peters pursued the 'hypotheses of a cultural and intellectual trickle-down effect' (6) of these journals. It is true, he wrote, that in the short run 'small and dedicated groups of cultural or intellectual aficionados do not have much immediate political or cultural impact on the broader social, cultural and political scene' (6). However, he writes that 'if we take a longer perspective' and consider 'deeper cultural changes and innovations and the development of influential public ideas' (6), cultural journals can play a role for the testing and probing of new ideas and arguments first within an – admittedly – elite readership, which eventually influence and determine the debates once they trickle into the political and societal mainstream.

British novelist and columnist Geoffrey Wheatcroft similarly maintains that not only mass circulation papers have the power to influence debates. He suggests that 'it would be perverse to argue that "power of the press" is in inverse ratio to circulation, but a case can be made that these reviews have often been more truly influential than mass newspapers, which are looked at rather than read' (Wheatcroft 2006: 6). This is not to suggest that in truth newspapers are 'not being truly read', but not to establish influence only through the parameter of the size of the print run. In some cases, daily newspapers even report on these journals: although this is an exception, rather than a larger trend throughout Europe, the German daily *Frankurter Allgemeine Zeitung*, for example pays observance to the journals' output in its *feuilleton* pages by featuring regular digests of selected cultural journals. So while journals are undoubtedly small, their writing addresses the multipliers of public opinion and meaning, such as academics or other journalists from larger newspapers who are in a position to influence and initiate debates.

The next question is then to what extent the reach of such publications can be feasibly said to reach *across* national borders, and extend to the European media sphere. There are numerous complex structural and also financial reasons why journals are today to a large extent rooted in a 'national' context, which are only briefly sketched here.[2] Abraam de Swann (Swaan 2007: 139) has pointed out that the prototype of the 'European intellectual' hardly exists anymore in a time when most intellectuals are bound to a specific institution, publishing house, or university, which are largely oriented towards a domestic environment. This 'institutionalization' of the intellectuals has contributed to a certain 'nationalization' of the intellectual production, Swaan points out. Language, and the difficulties involved in the translation of articles are one of the main reasons why many journals only reach a limited, mainly national audience. Translation costs are considerable, and therefore building up a true European readership is difficult – unless of course the writer happens to already write in English, Europe's lingua franca. Diversity of languages inevitably also raises questions of distinctive styles and specific cultural references, which do not always resonate with different audiences, yet the main point here is that translations, one of the prerequisites for textual exchange in the public sphere, is a costly and lengthy process and therefore not always economically viable for journals.

In short, cultural journals are not, simply by virtue of their cosmopolitan outlook automatically more likely to fulfil the criteria of a European public sphere, with the elements of transnational debates, dialogue, exchange of texts and authors, which this would require.Bearing these caveats in mind, the Internet has in recent years however opened up new avenues to facilitate exchange and dialogue between these journals. For example the German-language online journal *Perlentaucher* and its English-language sister publication *signandsight* collate an international weekly round-up of cultural journals. This review, which sums up the contents from the latest edition of European cultural journals in the form of a newsletter, is free to subscribers and accessible on the website.

Another Internet project which has consistently worked on promoting a European perspective is *Eurozine*, the Vienna-based network of European cultural journals which links up more than 50 partner journals and associated magazines from all over Europe. It publishes and translates entire articles from its partner journals and provides a useful overview over different debates taking place in the European countries. Both *Perlentaucher* and *Eurozine* also facilitate a European network by organizing conferences for the editors of these journals, together with newspaper editors, thus promoting more textual exchange and dialogue between them.[3] The final section will return to some examples from *Eurozine* in order to illustrate the type of texts and debates that can form part of an ongoing process of European identity formation.

European identity in the public sphere

Moving on from this general overview, the following section will provide a theoretical discussion of the framework of the European public sphere and its relevance for contemporary European identity formation. The aim here is to arrive at a more nuanced and considered framework for the relevance of these cultural journals and the type of texts and articles which they publish.

The debate around the European public sphere is usually tied to two overlapping main arguments. A large part of political science research addresses the role of the European public sphere in relation to the foundation of political legitimacy in Europe.[4] It is argued that a robust European public sphere would provide a remedy to the lack of democratic accountability and political legitimacy within the European Union. The public sphere, it is maintained, would provide the necessary 'deliberative' aspect on which European democracies depend for their legitimacy. According to this line of argument, the absence of an adequate debating and discussion space that amounts to a public sphere is considered as a decisive cause for the legitimacy – and hence democratic deficit of the European Union.

Secondly, it is contended that a functioning European public sphere would also address the weak and underdeveloped sense of European identity through the integrative processes of shared deliberation, communication and argumentation and would strengthen communal bonds and European-wide solidarity. Through the processes of debate and contestation which the public sphere thrives on, processes of identity formation are expected to take place, or in the words of the critics Eriksen and Fossum 'the binding force of words in communicative practices' (Eriksen and Fossum 2000: 2) will be able to take hold. Cathleen Kantner emphasizes for example that the development of a shared sense of identity depends on shared memory and experience that are exchanged and furthered crucially through communication processes in a public sphere (Kantner 2004: 81). Other social theorists also emphasize its relevance for identity formation. Craig Calhoun writes '[i]t is crucial to create public space within which people may engage each other in discourse – not just to make decisions, but to...make and remake their own identities' (Calhoun 1999: 228). In similar vein, Nancy Fraser notes that in her view 'public discursive arenas are among the most important and underrecognized sites in which social identities are constructed, deconstructed, and reconstructed' (Fraser 1992: 111).

As will be outlined in the following, this argumentative connection reveals on the one hand that the public sphere is bestowed with a large degree of constitutive power for the construction of identities. On the other hand however this connection also reveals some of the misgivings and reservations about identity formation processes.

Misgivings about identity formation

Expressed in a discursive context, 'identity' or specifically here European identity is implied when Europeans draw on a defined sense of 'Us' or 'We', and in doing so constitute the existence of a social community of 'Europeans'. That means that individuals relate themselves to a community to which they *feel* they belong and which they draw upon. Paul Ricoeur specifies that communal identities are made up 'to a large extent', of 'identifications with values, norms, ideals, models, and heroes, in which the person or the community recognizes itself' (Ricoeur 1992: 121). Hence, individuals identify with values, ideals that they make out and recognize as distinctively 'theirs'. Importantly, they do not only passively identify with certain values, norms and ideals but actively determine what these common values are in the first place. European identity is what Europeans define and construct as such: the values, norms and ideas that they consider to be 'European' – and those that are not. The question however that these approaches will have to take seriously at some point is: what should Europe come to stand for, to use Jan Ifversen's words, 'in a constructivist approach which involves a permanent deconstruction' (Ifversen 2004: 15) of what has been established? If identity is constantly renegotiated, constantly self-consciously observed as a process in the making, how and why can these constructions be assumed to have any bearing on our sense of identity as 'Europeans'? Social psychologists maintain here that for an identity to have any resonance, elements of recurrence and continuity as well as the possibility of providing a sense of positive self-identification must be part of this 'construction' (Breakwell and Lyons 1995: 26). Thus identity formation rests on construction, but these constructions have *real* consequences in that they can shape and alter collective and individual perceptions and self-understanding over time. It is contended here that identity formation depends on certain resources of a remembered past and on common cultural references and interpretation patterns, and not only on the positing of progressive political and civic European values as a desirable European identity.

Evidently, essentialist notions about identity play a completely marginalized role in the European context today. For example, any articulation of European identity which would invoke a primordial founding myth would be readily dismissed since what Ulrich Beck and Anthony Giddens have termed 'reflexive modernity', has make any recourse to pre-political myths to account for a collective identity unviable. Europeans are aware that they lack the foundation myths and stories to explain a common heritage and they are also aware that these myths cannot simply be created and embedded in society. After all, for every pre-political myth about a common European history, historians will be able to point to stories of divisions, wars and feuds that equally define European history. Contemporary European societies have relinquished the ability to tell, and more importantly to *believe* in myths without subjecting them to rational enquiry and critique. Relevant to note here are the intensive nation-building processes and identity-formation exercises in the nineteenth century which have been outlined most prominently by Benedict Anderson (Anderson 1991) and Eric Hobsbawm (Hobsbawm and Ranger 1983). As they point out, these processes depended on the effective dissemination of national myths and histories, made possible to a large extent through new forms of mass communication such as newspapers and literature which instilled a sense of national consciousness and awareness into the citizens of many European states. The awareness about these tricky nation-building processes, account perhaps for the wariness and considerable resistance with which attempts to construct identities on behalf of intellectuals, politicians, or institutions today are being met.

The wariness and resistance only half account however for the considerable misgivings about 'creating identities' that Europeans harbour today. Crucially, one is continually referred back to the legacy of two catastrophic twentieth-century wars and especially the 'civilizational collapse' in the form of the Holocaust which have led to a cautious and self-questioning tone about identity, in the traditional national context surely, but also with regards to *European* identity today. For example, in a newspaper editorial in the *Süddeutsche Zeitung* of January 2006, the two Swedish writers Rolf Gustavsson and Richard Schwartz urge caution towards any idea of a European myth which in their view is a dangerous idea

> because the idea of a unified Europe – a sort of United States of Europe – is based on the idea of a utopia which has to be fulfilled, and every utopia tends towards totalitarianism. Europe still has to pay off some of the mortgages that it incurred through its attempts to realize utopian visions, even though these attempts have long been compromised. Not too long ago, Hitler and Stalin were those who wanted to create a unified Europe (Gustavsson and Schwartz 2006: 11).

In this view, European identity is subject to potential misuse and exploitation on behalf of political interests. Unified identities far from creating cohesion, solidarity and cultural harmony or possibly even drawing on actual shared cultural meanings simply betray potentially dangerous utopian follies of grandeur. Not for nothing do intellectuals such as the Swiss novelist and essayist Adolf Muschg feel compelled to warily point out that 'productive self-doubt and continuous self-critique have been, and must in the future remain part of the guiding principle of European dialogue and identity formation' (Muschg 2005: 62). Despite these intellectual misgivings however, academic orthodoxy – with the exception of the most hardened functionalists probably – would concede that at least a modicum of European identity might be necessary for the durable integration of the European project.

The 'safe' zone of the public sphere

So if identity is 'somehow' necessary for European integration, how should such a potentially fraught enterprise be handled in order to avoid the negative implications that constructing identities entail? Enter the concept of the public sphere with its standards of rational and critical debate, investigation and self-critique; processes, which could then 'provide the basis for European identity as a reflexive project' (Heiskala 2001: 124). In the twenty-first century, European identity will not be created on the basis of spontaneous emotions, nor are European loyalties natural and preordained – it is the outcome of discursive debate, argumentation and agreement. If one accepts that the new form of political union that the European Union presents will be contingent on new forms of identity expression in the form of argumentative exchange, and in the light of the historical lessons that Europe has painfully undergone, it seems explicable in my view why the European public sphere is invested with so much hope in contributing to identity formation. The inbuilt 'safety measures' relating to the construction and expression of European identity in the form of rational deliberation and the ability for self-critique merit the public sphere as a desirable and valid locus for European identity that stays clear of allegedly unreflected and potentially unchecked expressions of allegiances, affinities and norms.

European identity and constructivism

Identity then is not being seen as simply 'out there', waiting to be discovered but rather something that needs to be articulated and constructed in the media sphere. According to Klaus Eder the 'production' (Eder 2001) of identities in modern societies is in fact *entirely* provided through communication that takes place within the public sphere. No longer do Europeans rely on the state or on religious authorities to generate a sense of self-recognition and understanding, but on communication staged by the media. With regard to the European case he maintains that intercultural communication will provide the platform from which a shared understanding can emerge and a (contingent) collective identity that is always aware of its own 'constructedness' can be staged and communicated. The premises from which European identity is analysed and studied today are thus; identity as expressed, communicated and staged, not pre-given and ordained; identity as contingent, discursive and preliminary, not fixed and solid, identity as expressed through communication processes and discursive practices, not as a wordless common understanding. This constructivist approach has become the 'progressive' norm because it contends that identities are subject to invention, revision and renegotiation and inherently 'contested, negotiated, contextual, contradictory' (Ifversen 2004: 15) while any suggestion of an essentialist view on identity that posits certain values, cultural traditions or characteristics as a given and primordial part of communal identity, is considered as best a sign of naivety, or worst of a retrograde parochialism.

By all means, self-critique and self-reflexivity should remain an absolutely vital part of the debate within the public sphere and in intellectual discourses. It would be foolish to propose to stop questioning the norms and values self-ascribed as 'ours', and become a bit less critical and a little more believing. Especially in the context of an intellectual production of European identity, which the cultural journals engage in, such a continuous construction and deconstruction is therefore to be expected, as noted above in reference to cultural journals' role in writing

European identities. The constructivist framework has crucially enabled the perspective of 'European identity as a process in the making' rather than presupposing fixed values and norms. Equally, the concept of the public sphere is a welcome and constructive one, since it frames the media output into a process of commenting, debating and arguing that *bears relevance* on cultural, political and social processes of European integration. Yet in the course of this, a certain type of discourse has become over-privileged as a 'valid' expression of 'European identity'.

Civic identity 'versus' cultural identity

With 'valid' are implied those discourses which also stress the constructed and perpetually provisional nature of European identity and which concentrate on politically progressive values. In recent attempts to forge out a positively defined European identity, the trend has been to separate cultural aspects which include common history, ethnicity and heritage from the civic/political ones. A civic understanding of European identity musters out political ideals of the European Union as potentially binding values for a new sense of European identity. They include the centrality of human rights, democracy, multilateralism, civil liberties and secularism; values which could be underlined through the introduction of a European citizenship.[5] The underlying concern here is that affective principles are 'irrational' and hence potentially divisive forces, as the history of European nationalisms have proved. Instead, this model proposes that positive 'civic' European values could be moulded into a sense of European identity that has – in the view of its proponents – left behind the allegedly divisive cultural and ethnic baggage of the nation states and moved on to a *legally* defined 'minimalist conception' of European identity, as termed by Eder (Eder 2001: 239).

These ideals are valuable in their own right, and are as a theoretical model certainly appealing. However, to what extent Europeans are prepared to accept such a 'minimalist', post-national conception of their identity and to espouse of cultural commonalities and historical allegiances appears questionable for reasons which have been outlined before. Firstly, they seem fairly abstract and theoretical to command a binding allegiance. Secondly, they seem too indistinguishable from the general 'Western' ideals to provide a distinct form of self-identification (Cerutti 2001: 1–31). Crucially however, they reduce or conveniently adapt 'identity' to serve as a bearer of chosen progressive political norms which are supposed to serve as a tool to politically legitimize the European Union.

Identity however does entail also questions of cultural and historical vectors, which in Europe are still pertinent and sometimes powerfully resonant. They involve questions of conflicting and differentiating memories of traumatic events; in the current European context those of the Second World War and the Holocaust and the post-war division are probably most relevant. In order for formulations of European identity to take hold, they can not only concern civic political aspects and ponder the continually invented nature of constructing identities but must delve into 'sticky' (Peters 2004: 5) components of identity formation that entail collective memories and cultural and historical interpretation patterns. Requisite to such a form of identity formation is, and here we arrive full circle at the European public sphere, the systematic 'exchange of memories' and 'reappraisal of narratives of the past and the plural reading of founding events' (Ricoeur 1995: 8) on a European scale. Ricoeur lays out the necessity for this in stark terms.

> [T]he history of Europe is cruel, wars of religion, wars of conquest, wars of extermination, subjugation of religious minorities, expulsion of reduction to slavery of religious minorities; the litany is without end. Europe is barely emerging from this nightmare. We know only too well what tendencies lead back to these horrors: the perverse recourse to a narrative identity which is devoid of the important correctives already noted, namely the examination of one's own stories and the entanglement of our stories with the stories of others. (Ricoeur 1995: 9-10)

Such a reappraisal of narratives of the past, and the examination of Europe's own stories does not mean that Europe must forever recount and atone for its past, as Ricoeur highlights in the above quote. Neither does such an approach will lead to all-encompassing answers to the question what exactly European identity denotes. Obviously European identity will not depend on any particular instantiation in which, as Brubaker has noted, we can posit or declare the sudden emergence of 'identity' as a neat and tidy end result. Instead, identities take hold – if we are prepared to accept that the European public sphere can fulfil this role – via a slow, continuous trickle in which changing perceptions 'permeate our ways of thinking and talking and making sense of the social world' (Brubakers and Cooper 2004: 16). In the complex multinational setting of contemporary Europe these will inevitably prove to be 'negotiable' and maybe even impossible to fixate. Nonetheless it must be legitimate to trace and aim to identify what these different 'stories' and historical narratives amount to. Probably it is impossible to come to a final understanding on a shared historical past, but at least it must be possible to put forward a more nuanced understanding that manages to escape an either uncritical self-celebratory tone on the great European cultural legacies and achievements nor a completely self-negating tone in which cultural and historical vectors are simply bracketed out of the equation.

Reassessing cultural journals: the example of *Eurozine*

With view to the above considerations, what role then can cultural journals play in articulating, testing and trying out new ideas and concepts as a tentative underpinning for an emerging sense of European identity? And how can they engage a sense of European identity, which would encompass the complex and contested arena of cultural and historical dimensions which the 'civic' values so conveniently sidestep? An example of this approach is outlined in this final part.

In recent years, debates have become more prevalent which touch upon the recent European history often in relation to the Second World War, the Holocaust and the subsequent post-war history with its division into Eastern and Western Europe. This current development can be partly understood as an attempt of the former Eastern European countries to reassess their own past, and to inscribe this history into the larger European framework. Frequently they touch upon discussions of national commemoration of the country's past, and the relevance thereof for a

European framework. After all, the inclusion, or – according to interpretation – the 'return' of Central/Eastern Europe into the European economic and political system, and finally in 2004 into the European Union, fundamentally altered the status quo of what had been until then primarily Western Europe. For many years however, the question to what extent Central/ Eastern Europe might change or alter Europe's perception of itself was not seriously considered. Only in the more recent past are these questions raised and expressed by these countries, and also recognized and listened to in the West. Of course these voices do not instantaneously synthesize into a new common understanding of how Europe sees it past; oftentimes, they are dissonant, sometimes antagonistic and deeply contested.

Yet with view to the necessity for a reappraisal of one's own past, a publication such as the aforementioned *Eurozine* for example, is in a position to engage with these texts which deal with questions of different forms of commemoration and memory in the individual European states, and their role in a European framework. Since *Eurozine* features such texts from its numerous partner journals, and is dedicated to translating them into the main European languages, it is in a position to publish texts which would normally not be accessible to a larger European-wide readership.

Some of the more recent examples of such texts include for example a pronounced East/West perspective, such as the article 'The Mémoire Croisée of the Shoah' (Kovács 2007) which deals with personal and social memories of the Shoah in Eastern and Western Europe. Other texts link the difficult commemoration of the communist past in Central/Eastern European directly in relation to their future in the newly emerging Europe such as 'The Geopolitics of Memory' (Zhurzhenko 2007). Other texts concentrate on a single country perspective – the national remembrance of the Second World War in Poland today, 'The Memory of World War II in Poland' (Ruchniewicz 2007), which is then discussed with view to the implications for Europe, or, to give another example, the commemoration of the Hungarian Revolution in 1956 and the (mis)perceptions surrounding it in Western Europe in the article 'Does a Civil War Mentality Exist in Hungary?' (Babarczy et al. 2007).

The point here is that *Eurozine* can become a true *forum* for expression of these different national debates and can provide a more systematic overview over the different discussions and attempts to inscribe or articulate a country's relationship to the larger European context. (http://www.eurozine.com/articles/2007-04-18-kovacs-de.html). The way in which *Eurozine* collates and systematizes these articles from its partner journals enables the readership to read them as parts of an ongoing process of dialogue and debate, which involves the question of competing and common European memories and narratives, and ultimately the question of its identity.

On such a basis, journals might be suitably placed to engage with these thick and contested aspects of 'identity', cultural and historical dimensions in a way which will not lead to a regressive and exclusionist retreat to essentialist positions on European identity. Instead, such a journal can include and acknowledge these potentially problematic cultural and historical aspects that are seen as somehow necessary but then dismissed on the grounds that they are invariably invented, irrational, or vacuous. The question of European identity also entails reaching into the conflicted realm of memory and of a – however contested – narrativization of the past. If these pools are tapped into, and if they are evoked in the public sphere with regard to divergent and possibly shared historical narratives and collective memories, a more encompassing and resonant sense of an emerging European identity might take hold.

Conclusion

This article has endeavoured to show that the dichotomy of the progressive, self-reflexive, liberal, civic attitudes on Europe and the outdated and unreflected culturally defined Europe is one that has been overstated and overdrawn. A functioning European public sphere *is* equipped to also negotiate and reflect on issues of a common historical past, common memory, on shared cultural legacies and to argue over the values and norms it wants to identity with. Rather than considering historical vectors as a threat to the new, shiny and unruffled 'post-national' European identities which are currently being idealized, this affective dimension should be an integral part of these discursive identities. For this to happen, however, it would be necessary to take seriously and consider legitimate expressions of the European identity discourse not as a mere 'strategic construction' but as an attempt – with all its possible misgivings – to write and formulate a narrative for this new political entity.

Notes

1. For a more detailed account of this see the chapter, 'Culture Wars'. In Judt, T. (2005) *Postwar: A History of Europe since 1945*. London: William Heinemann, pp. 197–226 and more extensively in Ackermann, U. (2000), *Sündenfall der Intellektuellen: Ein Deutsch-Französischer Streit von 1945 bis Heute* [*Fall of the Intellectuals: A German-French Argument from 1945 to the Current Day*]. Stuttgart: Klett-Cotta.

2. For a detailed account of these issues see: Charle, C., Schriewer. J. and Wagner, P. (eds) (2004), *Transnational Intellectual Networks: Forms of Academic Knowledge and the Search for Cultural Identities*. Frankfurt: Campus.

3. These include for example the media summits entitled 'Let's Talk European!' in Amsterdam, 4 June 2007 and in Prague, 29 June 2007 organized by *signandsight* and *Perlentaucher* (http://www.signandsight.com/service/1374.html), or the annual conference entitled 'European Meeting of Cultural Journals', organized by Eurozine (http://eurozine.com/).

4. A good overview of the current theoretical approaches can be found in Fuchs, D. (2007), 'European Identity and the Legitimacy of the European Union. Theoretical Considerations and Empirical Evidence'. Paper held at the International Garnet Conference 'The Europeans. The European Union in Search of Political Identity and Legitimacy'. University of Florence, May 25–26 2007 or also in Cerutti, F. (2006), 'Why Legitimacy and Political Identity are Connected to Each Other, Especially in the Case of the European Union'. Paper presented at the ECPR Joint Session of Workshops, Nicosia, April 2006.

5. For a discussion on European citizenship see amongst others: Delanty, G. (1995), 'Towards Post-National Citizenship', in *Inventing Europe: Idea, Identity, Reality*. London: Macmillan, pp. 156–63.

References

Ackermann, U. (2000), *Sündenfall der Intellektuellen. Ein Deutsch-Französischer Streit von 1945 bis Heute* [*Fall of the Intellectuals: A German-French Debate from 1945 to the Current Day*]. Stuttgart: Klett-Cotta.

Anderson, B. (1991), *Imagined Communities: Reflections on the Origin and Spread of Nationalism.* London: Verso.

Babarczy, E., et al. (2007), 'Does a Civil War Mentality Exist in Hungary?' At http://www.eurozine.com/articles/2007-08-30-interview-en.html. Accessed August 30 2007.

Beck, U. and Grande, E. (2004), *Das kosmopolitische Europa: Gesellschaft und Politik in der Zweiten Moderne.* Frankfurt a.M.: Suhrkamp.

Bödeker, H. (1990), 'Journals and Public Opinion: The Politicization of the German Enlightenment in the Second Half of the Eighteenth Century', in E. Hellmuth (ed.), *The Transformation of Political Culture: England and Germany in the Late Eighteenth Century.* Oxford: Oxford University Press, pp. 423–47.

Breakwell, G. and Lyons, E. (eds) (1996), *Changing European Identities: Social Psychological Analyses of Social Change.* Oxford: Butterworth-Heinemann.

Brubaker, R. and Cooper, F. (2004), 'Beyond "Identity"', *Theory and Society,* 29, 1–47.

Charle, C., Schriewer, J. and Wagner, P. (eds) (2004), *Transnational Intellectual Networks: Forms of Academic Knowledge and the Search for Cultural Identities.* Frankfurt: Campus.

Calhoun, C. (1999), 'Nationalism, Political Community and the Representation of Society or, Why Feeling at Home Is Not a Substitute Public Space', *European Journal of Social Theory,* 2: 2, pp. 217–31.

Cerutti, F. and Rudolph, E. (eds) (2001), *A Soul for Europe: on the Political and Cultural Identity of the Europeans.* Leuven: Peeters.

Cerutti, F. (2006), 'Why Legitimacy and Political Identity are Connected to Each Other, Especially in the Case of the European Union'. Paper presented at the ECPR Joint Session of Workshops, Nicosia, April 2006.

Darnton, R. (2003), *George Washington's False Teeth: An Unconventional Guide to the Eighteenth Century.* New York: Norton and Company.

Delanty, G. (1995), *Inventing Europe: Idea, Identity, Reality.* London: Macmillan.

Delanty, G. (2007), 'Peripheries and Borders in a post-Western Europe'. At http://www.eurozine.com/articles/2007-08-29-delanty-en.html. Accessed August 30 2007.

Eurozine, Partner Journals. At http://eurozine.com/journals. Accessed September 1 2007.

Esprit, Revue Internationale. At http://www.esprit.presse.fr/. Accessed September 1 2007.

Eder, K. (2001), 'Integration through Culture: The Paradox of the Search for a European Identity', in E. Klaus and B. Giesen (eds), *European Citizenship between National Legacies and Postnational Projects.* Oxford: Oxford University Press, pp. 222–69.

Eickelman, D. and Anderson J. (eds) (2003), *New Media in the Muslim World: The Emerging Public Sphere.* Bloomington: Indiana University Press.

Eriksen, E. and Fossum, J. (2000), 'Post-national Integration', in E. Eriksen and J. Fossum (eds), *Democracy in the EU: Integration through Deliberation?* London: Routledge, pp. 1–29.

Fossum, J. (2003), 'The European Union: In Search of an Identity', *European Journal of Political Theory,* 2: 3, pp. 319–40.

Fraser, N. (1992), 'Rethinking the Public Sphere', in C. Calhoun (ed.), *Habermas and the Public Sphere.* Cambridge: MIT Press, pp. 109–43.

Fuchs, D. (2007), 'European Identity and the Legitimacy of the European Union. Theoretical Considerations and Empirical Evidence'. Paper given at the International Garnet Conference 'The Europeans: The European Union in Search of Political Identity and Legitimacy'. University of Florence, May 25–26 2007.

Goldgar, A. (1995), Impolite Learning: Conduct and Community in the Republic of Letters 1680–1750. New Haven: Yale University Press.

Goodman, D. (1994), The Republic of Letters: A Cultural History of the French Enlightenment. Ithaca: Cornell University Press.

Gustavsson, R. and Schwartz, R. (2006), 'Die Unvollendete: Geduld mit Europa! ['The Unfinished Symphony: Patience with Europe!'], Süddeutsche Zeitung, January 12, p. 11.

Habermas, J. (1989), The Structural Transformation of the Public Sphere: An Inquiry into a Category of Bourgeois Society. Cambridge: MIT Press.

Heiskala, R. (2001), 'Our Time: Europe in the Age of Global Networks and Flowing Identities', in M. Kohli and M. Novak (eds), Will Europe Work? London: Routledge, pp. 111–27.

Hobsbawm. E. and Ranger, T. (eds) (1983), The Invention of Tradition. Cambridge: Cambridge University Press.

Ifversen, J. (2004), 'Europe and European Culture – A Conceptual Analysis', European Societies, 4: 1, pp. 1–26.

Judt, T. (2005), Postwar: A History of Europe since 1945. London: William Heinemann.

Kantner, C. (2004), Kein modernes Babel: Kommunikative Voraussetzungen europäischer Öffentlichkeit [No Modern Babel: Communicative Prerequisites of the European Public Sphere]. Wiesbaden: Verlag für Sozialwissenschaften, pp. 163–215.

Kohli, M. (2000), 'The Battlegrounds of European Identity', European Societies, 2: 2, pp. 113–37.

Kovács, E. (2007), 'The Mémoire Croisée of the Shoah'. At http://www.eurozine.com/articles/2006-05-22-kovacs-en.html. Accessed June 26 2007.

Lilla, M. (ed.) (1994), New French Thought: Political Philosophy. Princeton: Princeton University Press.

Lynch, M. (2003), 'Beyond the Arab Street: Iraq and the Arab Public Sphere', Politics and Society, 31, pp. 55–91.

Muschg, A. (2005), Was ist europäisch? Reden für einen gastlichen Erdteil [What is European? Speeches for a Hospitable Continent]. Munich: Beck.

Perlentaucher. At http://www.perlentaucher.de. Accessed January 15 2006.

Peters, B. (2004), 'Ach Europa: Questions about a European Public Space and Ambiguities of the European Project'. Speech given at the Seventeenth European Meeting of Cultural Journals, 'The Republic of Letters? Cultural Journals in a European Public Space'. Tallinn, Estonia, 14–17 May 2005. At http://www.eurozine.com/articles/2004-06-21-peters-en.html. Accessed December 3 2005.

Ricoeur, P. (1995), 'Reflections on a new ethos for Europe', in Philosophy and Social Criticism', 21: 5–6, pp. 3–14.

Ruchniewicz, K. (2007), 'The Memory of World War II in Poland'. At http://www.eurozine.com/articles/2007-09-05-ruchniewicz-en.html. Accessed September 5 2007.

Secor, L. (2005), 'Fugitives: Young Iranians Face a Hard-line Future', New Yorker, November 21, pp. 62–76.

Signandsight, Magazine round-up. At http://www.signandsight.com/features/1524.html. Accessed January 15 2006.

Signandsight, 'Let's Talk European!' At http://www.signandsight.com/service/1374.html. Accessed July 14 2007.

Swann de, A. (2007), 'The European Void: the Democratic Deficit as a Cultural Deficiency', in J. Fossum and P. Schlesinger (eds), *The European Union and the Public Sphere: A Communicative Space in the Making?* London: Routledge, pp. 135–54.

Trenz, H.-J. (2007), 'Quo Vadis Europe?'Quality Newspapers Struggling for European Unity', in J. Fossum and P. Schlesinger (eds), *The European Union and the Public Sphere: A Communicative Space in the Making?* London: Routledge, pp. 89–110.

Wheatcroft, G. (2006), 'Left within the Pages'. *Times Literary Supplement*, July 28, pp. 6–9.

Zhurzhenko. T. (2007), 'The Geopolitics of Memory'. At http://www.eurozine.com/articles/2007-05-10-zhurzhenko-en.html. Accessed May 5 2007.

14

INTELLECTUALS, MEDIA AND THE PUBLIC SPHERE

Peter Madsen

Abstract

Intellectuals and the public sphere are discussed under two aspects: (1) intellectuals' attitudes to the public sphere and media, (2) intellectuals' activities in the public sphere. In general relations between intellectuals and the public sphere are considered with a view of relations to media and institutions behind the media. Three themes in early articulations of opinions on the public sphere are highlighted: (1) defence of freedom of press and speech (Görres, Marx), (2) conservative critique of the public sphere (Kierkegaard, Heidegger), (3) critique of the public sphere as diversion and entertainment (Balzac, Kraus). With a focus on in particular the post-war period a number of publications are taken up as media for intellectuals, the creation of new quality newspapers is discussed in relation to the formations of a new reading public as a consequence of expansion of higher education and increase in women's participation in the labour market.

Keywords

Intellectuals, public sphere, media, entertainment, *feuilleton*, quality newspapers

> Such men have lost the last remnant of feeling, not only for philosophy, but also for religion, and have put in its place a spirit not so much of optimism as of journalism, the evil spirit that broods over the day – and the daily paper. (Friedrich Nietzsche)[1]

Introduction

To take part in discursive exchanges in the public sphere is essential to intellectuals. In so far questions concerning media and institutions that are channels for such exchanges are closely related to the role of intellectuals. The concept of the public sphere as such is implied in the concept of intellectuals. Nevertheless intellectuals and their opinions are more often than not analysed independently of questions concerning the public sphere, media and institutions. It was a main point in Jürgen Habermas' classic articulation of the structural changes in the public sphere, that the emergence of 'bourgeois' society coincided with a shift from a 'representative' public sphere as a sphere of presentation of power towards a public sphere that mediated between society and state, a public sphere in which the interests and opinions of citizens could counteract and – ideally speaking – develop towards consensus, even if the result in practice in the main was articulations of opposed interests and opinions within consensus about framing conditions. In these processes intellectuals hold a prominent position.

The concept of 'intellectuals' is, of course, fluid. Jean-Paul Sartre provided a striking formula, i.e. an intellectual is someone who interferes in matters that are none of his or her business, or – expressed in a more technical manner: a person may be professionally competent in a specific field, yet the role as an intellectual is to go beyond that field (Sartre 1972). There are no clear delimitations here; we might also say that by bringing his or her specific competence to bear in public debate the specialist takes on the role as intellectual. We do even find people that are specialist in bringing their opinion to bear in the public sphere, professional intellectuals, as it were, journalists that work as commentators or columnists. In all of these cases it is about a specific *function* in the public sphere, a function that goes beyond mere letters to the editor in newspapers, a true intellectual is an *opinion maker*. From the point of view of theories of the public sphere relations between intellectuals, media and institutions are thus of paramount interest.

Intellectuals on the Public Sphere
Defense of freedom of the press

What were the attitudes of the intellectuals towards the public sphere that was per definition their field of action? In 1814 the German publicist Joseph von Görres expressed a number of classic elements in defence of freedom of press and speech:

> What everybody desires and wants shall be expressed in the newspapers; what is depressing and troubling everybody may not remain unexpressed; there must be somebody who is obliged to speak the truth, candid, without reservation, and unfettered. For, under a good constitution the right of freedom of expression is not merely tolerated but is a basic requirement; the speaker shall be looked upon as a holy person until he forfeits his rights by his own faults and lies. Those who work against such freedom leave themselves open to the charge that the consciousness of their own great faults weighs heavily upon them; those who act justly do not shun free speech – it can in the end lead only to 'honor be to whom honor is due'; but those who are dependent on dirt and darkness certainly like secretiveness.[2]

Some 30 years later a somewhat more speculative version of the same principles were underscored in *Rheinische Zeitung*:

The free press is the ubiquitous vigilant eye of a people's soul, the embodiment of a people's faith in itself, the eloquent link that connects the individual with the state and the world, the embodied culture that transforms material struggles into intellectual struggles and idealises their crude material form. It is a people's frank confession to itself, and the redeeming power of confession is well known. It is the spiritual mirror in which a people can see itself, and self-examination is the first condition of wisdom. It is the spirit of the state, which can be delivered into every cottage, cheaper than coal gas. It is all-sided, ubiquitous, omniscient. It is the ideal world which always wells up out of the real world and flows back into it with ever greater spiritual riches and renews its soul.[3]

In his polemics against contemporary politicians Karl Marx not only stressed the principles of a free press and thus opposed censorship but also pointed to economic circumstances:

Freedom of trade, freedom of property, of conscience, of the press, of the courts, are all *species* of one and the same genus, of *freedom without any specific name*. But it is quite incorrect to forget the difference because of the unity and to go so far as to make a *particular species* the measure, the standard, the sphere of other species. This is an *intolerance* on the part of one species of freedom, which is only prepared to tolerate the existence of others if they renounce themselves and declare themselves to be its vassals...To make freedom of the press a variety of freedom of trade is a defence that kills it before defending it, for do I not abolish the freedom of a particular character if I demand that it should be free in the manner of a different character?...*The primary freedom of the press lies in not being a trade*...Of course, the press exists also as a trade, but then it is not the affair of writers, but of printers and booksellers. However, we are concerned here not with the freedom of trade of printers and booksellers, but with freedom of the press.[4]

Ideal and commerce may be at odds in spite of a common reference to freedom. In his critique of abstract liberalism Marx is among the pioneers.

Critique of the public sphere

Søren Kierkegaard was in many respects a conservative. This is particularly obvious in his critique of modernity as it is articulated in *A Literary Review*,[5] a short book he published in his own name (contrary to most of his well-known works that were published under various pseudonyms). The second section, under the headline 'The Present Age', unfolds a firm rejection of modernity, in particular the public sphere. This piece of writing was, particularly in the early part of the twentieth century, an influential contribution to social criticism.[6] Towards the end of this section Kierkegaard summarizes his diagnosis of his time:

> When the generation, which has in fact itself wanted to level, has wanted to be emancipated and to revolt, has wanted to demolish authority and thereby in the scepticism of association has itself occasioned the hopeless forest fire of abstraction, when through leveling by means of scepticism of association the generation has eliminated individualities and all the organic concretions and has substituted humanity and numerical equality among men, when the generation momentarily has entertained itself with the broad vista of abstract infinity...then the individuals have to help themselves, each one individually. (107-8)[7]

Kierkegaard's critique is aimed at epochal features: levelling, revolts, emancipation, critique of authorities are prominent features of his age, the age that in German is labelled Vormärtz, i.e. as anticipating the revolutions in 1848. Along with these features goes the principle of 'association', that is collective organization. In an organization (as well as in individual self-comprehension as member of a group) each individual may be substituted, the individual is only determined by common interests. As Kierkegaard wrote in a note in his diaries: 'The crowd is really what my polemics is aiming at...I wanted people to pay attention that they do not squander and waste their life. (I want to point its own ruin out to the crowd).'

Readers of A Literary Review have first and foremost paid attention to Kierkegaard's critique of his times, of 'our age'. The principle of association is, he wrote:

> an evasion, a dissipation, an illusion, whose dialectic is as follows: as it strengthens individuals, it vitiates them; it strengthens by numbers, by sticking together, but from the ethical point of view this is a weakening. Not until the single individual has established an ethical stance despite the whole world, not until then can there be any question of genuinely uniting...Formerly the ruler, the man of excellence, the men of prominence each had his own view; the others were so settled and unquestioning that they did not dare or could not have an opinion. Now everyone can have an opinion, but there must be a lumping together numerically in order to have it. (106)

Kirkegaard further stated that 'public opinion' is the worst, it is 'an unorganic something, an abstraction' (106). In Kierkegaard's view public opinion is brought forward by the press, and the press turns the individuals into 'the public', which is 'pure abstraction' (104), like the press itself: 'Together with the passionlessness and reflectiveness of the age, the abstraction "the press" (for a newspaper, a periodical, is not a political concretion and is an individual only in an abstract sense) gives rise to the abstraction's phantom, "the public", which is the real leveller.' (93). Kierkegaard's notion of abstraction is clearly linked to the concept of levelling, but also a much broader critique of modernity and public life: 'For the levelling really to take place, a phantom must first be raised, the spirit of levelling, a monstrous abstraction, an all-encompassing something that is nothing, a mirage – and this phantom is the public.' (90) The driving force in levelling is envy that is derived from search for equality: 'The dialectic of the present age is oriented to equality, and its most logical implementation, albeit abortive, is levelling, the negative unity of the negative mutual reciprocity of individuals.' (84)

Equality, levelling, association – press, public opinion, the public, these crucial themes in Kierkegaard's critique of modernity may be summarized as abstraction and de-individualization. The aim of the critique is to open up for a religiously oriented individual inwardness: 'the separation of the religious individual before God in the responsibility of eternity' (86), 'the separateness of individual inwardness in the religious life' (87) in 'equality before God and equality with all men' (89), i.e. true equality as opposed to social equality as it is an ideal in political discourses in the public sphere.

Kierkegaard's diagnosis of 'the present age' has again and again been read as a prophetic critique of modernity and has had its impact on a number of writers. The influential philosopher Martin Heidegger no doubt took impression from Kierkegaard's book in his discussion of what he called 'das Man', the impersonal 'they', in his main work Being and Time (Sein und Zeit) from 1929. Behind the veil of his particularly abstruse prose the contours of a well-known conservative argument and a resolute rejection of the public sphere is clear enough:

All prominence is tacitly held down...Distance, the average, levelling constitutes as the ways of being of das Man what we call 'the public' (Öffentlichkeit)...The public obscures everything and presents what it has covered over as the already known and for every man accessible...Everyone is the other and nobody is himself...Man is...dependency and Uneigenlichkeit [i.e. absence of authenticity, PM]. (Heidegger 1979: 127–8 (§27))

Heidegger's affinity to Kierkegaard is obvious; both have since appealed to many intellectuals.

Diversion: the feuilleton

Le feuilletoniste, Balzac wrote, 'vit sur les feuilles comme un ver a soie, tout en s'inquiétant, comme cet insecte, de tout ce qui file' (Balzac 1902: 188) – the contributor to the feuilleton is living like a silk worm on the pages or leaves while he – just like that insect – is anxious about everything that is moving, drawing attention, leaving a trace. The feuilleton is a small feuille, leaf or page: from the early nineteenth century the word became the denomination for a section in periodicals, Le Journal des Débat was the first to establish a similar section, where a variety of texts related to the cultural scene should attract the attention of the readers. Initially the idea was that the readers thereby should be attracted to the other sections of the newspaper – like political commentaries, but increasingly the interest to attract advertising stimulated the newspaper business' interest in the feuilleton (more on this subject in Madsen 2005). According to Balzac Paris is the home of the feuilleton:

The feuilleton is a creation that only belongs to Paris, and could not exist anywhere else. In no other country could one find such spiritual exuberance, such ridiculing in all notes (sur tous les tons), that stupid waste of treasuries of reason, these characters devoted to a state of fireworks, to a weekly line up that is immediately forgotten, and who should be faultless like the almanach, have the lightness of a dentelle, and embellish the newspapers dress with furbelows every monday. Today everything in France has its feuilleton...This lively spiritual productivity makes Paris the most entertainment seeking (*amuseuse*) metropol today, the most brilliant, the most curious ever. It is a perpetual cream. People, ideas, systems, entertainment (*plaisanteries*), literature and governments are consumed to such an extent that it would make the vessels of the Danaïds envious. (191)

Balzac is quoted here from his 'La Monographie de la Presse Parisienne' from 1843 (Balzac 1902). Its first printing was as a contribution to two volumes entitled *La Grande Ville, Nouveau Tableau de Paris, Comique, Critique et Philosophique* (ed. Paul de Lock, Balzac, Dumas, Soulié, Gozlan, Briffault, Ourliac, etc., Paris, 1844). The *feuilleton* is an urban phenomenon, it belongs to the big city. But what is it?

According to Balzac the public sphere is swollowed up by the *feuilleton*, it is turning all kinds of serious intellectual activity into material for easy entertainment, it is devoted to immediate excitement (fireworks) and is primarily concerned with popular culture of similar leanings. The *feuilleton* is ephemeral like fashion, it is about embellishment of the immediate situation, and it is soon forgotten. The *feuilleton* is in absolute opposition to serious culture. It is an early version of the culture industry.

The institutionalization of the *feuilleton* was *typographical*, it was the section below a line across the second and the third page in *Journal des Débats*. It was a space for all kinds of texts related to the public sphere and in particular, but not exclusively, the cultural sphere. At least four types of texts can be singled out: (1) notes on culture and politics, (2) reviews, (3) serialized novels, i.e. the *feuilleton*-novel, and (4) the *feuilleton* in the narrower sense, which is at stake in the present context. Serialized novels were an important part of nineteenth-century literature. The other three types of texts do all have a personal touch. This is one of the recurring themes in the debate about the *feuilleton*. Some commentators deplore it. In other cases the personal touch is just what the *feuilleton* is about. The theme here is the kind of *feuilleton* which is neither short commentaries, nor serialized novels, nor reviews in the ordinary sense. What is it then?

Thus far we can bring together some of the earlier characterizations. The *feuilleton* is a text *published in a newspaper* (or similar periodical) *for a broad audience*, if not a mass market, it is concerned with *a broad range of subjects*, primarily of a cultural character, but not excluding politics, science and social issues. It is intimately related to the big city – not only as a media phenomenon, but also when it comes to subject matter and themes treated in the *feuilleton*. And it is a kind of text that thematizes the author. The *feuilleton* is characterized by the *personal touch*. *It is about one inhabitant of the big city relating to fellow citizens by way of a modern mass medium.*

The question concerning the relation between the subjective and the objective is a general question in debates about the *feuilleton*, perhaps most poignantly discussed by Karl Kraus in his diatribe against the feuilleton 'Heine und die Folgen', 'Heine and What Followed' (Kraus 1979): 'Without Heine, no *feuilleton*' (171) – in German, that is. Heine introduced French manners of writing to the German language, and the consequence was, that 'German purpose is now ornamented with French ésprit' (170), 'Even in the style of the most modern impressionist journalism the Heinean model does not deny itself' (170–71). The issue is the relation between form and content, but at the level of imagery it is about bodies and women:

> But form, this form that is only an envelope for content, and not content itself, only clothing for the body and not the spirit's flesh, this form had to be discovered in order to appear. Heine made that discovery…[Heine] has unbuttoned the corset of the German language so much that any shop assistant can now finger her breast. The awful aspect of the scenery is the identity of these talents, they are alike just like one rotten egg resembles another. (172, 174)

Here shop assistants, rotten eggs and *feuilletonistes* are one and the same, and they are all alike. This is one of the recurrent themes in the critique of mass culture: social denigration of lower classes and critique of uniformity as opposed to the unique, represented by the intellectual or the creative artist. But there is more in Kraus' critical account of the feuilleton, where he finds a 'confusion of the spiritual and information' (175). The jounalist

> always has the largest themes and in his hands eternity can become news, but it becomes outdated just as easily. The artist articulates day, hour, minute. The occasion may be limited and determined by time and location, but the growth of his work is so much more free and boundless as it was separated from the occasion. What lives by the subject matter dies with it. What lives in language lives by language.

Real art in literature is a question of language and liberation from the occasion, the *feuilleton* is linked to the occasion and only uses language as an ornament to give it atmosphere. As a contrast to the shop assistant fingering the breast of the German language Kraus depicts true love: 'Heine always had his way with language. It never brought him to silent ecstasy. Its grace never brought him on his knees. He never followed language which does not give itself away to a profane reader's gaze so far that love might begin.' (192) Karl Kraus' oeuvre is a paradox. His aesthetics, his view of language is so far as one might imagine from journalism, but the majority of his writings were published in his weekly journal *Die Fackel*, in many respects structurally a *one man feuilleton*, replete with short notes, polemical short pieces, aphorisms, essays and occasional poems. A living and writing contradiction, and thus a magnificent witness to what has been called the age of the *feuilleton*. There is nothing new to this paradox, though. Conservative publicists in the eighteenth century like Jonathan Swift had to live with a similar dilemma: to publish a critique of publishing as such.[8]

In Horkheimer and Adorno's well-known chapter on 'Culture Industry' in *The Dialectic of Enlightenment* (1947, English translation 1996) a number of critical themes go together, among them in particular, as the title indicates, the intertwinement of economic interest and cultural products that had Balzac's as well as Marx' attention. From Marx (through Georg Lukács and thus linked to Max Weber's stress on rationalization) the theme of reification provides a conceptual frame for Horkheimer and Adorno. An affinity to (as well as influence from) Karl Kraus is further obvious in the opposition between true art and cultural industry, in this respect their version of critical theory is related to the opposition between mass and elite, although the mass in their account is so to speak a product of the culture industry rather than in and of itself a danger for an elite.

Intellectuals in the public sphere

Intellectuals like Görres, Marx, Kierkegaard, Balzac and Kraus articulated attitudes to the public sphere, the press and its institutions that since their times have been prominent, despite considerable historical changes. Freedom of press and speech still has to be defended, economic interests still interfere with the ideal aspects of publication, conservative critique of political organizations and ideals of social equality still abounds, and the nexus of entertainment and business is still exposed to critique that regards diversion as an ubiquitous evil of modern times. There are however also important changes. The opposition between elite and masses that not only was prominent in professional sociology but was widespread in all kinds of discourses in the early twentieth century has in the European context gradually been substituted by a broad democratic consensus, particularly after the Second World War.

It is in the context of this ideological and political change Habermas' historical reconsidering of the public sphere in his pathbreaking work *Strukturwandel der öffentlichkeit* belongs (1962, English translation 1991; Habermas 2006 is a recent discussion of themes related to the public sphere). During the same period substantial changes have taken place in the educational composition of European populations, what is often described as mass education represents in short a gradual transformation of 'masses' into an educated public. The result is that the public sphere in the twenty-first century relates to a quite different public compared to what was the case in earlier periods when the public in many respects was a limited educated group or was divided between a similar group and a substantially less educated 'mass'. It should be remembered, of course, that e.g. the press of the workers movement as well as popular publishing of books (and the *feuilleton* novels of the press) did reach over the gap between educated elite and less educated 'masses'. Yet the composition of the contemporary public does seem to correspond to a change in the character of European newspapers during the last decades, as I will argue at the end of this chapter.

Institutions of the public sphere are of many sorts: the book is a medium, a publishing house is an institution; a newspaper is a medium, a newspaper house is an institution. Newspaper houses and publishing houses are economic operations, intellectuals provide not only ideas and opinions they simultaneously provide raw material for the production of commodities. Public universities are institutions of a different kind, that are governed by more or less direct political decisions, yet many universities are increasingly getting involved in the economic circuits and thus to some extent governed by priorities that are derived from the market. The development of electronic media has changed the character of the public sphere, and thus the ways in which the function as intellectual may be orchestrated. From a historical point of view technological changes and changes in the balance between the various institutions and media affects the roles of intellectuals. A modern intellectual must work on being 'mediatized', preferably on the TV screen, and most efficiently by hosting a TV programme (as e.g. the German cultural historian Rüdiger Safranski). This is quite different from the role of Jean-Paul Sartre that was not least based on his magazine *Les Temps Modernes*, the role of Raymond Aron as columnist in the newspaper *Le Figaro*, Theodor W. Adorno's public appearances in radio programmes in Hessischer Rundfunk – or the philosopher Martin Heidegger's role as a university professor whose teaching attracted wide attention. From the university teacher through the magazine editor or newspaper columnist to the TV star the roles of intellectuals are manifold. Although there are obvious historical changes theses types of function are in play simultaneously.

Demands for freedom of press and speech related to a view of the public sphere as a positive factor were countered by perceptions of the public sphere as a medium for levelling and erosion of *Eigenlichkeit* (authenticity); this opposition is politically speaking often related to progressive and conservative trends respectively. Across the political spectrum a variety of critiques of entertainment, diversion and cultural industry are prominent. Yet all of these attitudes and opinions were expressed in the public sphere. Its institutions and media were used by its critics too. The enlightenment is not least remembered for the great *Encyclopédie* that Diderot and d'Alembert published, yet it was not the only such work. An encyclopedia is complicated project, though.

The typical medium for intellectuals is the magazine (if we do not think about the book), yet the newspaper is also important. In the Danish context the Brandes brothers established the magazine *Det nittende Aarhundrede* (*The Nineteenth Century*) and the newspaper *Politiken* in opposition to a press that was hostile towards their left liberal ideas. Georg Brandes' immense publicist activity reached over most of Europe ('The Good European' Nietzsche called him); he was the incarnation of an intellectual, taking up all kinds of subjects, including politics of the day, in articles to magazines and newspapers. Balzac published serialized novels in periodicals and tried his hand as publisher of a magazine; Marx was during his entire lifetime busy as a journalist; Kierkegaard published books and towards the end of his life the controversial periodical pamphlet *Øjeblikket* (*The Instant*, i.e. the critical or decisive moment); Heidegger was a classic university professor, his preferred medium of publication was the book; Karl Kraus, the indefatigable critic of what he considered to be the decay of the public sphere wrote next to all the contributions to his magazine (or pamphlet) *Die Fackel*. The central Spanish intellectual José Ortega y Gasset is another interesting example, 'an aristocrat in the public sphere', he called himself. He feared 'mass man' and was simultaneously everything else than a withdrawn intellectual, he was to the contrary a no less fatigable publicist than Georg Brandes. He established a publishing house, founded the important magazine *Revista de Occidente* (from 1923), and he wrote columns for newspapers. Another prominent example is Jean-Paul Sartre, one of the most important intellectuals in France during the first decades after the war with his magazine *Les Temps Modernes*, a magazine that also exemplifies how a number of important new periodicals came to life after the war, among the newspapers *Le Monde* was prominent (from 1944).

Just like Sartre wanted to promote a specific view of culture and politics, Perry Anderson and his group in a different historical moment developed *New Left Review* with a distinct program during the 60s. Anderson even wrote a programmatic essay on 'Components of the National

Culture' (Anderson 1968) in order to point out what he considered to be deficiencies in British intellectual life. Mid-way between magazines and newspapers the weeklies have had an important intellectual role. We are here on the way into the domain of journalism proper. Rudolf Augstein founded *Der Spiegel* in 1947 – in his own words in order to 'win the conquered Germans back for human culture'. In 1950 the first issue of *L'Observateur Politique, Économique et Littéraire* was published by a group of former resistance fighters. The weekly was turned against French colonialism and represented in general left-wing positions. In 1964 this weekly became the well-known *Le Nouvel Observateur* (after changes of name to *l'Observateur Aujourd'hui* in 1953 and *France Observateur* in 1954).

In Italy *L'Espresso* started in 1955 as a centre-left mouthpiece for modern Italy – and in opposition to the dominating Christian-Democratic party. Eugenio Scalfari became editor in 1963 and in 1976 he established the daily *la Repubblica*. Once again an example of institutionalization in the form of a medium of a specific intellectual horizon with one prominent intellectual or a number of intellectuals as driving forces. Umberto Eco has been a long-time contributor to *L'Espresso*. In Spain the daily *El País* was founded in 1976 a few months after the death of Franco. It became Spain's most important daily, it is oriented towards Europe and its leanings are centre-left. The creation of the *Independent* in England in 1986 was partly motivated by opposition to Rupert Murdoch's take-over activities that threatened freedom of the press. In 2000 60 per cent of the readers supported Labour, in 2004 39 per cent supported the Liberal Democrats and 36 per cent Labour (i.e. 75 per cent centre-left). The readers have been characterized as 'politically moderate, liberal, quite well educated...and interested in issues about the environment' (*Wikipedia:The Independent*, accessed 01.07.08).

A new newspaper reading public?

Why has it been possible to establish and continue publication of these important centre-left quality newspapers during the last decades of the century? *Libération* in Paris, *die tageszeitung* in Berlin and Adam Michnik's *Gazeta Wyborcza* could be added to this list. The points of departure are obviously specific (Parisian Maoists, activists in Berlin, political opposition in Poland, Italian modernizers, post-Franco Enlightenment, anti-monopolistic opposition in London) and so are the various historical moments. Yet there are, it seems, also common features, not only the political positions, nor just that this is usually considered to be the age of television, not the age of newspaper reading, but also that this is the age of considerable demographic changes, on one hand because women in a massive scale have entered the working market, on the other hand because the general level of education has been lifted, not least among women. Questions concerning the public sphere should include not only the intellectuals, the media and the institutions, but also the composition of the public in the specific historical process.

From a broader European point of view attention should be paid to a variety of activities that go beyond the borders. On the economic side the financial organization behind *El País* co-owns the financial organization behind the *Independent* (another interesting story is that Silvio Berlusconi was just about to get control of *L'Espresso* and *la Repubblica* through his acquisitions of publishing houses). When it comes to content the *Guardian Weekly* includes material from

Le Monde (and from the *Washington Post*). A selection in English from *El País* is included in the Spanish edition of *Herald Tribune*. There are more examples of these kinds of collaboration. Most striking are perhaps the 67 editions in 26 languages of *Le Monde Diplomatique* (several of them as supplements to newspapers) – beyond the borders of Europe, wherever they are drawn. Yet also *Lettre Internationale* should be remembered. It was founded by the Czech dissident Antonin Liehm in the 80s as a forum for European intellectuals beyond the iron curtain, and it is still an interesting medium for European essays and is published in Paris, Berlin, Madrid, Rome, Budapest, Buakarest, Sofia, Skopje and (until recently) Copenhagen. The editor of the German edition was among the initiators of *die tageszeitung*.

Eurozine, an Internet-based forum for distribution of essays from cultural journals in the European sphere, must be highlighted in this context. This remarkable institution continues and renews the role of the cultural journal as a medium for intellectuals by way of creative use of the potentials of the Internet (see also Tessa Hauswedell's chapter in this volume). Similarly the homepage *Perlentaucher* (and its English language equivalent *signandsight*) digs up and distributes contributions from newspapers and magazines; this homepage has even been medium for an inter-European debate among intellectuals on questions concerning Muslims in Europe, a piece of European public sphere. A related operation is the weekly homepage (with archive) *Eurotopics* (in English, German and French) that is created by the German Federal Agency for Civic Education (Bundeszentrale für politische Bildung)

The general picture has thus changed quite a bit, in terms of media as well as in terms of public, yet in a formulation of principles from *die tageszeitung* in Berlin it is clear how general principles that hark back to the Enlightenment and the early nineteenth century go together with relations to specific historical circumstances:

> *taz* is committed to a critical public sphere. It takes its stand in defence of and for progress of Human Rights and does in particular give voice to positions that in front of political powers do not gain hearing. *taz* is in opposition to all kinds of discrimination. To the editors freedom is freedom for those who think differently, democracy depends on each individual's democratic rights. The newspaper is obliged to give veracious accounts...The editors repudiate all attempts at influence, all sorts of pressure from individuals, political parties, or economically, religiously or ideologically guided groups... In the firm belief that the world cannot be described from an exclusive German or European point of view, domestic and foreign themes have the same rank. (*Wikipedia: die tageszeitung*, accessed: 01.07.08)

The significant number of quality newspapers that were established during the last decades have imposed themselves as major media – even the smaller *taz* has the seventh largest distribution in Germany, *Libération*, the *Independent*, *El País* and *la Repubblica* are among the most important if not *the* most important newspapers in their respective countries. These quality papers – this is the thesis here – represent a new relation between newspapers as fora for intellectuals and their public which in its composition is a result of the expansion of higher education and the changing role of women in Europe. Although all of this may seem like a reason for optimism, there are severe economic problems ahead. *Die tageszeitung* survives e.g. on the basis of modest salaries to its employees. In Spring 2007 *Die Zeit* brought this headline: 'Will the Fourth Power Come Under the Hammer?' It was prompted by rumours that the majority of the shares in *Süddeutsche Zeitung* might come up for sale. There are more stories of this kind. Economic problems for many newspapers stem from declining income from advertising. Newspapers are also businesses. The story in *Die Zeit* provoked a commentary from Jürgen Habermas arguing that it would be a responsibility of the state to seccure the survival of quality newspapers:

> public communication is a force that stimulates and orients citizens' opinions and desires, while at the same time forcing the political system to adjust and become more transparent... From a historical point of view, there is something *counter-intuitive* in the idea of reigning in the market's role in journalism and the press. The market was the force that created the forum for subversive thoughts to emancipate themselves from state oppression in the first place. Yet the market can fulfil this function only so long as economic principles do not infringe upon the cultural and political content that the market itself serves to spread. (Habermas 2008: 136–137)

It could even be argued that it should be a task for the European Union to secure that democracy in Europe includes a democratic public sphere.

Notes

1. Nietzsche 1965: 346.
2. Joseph Görres in *Rheinischer Merkur*, July 1 and 3, as quoted in Leo Löwenthal 1961: 12, cf. also Best and Kellner 1990: 26.
3. Karl Marx in *Rheinische Zeitung*, no.135, 15. maj 1842.
4. *Rheinische Zeitung*, no. 139, Supplement, 19. maj 1842
5. En litterair Anmeldelse. To Tidsaldre, 1846. The text has been published with a variety of titles in English, among them: Two Ages: *The Age of Revolution and the Present Age. A Literary Review* (trans. Hong and Hong), Princeton UP: Princeton, 1978, the second part of the book also as *The Present Age* or as *Critique of Our Time*. The point of departure was a novel by a Danish author entitled *Two Ages*.
6. As Allan Janik has argued (Janik 1984).
7. Here and in what follows references are by page to Kierkegaard 1978: *Two Ages*.
8. As Christian Thorne points out (Thorne 2001).

References

Anderson, Perry (1968), 'Components of the National Culture', *New Left Review*, 1: 50 (July–August), pp. 3–57.

Balzac, Honeré de (1902), 'Monographie de la Presse Parisienne', in *Oeuvres Complètes de H. de Balzac. Oeuvres Diverses, Vol. I*. Paris: Société d'éditions litteraires et artistiques, pp. 125–227.

Best, Steven and Kellner, Douglas (1990), 'Modernity, Mass Society, and the Media: Reflections on the Corsair Affair', in Robert L. Perkins (ed.), *International Kierkegaard Commentary: The Corsair Affair*. Macon: Mercer University Press, pp. 23–61.

Habermas, Jürgen ([1962]1991), *Strukturwandel der Öffentlichkeit* [*The Structural Transformation of the Public Sphere*]. Cambridge: MIT Press.

Habermas, Jürgen (2006), 'Political Communication in Media Society: Does Democracy Still Enjoy an Epistemic Dimension? The Impact of Normative Theory on Empirical Research', *Communication Theory*, 16, pp. 411–26.

Habermas, Jürgen (2008), 'Medien, Märkte und Konsumenten – Die seriöse Presse als Rückgrat der politischen Öffentlichkeit', in *Ach, Europa*. Frankfurt am Main: Suhrkamp, pp. 131–137.

Heidegger, Martin (1979), *Sein und Zeit*. Tübingen: Max Niemeyer.

Horkheimer, Max and Adorno, Theodor W. ([1947]/1996), *Dialektik der Aufklärung* [*The Dialectic of Enlightenment*]. London: Verso.

Janik, Allan (1984), 'Haecker, Kierkegaard, and the Early Brenner: A Contribution to the History of the Reception of *Two Ages* in the German-Speaking World', in Robert L. Perkins (ed.), *International Kierkegaard Commentary: Two Ages*. Macon: Mercer University Press, pp. 189–221.

Kierkegaard, Søren (1978), *Two Ages: The Age of Revolution and the Present Age. A Literary Review* (trans. Hong and Hong). Princeton: Princeton University Press.

Kraus, Karl (1979), 'Heine und die Folgen', in *Magie der Sprache*, Frankfurt am Main: Suhrkamp, pp. 169–92.

Löwenthal, Leo (1961), *Literature, Popular Culture, and Society*. Palo Alto: Pacific Books.

Madsen, Peter (2005), 'Feuilleton', *ProForma: Quaderni di Germanistica*, 3, pp. 149–58.

Nietzsche, Friedrich (1965), *The Philosophy of Nietzsche*, G. Clive (ed.). New York: New American Library.

Sartre, Jean-Paul (1972), *Plaidoyer pour les Intellectuels*. Paris: Gallimard.

Thorne, Christian (2001), 'Thumbing Our Nose at the Public Sphere: Satire, the Market, and the Invention of Literature', *PMLA*, 116: 3 (May), pp. 531–544.

15

(De)Constructing European Citizenship? Political Mobilization and Collective Identity Formation Among Immigrants in Sweden and Spain

Zenia Hellgren

Abstract

The political construction of a European citizenship and a 'European identity' is a project whose support among the diverse European peoples is uncertain indeed. Questions as how notions of citizenship, collective identity and the more abstract sense of belonging to a community are being transformed by immigration are becoming increasingly salient in national and European discourse and policy. This article looks at the role immigrants themselves as social and political actors play in such political and cultural dynamics.

Keywords

citizenship, collective identity, interest, immigrant claims-making

The immigrant experience

In this article, I discuss two social movements built on different forms of immigrant identities, focusing on their implications for social membership and collective identity in contemporary Europe. Different from many scholars within the field of multiculturalism, I do not see immigrants and their descendants necessarily as bearers of stronger cultural identities or traditions than the autochthonous population,[1] but seek to move beyond stereotypical perceptions of culture and difference.

My case studies of the Swedish anti-discrimination movement and the Spanish movement for undocumented immigrants' rights both represent political mobilizations with a trans-ethnic and universalist[2] form of claims-making. The two movements emerged in societies with very different institutional settings and histories of immigration and integration of immigrants. Yet, both are now experiencing activism around the mobilization of immigrant groups. Both movements are cases in which collective identities are being defined and redefined, suggesting that varied particularist and/or hybridized identities unite under a common frame that transcends ethno-cultural, national or other divides. There are indeed important differences between the two movements. Mobilizing to combat ethnic discrimination appears consistent with European (and national) policy aims. Conversely, the 'papers and rights for all' movement in Spain directly contests European immigration policies. Nevertheless, I find that there are similarities between these groups, and that an *immigrant* experience that is shared by ever more Europeans potentially could form a base for future, more inclusive collective identities.

Immigrants mobilizing against discrimination most likely have formal rights and their basic needs are covered by the social rights of the society in which they reside; undocumented immigrants are at a different level of struggle. Yet, immigrants with different legal statuses, ranging from nationalized citizens through workers with temporary residence permits and those with no formal right to stay, all coexist in European societies and constitute parts of the multicultural panorama. Indeed, statuses can change, and the Spanish case supports the thesis that immigrant claims-making might follow some kind of Maslowian hierarchy of needs, starting with claims for the right to immigrate and ending with participation on equal terms with the majority population within all spheres of society. Recently arrived, undocumented immigrants initially struggle for residence permits. As they become increasingly established in society their demands shift towards citizenship, voting rights and non-discrimination.

Besides actual political mobilization, immigrants modify everyday life and practices in the societies where they live through just being there. In some cases, their presence influences the very way meanings of citizenship are understood on an interpersonal level. Perhaps the irregular immigrants in Spain constitute the clearest example of this. They take part in society in a variety of ways; they go to the doctor, have their children in school and work for months, years or even a lifetime, but constantly live with the risk of being disclosed and expelled. Formal membership categories, including legal residence or citizenship, however do not automatically lead to social inclusion. The Swedish case shows that exclusion and discrimination operate through subtle mechanisms; through common people's reproduction of ethnic boundaries in everyday life. Representing individuals who share experiences of non-belonging, the two movements I study challenge these boundaries at different levels. Their activism could therefore, in a broader sense, be interpreted as immigrants' struggle for a place within the new Europe that is taking shape. More importantly, not only do they have to find a place within given contexts, but also participate in processes that redefine such contexts.

Collective identity and common interests

Much has been said over the last years about the 'cultural turn' in social sciences. Culture has become a key concept, and recognition of cultural specificity the political goal that follows the multiculturalist agenda. Some have argued that this shift took place at the expense of a focus on – continuing and deepening – social and economic inequalities (inequalities which paradoxically might have particularly severe effects for immigrants and minority groups).[3] Others claim that multiculturalist scholars often fail to problematize the actual meaning of 'culture' and its relation to the equally complex concept 'identity', taking for granted that a culture always is good for the individuals defined as its members, and that internal identification with the group is strong.[4] Furthermore, claims for the 'right to difference' might unintentionally support the ultra-rightist thesis that different ethnic groups should not mix. The strongest version of multiculturalism paradoxically tends to use arguments similar to the discourse of cultural racism (Stolcke 1994).

When talking of culture and identity, these concepts are often intertwined and apparently treated as more or less synonymous. Appiah (2005) argues that what initially is defined and referred to as immigrants' culture (by themselves or by others) tends to become blurred as generations pass by, leading to greater cultural hybridization – and homogenization. As a result of this development, Appiah concludes that identity and culture are increasingly decoupled, as 'it is getting harder to identify as a cultural group' (ibid.: 115). In his comment to Charles Taylor's (1994) call for a politics of recognition, Appiah problematizes the multiculturalist emphasis on group identity and highlights that the concept of identity embraces both a collective and an individual dimension. According to Appiah, the politics of recognition focuses exclusively on the collective dimension of identity and therefore simplifies its meaning. Thereby, Appiah argues, a potential conflict between the self and the group identity emerges, particularly as collective identity often is based upon a simplified perception of the presupposed homogeneity of groups. The politics of recognition risk being forcing and inhibiting for the individual, if they demand the politicization of private identities through a predefined image of how, for instance, 'Blacks' or 'homosexuals' are supposed to be, and what interests they are supposed to have (Appiah 1994).

A multiculturalist view on ethnic minorities' political interests tends to emphasize their cultural identity. The debate on multicultural policies therefore focuses on 'cultural rights', as the right for ethnic groups to maintain their traditions, and perhaps be granted exemptions from national law and majority rules and norms. Yet, collective identification – assumingly a precondition for political mobilization – among immigrated groups does not have to be based upon a common culture or ethnicity. Benhabib (2002: 123) poses the rhetorical question 'Why should members of the same ethnic community share a comprehensive worldview...cannot a Russian as well be an anarchist, a communist, or a slavophile?' From this point of view, it makes more sense to imagine a political identity based on common interests, instead of politicizing predefined notions of collective identity.

Which common interests could then be expected to form the basis for immigrant political mobilization? Mezzadra (2005: 118) defines the *common experience of non-belonging* as the basis for reciprocal identification among undocumented, 'paperless' immigrants. As I previously have stated, full inclusion furthermore implies more than a set of formal rights. Also regular immigrants, and even their children and grandchildren, are confronted with hostility or distanciation in societies where they – in spite of being born there, and perhaps not knowing any other mother tongue than the language spoken by the majority population – still are not considered as part of the same national identity (Lipponen et al. 2006). Immigrants' political interests might in this view spring from them – in Fraser's (2003b) Weberian framework – *not being recognized as a peer in social life*. This experience could be a potential basis for the formation of a universalist collective and political identity, that unites people across ethnic, national, religious or other divides through the shared situation of being – or being defined as – an immigrant.

Let us now imagine the immigrant as a social and political actor, underlining the difference between ethnic and cultural *belonging* and the *situation* in which an immigrant encounters him- or herself. Being an immigrant is not an established identity. It is a legal status and a life history that very well might be transformed into an identity, alongside – and under certain circumstances perhaps above – other collective, ethno-cultural and individual dimensions of the utterly complex phenomenon we call identity. A political mobilization that reclaims rights for immigrants does therefore not necessarily imply an agenda that also demands the recognition of these immigrants' cultural identities, although neither does it exclude this possibility.

The immigrant as a social and political actor
The diversity both within and between many ethno-cultural groups might certainly lead us to question the idea that there would be a common identity strong enough to form the base for political mobilization. Yet, without being explicitly political, immigrants organizing their lives between the homeland and the host country do practice a kind of non-institutional 'transnationalism from below' that – when these immigrants establish themselves in a country without having the formal right to reside there – challenge state policies for territorial access and citizenship by their very presence. If immigrants define a common interest in acquiring more rights in the society where they reside, and subsequently to participate on equal terms with the majority population in all – formal and informal – aspects of life, there is indeed more potential for such transethnic collective identities to take shape. Furthermore, immigrants do participate as social actors in their new homelands; on the labour market and in everyday life. They create bonds to compatriots, to immigrants with different origins, and to people from the autochthonous population. One might therefore view the formation of collective identities and political interests as a simultaneous and interrelated process.

Social movements, as the workers' or the women's movement, were once successively politicized through the definition of injustices shared by collectives of individuals. One could say that ideology starts to take shape with such a discovery – the transgression from being a *class in itself* to a *class for itself*, speaking with Marx. The definition of common interests thus precedes the formation of a collective identity in these cases, similar to what Tilly (1978) observed in his earlier work. The idea that immigrants need a political voice of their own is based upon the presumption that there are specific 'immigrant' interests. As for feminism, which starts with the revelation of patriarchal power structures, a political immigrant identity could presuppose that there is an ethnic status hierarchy, where the opportunities of every individual are related to his or her ethnicity.

Multiculturalist thought sometimes risks to culturalize immigrants and ethnic minorities, by assuming that their political interests are related to strong cultural identities and traditions. A culturalized view on immigrants as political actors might make one assume that their political interests primarily are related to their 'cultural community', as the survival of ancient traditions or exemption from national law for marriage practices or sexual education. Such claims are certainly heard, and reflect the kind of value-conflicts that probably are inevitable in multi-ethnic societies (Banakar 1994). Of greater interest for this article are however the immigrant actors who do not primarily represent an ethnic group or another way of life, but who demand participation in society on equal terms. This is perhaps even more politically controversial, as it potentially challenges status quo: power structures and privilege systems created and upheld by the ethnic majority population. It does also contain a possibility for broadened collective identities and categories of inclusion in multi-ethnic societies, where identification not only transcends ethno-cultural boundaries between immigrant groups, but also between immigrants and ethnic majorities.

New claims for social membership
The two movements I study, the Spanish 'papers and rights for all' movement and the Swedish anti-discrimination movement, are both mobilized around collective interests rather than group identity. Diverse group identities are subordinated to the universal aims of the movements (residence permits and equality of opportunities, respectively), and interests in turn give rise to new political identities, reflecting the way interest and identity are intertwined in political mobilization processes. Both movements challenge status quo, although in different ways. While the former challenges the fundaments for territorial control and EU border policies, the latter is formally supported by state and EU policies but pose challenges to national power structures. Immigrants' experience of exclusion and discrimination is universal in the sense that it transcends cultural particularities.[5] I suggest that this experience forms the potential basis of a more universalist framing of rights, and a collective identity that both might trigger political mobilization and confrontation, and constitute a fertile source for the shaping of inclusive collective identities and future citizenship categories.

In this context, I wish to highlight the dual dimension of the citizenship concept. Formally, citizenship is a legal status, which brings about certain rights and obligations as a recognized member of a nation. A more sociological definition of citizenship would however focus on an individual's role as an actual member of society: participation in everyday life, institutions and organizations, social relationships and responsibilities, etc. It could also embrace an identity dimension: to identify with the local community or neighbourhood. Such identification, rather than symbolic identification with a vague and outdated notion of 'national identity', would thus form the base for a more participative form of citizenship at the grassroot level. When I talk of the potential impact of immigrant mobilization on meanings of citizenship, I am primarily interested in this definition, without excluding the possibility that new forms of social membership could lead to changes in legal criterias for citizenship.

Holston and Appadurai (1999: 3–13) have suggested that the city increasingly is the arena where citizenship takes shape, and that it might even be replacing the nation as the actual *lived* space where claims are raised and diverse forms of membership are being practiced. In both my Swedish and Spanish case, place seems to play an important role for the construction of new forms of claims-making and meanings of social membership. As we shall see, suburban identity is crucial for Gringo, the Swedish anti-discrimination actor that most explicitly has aimed at constructing new collective identities. In this case, it refers rather to a symbolic meaning of 'suburban' as an underdog identity, uniting second generation immigrant and working-class youth, than to the actual streets and squares of Swedish suburbs. In Spain, or more specifically in Barcelona where I conducted my study, the division in *barrios*, local neighbourhoods that often have a village-like character, is central. Neighbour associations are nodes of social life, where both local *fiestas* and political protests are organized. These associations have supported undocumented immigrants claims, and they furthermore symbolize the remaining local and informal character of Spanish society: integration into everyday life in a local neighbourhood has little to do with official documentation.

Immigrant identity-formation and claims-making within two different structures

Geographically, Sweden and Spain are about as far away from each other as two countries can be within European borders. They are far apart in other senses as well; politically and socially. Immigration politics might be increasingly Europeanized; integration and 'multicultural' policies are however still nationally defined (though often influenced by European directives, specifically regarding the agenda of anti-discrimination). Simultaneously, media and political discourses as well as people's everyday practices and attitudes vary among countries and regions, meeting immigrant actors with support or hostility. In this section, I shall briefly present two movements that I have been researching over the last years. My concern is primarily with how these actors define collective identity and interest, and what implications this in turn has for national and European citizenship.

The 'papers and rights for all' movement in Spain

The organization of undocumented immigrants in Spain started to emerge during the late 1980s. Immigrants from third-world countries, most of whom had no legal residence or work permits, started to meet and establish close contacts with people sharing their situation in certain Spanish areas and communities. An awareness of their situation and a desire to change this situation took shape. In 2001, the mobilization escalated through a massive protest against the reinforced Alien Law. The platform 'papers for all', who demanded unconditional regularization of all undocumented immigrants in Spain, played a leading role during the protests, and was frequently present in mass media. Both my own research and another sociologist's fieldwork (Laubenthal 2004) indicate that emotion-laden articles with titles as 'They Ask for Help to Legalize their Situation' and 'Death Does not Need nor Ask for Papers' (*La Opinión*, 5 January

2001; *La Opinión*, 7 January 2001) helped forming a discourse that supported the mobilization out of sympathy and humanitarianism. Social movement research consistently argues that mass media's importance for the outcome of political mobilization increases, as public discourses that may support or reject a movement's agenda largely are shaped by TV and newspapers (Klandermans and Goslinga 1996).

In Barcelona, eight churches were squatted and turned into 'immigrant camps' during January and February 2001, supported by 'papers for all', NGOs, trade unions, Christian organizations, neighbour associations, organized squatters[6] and the public. Several manifestations and public protests against the law took place during this time, and the streets and squares of the city centre filled with demonstrators. Even the Pope made a statement in favour of the protesting immigrants, which surely had a heavy weight in Catholic Spain. As the mobilization was intensified, representatives among the immigrants' rights advocates were invited to negotiations with government officials. Finally, 334,882 out of 615,377 applications for regularization were approved during the amnesty of 2001. Since then the movement persists, although mobilization intensity varies strongly. A major regularization of undocumented immigrants has occurred since then, in 2005, but it is more unclear what role the movement played at that time.

The irregular immigrants who started the mobilization process in 2001 appeared to act out of desperation rather than strategy, particularly at the initial stage. The one-issue character of the 'papers' furthermore creates a situation where it is uncertain whether immigrant actors will remain politically active once they achieve their permits. The shaping of a coherent political struggle and claims-making discourse among immigrants, directed at a wider range of demands than the acquisition of the papers, is an ongoing process whose outcome is yet unclear. There is possibly a dividing line between immigrants who become organized in associations with broader agendas, and those who exclusively are involved in the 'papers for all' movement, as between those with a trans-ethnic discourse and those who mainly advocate their own ethnic groups' particular interests.

There are also pan-ethnic identities as the Latin identity that unites many immigrants of Latin American origin, besides their particular ethnic identities and their overall immigrant identity, while Africans and some Asian groups as the Pakistani have been particularly present within the 'papers for all' movement. Latin American immigrants have obviously not suffered from the same language problems as other immigrants, experienced greater cultural proximity – and acceptance – from Spanish society. Some of them also come from countries with governmental agreements that gave them easier access to Spanish citizenship. This has however changed over the last years. The inflow of irregular immigrants from the poorest Latin American countries, as Bolivia, Ecuador and Peru, has increased rapidly. These groups can often not count on the support from strong and well-organized local ethnic communities as many other Latin Americans, and might experience that they share more interests with undocumented Moroccan construction workers than well-established Argentinean architects or psychologists.

In immigrant associations based on ethnicity, irregular immigrants are furthermore as present as legalized, and liberalizing immigration laws and facilitating access to the 'papers' is generally a central concern for all these groups although not their only or primary goal. The one-issue character of the 'papers for all' movement is also changing: it recently broadened its agenda to include the more general focus on 'rights' for immigrants (papers and rights for all). If such a development takes place, it implies increasing similarities with my other case of the anti-discrimination movement in Sweden, and reflects the emergence of more universalist immigrants' rights discourses and movements in Europe.

Identification with an immigrant experience is central for the movement 'papers and rights for all'. To bridge cultural particularities and discrepancies between immigrant communities is a central and explicit aim for the movement.

> Now, what is most important is that all forces are being united. If we al participate and concentrate on the situation that affects us, and we all have to participate no matter what...there are other things too but we must focus on what is really important, because we are not in our own countries now. (Lina, Activist, 2006)

A trans-ethnic immigrant identity also emerges from the informal encounters at squares and work places as well as from political engagement and consciousness, supporting the thesis that interest and identity formation is a simultaneous and mutually enforcing process.

When following the movement's activists as they demonstrate from time to time on the streets of Barcelona, the catchphrase 'We are all immigrants' is constantly repeated. In the movement's internal publications, the collective 'we' is also defined as 'immigrants':

> There is no need to further explain the difficulties immigrants face today: more than million without papers, problems with renovations of permits, a strong repression both inside and outside national borders, discrimination and criminalization of whole immigrant communities...With this situation in mind, we will aim to establish a broad framework for continuous work and struggle, which actively will look for collaboration among all persons and organizations willing to participate in the united struggle for the rights of immigrants. (From papers and rights for all's communiqué *Jornada de Reflexión*, April 8 2006, my translation from Spanish)

Within the movement, where a Marxist-sounding discourse is often used, the more universalist notion of global workers' interests may discursively include the concept of an exploited immigrant (as a sub-category to the former), which is more rooted in the mobilizing immigrants' own experiences. The same agenda is thus embraced both by Spaniards (who interpret the politicized immigrant identity as part of the workers' struggle) and immigrants (as it is based upon their narratives).

The movement for irregular immigrants' rights has, as Solé and Parella (2003) state, made evident that non-Parliamentary action is an important instrument to achieve rights in countries as Spain and France, where the 'paperless' immigrants relatively successfully have mobilized to demand regularization of their status. Besides the existence of large informal labour markets, Southern European countries seem to be characterized by a high degree of scepticism towards authorities and state control compared to Scandinavia.

Suárez (2004: 104–28) argues that there are multiple factors in Spain impeding the implementation of strict immigration control policies in accordance to EU norms. This increases opportunities for actors who demand regularization of undocumented immigrants. Ambiguousness in relation to immigration policies both at the administrative level and among the Spanish public are important such factors. Suárez describes the 'legitimization of legality' as a symbolic component of Spain's transgression to a modern European country, which not yet has become integrated in people's relationship towards the state. In a rural community in the south of Spain, factors such as an informal economy, strong local ties and loyalties and little identification with the central state or with an abstract European identity, provide a structure that both might produce hostility towards outsiders as immigrants, but also, once they have become accepted, integrate them into a local community that cares little of legal statuses. In Spain, state control and bureaucracy are typical targets for popular jokes about corruption and abuse of power. Traditional structures of a certain communitarian self-help and non-control still remain alongside the rapid Europeanisation and modernization processes, which provides potential for more participative citizenship practices.

This meaning of citizenship is exemplified by the salient neighbour associations in Barcelona, as they embrace immigrants in their ongoing project of constructing citizenship from below. They actively try to build links between the immigrated and the autochthonous populations through local activities. Identification with the local neighbourhood is the common reference point, and the objective is to 'promote solidarity, equality and coexistence among the neighbours'. Neighbour associations also played a central role in supporting the immigrants who locked themselves up in churches during the protests of 2001, and the umbrella organization FAVB (Federation of Neighbour Associations in Barcelona) currently accommodates 'papers and rights for all's main office. FAVB presents its programme under the slogan 'More than 30 years constructing citizenship', and aims to function as the 'little citizen's' guardian against authorities' potential abuse of power. The neighbour associations of FAVB represent something central for the Spanish structural context: the importance of (informal) bonds between people in the local community – which apparently remain strong also in a metropolis as Barcelona – and the suspiciousness towards authorities.

The 'papers and rights for all' movement challenges common perceptions of citizenship and political agency, as it represents the political voice of those who have no formal right to express such a voice. The claims of irregular immigrants are ideologically founded on the notion of universal human rights. Hence, the rights and claims of the individual do in this case not only transcend the citizen (Soysal 1994: 142), but reach beyond all forms of territorial boundaries. The definition of citizenship applied by FAVB furthermore lies close to Suarez' participative citizen concept. Irregular immigrants in Spain contest current citizenship categories and European policies, both through their actual ways of life and their political organization.

Increased bonds between these immigrants and the autochthonous population, within the social movements, neighbour associations, or in everyday life, strengthen ties between people at the grassroots level and do somehow represent the emergence of a new kind of (informal) citizenship.

The Swedish anti-discrimination movement and Gringo

In Sweden, the situation is different from Spain in several ways. The extensive shadow economy that characterizes Southern European countries, and makes it possible for irregular immigrants to find work, is virtually non-existent in Scandinavia. This is largely due to the organization of the labour market, where unions have a strong bargaining position that prevents wage dumping. Immigrants in Sweden often hold Swedish citizenship, and although there clearly is a relationship between immigrant background and belonging to the lower social classes, precarious life conditions comparable with those many immigrants in Spain experience are extremely rare (Schierup et al. 2006).

Labour immigration has often been framed as a threat by Swedish unions, undermining legitimacy for claims as 'the right to migrate' (Hellgren and Hobson 2008). There is thus clearly a lack of opportunity for a 'papers for all' agenda in Sweden, and no such movement exists here (although there has been some mobilization for the rights of refugees, who seemingly attract more sympathy than 'economic migrants'). In a society where state control reaches far and is highly supported by its citizens, and leading a fairly normal life without a social security number is virtually impossible, there is little space for the development of 'informal citizenship'.

The anti-discrimination agenda, however, apparently appeals to basic ideals for Swedish society: justice and equality of opportunities. Consequently, Sweden has adopted EU directives against ethnic discrimination and reformed discrimination laws to make them significantly stricter,[7] although several anti-discrimination lawyers and activists claim that there is a wide gap between law and practice (Hellgren 2005). Immigrants' struggle for inclusion appears in the Swedish context to be primarily a question of challenging social structures where a notion of Swedishness still invisibly divides people into 'A and B citizens'. Anti-discrimination groups consequently advocate for a more inclusive notion of national identity, and, more controversially, for ethnic quotas and affirmative action.

The increased emphasis on ethnic discrimination in Swedish society has also resonated in the agendas of ethnic and immigrant organizations. Aytar (2004: 70) argues that the immigrant organizations in Sweden currently undergo important changes regarding the framing of their agendas. His research shows that they increasingly focus on the country where they live instead of the ethnic homeland or their own ethnic group. Within this new direction of immigrant activism, anti-discrimination appears to be a main thread that connects politically or organizationally active immigrants' interests. All immigrant actors I have interviewed during my studies did share the experience of having been a victim of ethnic discrimination. To change discriminatory structures and practices is thus an objective that obviously unites immigrants (of certain characteristics)[8] across ethnic divides.

Among the multitude of Swedish anti-discrimination actors, Gringo has been the one that most explicitly focuses on collective identity and discourse formation. Most anti-discrimination organizations underscore that nothing influences public opinion more than media, and that the image of immigrants transmitted by mainstream TV and newspapers is generally negative and stereotyped. To challenge this trend, Gringo started their own magazine in 2004, which soon became quite a success story (http://www.gringo.se). The members have frequently been invited as 'multicultural consultants' by companies and politicians, participated in public investigations and have been involved in several projects to promote young people from disadvantaged housing areas. Gringo is explicit about their method: 'being political without this being noticed' as they think an overtly politicized and confrontational approach might be counter-productive, and consider media a more efficient tool to accomplish change than traditional political processes. Gringo, along with other anti-discrimination actors, defines the main target for change as everyday people's attitudes rather than policies and laws.

Founder, editor and leading figure, Swedish-Kurd Zanyar Adami,[9] started Gringo as a reaction to the discrimination he experienced himself. Initially, he called the ethnic youth associations to organize a broad, trans-ethnic mobilization. They were however not interested in such an agenda, but maintained their emphasis on ethnic identities. According to Adami, these organizations mainly 'want to preserve their own culture and live in a parallel Sweden' (Interview, 2005). Contrastingly, Gringo promotes a collective identity which embraces both Swedish and different ethnic and immigrant identities. Members are both individuals who have grown up in multi-ethnic areas and whose identities are shaped by this experience, and actors who have turned their experiences into a broader project. Gringo has also created its own characteristic vocabulary, where references to suburban identity, Swedishness and 'immigrantness' in a humoristic, ironic and often provocative fashion are key.[10]

For Gringo, identification with the 'million programme suburbs'[11] (which they believe generally are negatively pictured in mainstream media)[12] becomes the link that transcends ethnic divides and simultaneously embraces a wide range of particular identities. One Gringo member says that while suburban identity is commonly taken for equal to an immigrant identity, it is rather a question of 'underdog solidarity' (which, in turn, includes an immigrant identity). This definition thus implies a more universalist identification than the one shared by immigrants and ethnic minorities: an experience of exclusion that also is shared by parts of the ethnic majority population.

The 'Gringo identity' is clearly defined by cultural hybridization, where particular ethnocultural identities mix with the majority culture and meet in new forms of Swedishness. Part of Gringo's project is, in their own words, to 'update Swedishness' by the construction of a national identity that both immigrants and ethnic Swedes can identify with. Suburban language is a concrete representation of cultural hybridization: a mix of Spanish, Arabic, English, Swedish and other languages' words and expressions.[13] This hybridization emerges where children of immigrants grow up side by side with Swedes in multi-ethnic neighbourhoods. The Gringo members emphasize the difference between first- and second-generation immigrants, or, as also the immigrated respondents consider themselves part of the second category: between those who grew up in Swedish 'melting pots' compared to those who came later in life, with different cultural baggage:

> The new generation of *blattar* is very different from the first. SIOS [an umbrella organization for ethnic minority associations in Sweden] represents the first generation, they long back somehow, and they don't see this as their country. They don't think they have the right to demand things, and they care much about conserving their culture because they are afraid it will be dissolved. But for us...Sweden is my country. And the second generation is quite homogeneous. People meet in an immigrant identity that is being assigned to us. (Zanyar, Gringo member, 2005)

> The first generation was a very heterogeneous group, they came from half of the world. The idea with Gringo is that the second generation can be generalized; unlike the first, there are common experiences. We have grown up in Sweden but all tasted exclusion, which is very much related to class. Our culture, which has developed in the million program suburbs, has been devalued. (Pedro, Gringo member, 2005)

Though immigrants and Swedes thus could (and in Gringo's view, ought to) meet in a shared and new collective identity, particular immigrant experiences exist alongside the perception of being Swedish, but not being recognized as such. Collisions with the majority society are perceived as related to immigrant claims-making and demands to be treated as peers:

> Looking at our parents...They were grateful for their right to be here and have democratic liberties. But our generation doesn't feel this gratitude, because we see ourselves as Swedes. We are here to build Sweden just as anyone else and demand our rights, we demand to be your equal. And then the problems start immediately. (Zahra, Gringo member, 2005)

Despite some more universalist ambitions, as to embrace Swedes from all kinds of social classes and ethnic backgrounds, as well as to promote a more inclusive European identity with the ultimate ideal being their version of a cosmopolitan 'citizen of the world' concept, it remains clear that Gringo departs from an underdog perspective. The suburban identity might be rooted in the actual physical neighbourhood, but it also contains a more abstract dimension; a transnational 'suburban identity' with a mobilizing potential that springs from misrecognition.

> Maybe we will be Europeans, or citizens of the world. It is a bit like Marx, workers all over the world unite. People from the suburb here can really relate to people from suburbs in Paris or London or Greece, the same things are going on. I think you can identify as a Swede but that will only be a part of your identity. (Lisa, Gringo member, 2005)

> In the suburbs, talking to people in the streets...It is hard to control the movements that are emerging. The frustration and anger people feel makes our task a bit ambiguous,

we don't want riots. There is an immense power in the suburbs, but we have been fooled all our lives. We have been told that we are not good enough, that we live in bad neighbourhoods, and when you realize that you have been fooled...I want to open people's eyes and make them see themselves. (Zanyar, 2005)

Gringo has clearly influenced what is spoken of and how this is spoken of, creating its own, alternative discourse. Their 'trend-setting' function seems to have been one of their strengths, and they are explicit about their ambition to give young, non-established people an opportunity: these are then fostered in the 'Gringo way of thinking' and can bring their (new) perspectives with them when they proceed to work at other magazines, newspapers, TV or radio channels or otherwise. From this point of view, Gringo's successfulness has doubtlessly been an opportunity that gives voice to people who hitherto have had little chances to influence public debate and discourse. Lately, Gringo has however had some financial problems, and its future is currently uncertain. It remains to be seen whether Gringo manages to remain visible after the media honeymoon is over.

Gringo's discourse contains potential as a source of inspiration for the redefinition of national identity, if it has the impact on people's hearts and minds its advocates hope and aim for. In any case, it is the most explicit intent of a public actor to achieve such changes that has entered the Swedish scene so far. Their discourse furthermore implies that immigrant or ethnic identities intersect with social class, and that disadvantage not only is a question of ethnic status hierarchies but of socio-economic ones as well. This, in turn, opens for a broader identification where both disadvantaged immigrants and Swedes could define shared interests.

Concluding remarks

In the beginning of this paper, I positioned myself as critical towards the multiculturalist view on immigrants as bearers and representatives of particularly thick notions of cultural identity. With the two cases of the anti-discrimination movement/Gringo in Sweden, and the 'papers and rights for all' movement in Spain, I have showed that identity and interest are intertwined in the formation of ethno-culturally hybridized collective identities. Theoretically, I have referred to Mezzadra and Fraser, defining the basis for immigrant mobilization as the *common experience of non-belonging* and the claim to be *recognized as peers in social life*.

Evidently, there are important differences between the movements. Perhaps one could say that while the irregular immigrant activists in Spain fight for basic rights and legal inclusion, anti-discrimination activists in Sweden reclaim recognition of their equal worth and inclusion in a more symbolic sense. The Spanish movement would then to a higher extent emphasize collective *interest* and aim at *redistribution*, while the anti-discrimination movement (and particularly Gringo) seeks to reform national *identity* and aim at *recognition*. Yet, it would be far too simplistic to make such a division and leave it to that. Exclusion operates at different levels, but effects are similar: perpetuated precariousness; lacking opportunities to ascend in society; a damaged self-image. Both movements furthermore make references to status hierarchies that are universal in the sense that they are not merely defined by ethnicity but also by class, implying intersections between their agendas and autochthonous groups of disadvantaged in relation to the current power structures. Nevertheless, the definition of a shared *immigrant experience* is crucial for these groups, and particularistic – not in the strongly multiculturalist sense of ethno-cultural identity as it cuts across ethnic divides, but in the sense that it does not embrace autochthonous experiences.

My research suggests that the construction of more inclusive citizenship categories presupposes the inclusion of both ethnic minorities and majorities within what Benhabib (1992) has characterized as universalist principles with particularist perspectives. The movements I study highlight important dilemmas at two different levels: at the level of citizenship, how to include the majority society into more inclusive collective identity formations; and at the level of struggles among disadvantaged groups, how to achieve their aim to bridge ethnic particularities and construct broad agendas with strong mobilizing power. The irregular immigrants that become political actors furthermore highlight the ongoing and increasing tensions between national and European border policies, informal labour markets and the limited right to mobility that is defined by global status hierarchies.

Without claiming that these are solutions to such dilemmas, I suggest that the same movements also reflect opportunities. At the mobilization level, shared experiences of exclusion transcend ethnic divides and form the basis for a stronger political voice that unites the ever larger numbers of immigrants and ethnic minorities that are not recognized as peers in social life. The way Spaniards within the 'papers and rights for all' movement interpret 'immigrant' as part of a broader worker's identity, and the way Gringo defines collective identity as based on suburban roots, however indicate that parts of the majority populations share immigrant activists' interest in challenging current power structures. At the level of citizenship, immigrants and autochthonous share experiences through everyday life in local neighbourhoods. This interaction might give rise to new constructions of informal forms of 'citizenship', in a participative rather than a legal sense, which in turn fosters broader identifications. The arena where these changes occur furthermore plays a central role: perhaps could the neighbourhood (be it the *barrio*, the suburb or the whole city) function as a 'construction site' for the shaping from below of a kind intercultural and *rooted cosmopolitan* (Appiah 2005) identities that can bridge unnecessary discrepancies between the universalist and the particular in multi-ethnic societies. This is what Stevenson (2003) suggests in his intent to combine multiculturalist and cosmopolitan perspectives, and this is what I believe to be the strongest indicator that these new social movements could be fertile sources for the shaping of more inclusive collective identities and future citizenship categories.

Notes

1. Although 'culture' and strong ties to the ethnic community indeed often increase in importance in exile.
2. Trans-ethnic means that it cuts across ethnic divides, which may or may not include the majority population. The term universalist is in this context used in the meaning that an agenda, a claim or otherwise has the ambition of representing general or 'universal' as opposed to particular interests or identities.

3. See, for instance, the work of Nancy Fraser and Brian Barry.
4. Bhiku Parekh (2000, etc.) is among the most well-known advocates for such strong multiculturalism.
5. Although this experience is evidently racialized. The word 'immigrant' is in itself a marker of status. A Northern American researcher recruited to work for a medical company in Europe would obviously not be considered an *immigrant*. The mobilizing immigrants are mostly those who are disadvantaged by global status hierarchies with roots in colonialism, identified as 'Others' in relation to the white, Western hegemony (de los Reyes and Mulinari 2005).
6. Links between the Spanish *okupa* movement of squatters occupying empty flats and houses and protesting against real estate speculation, and irregular immigrants, were established during the 1990s. Shared experiences of precarious housing and laboUr market situations created bonds between the collectives, and squatters from Barcelona periodically participated in the platform 'papers for all' (Morén-Alegret 1999: 191).
7. Which according to several NGO actors was the result of their intensive lobbying in Brussels, at a time when political receptiveness was high due to the fear of increasing right-wing extremism in Europe.
8. Remember the earlier notes on global status hierarchies and racialization.
9. As Zanyar Adami is by now such a well-known public person in Sweden, it would make no sense to try to obscure his identity. The names of the other Gringo members are however fictitious.
10. Immigrants are by Gringo generally referred to with the normally highly degrading word 'blatte', which perhaps best could be described as something like a mix of 'immigrant' and 'nigger': a 'blatte' is never white, but can have any nationality. Swedes, in turn, are assigned the also degrading denomination 'svenne'. To play with stereotypes and make negatively loaded words their own (which can be compared to the use of the word 'nigger' by Blacks in the US) is by Gringo considered an efficient method to 'disarm' these.
11. The so-called 'million programme' was a governmental project initiated in the early 1960s, to build 1 million apartments in ten years outside the big cities, to meet the urgent need of housing in an age of quick urbanization. These are characteristically defined by high concrete buildings, large parking lots and clear physical separation from the city. The 'million programme suburbs' soon largely became residential areas for people with few financial resources, as immigrants and socio-economically disadvantaged Swedes.
12. Gringo has recently produced a report together with TCO and the National Integration Board, where 1,000 inhabitants in three 'million programme suburbs' were interviewed about how they perceive the media image of their neighborhoods. Around half of the interviewees perceived that their suburb is being represented in a negative or a very negative way by mass media, and a third that this has negative consequences for their job opportunities (Bilden av förorten 2005: 5).
13. The fact that the Arabic word for darling, 'habibi', was recently included in the official Swedish national dictionary (*Svenska Akademins Ordlista*) must be considered a new recognition of such hybridized language.

References

Appiah, K. A. (1994). Identity, Authenticity, Survival. In Gutman, A. (ed.), *Multiculturalism: Examining the Politics of Recognition*. Princeton: Princeton University Press.

Appiah, K. A. (2005). *The Ethics of Identity*. Princeton: Princeton University Press.

Aytar, O. (2004). Kommunikation på olika villkor – om samrådet mellan invandrarorganisationerna och svenska staten [Communication on Equal Terms – About the Communication between the Immigrant Organizations and the Swedish State] in Föreningsliv, makt och integration. DS 2004:49.

Banakar, R. (1994). Rättens dilemma. Om konflikthantering i ett mångkulturellt samhälle [The Dilemma of Law. Managing Conflicts in a Multicultural Society]. Lund: Bokbox förlag.

Benhabib, S. (1992). Situating the Self. Gender, Community and Postmodernism in Contemporary Ethics. Cambridge: Polity.

Benhabib, S. (2002). The Claims of Culture. Equality and Diversity in the Global Era. Princeton: Princeton University Press.

Bilden av förorten – så ser medborgare i Hjällbo, Rinkeby och Rosengård på förorten, invandrare och diskriminering (2005) [The Image of the Suburb – How Citizens in Hjällbo, Rinkeby and Rosengård view the Suburb, Immigrants and Discrimination]. Report from the National Integration Board, TCO and Gringo.

de los Reyes, P. and Mulinari, D. (2005). Intersektionalitet. Kritiska reflektioner över (o)jämlikhetens landskap [Intersectionality. Critical Reflections upon the Landscape of (In)equality]. Lund: Lber förlag.

Fraser, N. (2003a). Shifting Paradigms? Recognition and Redistribution. In Hobson, B. (ed.), Recognition Struggles and Social Movements: Contested Identities, Agency and Power. Cambridge: Cambridge University Press, pp 21–35.

Fraser, N. and Honneth, A. (2003b). Redistribution or Recognition? A Political-Philosophical Exchange. London: Verso.

Hellgren, Z. (2005). Overcoming the Discrepancy between EU Anti-discrimination Directives and Persisting Discrimination at the National Level, report within the EU project CIVGOV, WP 3.

Hellgren, Z. and Hobson, B. (forthcoming during 2008): Gender and Ethnic Minority Claims in Swedish and EU Frames: Sites of Multi-level Political Opportunities and Boundary Making. In Roth, S. (ed.) Gender Issues and Women's Movements in the Expanding European Union, ed. Silke Roth, to be published during 2007, pp 211–236.

Holston, J & Appadurai, A. (1999). Cities and Citizenship. In Holston, J. (ed.), Cities and Citizenship. Durham and London: Duke University Press, pp 1–21.

Klandermans, B. and Goslinga, S. (1996). Media Discourse, Movement Publicity, and the Generation of Collective Action Frames. In McAdam, D., McCarthy; J. and Zald; M. N. (eds.), Comparative perspectives on Social Movements. Cambridge: Cambridge University Press, pp 312–338.

Laubenthal, B. (2004). La emergencia de las protestas de inmigrantes sin papeles en España: el caso de Murcia [The Emergent Protests of Paperless Immigrants in Spain: The Case of Murcia]. Paper presented at the conference "La Murcia Inmigrante. Exploraciones e Investigaciones" at the University of Murcia, 2.11.–5.11.2004.

Lipponen, Sami, Burns, Tom R. & Lilja, Maja (2006) På svenska villkor – om strukturell diskriminering i arbetslivet [On Swedish Terms – about Structural Discrimination in the Worklife]. Report within the Swedish governmental investigation on structural discrimination. (JU 2004:04).

Mezzadra, S. (2005): Derecho de fuga. Migraciones, ciudadanía y globalización [The Right to take Refuge. Migrations, Citizenship and Globalization], Madrid: Traficantes de sueños.

Morén-Alegret, R (1999). Integration(s) and Resistance. Governments, Capital, Social Organizations and Movements, and the Arrival of "Foreign Immigrants" in Barcelona and Lisbon. Doctoral thesis in Ethnic relations, University of Warwick, Centre for Research in Ethnic Relations (CRER).

Parekh, B. (2000). *Rethinking Multiculturalism. Cultural Diversity and Political Theory.* Harvard University Press.

Schierup, C., Hansen, P. and Castles, S. (2006). *Migration, citizenship and the European welfare state. A European Dilemma.* Oxford: Oxford University Press.

Solé, C. and Parella, S. (2003). Identidad colectiva y ciudadanía supranacional [Collective Identity and Supranational Citizenship] in *Papeles de Economnía Española*, no.98 2003, pp. 166–181.

Soysal Nhoglu, Y. (1994). *Limits of citizenship – migrants and postnational membership in Europe.* Chicago: The University of Chicago Press.

Stevenson, N. (2003). *Cultural Citizenship – Cosmopolitan Questions.* Maidenhead, Berkshire: Open University Press.

Stolcke, V. (1994). Europa: nuevas fronteras, nuevas retóricas de exclusion [Europe: New Borders, New Rhetorics of Exclusion]. In *Extranjeros en el paraíso* [Foreigners in Paradise]. Barcelona: Virus, pp. 235–267.

Suárez Navaz, L. (2004). *Rebordering the Mediterranean. Boundaries and Citizenship in Southern Europe.* New York and Oxford: Berghahn Books.

Taylor, C. (1994). The politics of recognition. In Gutman, A. (ed.), *Multiculturalism: Examining the Politics of Recognition.* Princeton: Princeton University Press.

Tilly, C (1978). *From mobilization to revolution.* Reading, Mass.: Addison-Wesley.

PART FOUR: MEDIA AND COMMUNICATION POLICY IN EUROPE

16

Misrecognitions: Associative and Communalist Visions in EU Media Policy and Regulation

Richard Collins

Abstract

A persistent theme in the affairs of the European Union has been the projection onto the media of problems that lie elsewhere. The absence of strong sentiments of attachment to the union by its 'citizens' is persistently blamed on deficiencies in Europe's media rather than being seen for what it is – an appropriate level and kind of engagement in the European Union as an 'associative' (Weber 1964) society; that is one bound together by reason not sentiment. This associative character of the EU is reflected in what can no longer be called the European Constitution but, in a delicate euphemism, the Reform Treaty[1] where there is scant consideration given to either the media, culture or to other sentimental, or 'communal' as Weber put it, issues. Nonetheless, although it is 'associative' principles that have principally driven European integration, 'communalist' concerns have long had, and continue to have, considerable salience in European policy and discourse, not least in the tormented progress of the Audio-visual Media Services Directive, the successor to the celebrated Television without Frontiers Directive.

Keywords

associative society, communal society, nationalism, functionalism, Television without Frontiers, Audio-visual Media Services Directive

Introduction

European policy, whether the 'high politics' of the Constitution or more specific areas, such as negotiation of the terms of the successor to the Television without Frontiers Directive (TVWF), develops rapidly. Commentaries on current issues risk rapidly passing their sell-by dates. In consequence I'll focus on structural issues, notably, the relationship between media representations of European Union politics and public perceptions; the extent to which the cohesion of the European Union depends on what Ernest Gellner (1983: 43) called the congruence of polity and culture; and the relationship between the media and what Max Weber (1964[1922]) called associative and communal forms of social organization.[2]

In 1982 the German MEP Wilhelm Hahn submitted his *Report on Radio and Television Broadcasting in the European Community* (European Parliament 1982) which stated, *inter alia*, that 'Information is a decisive...The vast majority of journalists do not 'think European'...Hence the predominance of negative reporting. Therefore, if European unification is to be encouraged, Europe must penetrate the media' (European Parliament 1982: 8).[3] A more nuanced, but strikingly similar, version of Hahn's arguments were rehearsed in the European Commission's *White Paper on a European Communication Policy* of 2006 which stated:

> The 'communication gap' between the European Union and its citizens is not new...people learn about politics and political issues largely through their national education systems and via their national, regional and local media...the 'public sphere' within which political life takes place in Europe is largely a national sphere...The media remain largely national... People feel remote from...the decision-making process and EU institutions...One reason for this is the inadequate development of a 'European public sphere' where the European debate can unfold' (European Commission 2006b: 4–5).

These sentiments, whether put forward in 1982 or 2006, are both representative and mistaken for they over-estimate and mis-recognize the importance of media and culture in the European Project.[4] Although there's an abundant scholarly literature questioning the thesis of strong and direct media effect, weak sentiments of attachment to the European Project by Europeans are often attributed to deficiencies in the media and the persistent consumption by Europeans of media works from outside Europe is seen as a threat to social and political cohesion and to the 'European Project'. Moreover, sentiments such as Hahn's mis-recognize the EU whose cohesion lies elsewhere, in being what Weber (1964[1922]) called an 'associative', rather than a 'communal', society: one bound together by 'rationally motivated adjustments' rather than by 'subjective feeling' (Weber 1964: 136). Obstacles to the European Project which lie in high politics are projected onto the media and thus mis-recognized. In high politics, the impasse presented by the stalled ratification of the European Constitution contrasts with the striking success of the EU in sustaining a 'dense web of commercial, economic, political and legal links' (Piris 2006)[5] though the achievement to which Piris testifies is insufficiently acknowledged because of belief in the necessary congruence of polity and culture (Gellner 1983) as a basis of social cohesion: a belief which attributes great importance to media of cultural reproduction.

In the domain of EU media and communications policy and regulation the Television without Frontiers (TVWF)[6] era, dominated by communalist questions of European identity, is giving way to a new era, that of the Audio-visual Media Services Directive (AVMSD),[7] which is likely to be focused on an associative issue – the extent to which freedom of expression may be safeguarded. Looking at the European Union in 2006 through 'communalist' eyes it may appear fragile and incomplete but through 'associative' eyes it appears as a remarkable achievement: the EU has enlarged our liberties, provided an economic framework for growing prosperity and economic security, built mutual confidence between its member states enabling us to remain at peace (with each other at least) and making negotiation of intra-European conflicts more tractable.

Although respondents to the Eurobarometer survey on 'the Future of Europe' wished for 'better information by the media' (Eurobarometer 2006: 12) and some respondents stated that 'the media often spreads word of problematic or negative aspects of the European Union' (Eurobarometer 2006: 21) the putative weakness of our affiliation to the EU is better attributed to the organization and conduct of high politics than to deficiencies of the mass media. Indeed responses to the German Presidency's attempts, in the first half of 2007, to restart the stalled constitutional process suggest that member states' own national high politics[8] were more important considerations than EU affiliation or cohesion.

Media representations and political disenchantment

At the risk of a banal insistence on the obvious, there are profound differences in values and visions attaching to Europe both within and between member states which cannot simply be ascribed to media influence – even in the UK, where Eurobarometer found 'weakness of positive perceptions and/or...abundance of criticism' concerning the EU to be 'a permanent feature' (Eurobarometer 2006: 9). Piquantly, an enquiry into BBC news coverage of the European Union, commissioned by the BBC's governors and undertaken in 2004 found grounds for the perception that BBC coverage of Europe is systematically biased in a pro-European way (BBC 2005: 3). Whether this inadequate treatment, because excessively positive, is damaging to the EU is an open question.

Nor can it be claimed that negative media coverage (whether or not excessively or unreasonably negative) has held back European unification. True, the rubric of 'ever closer union' in the Treaty can never, by definition, be achieved but the accession of seventeen new member states, the creation of the single market, the adoption of the Maastricht, Amsterdam and Nice Treaties, creation of the Eurozone (albeit not yet extending to all member states) – all since Hahn's statement – can hardly be judged insignificant steps on the road to 'ever closer union'. As François Duchene[9] commented, in the closing chapter of his biography of Jean Monnet, 'the European Community has already produced a political revolution' (Duchene 1994: 406) a revolution which should be seen in the context of only three other successful unforced political federations – Switzerland, the Netherlands and the United States – all of which, Duchene claims, unlike the EU 'came together in war against an overlord' (Duchene 1994: 408).

But, despite the BBC, there can be no doubt that much reporting of the EU in the United Kingdom is critical – even hostile (though critique focuses on what an Davidson, in the *Financial Times*, called 'high politics' whereas other aspects of EU policy and practice, such as trade liberalization and the single market, are viewed positively).[10] However, customarily the reporting of high politics in democracies, in the United Kingdom at least, is adversarial (see, the prime minister's Reuters speech of June 12 2007 which described the media as 'like a feral beast').[11] And, as the BBC has commented (in its own defence), 'An adversarial approach is the cornerstone of many key British institutions, such as Parliament and the courts. A robust exchange of views is acknowledged not as a way of generating heat but of casting light on a subject. Broadcasting is no different' (BBC 2005a: 3).

Despite the sentiments of Hahn and his epigones, one might think the absence of negative media coverage of the EU a greater cause for concern than its presence. How could the current high politics of the Union not be represented critically? Not only are they at an impasse but the blocked constitutional imbroglio perfectly epitomises the European 'democratic deficit'. Only four of the EU's member states, France, Luxembourg, the Netherlands and Spain, have actually permitted their citizens to vote on the Constitutional Treaty. Political parties remain organized at a national level and European Parliamentary elections are treated by voters and parties as a proxy for national elections. Moreover, the incomplete ratification of the Constitution is not the only sign of political disenchantment in the Union. The number of voters in successive elections to the European Parliament has fallen (from 63 per cent in the first election in 1979 to 45.7 per cent in the most recent election in 2004). If democratic decision-making is denied, one does not need to conjure into existence the bogy of the media to account for weak sentiments of attachment to the European Project.

The EU and media and communications policy

Let me turn from these observations about the media and the EU to the EU and the media. Although there are a number of live EU media policy issues, (such as media pluralism and concentration of ownership, the relationship between public service broadcasting and competition policy and regulation, and the drafting and discussion of a replacement to the Television without Frontiers (TVWF) Directive), these concerns are embedded in a macro-context where neither the Constitution nor the extant treaties say much about media and communications: the Constitution refers to freedom of expression, network infrastructure building and the audio-visual sector only as a subset of artistic creation.

Article II-71 on freedom of expression and information provides that:

1. Everyone has the right to freedom of expression. This right shall include freedom to hold opinions and to receive and impart information and ideas without interference by public authority and regardless of frontiers.
2. The freedom and pluralism of the media shall be respected.

This provision may seem banal because so familiar from Article 10 of the European Convention on Human Rights (ECHR), Article 19 of the UN Universal Declaration of Human Rights, Article

11 of France's Declaration of the Rights of Man and of the Citizen, Article 5 of the German Basic Law, the United States' Bill of Rights and in many other national instances. However, Article II-71 is not hedged around with exceptions as is the corresponding Article 10 in the European Convention on Human Rights.[12] It entitles EU 'citizens' to transgress rhetorical boundaries, offend, verbally and in writing, against established cultural codes and conventions and assert, in speech and writing, their differences.

In order to bring together the varied expressions sanctioned by Article II-71 the Constitution text provides for the Union to exercise powers to develop communication networks. Section 8 of the Constitution, Trans-European Networks Article III-246, states:

1. To help achieve the objectives referred to in Articles III-130 and III-220 and to enable citizens of the Union, economic operators and regional and local communities to derive full benefit from the setting-up of an area without internal frontiers, *the Union shall contribute to the establishment and development of trans-European networks in the areas of transport, telecommunications and energy infrastructures.*
2. Within the framework of a system of open and competitive markets, action by *the Union shall aim at promoting the interconnection and interoperability of national networks as well as access to such networks.* It shall take account in particular of the need to link island, landlocked and peripheral regions with the central regions of the Union. (My emphasis).

Here, it's worth noting that these constitutional provisions apply only to telecommunications networks, that is to 'carriage' and what we might name 'associative' infrastructure. Weber foreshadowed such an exercise of political authority and prioritization in referring to 'extremely important conditions in the fields of communication and transportation' and identified 'the services of the railway, the telegraph and the telephone' (Weber 1964: 339).

As regards content and culture, the Preamble to the Constitution proclaims Europe to be 'a continent open to culture, learning and social progress' and in Article I-3, part of cl. 3 affirms, 'It shall respect its rich cultural and linguistic diversity, and shall ensure that Europe's cultural heritage is safeguarded and enhanced'. Again, these are essentially permissive provisions, accepting of difference but not ones which foster a communalist Union. The Constitution empowers the Union only to take *supporting* action in respect of culture – attributing significantly less importance to culture at the European Union level[13] than to telecommunication networks or to, say, agriculture, energy, the environment and transport.

Chapter V, Section 3 Culture, Article III-280 provides:

1. The Union shall contribute to the flowering of the cultures of the member states, while respecting their national and regional diversity and at the same time bringing the common cultural heritage to the fore.
2. Action by the Union shall be aimed at encouraging cooperation between member states and, if necessary, supporting and complementing their action in the following areas:

(a) improvement of the knowledge and dissemination of the culture and history of the European peoples;

(b) conservation and safeguarding of cultural heritage of European significance;

(c) non-commercial cultural exchanges;

(d) artistic and literary creation, including in the audiovisual sector.

3. The Union and the member states shall foster cooperation with third countries and the competent international organizations in the sphere of culture, in particular the Council of Europe.

4. The Union shall take cultural aspects into account in its action under other provisions of the Constitution, in particular in order to respect and to promote the diversity of its cultures.

There is, of course, also the transposition into the draft Constitution of the celebrated 'Amsterdam Protocol' – the Protocol on the System of Public Broadcasting in the member states – as Protocol 27 of Part IV of the draft Constitution. But, essentially, the protocol is a subsidiarity provision which makes clear that member states may establish public service broadcasting services but only if so doing does not adversely and disproportionately affect competition and trade.[14] We have a paradox – there is little about media and communications explicitly defined in the European Union's formal constitutional texts yet the impact of the EU on media and communications in Europe has been considerable: establishment of the single market in television, liberalization of telecommunications across the member states are inconceivable except in the context of the EU. The impact principally has come by applying basic treaty provisions to European communication markets.

The TVWF Directive, described by the European Commission as the 'cornerstone of the European Union's audiovisual policy' (see http://europa.eu/scadplus/leg/en/lvb/l24101. htm, accessed 22 August 2006), came into being as a market integration measure. And the most comprehensive set of measures taken by the EU in media and communications, the telecommunications liberalization package of 2000 (which included the e-Commerce Directive) and a succession of judgements in the ECJ judgements (see the useful portal at http:// ec.europa.eu/comm/avpolicy/info_centre/library/case_law/index_en.htm, accessed 14 July 2006) underpin this emphasis. The EU's major initiatives in media and communications have been on what, more than ten years ago when I drew a distinction (Collins 1994) between liberal and *dirigiste* EU policy visions, I called the liberal side (although I now think this distinction would better have been defined as between *associative* and *communalist*).

Why the success of *liberal/associative* initiatives? Because the terms of the European Treaty, and the Constitution, are fundamentally friendly to a liberal market order; liberals go with the flow, *dirigistes* swim against it. Nonetheless, *liberal/associative* initiatives have been balanced on the *dirigiste/communalist* side by defensive battles to mitigate the effect of the operation of markets, such as the Amsterdam Protocol (Protocol 27 of the Constitution, p. 379), the MEDIA Programme (to be expanded to MEDIA PLUS, see http://ec.europa. eu/comm/avpolicy/media/index_en.html, accessed 14 July 2006) and the reining back of some of the maximalist liberal proposals in the Convergence Green Paper (European Commission 1997).

The historical shaping of EU media and communications policy

When the Treaty of Rome was promulgated, in 1957, it's doubtful whether anyone imagined that its provisions would apply to posts, telecommunications or broadcasting all of which[15] were then organized as national monopolies. The competition provisions of the Rome Treaty, so central to Monnet's vision of the European Communities, were unlikely to have been thought applicable to broadcasting and telecommunications – not least because there was little inter-state trading of these services. Yet the creation of a single market and the competition provisions of the Treaty, revised and reissued in the Constitution, have profoundly reshaped European broadcasting and telecommunications.

Cable relay systems, high-powered communication satellites, fibre-optic cables, digital compression and the adoption of GSM and IPTV standards have intensified competition, integrated markets and eroded national authority over electronic communications. But whilst there now hundreds of separate television channels available to European viewers and significant levels of intra-European trade in broadcasting services, broadcasting is clearly a less fully integrated and Europeanized a market than is telecommunications. For two reasons: first, intra-European linguistic and cultural differences continue to both inhibit development of pan-European services (see, *inter alia*, Collins 1998); and, second, member states continue to exert, and strive to maintain, significant levels of national control in broadcasting – as the support of almost half of member states (the 'gang of thirteen') for replacement of the 'country of origin' principle of TVWF by a 'country of reception' principle in the draft Audio-visual Media Services Directive (AVMSD).

Nonetheless, the combination of technological change and the liberalization of markets, playing out the logic of the provisions of the Treaty of Rome, changed the European media and communication landscape. New technologies made it possible for broadcasting (and telecommunication) services to be efficiently provided from outside member states and a succession of ECJ judgements (see, *inter alios*, Sacchi, Debauve and Mediawet I)[16] have demonstrated the legality of such activities. In 1984 the celebrated Television without Frontiers Green Paper (Commission of the European Communities 1984), foreshadowing the TVWF Directive (European Council 1989), opened the door to liberalization of member states' television broadcasting markets under the cloak of European integration conveniently provided by the European Parliament's earlier Hahn Report (European Parliament 1982) which asserted that a European identity, cultivated by European media, was required if European union was to be achieved. Hahn stated:

> European unification will only be achieved if Europeans want it. Europeans will only want it if there is such a thing as European identity. A European identity will only develop if Europeans are adequately informed. At present, information *vis a vis* the mass media is controlled at national level (European Parliament 1982: 8).

TVWF to AVMSD

Television without Frontiers brought together both associative and communalist elements of the 'European Project': market integration, liberalization and associationism on one hand and European identity building and communalism on the other. The term 'identity', used by Hahn, became a central focus of European broadcasting and audio-visual policy throughout the next two decades.[17] European identity politics both provided a convenient rationale for advocates of protection and subsidy of the film and television sector and also expressed the conviction of many that European political institutions would lack legitimacy and durability if the political structures of the EU were not made congruent with a European cultural identity. Essentially, European identity politics projected onto a large canvas the classically nationalist scenario of welding polity and culture together (Gellner 1983). But whereas classic nationalism sought to give political expression to an antecedent cultural community the European identity project sought to create a European cultural community, through the modern mass media, in order to sustain and legitimize an antecedent political institution – the European Community/European Union.

Various attempts were made to enact Hahn's scenario through pan-European television services (see *inter alia* Collins 1998) but the most important actual outcome has been to intensify competition within national broadcasting markets rather than to foster a pan-European cultural identity. Integration of EU television markets has made possible establishment of pan-European media firms, such as Bertelsmann/RTL and Canal+, and has enabled some firms to overcome European linguistic and cultural differences and offer a portfolio of products across the EU – Endemol and FremantleMedia are cases in point. But the policy has had some perverse effects. As the number of European television channels has risen, so the proportion of television programming of non-European origin (notably in fiction and entertainment) has grown (see *inter alios* the yearbooks of the European Audio-visual Observatory e.g. European Audio-visual Observatory 2005).[18]

Moreover, the range of imported television programmes has narrowed as importers have maintained imports from the USA and thus squeezed out works from other non-member states: for example Canadian television exports to the EU fell from $611 million in 1999/2000 to $270 million in 2004/5 – a fall attributed to 'increased demand for domestic programming in the European Union' (see CRTC 2006: para. 7). And benefits have accrued disproportionately to large EU member states[19] (although member states' own support policies, as Graham (2005: 17) found, have 'acted as barriers to cross-border trade, thus possibly inhibiting cultural exchanges among member states'). These factors provide the context in which the drafting (current at the time of writing) of the successor to Television without Frontiers (TVWF), the draft Audio-visual Media Services Directive (European Commission 2005), has taken place.

New points of contention have appeared – rather than the perennial conflict over European content quotas and thus, putatively, over European identity, the main points of debate have been the country of origin principle; extension of the scope of the Directive to 'non-linear' online services; and stronger duties of protection from unwanted and harmful content [notably protection of minors and the incitement of hatred). The question of EU cohesion, whether associative or communal, has been displaced by those of the relative importance of national or EU jurisdiction and the extent to which jurisdiction can effectively be exercised in new circumstances.

Country of origin or country of reception?

The keystone of the single market in television, embodied in the TVWF Directive, has been the country of origin principle, whereby goods from other EU member states are treated in the same way as domestically produced goods. European Court of Justice (ECJ) case law[20] qualified this principle somewhat enabling, under certain conditions, a member state (MS1) to apply its own rules to broadcasts from another member state (MS2). The AVMSD promises to build on ECJ precedents so that MS1 would be able to exercise 'country of reception' powers if, first, broadcasts from MS2 are directed at MS1 and, second, establishment of an enterprise in MS2 was done to evade MS1's rules.

Thirteen member states proposed radical change to the 'country of origin' principle of TVWF proposing that the AVMSD should be based on a country of reception principle.[21] This means that a receiving member state would be able to discriminate against exogenous services which did not conform to its rules thus seriously compromising the single market in television. Putting the country of origin principle into play puts at issue wider normative relationships between politics, economics and culture in EU television and the degree to which subsidiarity should apply in broadcasting regulation. Seen from a European integrationist point of view the country of origin principle is vitally important. But from another point of view, the country of origin principle has unleashed a race to the bottom where cherished measures, such as keeping children's television free of advertising or requiring a programme schedule that balanced information, education and entertainment, have been, or are in danger of being, washed away. In this view of things, the country of reception, and national jurisdiction, is seen as the locus where citizens' and consumers' interests can best be secured.

Extending the scope of the Directive

The Commission also proposed to extend the scope of the AVMSD beyond conventional television broadcasting. This, from one point of view, makes eminent sense: new technologies and standards have made delivery of television like services in ways which would fall outside the TVWF Directive. But, from another point of view, the AVMSD threatens to do too much by chilling entry and innovation. The United Kingdom national electronic communications regulator, Ofcom, has proposed that, rather than attempting to distinguish between linear and non-linear services – a distinction which Ofcom believes is hard to sustain – the Directive 'should be limited in scope to cover only those services which "look and feel" like television broadcasting (e.g. television delivered over IP networks – IPTV)' (Ofcom 2006: 3) because consumers expect more protection in respect of such services.

Protection from harm and offence

Consumer expectations, and/or intensified elite concern over Internet content, led to inclusion in the draft Directive of the clauses: 'member states shall take appropriate measures to ensure that audiovisual media services under their jurisdiction are not made available in such a way that might seriously impair the physical, mental or moral development of minors' and 'member states shall ensure by appropriate means that audiovisual media services and audiovisual commercial communications provided by providers under their jurisdiction do not contain any incitement to hatred based on sex, racial or ethnic origin, religion or belief, disability, age or sexual orientation' (European Commission 2005: 24). These provisions may seem unexceptionable – who could reasonably object to preventing serious impairment of the development of minors or to prevention of incitement to hatred? But, because of the difficulties of distinguishing between services accessible to minors and those for adults and also in distinguishing reliably what will 'seriously impair' and constitute 'incitement to hatred' such measures promise (or threaten) to generally effect the character of electronic media content throughout the EU and, some fear, thereby to chill freedom of expression.

Television and the European project

Discussions of the potential scope and content of the AVMSD undoubtedly reflect the impact of technological change on established broadcasters and on the effectiveness of viewer protection but also concern the scope and character of the 'European project'. The country of origin principle, formerly seen as indispensable to realization of the 'European project', by both 'liberals/associationists' (for its single market effect) and 'dirigistes/communalists' (for its potential to bond European television viewers into a collective European identity), has come under attack for its, putative, commercialization of European broadcasting and for thus increasing demand for non-European programming.

Identity, Europe and cohesion

Traditionally, the case for extending EU competencies in media and communications and for an enhanced role for Media and Communications in the 'European project' has rested on the communalist presumption that European identity must be fostered in order to strengthen political legitimacy and strengthen social cohesion in the EU: unless the EU is grounded in a sentiment of belonging shared among European citizens – in Weber's terms 'communalism' – it will lack viability and durability.

The belief that the legitimacy and durability of political institutions, states, depends on their symmetrical relationship to cultural communities, nations, is both pervasive and long established. National states in which the principle, as Gellner put it, of political and cultural congruence (Gellner 1983: 43) exemplify the normative model. Given the pervasiveness of nationalism in Europe, the cradle of nation states, it's not surprising that the doctrine of nationalism – that is of a congruence between polity and culture – is projected onto the EU. But there are obvious difficulties in creating what Eurobarometer called a 'European cultural supra-nationality' (Eurobarometer 2006a: 44); that is in making polity and culture congruent on a European scale. Language provides the most obvious case in point – the EU has twenty official languages. But as well as similarity *within* the putative national political community the nationalist project also requires difference from those *outside* the putative community. But much of what Europeans share, they share with others beyond the continent of Europe and attempts to define a communalist European identity, shared only by those under the umbrella of a European political institution and distinguishable from other identities, are thus likely to end only in disappointment and frustration.

This issue has, in our domain at least, focused for the last couple of decades on the 'problem' of European consumers' taste for American media and on a sometimes frantic effort to build European cinema and television production which could succeed in displacing America from the viewing habits of Europeans[22] and overcoming what Hoskins and Mirus (1988) called the low cultural discount[23] which attaches to American product in European markets. But latterly the steam seems to have gone out of concern about the possible erosion of difference between European and American identities and cultures under the influence of films and television programmes from the United States. Perhaps because the foreign policy and practice of the USA has over the last five years or so alienated the sentiments of many Europeans (and many Americans). And also because of a recognition that the impact of American audio-visual works, both economically and culturally, has been somewhat less than was once feared we no longer believe, as once we seem to have done, that Europe is so fragile as to be overturned by one more percentage point of Hollywood product on European screens.

As the EU has grown and as its constituent parts have become more multicultural and multi-ethnic, so the difficulties of realizing the politico-cultural congruence mandated in nationalist theory have nudged sentiments towards acknowledging that the classic political nation-state structure, based on mutually supporting and symmetrical political and cultural institutions, is neither necessary nor inevitable. Migration has undoubtedly contributed enormously to such a change in thinking but so too has the EU itself had an enormous impact in 'de-singularizing' the allegiances and identities of its citizens. We all inhabit European as well as national identities.

Association, functionalism and Europe

But if culture is not to be the European social glue, as communalists advocate and prescribe, then what is? First, I think it's important to acknowledge that the EU has survived, thrived and grown for nearly 50 years. It is a fantastic and unprecedented achievement. But its principle of success has not been that of a nationalist congruence between polity and culture. Rather it's been the functionalist 'methode Monnet' – a system of engendering political cohesion not on the basis of a common culture or language but of creating facts and acts which force new relationships and new forms of collaboration. The successes and strengths of the EU are rooted in association (as Weber puts it), and in 'functional' (as Mitrany puts it) relationships between Europeans and EU member states, rather than in communalism and congruence between polity and culture.

The functional model of European integration was formulated explicitly by David Mitrany in his last major work *The Functional Theory of Politics* (Mitrany 1975). One of Mitrany's disciples summarized the functional theory as the idea that man (sic) can be weaned away from his loyalty to the nation state by the experience of fruitful international co-operation; that international organization arranged according to the requirements of the task could increase welfare rewards to individuals beyond the level obtainable within the state...individuals and organizations would begin to learn the benefits of co-operation and would increasingly be involved in an international co-operative ethos, creating interdependencies' (Taylor in Mitrany 1975: x).

At least some of this may seem somewhat starry-eyed, 'an international co-operative ethos' perhaps overstates the level of peace and harmony which reputedly informs meetings of the European Council. But it's surely right to claim that common institutional structures do create interdependencies. And that's the core of the 'methode Monnet' – trerchantly asserted by Monnet himself: 'While fifty-five countries were meeting in Lome or Brussels to seek their common interests, our diplomats were holding pointless debates about European identity' (Monnet 1978: 499). The focus on culture and identity that our professional field leads us towards sometimes leads us to mis-recognize the achievements, the robustness and the proven worth of functional, rather than nationalist, methods of building Europe. For the European Union is an instance of what Weber identified as an 'associative', rather than a 'communal', society:

> A social relationship will be called 'communal' if and so far as the orientation of social action – whether in the individual case, on the average, or in the pure type – is based on a subjective feeling of the parties, whether affectual or traditional, that they belong together. A social relationship will, on the other hand, be called 'associative' if and in so far as the orientation of social action within it rests on a rationally motivated adjustment of interests or a similarly motivated agreement, whether the basis of rational judgement be absolute values or reasons of expediency (Weber 1964[1922]: 136).

Weber's distinction between associative and communal relationships echoes the well known distinction (which Meinecke 1970[1907]) made, and which has been comprehensively explored by Smith 1991, 1995) between 'civic' and 'ethnic' nationalism. It also suggests resonances of Toennies' (1988) distinction between 'gesellschaft' and 'gemeinschaft'. Smith asserts that associative, or civic, societies are a majority of contemporary states: he states that fewer than 10 per cent of United Nations member states are nation states (Smith 1995: 86).

In contrast to Television without Frontiers, where much debate focused on the 'communalist' question of European content quotas, the draft Audio-visual Media Services Directive suggests a shift towards a more 'associative' frame of reference. Certainly, the two central issues (of country of origin v. country of reception as a locus for regulation and the scope of the Directive, whether (and if so how) 'broadcasting' principles and practice are to be projected onto new media, suggest a different set of concerns and assumptions.

Coming to terms with media change: the draft AVMSD and convergence

The proposal to extend the scope of the TVWF Directive by applying television (linear service) regulation to non-linear services represents one way to address the challenges posed by convergence. Convergence is generally understood to be the effect of digitalization in eroding distinctions between different networks, technologies and established systems of service delivery. The European Commission, in its Green Paper on Convergence (European Commission 1997), asserted that 'digital technology now allows both traditional and new communication services – whether voice, data, sound or pictures – to be provided over many different networks'. Convergence also makes different networks and services substitutable and thus opens up the possibility of a particular service being provided under different regulatory regimes: for example, a film might be accessible via broadcast television, theatrical exhibition, video on demand (VoD) or purchase/rental as a DVD or video cassette.

The Commission's Convergence Green Paper of 1997 identified three alternative regulatory responses to convergence:

1. Current vertical regulatory models would be left in place. This means that different rules apply in telecommunications and audiovisual/broadcasting sectors, and to a lesser extent in publishing and IT.
2. Develop a separate regulatory model for new activities, to co-exist with telecommunications and broadcasting regulation.
3. Introduce a new regulatory model to cover the whole range of existing and new services (European Commission 1997: 34).

Each of the Commission's three proposals would, if implemented, impact differently on established regimes in different member states. The case of Germany exemplifies the difficulties which would attach to either of options 2 and 3: because the German Basic Law, the Grund Gesetz, specifies broadcasting jurisdiction resides with the Laender and Telecommunications with the Bund: implementation of regulatory convergence across broadcasting and telecommunications in Germany would be very difficult. The federal division of powers in Belgium poses analogous challenges. The third option identified by the Commission admits the possibility of establishing the 'new regulatory model' as either a projection of the old onto the new or the new onto the old.

Convergence and substitutability poses obvious challenges to established regulatory regimes, including TVWF. If a work is regulated under the TVWF regime when accessed via broadcast television and under another, notably the e-Commerce Directive, when retrieved via a VoD network there are obvious possibilities of regulatory arbitrage and evasion. The AVMSD is drafted so as to apply to online (non-linear) services the same type of regime as has operated in broadcast television – it is thus a version of options 1 and 2 canvassed by the Commission – though it is as yet unclear, and a matter of intensely disputed interpretation among those contributing to the consultation and drafting process, precisely what will be included and what excluded from the scope of the AVMSD.

The draft AVMSD and freedom of expression
The draft AVMSD further poses the challenge of proportionality – of extending an established remit in new circumstances but without extending it too far. Criticism of the draft AVMSD

contends that the AVMSD extends the reach of regulation too far, e.g. to blogs and online newspapers, and that its effect will be to chill and compromise the right to freedom of expression featured in the Constitution (Article II-71).[24] In this respect the terms of the draft AVMSD contrasts with the EU position defined in the e-Commerce Directive where the importance of freedom of expression is stated explicitly.[25]

It's important to acknowledge that (except for some absolutists) the issue aroused by the AVMSD is not one of regulation or no regulation but of the appropriate level and manner of regulation. Freedom of expression is a hard doctrine, the entitement to freedom of expression is meaningful only in hard cases – if freedom of expression does not extend to 'speech' that some find offensive and to expression that some may judge harmful, a right to freedom of expression is an empty right. Few argue that there are no cases where an exception to a general entitlement to freedom of expression should not be made.

However, there is then the important second order issue of whether exceptions, such as those respecting minors,[26] should be a matter for the law in general or for statutory regulation. Or, putting a specific case, should the Internet and/or broadcasting be subject to regulation beyond that which applies generally to speech and writing? If it is judged that, on balance, it is better to rely on the law in general rather than on sector specific statutory regulation, and I think this is the direction in which the current now flows, then the role of self- and co-regulation is likely to become more important (as the AVMSD signals). It is clearly better that relevant instutitions develop their own codes and procedures to foster lawful behaviour just as it is better that each of us as an individual acts lawfully of our own volition rather than because we are compelled to do so by a vigilant policing.

If the era of TVWF was one where debate and concern focused on the communalist issue of collective cultural identity then it seems likely that the era of the AVMSD will be one of concern about the associationist issue of freedom of expression. In the United Kingdom at least the context in which the AVMSD is under consideration is one of increasing government pressure on freedom of expression. It would be comforting to believe that the United Kingdom was exceptional among EU member states in this respect. Porter (2006) provides a convenient (and chilling) account of recent United Kingdom government initiatives in this area. The provision of the Communications Act 2003 that Ofcom must have regard to the need only to secure 'an appropriate level of freedom of expression' (Communications Act 2003: 1.3.(4) (g)) is also eloquent. As too is the government's publication of its *Consultation on the Possession of Extreme Pornographic Material* (Home Office and the Scottish Executive 2005) which proposes suppression of lawful material distributed over the Internet. Moreover, the Racial and Religious Hatred Act 2006, despite successive Parliamentary defeats which led to softening of the government's original drafts, contains provisions bearing on freedom of expression which were first presented in the Anti-Terrorism, Crime and Security Bill in 2001 and then in the Serious Organized Crime and Police Act 2005. These are to the effect that use or display of threatening words with the intention of stirring up religious hatred is to be unlawful. The effect of the Act is unlikely to do other than chill the exercise of our entitlement to freedom of expression.[27]

Perhaps surprisingly, but one must never overestimate the coherence of so large and baggy a beast as a government, the United Kingdom has argued in its contribution to the drafting of the AVMSD that the inclusion in the draft Directive of a clause (3e at the time of writing) which requires member states to ensure that audio-visual media services do not contain any incitement to hatred[28] is too broadly drawn and would have a negative effect on freedom of speech. The United Kingdom also argued that the unified application of a single policy to broadcasting and on-demand services would have a diproportionate and adverse impact on freedom of speech (see DCMS 2006). Similar arguments for distinguishing between broadcast and online services have been made elsewhere.

The free expression civil society organization Article XIX's response to the Council of Europe's proposals to apply regulations devised for broadcasting to the Internet (and in particular the institution of a right of reply in respect of Internet publication) brings home the potential adverse impact of the AVMSD proposal to apply broadcasting (linear) regulation to online (non-linear) services. As Article XIX argues, such a strategy would not recognize or appropriately acknowledge the distinct characteristics of the Internet (see Article XIX 2003: 7–8) as it cogently argues using the example of the 'right to reply' entitlement enshrined in the TVWF.

Conclusion

> The statist conception of the nation has to be replaced by the social and the cultural conception. The nation can no longer be defined by the creation of a unitary space in which citizenship transcends social and cultural diversity. It must be characterised by the quest for inter-cultural communication and social solidarity. It must be a united society that brings people closer together and tears down barriers, but in cultural terms it must encourage a dialogue (Touraine 2000: 227).

The word 'conclusion' suggests a firmer and more confident closure than is probably appropriate to this paper. The cluster of linked propositions and commentary which precedes these closing comments do not point towards a clear conclusion but rather towards two kinds of further propositions.

First, a situated and specific proposal which derives from my analytical commentary on the draft AVMSD where I argued that there are three novel structuring forces at work in contemporary EU broadcasting policy. Notably, a significant resiling from the established governing principle of European broadcasting policy, the country of origin/single market principle; an as yet unresolved debate about whether consistency in regulation is best achieved by projecting broadcasting regulatory principles and practices onto new media or vice versa; and a shift in the fundamental value debate that informs EU audio-visual and broadcasting policy from communalist to associationist questions.

And second, a proposition of greater generality, that the relative importance of the media and European high politics has often been mis-recognized and that the turbulence in the course of the European project which we are now experiencing is better understood as arising from the conduct and character of European high politics rather than from media representations.

Here a caution is appropriate and salutary: generalization about the EU is dangerous. Each of the 27 member states has a different formation, a different perspective and a different set of practices. Generalization, based as mine is (and perhaps of most of us) on long-standing experience of only one of the 27 is likely to be speculative and possibly inaccurate. Moreover, United Kingdom perspectives are sometimes thought to express the very particular perspective of what Stephen George (1990) referred to, the United Kingdom as the EU's 'awkward partner'. Perhaps so, but perhaps each of the 27 constituent states has its own awkwardness. And if so we may better conduct our common European affairs and secure our common European interests by thinking of ourselves as engaged in a Weberian associative project, where principles of cohesion and collaboration are largely functional (in Mitrany's sense) rather than communal and resting on strong cultural affinities and communalities.

The EU has shown that a multicultural, multi-linguistic political community can survive, thrive and benefit those who live in it without the 'thick', visceral, shared experience of strong cultural community and mutual identity recognition. Indeed I think this is one of the great achievements of the EU. It has demonstrated that shared language and cultural values are not essential to the creation and maintenance of durable and effective political institutions. Of course, there are difficulties in the EU enterprise which are not present, or not so insistently present, in national political enterprises but so too are there possibilities and successes which go beyond what's achievable under a classically national umbrella. And the national umbrella looks more and more leaky in a world where sovereignty must more and more be shared if it is to be exercised effectively and in a world where fewer and fewer of us are covered by normative national umbrellas as our European societies pluralize and become more multicultural, multi-linguistic and multi-ethnic.

We have the opportunity to realize our communalist and associative relationships at different levels and through different institutional forms. As Alain Touraine has argued, statehood and (national) identity need to be decoupled. I find his argument no less convincing in the context of the EU than I do in the context of nation states.

Notes

1. The bulk of this chapter was drafted before the Constitution was re-nominated as the Reform Treaty and before the final version of the AVMSD was agreed.
2. See my 'Associative or Commun/e discussion of these terms.
3. This, widely quoted, section of the text of the report is reproduced at p. 8 in the European Parliament's compilation of working documents 1-1013-81 of 23 February 1982 which is conveniently available online at the University of Pittsburgh's site http://aei.pitt.edu/3120/01/000057.PDF. Accessed 16 June 2007.

4. I use this imprecise term to refer to the commitment to the 'ever closer union' defined in the preamble to the European Treaty, see text at OJC 191. 29.7.1992

5. Piris was chair of the legal secretariat dealing with the drafting of the Constitution.

6. The Television without Frontiers Directive was promulgated in 1989 (see European Council 1989).

7. See European Commission 2005.

8. I think of Poland's concern for the weight of its vote in EU decisions, France's excision of high-level references to 'competition' in the Treaty, the Netherlands' concern for the sovereignty of its Parliament, the United Kingdom's derogation from certain codification of human rights principles in the Treaty and so on.

9. Duchene is described in his obituary (*Independent*, 25 July 2005) as having had a 'close working relationship' with Monnet. See http://www.sussex.ac.uk/sei/documents/independent_obituary_-_duchene.pdf. Accessed 16 June 2007.

10. Davidson stated 'the antithesis between high politics and pragmatic trade liberalization has been the most consistent theme in the running policy debate between the members of the Community, and it has regularly pitted the United Kingdom against the original Six' (*Financial Times*, 19 January 1993, p. v).

11. At http://www.pm.gov.uk/output/Page11923.asp or http://www.telegraph.co.uk/news/main.jhtml?xml=/news/2007/06/12/nmedia212.xml. Accessed 16 June 2007.

12. Article 10.2 of the ECHR states 'The exercise of these freedoms, since it carries with it duties and responsibilities, may be subject to such formalities, conditions, restrictions or penalties as are prescribed by law and are necessary in a democratic society, in the interests of national security, territorial integrity or public safety, for the prevention of disorder or crime, for the protection of health or morals, for the protection of the reputation or rights of others, for preventing the disclosure of information received in confidence, or for maintaining the authority and impartiality of the judiciary'. At http://www.pfc.org.uk/legal/echrtext.htm. Accessed 14 July 2006.

13. Many member states, of course, attribute great importance to cultural policy and may consequently regard it as more appropriately addressed as member state level.

14. The relevant text states: 'insofar as such funding is granted to broadcasting organisations for the fulfilment of the public service remit as conferred, defined and organised by each Member State, and insofar as such funding does not affect trading conditions and competition in the Union to an extent which would be contrary to the common interest, while the realisation of the remit of that public service shall be taken into account'.

15. Use of absolutes, such as 'all', are (almost) invariably lethal to the writer. There are (almost) always exceptions – such as the telephony cooperatives of the Nordic countries, municipal telephony in Hull England (and some Nordic countries), the Laender broadcasters in Germany (both Hull and the Laender broadcasters were publicly owned local monopolies) and non-national radio services (such as Radio Free Europe). But despite such exceptions monopolies prevailed throughout Europe and exceptions to this rule were principally located outside the 'six' who were parties to the Treaty of Rome.

16. See the classic cases: Sacchi, Case 155–73. Judgment of the Court of 30 April 1974. At http://eur-lex.europa.eu/LexUriServ/LexUriServ.do?uri=CELEX:61973J0155:EN:NOT. Accessed 14 July 2006; Debauve, Case 52/79. Judgment of the Court of 18 March 1980. At http://eur-lex.europa.eu/LexUriServ/LexUriServ.do?uri=CELEX:61979J0052:EN:NOT. Accessed 14 July 2006 and

Mediawet I. Case C-288/89. Judgment of the Court of 25 July 1991. At http://eur-lex.europa.eu/LexUriServ/LexUriServ.do?uri=CELEX:61989J0288:EN:NOT. Accessed 14 July 2006.

17. But the term 'identity' is absent from the Constitution. A keyword search found two uses of the word 'identity' – one in connection with the status of churches (Article I-52) and one in connection with identity cards (Article III-125).

18. Although the Commission found (European Commission 2006) that (in fifteen member states surveyed in 2002) European works accounted for 66 per cent of EU TV.

19. For example, more than half the UK's 2004 TV exports went to Europe (ONS 2005: Table 5).

20. See Case C-23/93 TV 10 SA v. Commissariaat voor de Media, paragraph 21.

21. In the Draft Services Directive the country of origin principle was adopted for some sectors but not for either telecommunications or audio-visual services (see European Commission 2004b and 2006a).

22. It's worth noting that the European view of the USA is by no means fixed – earlier moments in the formation of the 'European project' were distinguished by pervasive expressions of philo-Americanism, not least by Monnet and other founding fathers of the EU such as Hallstein.

23. Hoskins and Mirus (1988: 500) define this as "A particular programme, rooted in one culture, and thus attractive in that environment, will have a diminished appeal elsewhere as viewers find it difficult to identify with styles, values, beliefs , institutions and behavioural patterns of the material in question".

24. A further node of opposition to the AVMSD rests on the belief that the AVMSD will inhibit innovation, raise prices to consumers and slow the responsiveness of services to consumer demands.

25. Cl. 9 of the preamble states: 'The free movement of information society services can in many cases be a specific reflection in Community law of a more general principle, namely freedom of expression as enshrined in Article 10(1) of the Convention for the Protection of Human Rights and Fundamental Freedoms, which has been ratified by all the member states; for this reason, directives covering the supply of information services must ensure that this activity may be engaged in freely in the light of that Article, subject only to the restrictions laid down in paragraph 2 of that Article and in Article 46(1) of the Treaty; this Directive is not intended to affect national fundamental rules and principles relating to freedom of expression'.

26/ See, inter alios, the Commission's Recommendation on Protection of Minors and Human Dignity at http://ec.europa.eu/comm/avpolicy/reg/minors/index_en.htm, accessed, 12.08.08 .

27. See Racial and Religious Hatred Act 2006 Chapter 1. At http://www.opsi.gcv.uk/acts/acts2006/20060001.htm. Accessed 7 July 2006.

28. Based on sex, racial or ethnic origin, religion or belief, age or sexual orientation.

References

Article XIX (2003), Memorandum on the Draft Council of Europe Recommendation on the Right of Reply in the New Media Environment. London. Article XIX. At http://www.article19.org/pdfs/analysis/council-of-europe-right-of-reply.pdf. Accessed 11 July 2006.

BBC (2005), BBC News Coverage of the European Union. Independent Panel Report. At http://www.bbcgovernors.co.uk/docs/reviews/independentpanelreport.pdf. Accessed 11 July 2006.

BBC (2005a), The European Union – Perceptions of the BBC's Reporting: Management's Response. At http://www.bbcgovernors.co.uk/docs/reviews/eu_management_response.pdf. Accessed 21 July 2006.

Collins, R. (1994), Broadcasting and Audio-visual Policy in the European Single Market. London: John Libbey.

Collins, R. (1998), *From Satellite to Single Market: New Communication Technology and European Public Service Television 1982–1992*. London: LSE Books/Routledge.

Collins, R (2000), 'Associative or Communal Society? The Globalization of Media and Claims for Communality', in P. Askonas and A. Stewart (eds), *Social Inclusion: Possibilities and Tensions*. Basingstoke and London: Macmillan, pp. 186–204.

Commission of the European Communities (1984), *Television without Frontiers. Green Paper on the Establishment of the Common Market for Bradcasting especially by Satellite and Cable*. COM (84) 300 final. Luxembourg: Office for Official Publications of the European Communities.

Communications Act (2003) Chapter 21. At http://www.opsi.gov.uk/acts/acts2003/20030021.htm. Accessed 29 June 2007.

CRTC [Canadian Radio-television and Telecommunications Commission] (2006), *Broadcasting Notice of Public Hearing CRTC 2006–5. Review of Certain Aspects of the Regulatory Framework for Over-the-air Television*. Ottawa: CRTC. At

http://www.crtc.gc.ca/archive/ENG/Hearings/2006/n2006-5.htm?Print=True. Accessed 11 September 2006.

Duchene, F. (1994), *Jean Monnet: The First Statesman of Interdependence*. New York: Norton.

Eurobarometer (2006), 'The Future of Europe – May 2006'. At http://www.europa-kommissionen.dk/upload/application/e945369f/future_of_europe.pdf. Accessed 11 September 2006.

Eurobarometer (2006a). 'The European Citizens and the Future of Europe'.

At http://ec.europa.eu/public_opinion/quali/ql_futur_en.pdf. Accessed 12 July 2006.

European Audiovisual Observatory (2005), *Yearbook* (5 volumes). Strasbourg. European Commission (1997), *Green Paper on the Convergence of the Telecommunications, Media and Information Technology Sectors, and the Implications for Regulation*. COM (97) 623: 3.12.1997. Brussels: European Commission. At the portal site: http://europa.eu.int/ISPO/infosoc/telecompolicy/en/comm-en.htm. Accessed 18 July 2006.

European Commission (2003). *Green Paper on Services of General Interest*. COM (2003) 270, 21.5.2003. Brussels: European Commission.

European Commission (2005), *Proposal for a DIRECTIVE OF THE EUROPEAN PARLIAMENT AND OF THE COUNCIL AMENDING COUNCIL DIRECTIVE 89/552/EEC on the Coordination of Certain Provisions Laid Down by Law, Regulation or Administrative Action in member states Concerning the Pursuit of Television Broadcasting Activities*. COM(2005) 646 final 2005/0260 (COD). Brussels: European Commission. At

http://ec.europa.eu/comm/avpolicy/docs/reg/modernisation/proposal_2005/com2005-646-final-en.pdf. Accessed 15 July 2006.

European Commission (2006). *Fifth Report from the Commission to the Council, the European Parliament, the European Economic and Social Committee and the Committee of the Regions on the Application of Directive 89/552/EEC 'Television without Frontiers'*. COM(2006) 49 final. Brussels: European Commission. At http://eur-lex.europa.eu/LexUriServ/site/en/com/2006/com2006_0049en01.pdf. Accessed 11 July 2006.

European Commission (2006a). *White Paper on a European Communication Policy*. COM (2006) 35 final. Brussels: European Commission. At http://ec.europa.eu/communication_white_paper/doc/white_paper_en.pdf. Accessed 19 September 2006.

European Communities (2005), *Treaty Establishing a Constitution for Europe*. Luxembourg: Office for Official Publications of the European Communities. At http://europa.eu/constitution/en/lstoc1_en.htm. Accessed 12 July 2006.

European Parliament (1982), *Report on radio and television broadcasting in the European Community on behalf of the Committee on Youth, Culture, Education, Information and Sport.* [The Hahn Report]. PE Document I-1013/81.

European Council (1989), *Directive on the Coordination of Certain Provisions Laid Down by Law, Regulation or Administrative Action in member states Concerning the Pursuit of Television Broadcasting Activities. 89/552/EEC.* Official Journal L 298. 17.10.1989. P. 0023–0030.

Gellner, E. (1983). *Nations and Nationalism.* Oxford: Blackwell.

George, S. (1990), *An Awkward Partner: Britain in the European Community.* Oxford: Oxford University Press.

Graham, D. and Associates (2005), *Impact Study of Measures (Community and National) Concerning the Promotion of Distribution and Production of TV Programmes Provided for Under Article 25(a) of the TV Without Frontiers Directive. Final Report.* Brussels: The Audio-visual, Media and Internet Unit. Directorate-General Information Society and Media. European Commission. At http://ec.europa.eu/comm/avpolicy/docs/library/studies/finalised/4-5/27-03-finalreport.pdf. Accessed 14 September 2006.

Hartz, L. (1964), *The Founding of New Societies: Studies in the History of the United States, Latin America, South Africa, Canada and Australia.* New York: Harcourt Brace and World.

Home Office and the Scottish Executive (2005), *Consultation on the Possession of Extreme Pornographic Material.* London: Home Office. At http://www.homeoffice.gov.uk/docs4/Consultation_Extreme_Pornographic_Material.pdf. Accessed 2 September 2005.

Hoskins, Colin, and Mirus, R. (1988), 'Reasons for the U.S. Dominance of the International Trade in Television Programs', *Media, Culture and Society,* 10: 4, pp. 499–515.

Meinecke, F. (1970[1907]), *Cosmopolitanism and the National State.* Princeton: Princeton University Press.

Mitrany, D. (1975), *The Functional Theory of Politics.* Oxford: Martin Robertson.

Monnet, J. (1978), *Memoirs.* London: Collins.

Ofcom (2006), *Ofcom Position Paper – Scope. On the Proposal for a DIRECTIVE OF THE EUROPEAN PARLIAMENT AND OF THE COUNCIL AMENDING COUNCIL DIRECTIVE 89/552/EEC on the Coordination of Certain Provisions Laid Down by Law, Regulation or Administrative Action in member states Concerning the Pursuit of Television Broadcasting Activities COM(2005) 546 final (Television without Frontiers).* London: Ofcom. At http://publicaffairs.linx.net/public/eu/audiovisual/Ofcom_Mini_Paper_Scope.pdf. Accessed 15 July 2006.

ONS [Office for National Statistics] (2005), *International Transactions of the UK Film and Television Industries, 2004.* London: Office for National Statistics. At http://www.statistics.gov.uk/pdfdir/itf1005.pdf. Accessed 11 September 2006.

Piris, J. -C. (2006), *The Constitution for Europe: A Legal Analysis.* Cambridge: Cambridge University Press.

Porter, H. (2006), 'Blair Laid Bare: the Article That May Get You Arrested', *Independent,* 29 June. At http://news.independent.co.uk/uk/politics/article1129827.ece. Accessed 14 July 2006.

Smith, A. (1991), *National Identity.* London: McGraw-Hill.

Smith, A. (1995), *Nations and Nationalism in a Global Era.* Cambridge: Polity.

Toennies, F. (1988[1887]), *Gemeinschaft und Gesellschaft* (ed. and trans by C. P. Loomis (1957) as *Community and Society*). New Brunswick: Transaction.

Touraine, A. (2000[1997]), *Can We Live Together? Equality and Difference* (trans D. Macey). Cambridge: Polity.

Weber, M. (1964[1922]), *The Theory of Social and Economic Organization.* New York: The Free Press.

17

BETWEEN SUPRA-NATIONAL COMPETITION AND NATIONAL CULTURE? EMERGING EU POLICY AND PUBLIC BROADCASTERS' ONLINE SERVICES

Hallvard Moe

Abstract

Since the early 1990s, the EU has gained an important political role as it tries to manoeuvre between conflicting interests in regulating public service broadcasting. At the outset, the activities are granted a privileged exemption from the prevailing competition law approach. Yet, this position is increasingly challenged. The chapter identifies key tendencies in, and discusses potential implications of, the emerging approach in relation to public broadcasters' online services. Further, the chapter suggests a way forward that seeks to acknowledge both ample room for national peculiarities to be played out, and the prospective autonomous cultural and democratic functions of new media services.

Keywords
public service broadcasting, media policy, Internet, European Commission, state aid

Introduction
The ideal of organizing broadcasting as a public service firmly founded in national cultural policy aims has retained a substantial position across Europe. And public broadcasting institutions are still main beneficiaries of broadcast media's privileged regulatory status. Yet, over the last decade, this arrangement has been challenged on at least three fronts.

First, the idea of fundamentally national media has grown more contested. Boundaries are blurred on several levels; from content production, via ownership and policy to media use. On a regulatory level, the challenge can be concretely related to the emergence of the European Union as a supra-national media policy actor. Second, consumer, industry and competition law considerations are seemingly being ascribed more weight in media policy. Current developments in public service broadcasting can be seen as 'another stage of redefining the media as a sector of the economy, and media policy from a "cultural" into an "industrial" one' (Jakubowicz 2004: 279). Third, digitalization and convergence challenge media policies' separation of radio and television from other media. Even public broadcasting institutions have expanded onto new platforms. Most evidently, much of their Internet activities – from text-based news provision, via games to user-generated video content – seem to represent something far removed from their traditional remits. This is a key development in these institutions' efforts to redefine themselves from public service broadcasting to public service media.

Due to different historical developments, implementations of the common ideal of public service broadcasting have differed significantly between nation states.[1] Thus far, variations are also found in approaches to public broadcasters' online services (Moe 2008). This chapter scrutinizes how emerging EU policy – represented by state aid rules – impinges in this situation. What are the tendencies in, and implications of, the EU's approach for the development and status of public broadcasters' online services?

I analyse three cases. The British BBC, the NRK from Norway and Germany's the ARD and the ZDF have all been subjects of complaints from commercial competitors for violation of EU state aid rules.[2] These complaints have resulted in processes which bring light on emerging EU policy. All three processes I focus on deal in different ways with the status of online activities in the public broadcasters' remits. Through the analysis, I explore the presumption that the supra-national actor's focus on competition law represents a contrast to cultural policy considerations in each member state. An aim is to provide an illuminating case for wider discussions both of the future of public service broadcasting, and of relations between national and supra-national policy actors.

I first contextualize EU policy on public service broadcasting, elaborating on the relevant state aid rules. Next, the three cases – and the involved parties' argumentation – are scrutinized, and discussed in connection to each other. On this basis, I identify tendencies in, and implications of, the incipient EU policy approach. I further suggest a way forward seeking to acknowledge both potential autonomous cultural and democratic functions of public broadcasters' online services, and the necessity of ample space to let national peculiarities be played out.

EU policy and public service broadcasting

The EU's policy approach to the media can be explained by contrasting an economic perspective with a cultural and social one (Jakubowicz 2004: 277ff; see Nitsche 2001; Sarikakis, 2004: 19ff). The first concentrates on commercial competition, technological innovation and consumer choice. The latter is dedicated to defending the public interest, curbing the power of leading market actors and securing social equality. There is a constant conflict between the two perspectives – with the economic one having the upper hand (Jakubowicz 2004: 279). Emerging EU policy on public service broadcasting can be understood in this context.

The Union's policy impinges on the broadcasters' public service activities through the general content regulation of the audio-visual sector. The main directive is Television without Frontiers, last revised in 2007, which lays down rules for advertisement, European programme quotas, etc.[3] A second, more implicit way of control is via general EU law. For the present discussion, the most relevant part is the state aid rules, administered by the Directorate General Competition under the European Commission. The rules set out to harmonize market conditions in order to make a level playing ground for businesses, and have constituted the founding for commercial competitors' attacks on public broadcasters. Importantly, within the EU, competition law has a 'much higher value' (Harrison and Woods 2002: 498; Sarikakis 2004: 19ff) compared to social and cultural policy.

According to the EU, support from means controlled by the state is state aid if it distorts, or threatens to distort, competition by favouring certain actors; and affects commerce between member states. And state aid is illegal (EU 1997: art. 87, 88). There are, however, some exceptions. The one applicable for the present matter is for so-called services of general economic interest. Services of general economic interest are those the EU finds unfit for the free market. They are services all members of a society should have equal access to, deemed socially important in the long term. Examples are network industries like transport and energy, or libraries and health services. Public service broadcasting belongs to this category. This status makes it possible for the EU to accept licence fee-funding, labelled as state aid.[4]

A protocol to the Treaty of Amsterdam of 1997 laid down the EU's fundamental attitude towards public service broadcasting. It acknowledged that 'the system of public broadcasting...is directly related to the democratic, social and cultural needs of each society and to the need to preserve media pluralism' (EU 1997: protocol no. 32). Further, each member state was free to define, organize and fund public service broadcasting as it saw fit, as long as it did not 'affect trading conditions and competition in the Community to an extent which would be contrary to the common interest' (EU 1997: protocol no. 32).[5] Despite this clarification of the basic status, uncertainties remained. Pressing questions related to the scope of activities and separation of public services from purely commercial activities.

In 2001, the Commission published a communication that sought to end these ambiguities. It awarded each member state the right to define a 'wide' remit, also in order to secure a certain level of audience shares (EC 2001: 8). Additionally, the remit could 'include certain services that are not "programmes" in the traditional sense, such as on-line information services' (EC 2001: 8). If so, these services should address the same democratic, social and cultural needs of the society as the radio and television programmes do. In closing, the Commission described its own role as to merely check for manifest errors.

This would apparently secure both leeway for national differences, and the possibility for extending the public service remit beyond broadcasting to include online services. As David Ward (2003; also Harcourt 2005: Chapter 3) argues, we should not portray the EU as leading a one-sided attack on national cultural policy. The Commission has not been unsympathetic to public service broadcasting.[6] However, as I now turn to scrutinize some recent cases of complaints on public broadcasters' funding and Internet activities, a picture materializes that illustrates several problematic implications. The interesting question is what public broadcasters' position as an exception from competition rules means for the status of their online services. Is the 'free zone' expanded or in danger of being scaled down? Does the assumed distinction between a supra-national competition law perspective and national culture policy apply?

BBC: Incorporating an online syllabus?

The pilot for *BBC Online* was introduced in 1997 as a result of explicit ambitions for an 'online public service' (Graf 2004: 18). The website, re-branded bbc.co.uk, has since its inception been granted status by the British government as a part of the licence fee-funded core public service provided by the BBC (Moe 2008).

In the spring of 2002, the BBC applied to the Department for Culture, Media and Sport (DCMS) seeking approval for an addition to its publicly funded web service. The *Digital Curriculum* should comprise interactive learning materials in support of the school curriculum. Apparently, it 'would be a further development of the high quality educational materials which the BBC has provided...since the 1920s' (BBC 2002: 1). In January the following year, the government gave its consent, communicating hopes that the scheme would 'stimulate, support and reflect the diversity of the UK' (DCMS 2003: 4). The next month, Research Machines plc, a commercial provider of online educational services, filed a complaint to the Commission, claiming the new service was in violation of state aid rules. The complainant argued that the scheme did not clearly define what was included in and excluded from the *Digital Curriculum*, and also pointed to the fact that the approval was not limited in time (EC 2003). In sum, the company feared the economic consequences for private actors.

The proposal and its planned licence fee-funding constituted state aid, according to the Commission (EC 2003: 5–7). But was it existing or new aid? In the first instance, the *Digital Curriculum* would be regarded as merely another service from the BBC, legitimate as an element in the service of general economic interest already provided by the institution. Both the British government and the broadcaster meant this was the case, bearing in mind the BBC's long tradition for educational services. 'The opportunity to make a difference to learning in this country lies deep at the heart of the BBC's Reithian remit', stated then-Director General Greg Dyke; 'across TV, radio and online' (BBC 2003: 1).

The Commission did not subscribe to this reasoning. It asserted that an online educational service only fell within existing aid 'to the extent that it remains closely associated with the BBC's "television and radio services"' (EC 2003: 8). The Commission found the association in the *Digital Curriculum* case too open, describing the plan as 'a digression' from markets in which the BBC previously had been active (EC 2003: 8). Consequently, the proposed service could not be part of the institution's public service broadcasting remit.

Instead, the question was if the scheme could be accepted as an independent, new service of general economic interest, warranting new state aid. The Commission answered yes, not only with reference to relevant articles in the Treaty, but also including two additional considerations: the expected market impact would be reduced by subsidies for commercial actors; and quality education is one of the objectives of the European Community (EC 2003: 9ff). In conclusion, the Commission had no objections to the planned *Digital Curriculum*. However, as the complainant underlined, the decision affirmed important limitations to the BBC's scheme in order to protect commercial interests (Research Machines 2003).

Over two years later, in January 2006, the service was finally launched under the name *BBC jam*. The institution claimed to keep a 'continuing dialogue' with the private sector to 'ensure that BBC jam complements educational resources available commercially' (BBC 2004: 1). However, objections from private competitors remained strong (see Dodson 2006). New complaints were sent to the Commission, asserting the BBC had contravened the original conditions. The Commission in turn requested a new review of *BBC jam* – in addition to one already planned for 2007. In an unprecedented move, the newly constructed BBC Trust reacted by suspending the whole service in March 2007, and ordering BBC management to come up with fresh ideas (BBC Trust 2007). At the time, merely 10 per cent of the planned service had even been launched. The closing affected about 170,000 registered users, nearly 200 employees and 25 commercial content providers, some of which sought compensation from the BBC for breach of contract (Deans 2007; Gibson 2007). A further consequence was a new complicated round of competition law initiated considerations impinging on the BBC's effort to take its educational purpose beyond radio and television.

In sum, the *Digital Curriculum* case defined the basic components of the emerging policy approach: the Commission had published its specified view on the role of public service broadcasting – stressing the relation to social, cultural and democratic needs in each society as key concepts in assessing their activities – two years prior to the original decision. Yet, the approval of the *Digital Curriculum* made no reference to these phrases or to the protocol from the Amsterdam Treaty. This could be seen as a violation of primary European law (Wiedemann (ARD) 2004: 8; see Mortensen 2008: 221ff). The decision was furthermore problematic due to its implications for the delimitation of public broadcasters' online services. It marked a shift as more weight was now given to market impact arguments (Humphreys 2007: 107–8; Michalis 2007: 237).

A competition law rationale defined the proposed scheme as outside the existing public service broadcasting remit: the Commission pointed to the situation for commercial competitors, and deemed the *Digital Curriculum* as belonging to a market too far beyond BBC operations. The resulting decision took a restrictive approach. It introduced the criterion 'closely associated' to radio and television programmes as a measure of online activities' public service value. Only via a detour was the curriculum endorsed, uncoupled from the broadcaster's remaining service. The decision was a clear rejection of the British government's approval of the BBC's right to include the *Digital Curriculum* in its existing public service remit.

There is a further problematic issue: the argument of the British government is principally situated within competition law, concerned with making room for commercial actors. Even though the conclusions differ, the national authority thus relates to the context defined by the Commission – they refer to the same principles. It is interesting, then, how this compares to the arguments from national governments in the two other cases.

ARD and ZDF: the limits of the remit online

In April 2003, the lobbyist for German commercial electronic media actors, VPRT, complained to the Commission about both the ARD and the ZDF's lack of accounts separating licence fee-funded and commercial activities, and that e-commerce services were being paid for with public money.[7] The VPRT referred to a much discussed paragraph in the contract between the German states regulating the public broadcasters' activities. The paragraph limits the scope of their publicly funded Internet services to 'program accompanying services...with program related content' (Rundfunkstaatsvertrag §11(1)).[8] The regulation defines emerging activities on new platforms as activities in the periphery, as a means to support the implementation of the public service broadcasting remit (Moe 2008). It builds on the so-called 'development guarantee' granted the public broadcasters by a Constitutional Court decision in 1986, conceived to secure the institutions room for development facing new conditions (Humphreys 1994: 255ff). According to the VPRT (2003: 3) however, 'the public broadcasters' expanding internet activities (had) long since burst the restrictions laid out in the contract between the German states'.

The Commission's response attacked the status of online activities (EC 2005). Again, a main criterion was the presence of commercial actors: if a similar service already was provided on market terms, public broadcasters had to yield. A further decisive factor was the relation to conventional television and radio. The Commission doubted, for instance, that all online games and chat rooms always could be included in the remit. Chat rooms with a close association to broadcast programmes, or educational games, might be approved. But any chat room on any social relevant theme was not automatically accepted as a component of the broadcasters' public service. Several examples were discussed. One was the *Liebesalarm-community* – an online contact forum from ARD member WDR where the 'broadcasting-specific contribution to the process of opinion formation seems less distinctive' (EC 2005: 189). In its preliminary conclusion, the Commission stated that the German regulatory framework was not sufficiently clear.

Invoking the autonomy of member states on the issue, the ARD argued fiercely against this stand, and asserted that the regulation already 'clearly defines the online remit of ARD and ZDF' (ARD 2005a: 2). When it comes to the *Liebesalarm-community*, the ARD (2005b: 6–7) had a three-part argument: first, the community stood out from commercial alternatives through tighter control. Second, it was a necessary step in the institution's endeavours to reach young people. Third, the service did in any case not steal customers from private providers since the *Liebesalarm-community* in practice was more likely to be used to find contacts for hobby and leisure time activities, rather than as a place to look for partners.

The German government – formally speaking for the states – also countered the Commission's criticism: the controversial services were partly experiments with new media, and partly connected to, and providing interactive possibilities for, broadcasting content. Online games provided by the ARD and the ZDF, for instance, were special both in terms of quality, target groups and through their relation to radio or television programmes (Bundesregierung 2005: 3, 11).

The broadcasters and the government also made a more fundamental argument for public service media online: the Internet is a central information and communication instrument. Simultaneously, converging technologies make it irrelevant for users if content is delivered as traditional broadcasting signals or distributed over the Internet. The understanding of broadcasting has always been dynamic; from medium-wave radio in the 1920s, through to the satellite and cable distributed multi-channel television environments of the 1990s. In this context, online does not describe new content. It just represents the ongoing change of communication platforms. And the aforementioned 'development guarantee' affirms the public broadcasters' right to take part in these changes (ARD 2005b: 5–6; Wiedemann 2004: 8). In a similar tone, the German government claimed that services for mobile phones could not be singled out as an independent category in the remit. Rather, mobile phone networks merely represented an additional method for distributing content (Bundesregierung 2005: 3; also ARD & ZDF 2006: 4).

As a reply, the Commission sent a list of questions in early 2006. Its approach seemed to assume that the broadcasters were under direct political control, according to one commentator (Grothe 2006). The parties met again during the summer of 2006, and finally reached an agreement by the end of the year. In April 2007, the investigation was officially closed. In the settlement, Germany agreed to a long line of commitments. In addition to existing formulations restricting the scope of online public services, new services should be explicitly tested according to their contribution to 'editorial competition'; their financial impact; and their contribution to the same social, political and democratic needs that broadcasting fulfils (EC 2007: para. 328). Further, the German government should make a list of which services fall within and outside the public service remit. Paid-for download services and games will by default belong to the latter category. VPRT (2007) applauded the outcome. ARD Chairman Fritz Raff stated he felt 'relieved, but not like a winner' (quoted in Aretz 2007).

The end result approved of a quite wide range of public services online (see Schulz 2008 for a discussion of its regulatory consequences). Still, the German case points further in the direction indicated by the British case. Arguments are again firmly placed in the territory of competition law: potential implications for private actors trying to make a profit on similar services remain a key consideration. Further, the Commission focuses on closeness to traditional broadcasting as another main criterion. As shown, the German regulations were already strict in this regard

– far more so than the British. Yet, the Commission's understanding of 'closely associated' is even more rigid.

Although German policy, also incorporating extended self-regulations by the broadcasters, are among the most detailed of its kind, the Commission's tendency to go further than national authorities was confirmed in the call for clarifications of the remit online. The government stressed the protection national regulations provide for commercial initiatives. Thus, one admitted the weight of competition law arguments. However, the Commission remained unimpressed, and pushed for a stricter regime which aims to 'increase transparency and predictability for other operators' (EC 2007: para. 364). As a consequence, the Commission not only challenged the member state's authority to define public broadcasters' remits, it also indicated a stricter policy. In this sense, the trend from the British decision is amplified.

Another part of the argument may be even more problematic: a main difference between broadcast programmes and online services, the Commission would argue, is that the first is disseminated to everyone, while the latter is principally on-demand for individuals. On this basis, in reviewing the public service value of online activities, the Commission took different parts out of their environment, and assessed them individually. It did not, for instance, consider the *Liebesalarm-community* in relation to the ARD's total web presence. Rather, the Commission singled out the service, and asked for its broadcasting-specific contribution to German citizens' democratic, social and cultural needs. The approach marks a departure from the widespread practice of viewing the elements of the public service broadcasting remit as constituting a whole. An important question is if the same logic was applied in the Norwegian case.

NRK: the Internet services' place in the remit

In April 2003, the NRK's strongest competitor on television, TV2, filed a complaint to the EFTA Surveillance Authority (ESA) on alleged cross-subsidy of the public broadcaster's teletext and Internet services.[9] In contrast to the British and German sister organizations, Norwegian regulations have allowed advertising on these two parts of the licence fee-funded broadcaster's output. According to TV2, this arrangement gave the NRK an unfair advantage when trying to attract advertisers. During 2004, ESA extended the investigation to include the complete model for funding the NRK, and the definition of its remit (ESA 2005). Several problematic issues were identified. Here, I concentrate on those related to online services.

The presence of advertising is not the only controversial matter with the NRK's Internet activities: they also have had a somewhat unclear status in relation to the overall public service remit. During the spring of 2004, the Norwegian Ministry of Culture and Church Affairs (MCCA) affirmed that Internet activities were an 'important element of the information aspect of the public service remit' (MCCA 2004a: 13). The ministry found support for its view in the fact that the NRK was forbidden to engage in commercial activities prior to 2000. Thus, everything the institution was involved in at an earlier date – including its online presence – would have to be a public service (MCCA 2004a: 14).[10]

This attitude was confirmed as new statutes were introduced in the summer of 2004. They stated that 'the object of the NRK is to offer public service broadcasting...through radio and television, and on other media platforms' (MCCA 2004b: §3–1). The next paragraph defined the NRK's public service remit to include, firstly, the 'core activity' of two television channels and three nationwide radio channels, and secondly, 'other editorial activity including teletext services, internet and other media platforms suitable for communication of editorial content' (MCCA 2004b: §3–2). These formulations provided the broadcaster with a comparatively generous leeway (Moe 2008).

They were also highly problematic, according to ESA. In its preliminary conclusion, the Norwegian government's approach was discarded (ESA 2005). Instead, ESA assessed individual parts of the online activities in accordance with the overarching aim of catering to the democratic, social and cultural needs of society. Chat rooms and games were emphasized as controversial components. Could they be considered as services of general economic interest, and thus be eligible for licence fee-funding? In deciding, ESA built on the same criteria as the Commission did in the German case: 'The link to traditional programmes, the societal need as opposed to individual demand and the adequate offer of similar services by other operators are factors which might be relevant for such delineation' (ESA 2005: 24). Again, examples were selected from the website. A chat room called 'Open forum', for instance, inviting discussions 'independently of (the) NRK's programmes or channels', was accentuated as highly problematic (ESA 2005: 10, 23).

At the outset, ESA's requirements were met: the ministry admitted that NRK statutes 'could be more precise in regard to which new media services fall within the scope of the public service remit' (MCCA 2005: 23). Yet, the competition law approach was rejected on a fundamental level, as the Norwegian government argued for a much more dynamic approach to the question:

> (I)nteractivity, fragmentation, niche services and catering to individual needs is precisely what defines new media services and distinguishes them from traditional media...This new relationship between content providers and consumers (sic) presents considerable new opportunities for the media, including public service broadcasters (MCCA 2005: 24).

EU state aid rules could not block a remit from keeping with the technological and social development. From this perspective, the medium of distribution was secondary, and the scope and extent of the NRK's remit had to be allowed to 'evolve' (MCCA 2005: 25).

Not surprisingly, the NRK supported such an understanding. Then-Director General John G. Bernander read the statutes as a duty to be present on all platforms, wherever there was public demand. New platforms could also serve as 'new vehicles' for public service, giving 'broadcasters more chance to provide signals in a more efficient manner to minorities' (Bernander 2005: 3). As an example, he mentioned easily accessible news in Sami for indigenous people, distributed to mobile phones.

In April 2006, the Norwegian government did acknowledge the need for more specific regulations, explicitly stating that 'services offered (on) new media platforms must meet the democratic, social and cultural needs of the population' (MCCA 2006a: 8-9). But, the statement underlined; 'an obligation to ensure a sufficient link to the traditional broadcasting programmes is not planned to be included in such a specification' (MCCA 2006: 2). The parties met during the summer, and by autumn ESA seemed to take a somewhat more cautious approach. It admitted that interactive services could be of general economic interest, and called their criteria '"suggestions", "ideas for elements" in an assessment of new media services' status' (ESA 2006: 1). As a response, the Norwegian Ministry commenced work on a White Paper on the future of public service broadcasting. Here, the issues raised by ESA should be 'thoroughly discussed' (MCCA 2006b: 1).

Published in May 2007, the White Paper did indeed propose a revision of NRK statutes. It also confessed that the issue of Internet services' place in the remit had never been debated by Parliament – and that the development thus far had been directed by the NRK's own priorities (MCCA 2007a: 99). It suggested abolishing the separation between broadcast 'core activities' and the rest, thus explicitly equalizing Internet services' status with traditional radio and television. Further, all 'editorial activities' online were to be included in the remit. This included even 'user-generated material' (MCCA 2007b: 2). Potential new services would be assessed also with regards to their market impact. The liberalist People's Party (*Fremskrittspartiet*) notwithstanding, Parliament showed its support to the government's approach, holding it vital that 'the NRK are enabled to fulfil its remit independently of technical platforms' (Familie- og kulturkomiteen 2007: 27). As of February 2008, the ESA case was still pending.

The emerging EU approach is also found in the Norwegian case. The criteria that Internet services need to be closely related to broadcasting programmes; assessed individually; and not cause undue distortion of the market were formulated more explicitly. At the outset, social needs were again contrasted with individual demand: while ESA finally admitted that interactive services could be a public service, these were still treated differently. Though the parties may seem somewhat reconciled in the latter case documents, the Norwegian government does not touch on the key question of whether online services need to be more or less closely linked to existing broadcasts, and if they should be assessed individually without much consideration of contexts. This somewhat evasive approach fails to thoroughly tackle the issue of the status of the public broadcasters' online activities. I now turn to discuss the implications of the emerging EU policy approach, and suggest a direction forward which could lead to a more fundamental engagement with this issue.

Implications – and a possible way forward

Three tendencies can be identified in the Commission's approach. The first goes towards assigning public broadcasters a supplementary role online: new offers need to be notably different from existing commercial ones. Public service should only complement what the market takes care of. The second tendency regards assessment of individual public services: the Commission goes from considering whole schedules and channels to looking at single parts of

Internet activities. In this assessment, a tentative division has been sought between services tailored to individual demands as opposed to societal needs. The third tendency deals with the concrete function of new media activities – they are seen as accompanying or supporting broadcast programmes, not as autonomous. Importantly, a problematic accumulation of arguments is clearly at work: despite questionable founding and strong protests, once the Commission introduces an argument, it seems destined to be used in the following cases.

Taken together, the three tendencies illustrate implications of the emerging competition law approach on the regulation of public broadcasters online. The Commission's demand for a level playing field introduces a perspective clearly contrasting traditional conceptions about the role of the institutions. The aim is to expand the playing field, to make these kinds of online services subject to competition law, and create a bigger space for commercial competition. A first consequence is that the 'free zone' granted public broadcasters is not expanded online in step with new technological developments and social requirements. A second consequence is less weight given to national differences.

Each nation continues to have its unique social, cultural and economic developments. A public broadcasting institution's concrete scope still needs to adapt to such developments, and to the remaining media actors – commercial and non-commercial – in each society. On the way forward we must acknowledge the need to reserve ample room for national differences to be expressed in the regulation and organization of public service media institutions. This implies shifting the balance from supra-national competition law concerns towards national cultural policy aims. Countering the first tendency of the emerging approach, this would mean recognizing public broadcasters as more than supplements online. They should be allowed to offer more than what commercial market actors do not care for.

While calling for a greater emphasis on cultural policy considerations in the assessment of the institutions' possible functions in their societies, I do not suggest a total abandonment of competition law. In a similar way, I do not argue for wresting all authority from the EU or the Commission on the issue. The question is rather how especially the Commission can be influenced to move in a different direction. Importantly, we should not see the links between, one the one hand, the national level and cultural policy and, on the other hand, the supra-national level and competition law as mutually exclusive: the EU still admits the importance of a space for communications outside the market, based on cultural or social policy aims. As Frands Mortensen has underlined, the Treaty includes passages which stress cultural policy considerations. Yet, to the extent these are taken into consideration, the Commission tends to focus on high culture. Analysing and attacking this understanding could yield results in the long run (Mortensen 2005: 105ff; also Harcourt 2005: 89).Vice versa, as evident from especially the British and, to a lesser extent, the German case, national regulations of public service broadcasting clearly relate to, and build on, a competition law rationale when relating to the status of online services. In this sense, the assumed contrast between the EU and member states does not apply. Nevertheless, while the shift in balance may be attainable on a supra-national level, it is chiefly through the member states that an approach more attentive to cultural policy concerns can be initiated. For starters, this can be done by steering clear of a pure competition law argument.

A cue can be taken from the Norwegian government's argumentation, scrutinized above. Interestingly, not only did this go quite far in defending a wide and dynamic definition of the public service remit; the character of the argument is also interesting. The British defence of the *Digital Curriculum* concentrated on moderating its market impact. The Germans defended the ARD and the ZDF websites by stressing similarities between broadcasting and new media: the Internet first and foremost provides a new form of distribution. In contrast, the Norwegian argument clearly pointed to differences, to new possibilities in online communication. These present public broadcasters with new opportunities in carrying out their remits. In the Norwegian Government's defence, this potential had a clear relevance also for cultural policy. Although it does not disregard competition law, the approach at least hints at another emphasis.

This is an emphasis of the potential inherent in the incipient services – a potential that should be acknowledged as valuable for public service purposes. The Internet can for example be exploited to reach new audience groups; let new and hitherto silenced voices be heard; and build connections between more or less isolated parts of the public sphere (e.g. Murdock 2005). Some of these functions clearly extend those of broadcasting, while others have quite different characteristics. All these possibilities should be taken advantage of. General discussion forums decoupled from a broadcast schedule, for instance, may be utilized to achieve public service aims. Such services could be valuable in themselves, as well as in their context. The criterion should be their autonomous, not their broadcast-specific, contribution. This would counter the second tendency in the Commission's approach where the Internet is just an auxiliary channel, relegated to support broadcasting programmes.

Despite recent admissions from ESA, there is an attempt throughout the three cases to separate services constructed especially for individual demands from those that deserve a public service status. This is a somewhat diffuse delineation, and one in danger of confusing the form of reception (broadcasting/on-demand) with the form of needs (societal needs/individual needs) (see Mortensen 2008). If the Commission by individual demand assumes some form of activity where users provide information and make choices, the separation gets even more difficult. Interactivity is a central characteristic of many online media services. Refusing its value seems highly problematic. Stressing the division would not only undermine the potential for using online communication to fulfil public service tasks, it could also lead to a major challenge for the very regulation of public broadcasters in a digital media system. The transformation of broadcasting to on-demand services is a leading promise of digital technology. Regardless of the actual speed and extent of this transformation; with the Commission's logic we could end up in a situation where each radio and television programme is assessed only in isolation. The result would clearly be a move towards a narrower definition of the remit, away from comprehensive understandings.

Yet, the Commission's emerging approach seems to force its logic even onto the broadcasters themselves. As shown, in an attempt to meet the imposed requirements, the ARD and the ZDF, for instance, underlined how mobile phones are not much more than a new way of distributing the same old content, a new channel for spreading radio and television. Thereby, the public broadcasters contribute to downplay any innovative potential. In my view, the institutions should be encouraged to take a more exploratory and open approach to new platforms. This means underlining that the Internet and other platforms represent something different – in addition to serving as auxiliary distribution channels.

A shift in the balance between supra-national competition concerns and nationally based cultural policy motives would also question the third tendency: dismantling a broadcaster's total output to assess online elements individually. On the one hand, it is not difficult to understand the logic behind this trend: all aspects of the institutions' licence fee-funded activities are required to be accounted for in order to prevent misuse of public money. This process is hardly feasible, one could argue, without taking the service to pieces. Importantly, the approach is not new – it follows the general development of New Public Management. More specifically, it has also been applied by the Commission in earlier cases regarding television programmes (see Harrison and Woods 2002: 494ff).

On the other hand, public broadcasters were originally created to provide a coherent service, made up of different programme formats, genres and communicative modes. By putting together a mixed menu of news, information and entertainment, citizens were potentially exposed to a wide range of content and opinions. Obviously, significant social and technological developments have challenged this design. Still, the idea that public broadcasters' output constitutes a whole remains strong. As noted, both the Commission and national authorities stress the advantages of granting them a comprehensive television and radio service – also including shows that aim at large audience shares. Of course, television and radio programmes are criticized and analysed separately – also in relation to public service criteria. However, their place in the institutions' general output and the specific channels' schedule is seldom ignored. In this way, when we discuss whether a popular talk show belongs on public service television, it matters how many airings it has per week, when its slot is and what other shows the channel broadcasts the same day. We understand each programme in its context. There is a constant need for public broadcasters to stand out. Still, a programme is not dismissed due to its category or genre alone. A similar criterion could be practised for new activities.

In sum, I argue that we on the way forward would profit from a more nuanced approach. This approach should ascribe due weight to established practices of public service broadcasting policy, also founded in national cultural policy concerns, and simultaneously acknowledge the innovative potential offered by new media platforms.

Concluding remarks

Scrutinizing three recent EU state aid cases against public broadcasters, this chapter has discussed the content and consequences of the emerging EU policy approach for such institutions' online services. I have identified three key tendencies. The first is based on market impact. It downgrades public broadcasters to merely complement what commercial actors take care of. The second goes towards testing individual internet services disconnected from their context. The final tendency is to see online as accompanying broadcast programmes, not as autonomous in a public service remit.

The implications of this supra-national competition law approach, I have argued, is that public broadcasters are in danger of being left stranded, instead of enabled to take their public purposes further on new media platforms. Different forms of Internet communication can be exploited to fulfil public service aims – both to reach citizens and to connect them. I have suggested that this potential may better be realized if we shift the balance somewhat from supra-national competition law concerns towards nationally founded cultural policy considerations.

Such an approach would obviously appeal to the public broadcasters. Corresponding elements can be found in their arguments (e.g. Jarass (1997: 37ff) for a German perspective; EBU (2006) and Nissen (2006: 26ff) for a European). Still, the approach also entails considerate requirements. In closing, I will highlight two of the most pertinent.

Assessing individual elements in their context indicates a need to pay attention to interconnections between the components. If public broadcasters are to provide meeting points for dispersed publics online, and legitimize a wide-ranging line of services, components need to be seamlessly interwoven. This can be promoted through extended and thorough linking, and by making the public broadcasters' role in each service clearer. In short, the institutions must strive to present their total output – on- and offline – as a whole. The *Liebesalarm* site, for example, has its own domain name, neither directly related to the ARD, nor to the regional WDR. The service could appear as better integrated into the remaining activities by quite easy measures. Admittedly, compared to television and radio, the Internet's structure makes the job of creating an incorporated service harder. It is, nevertheless, an indispensable task.

Just as essential and challenging is the stress institutions need to put on exploiting the potential for new communicative forms inherent online. If new services are going to be more than mere extra channels, they must offer something innovative. Despite some exceptions, an unrealized potential clearly remains (see Carpentier 2003; Macdonald 2007; Puijk 2004). Public broadcasting institutions have both disadvantages and advantages in trying to realize this potential: one the one hand, they are big, and may be stuck in traditional ways of thinking about communication and production. Possible contributions offered by novel, more 'ground-up' initiatives, for instance emerging from the civil society, should most certainly not be disregarded (see Harrison and Wessels, 2005). On the other hand, experimentation and innovation have been intrinsic parts of public broadcasters' remits, yielding interesting results for decades. It is decisive to mobilize such a creative drive also on new platforms if their autonomous function is going to be recognized.

On the way forward there is a need for analyses of actual online services offered by public broadcasters. In addition, there is a need for fundamental discussions of the potential of different communicative forms online in connection with public service purposes – what we might label public service media online.

The struggle over public broadcasters' functions – of which online services make up a crucial part – is but one example of ongoing media policy discussions in a changing Europe. It is nevertheless quite an illuminating example: it shows how the two familiar perspectives of competition versus culture – permeating also other media policy debates – are played out by different interests on arenas with shifting importance. In so doing, the example is also relevant for those interested in challenging the wider policy field's balance between competition and culture.

Notes

1. See Born & Prosser (2001), Jakubowicz (2000), and Syvertsen (1999) for discussions of definitions and characteristics of public service broadcasting.
2. Despite not being a member of the EU, all relevant regulations are binding for Norway pursuant to the European Economic Area (EEA) Agreement.
3. See Krebber (2001) for a detailed analysis of the decision-making processes of the original version (from 1989), and the 1997 revision of the directive. In its current form, the directive is titled *Audiovisual Media Services Directive*.
4. Public broadcasters have protested heavily against defining licence fee money as state aid. The question remains disputed (see Holtz-Bacha 2006: 227ff; Mortensen, 2005).
5. See Sarikakis (2004: 103–19) for an astute analysis of the European Parliament's role in the process leading to the inclusion of this protocol.
6. See Harrison and Woods (2007: 290ff), Humphreys (2007), Michalis (2007: 230ff), Nitsche (2001: 129ff), and Mortensen (2008) for analyses of earlier cases, also against the BBC, the ARD and the ZDF.
7. The ARD and the ZDF are two autonomous organizations. However, in this case, they were attacked and defended themselves in unison.
8. All translations from German and Norwegian are my own.
9. In the field of state aid, the powers of ESA mirror the competencies of the European Commission. In the general discussion I therefore only refer to the Commission. See ESA (2007) for a general communication on its application of state aid rules to public service broadcasting. It corresponds to the 2001 EC communication (EC 2001).
10. This is at best a misleading claim: the NRK founded the subsidiary NRK Aktivum in 1997 to exploit the broadcaster's commercial values. In 2000, a further de-regulation made it possible to extend the commercial activities to include services unrelated to the public service remit.

References

ARD (2005a), 'European Commission Confirms Remit and Licence Fee Funding of ARD and ZDF'. Press release, 3 March.

ARD (2005b), 'VPRT-Beihilfebeschwerde in Brüssel. Kritische Fragen an die ARD und Antworten darauf'. Letter, 10 February.

ARD and ZDF (2006), 'Questionnaire – Public Consultation on Content Online in the Single Market'. Letter, no date.

Aretz, E. (2007), 'Wir fühlen uns erleichtert, aber nicht als Sieger.'At http://www.tagesschau.de/aktuell/meldungen/0,,OID6661896_REF1,00.html. Accessed 3 August 2007.

Bernander, J. G. (2005), 'NRK, pioneer'. *Diffusion Online*, 45.

BBC (2002), 'BBC Applies for Digital Curriculum Service'. Press release, 24 May.

BBC (2003), 'Approval for Digital Curriculum Puts the BBC at the Heart of Online Learning'. Press release, 9 January.

BBC (2004), 'Proposed Areas of Eclusion for *BBC jam*'. At www.bbc.co.uk/info/policies/digital_curriculum7.shtml. Accessed 30 July 2006.

BBC Trust (2007), 'BBC Trust Suspends *BBC Jam*'. Press release, 14 March.

Born, G. and Prosser, T. (2001), 'Culture and Consumerism: Citizenship, Public Service Broadcasting and the BBC's Fair Trading Obligations', *Modern Law Review*, 64: 5), pp. 657–87.

Bundesregierung (2005), 'Mitteilung der Bundesregierung an die Europäische Kommission Staatliche Beihilfen'. Letter, May 6, 2005.

Carpentier, N. (2003), 'The BBC's Video Nation as a Participatory Media Practice', *International Journal of Cultural Studies*, 6: 4, pp. 425–47.

Deans, J. (2007), 'Tinopolis Ponders BBC Jam Claim'. At http://media.guardian.co.uk/newmedia/story/0,,2034841,00.html. Accessed 6 July 2007.

DCMS (Department for Culture, Media and Sport) (2003), 'Tessa Jowell Gives Approval to BBC Digital Curriculum'. Press release, 9 January.

Dodson, S. (2006), '*BBC Jam* off to a sticky start'. At http://education.guardian.co.uk/elearning/story/0,,1724595,00.html. Accessed 8 August 2007.

EBU (European Broadcasting Union) (2006), 'EBU Comments to the EC Commission's Public Consultation Paper on Content Online in the Single Market'. Letter, 23 October.

ESA (EFTA Surveillance Authority) (2005), 'State Aid – Financing of NRK – Letter According to Article 17(2) in Part II of Protocol 3 to the Surveillance and Court Agreement'. Letter to MCCA, 12 May.

ESA (2006), 'State Aid – Financing of NRK'. Letter to MCCA, 10 October.

ESA (2007), 'The Application of the State Aid Rules to Public Service Broadcasting', *Official Journal of the European Communities* L 327, p. 21.

EC (2001), 'Communication from the Commission on the Application of State Aid Rules to Public Service Broadcasting', *Official Journal of the European Communities* C 320, pp. 5–11.

EC (2003), 'State Aid No N 37/2003 – United Kingdom BBC Digital Curriculum'. At http://ec.europa.eu/community_law/state_aids/comp-2003/n037-03.pdf. Accessed 9 August 2007.

EC (2005), 'Mitteilung der Generaldirektion Wettbewerb der EU-Kommission zur Finanzierung des öffentlich-rechtlichen Rundfunks in Deutschland'. Press release, 3 March.

EC (2006), 'State Aid: Public Service Broadcasting in Germany – Joint Press Declaration of European Commissioner Neelie Kroes and Minister-Presidents Kurt Beck and Edmund Stoiber'. Press release, 7 July.

EC (2007), 'State Aid E 3/2005 – Financing of Public Broadcasters in Germany'. Press release, 24 April.

EU (European Union) (1997), 'Treaty of Amsterdam', *Official Journal of the European Communities* C 340.

Familie- og kulturkomiteen (2007), *Innst. S. nr. 24: Innstilling fra Familie- og Kulturkomiteen om Kringkasting i en Digital Fremtid*.

Gibson, O. (2007), 'BBC Axes £150m Online Learning Service'. At http://education.guardian.co.uk/schools/story/0,,2034229,00.html. Accessed 6 August 2007.

Graf, P. (2004), *Report of the Independent Review of BBC Online*. Commissioned by the Department for Culture, Media and Sport.

Grothe, T. (2006), 'Fragenkatalog zum öffentlich-rechtlichen Rundfunk', *Epd Medien*, 13/2006.

Harrison, J. and Woods, L. (2001), 'Defining European Public Service Broadcasting', *European Journal of Communication*, 16: 4, pp. 477–504.

Harrison, J. and Woods, L. (2007), *European Broadcasting Law and Policy*. Cambridge and New York: Cambridge University Press.

Harrison, J. and Wessels, B. (2005), 'A New Public Service Communication Environment? Public Service Broadcasting Values in the Reconfiguring Media', *New Media and Society*, 7: 6, pp. 834–53.

Harcourt, A. (2005), *The European Union and the Regulation of Media Markets*. Manchester and New York: Manchester University Press.

Holtz-Bacha, C. (2006), *Medienpolitik für Europa*. Wiesbaden: VS Verlag für Sozialwissenschaften.

Humphreys, P. J. (1994), *Media and Media Policy in Germany – The Press and Broadcasting since 1945*. Oxford and Providence: Berg Publishers.

Humphreys, P. J. (2007), 'The EU, Communications Liberalisation and the Future of Public Service Broadcasting', *European Studies*, 24, pp. 91–112.

Jakubowicz, K. (2000), 'We Know it When We See It? Public Service Broadcasting: Definitions, Descriptions and Policy Dilemmas'. Working paper 2, The Changing Media-Changing Europe programme. At http://info.lut.ac.uk/research/changing.media/K.J.-Paper.html. Accessed 9 August 2007.

Jakubowicz, K. (2004), 'A Square Peg in a Round Hole: The EU's Policy on Public Service Broadcasting', in Bondebjerg, I. and Golding, P. (eds), *European Culture and the Media*. Bristol: Intellect Books, pp. 277–301.

Jarass, H. D. (1997), *Online-Dienste und Funktionsbereich des Zweites Deutsches Fernsehens*. ZDF Schriftenreihe Heft 53. Mainz: ZDF.

Krebber, D. (2002), *Europeanisation of Regulatory Television Policy: The Decision-making Process of the Television without Frontiers Directives from 1898 & 1997*. Baden-Baden: Nomos.

Macdonald, M. (2007), 'Television Debate, 'Interactivity' and Public Opinion: The Case of the BBC's "Asylum Day"', *Media, Culture and Society*, 29: 4, pp. 679–89.

Michalis, M. (2007), *Governing European Communications*. Lanham: Lexington.

MCCA (Ministry of Culture and Church Affairs) (2004a), 'Complaint – State Aid – Alleged Cross Subsidiation of Teletext and Internet Based Services by the Norwegian Broadcasting Corporation (NRK) – Information'. Letter to ESA, 25 May.

MCCA (2004b), 'Vedtekter for NRK AS'. At http://www6.nrk.no/informasjon/2005/NO/omnrk_vedtekter.htm. Accessed 9 August 2007.

MCCA (2005), 'State Aid – Financing of NRK'. Letter to ESA, 20 June.

MCCA (2006a), 'State Aid – Financing of NRK'. Letter to ESA, 24 April.

MCCA (2006b), 'State aid – Financing of NRK'. Letter to ESA, 13 November.

MCCA (2007a), 'St. meld. Nr. 30: Kringkasting i en digital fremtid'.

MCCA (2007b), 'State Aid Financing of NRK'. Letter to ESA, 21 May.

Moe, H. (2008), 'Public Service Media Online? Regulating Public Broadcasters' Internet Services – a Comparative Analysis', *Television and New Media*, 9: 3, pp. 220–38.

Mortensen, F. (2005), 'Er licensen til Public Service-institutionerne i Norden lovlig statsstøtte ifølge EU?', *Nordisk Kulturpolitisk Tidskrift*, 8: 1, pp. 84–119.

Mortensen, F. (2008), 'EU og statsstøtte til Public Service Broadcasting 1992–2005', in F. Mortensen (ed.), *Public Service i netværksksamfundet*. København: Samfundslitteratur, pp. 183–233.

Murdock, G. (2005), 'Building the Digital Commons', in G. F. Lowe and P. Jauert (eds), *Cultural Dilemmas in Public Service Broadcasting*. Göteborg: Nordicom, pp. 213–31.

Nissen, C. S. (2006), *Public Service Media in the Information Society*. Strasbourg: Council of Europe.

Nitsche, I. (2001), *Broadcasting in the European Union: The Role of Public Interest in Competition Analysis*. The Hague: T. M. C. Asser Press.

Puijk, R. (2004), 'Television Sport on the Web: The Case of Norwegian Public Service Television', *Media, Culture and Society*, 26: 6, pp. 883–92.

Research Machines plc (2003), 'RM Welcomes European Commission Decision on BBC Digital Curriculum Scheme'. Press release, 31 October.

Sarikakis, K. (2004), *Powers in Media Policy – The Challenge of the European Parliament*. Oxford: Peter Lang.

Schulz, W. (2008), *Der Programmauftrag als Prozess seiner Begründung. Vorschläge zu Verfahren und Organisation des 'Drei-Stufen-Tests' zur Selbstkonkretisierung des Funktionsauftrags öffentlich-rechtlicher Rundfunkanstalten*. Berlin: Friedrich-Ebert-Stiftung.

Staatsvertrag für Rundfunk und Telemedien. At http://www.lfk.de/gesetzeundrichtlinien/rundfunkstaatsvertrag/main.html. Accessed 3 August 2007.

Syvertsen, T. (1999), 'The Many Uses of the "Public Service" Concept', *Nordicom Review*, 20: 1, pp. 5–12.

VPRT (Verband Privater Rundfunk und Telekommunikation) (2003). 'Erklärung des Präsidenten des VPRT aus Anlass des Einreichens einer Beschwerde des Verbandes bei der Europäischen Kommission in Brüssel'. Press release, 24 April.

VPRT (2007), 'Kein Freibrief aus Brüssel sondern Verfahrenseinstellung auf Bewährung – Europäische Kommission stellt bei Rundfunkfinanzierung Verstoss gegen Europarecht fest'. Press release, 13 July.

Ward, D. (2003), 'State Aid or Band Aid? An Evaluation of the European Commission's Approach to Public Service Broadcasting', *Media, Culture and Society*, 25: 2, pp. 233–55.

Wiedemann, V. (2004), 'Public Service Broadcasting, State Aid, and the Internet: Emerging EU Law', *Diffusion Online*, 47/2004.

18

THE EFFECTS OF THE MEMBERSHIP PROCESSES OF THE EUROPEAN UNION ON MEDIA POLICIES IN TURKEY

Mine Gencel Bek

Abstract

The European Union's effects on media policies in Turkey are evaluated as two sides of a coin in this article which examines the political, cultural and economic dimensions of these effects. The EU in general with its culture and tradition of law has a democratizing effect on political culture and communication in Turkey especially through the legal changes made in order to become a member of the EU. However, the chapter argues that is hard to maintain that optimism when we turn to the economic and cultural spheres, characterized by the dominancy of market mechanisms in EU communication policies and the existence of an essentialist 'cultural difference' discourse in Europe. Thus, the effects of the EU policies have a dual structure: democratic in terms of reducing the power of the state in politics, but not sufficient in terms of limiting market forces.

Keywords
media policy in Turkey, the European Union, democracy, cultural identity, market mechanisms

Introduction
The relationship between Turkey and the European Union has a long history. After the first agreement, called the Ankara Agreement, which was signed on 12 September 1963, there were many agreements and protocols with the Community. Turkey's application for membership

was rejected, and Turkey remained an associate member until its candidacy was approved at the 1999 Helsinki Summit. It is possible to say that, especially since the candidacy was approved, the EU has become one of the most important elements of political culture in Turkey.

This chapter aims to trace the effects of the process of the EU membership on media policies. Legal political changes, activities related with NGOs, media policy of the EU and Turkey, and the characteristics of Turkish media industry are analysed in order to demonstrate the dual effects on media policy in Turkey. The questions being focused on as follows: what is the effect of the EU candidacy process on Turkey's media policy? What are the main elements of the EU media policy and to what extent this policy affects the media policy in Turkey? What is the role of the EU media policy and EU in general in the transformation of democracy in Turkey? How can we discuss this by taking into account the political, economic and cultural dimensions at stake?

The 1990s witnessed a major change in the media in Turkey with the end of the monopoly over broadcasting held by TRT (Turkish Radio Television). TRT, which started television broadcasting in 1968, has always been controlled by the state. Since TRT lost its autonomy in 1971, it cannot fully determine its content. With the advent of private media, the range of the ideological debate has been widened, and different forms of popular culture, which are not reflected by TRT, have been included in the private media. However, the private media is concentrated, and at the same time it is conglomerated. These commercial, concentrated and conglomerated structures have limits, shortcomings and are subject to dangers for democracy. They use the media as a weapon against their rivals driven by the main motive of maximizing profit. They are in harsh competition, which results in endless promotion campaigns. Also, the private media's close relationship with the state, and the continuation of the statist tradition, and private media incorporating elements of official ideology, maintaining the consensus when the issue is of 'national interest', should not be forgotten.

Media policies in the EU and Turkey

Irvan (1999: 264–65) analyses the principles concerning broadcasting contained in the earlier law regulating communications and argues that what this law aims to protect is the state, official ideology and big companies. Irvan's argument is still valid even after the changes to the law introduced in 2002. The regulation of the media involves different, competing interests including media owners who want to protect their property; the audience's demands for access; civil society organizations' desire for access to the media in order to express and disseminate their opinions; society's interest in maintaining a public interest function and the government's interest in protecting citizens' rights and addressing its opinions to them (Splichal 1999: 298). When we look at the process of drafting legislation in Turkey, it is seen that the interests of government and media owners, again, become dominant while the opinions of other actors are not sufficiently sought out.

Concerning the 'application' of the law and regulations, the situation that Irvan describes still continues: it is possible to argue that the principles of broadcasting protect the state; the regulatory authority of RTÜK controls mostly content; channels which are seen as 'opposing the state' are punished by means of content control. On the other hand, we also see the negative outcome of market mechanisms; 'structural' concerns are not taken into consideration as much as those related with content. Frequence allocation, the basic duty of RTÜK (now assumed by the Telecommunication Institution), has not been enforced for years, and so frequencies are used freely. RTÜK does not do much in terms of protecting pluralism and struggling against the concentrated media structure either. Even when channels violate the principles of advertising, and broadcast longer advertisements, RTÜK does not intervene sufficiently.

Thus, the media system in Turkey, like the media system in any other country reflects dynamics such as the country's specific history, conditions and social change (Kaya 1985), political culture (Mutlu 1999), and the 'professional culture' of broadcasters which determined whether media professionals are weak or powerful (Çaplı 2001). The question of how this professional culture is affected by broader social change can be answered only by examining the country's political culture and political economic structure. The differences between media policies in Turkey and other European countries are explained broadly by both the determining effect of political culture and political-economic structure by Kejanlioglu et al. (2001: 138). The authors argue that bringing rules and their implementation into conformity with international regulations; or bringing RTÜK into line with the policies of European countries are not considered important because commercialization is being prioritized over freedom of communication. Even though this chapter does not take the EU as an ideal model and does not take the view that harmonizing with Europe can solve all problems, what distinguishes this chapter is the argument that the EU also has positive effects on media policy in Turkey as it follows the EU harmonization process as a candidate for membership.

EU media policies have been criticized from many aspects. These can be briefly summarized as such: as a result of EU policies, small countries, it is argued, may be dominated culturally by the larger and stronger European countries (Spa and Lopez 1995: 222). The EU prioritizes commercial channels over public service broadcasting which have been affected negatively through the marketization of communication (Galperin 1999: 637, Golding and Murdock 2001). Digitalization (Naranen 2002) and convergence (Iosifidis 2002) and the effects of these processes on media ownership and media content are not taken into account by EU regulation. The regulation of content is already left to nation states with the justification that content is national, and that therefore its regulation should take into account the cultural and social needs of a society, and that this should be the member state's responsibility (Hills and Michalis 2000). According to Kaitatzi-Whitlock (1996), if broadcasting is transnational, its regulation also should be transnational; otherwise national measures will be inadequate in the struggle against concentration. Besides, the lack of content regulation, measures to prevent concentration – with its negative implications for pluralism – are also considered insufficient by other researchers (Semetko 2000; Hoffman-Riem 1992).

Ward (2001: 82) labels these critical views on EU policies, and especially those of Sophia Kaitatzi-Whitlock and Shalini Venturelli, the 'orthodox' view, arguing that they consider EU audio-visual policies responsible for the de-regulation of the sector,[1] and in contrast argues that the European Commission in particular, works towards democratizing communication more than is presumed (76). He acknowledges that competition policy is limited as a tool for regulating national media pluralism, but for him it is member states which fail to develop efficient policies for the protection of pluralism (Ward 2005). Ward also distances himself from critics by claiming that these views argue that the EU policies dismantle nation state's regulatory mechanisms. These discussions lead us to focus more on the relationship between the nation state and the EU. Are the member states really as powerful as Ward (2001: 90) argues? Is it the nation state that is responsible for the negligent regulation of the commercial sector with its political preferences?

Studies of the telecommunication sector in Turkey shows that exactly the opposite is the case. Haluk Geray explains how the World Bank and IMF have pressed for the privatization of PTT telecommunication services with the justification of decreasing the budget deficit and foreign debt stock. While the policies of such global power agencies have advocated the liberalizing of market mechanisms, TUENA (Turkish National Information Masterplan 1994–97)[2] constitutes an example of how more democratic strategies can be developed on a nation basis (Geray 2002: 144–45). Nordenstreng underlines the idea that nation states are still vital for the development of the third world. According to him, the state can not leave issues such as inequality and poverty to NGOs and civil society in developing countries; it has to deal with these issues itself. Therefore, globalization prevents development (Nordensteng 2001: 160).

Here, the main question is how to define the global and national/local, whether to consider the global as economic, market-oriented, pro-privatization; the national/local is understood in terms of a cultural, social and political forum. If we talk about communication, the question becomes whether to consider commercial media with de-regulation and public media with regulation in an antagonistic way (Servaes 1992: 80). This antagonist relationship is not fully exploratory in the Turkish case where it is hard to claim that national forces are democratic, while transnational pressures are not democratic. Turkey is not a country where the market model of global economic order replaced old national models based on public interest, if we use Venturelli's general theoretical remarks on communication (Venturelli 1993: 497). The main reason for this is the public-interest-oriented national model which serves democratic processes as a civic and cultural phenomenon (Venturelli 1993: 504) has not been experienced in fact, so that we cannot now talk about the dismantling of this model in the logic of globalization, as the history of Turkish media, especially the position of TRT show.

Despite the fact that the EU emerged in opposition to the dominancy of the main global power, the United States, it is also possible to consider the EU as a globalizing power if we follow Castells (1998: 318), who argues that EU integration is both a reaction to globalization and an expression of it. Then, it is possible to reflect on the EU in the light of discussions of globalization. Besides these views which criticise globalization for being not much a global and a novel process (Hirst and Thompson 1995; Boyer et al. 1996; Krasner 1994), as the 'universalisation of capitalism' (Wood 1997) or an ideology of neo-liberalism (Piven 1995) which brings about the end of the nation state (Deutsch 1981), there have also been some attempts to conceptualize globalization differently. Far from supporting globalization, these criticisms lead to alternative conceptions of globalization. For example, Pieterse criticises the identification of globalization with neo-liberalism. As a result of a critical examination of current neo-liberal globalization, he develops a concept of 'critical globalism' (Pieterse 1996: 555–56). Critical globalism includes not only 'market forces but also interstate relations, international agencies and civil society in its domestic as well as transnational manifestations'. Non-governmental organizations are seen as having a great potential in this kind of understanding of globalization (Pieterse 1996: 560).

Held's concept of cosmopolitan democracy can be thought of as another attempt to reconcile democracy and globalization. Held argues that democracy has to become a transnational affair which is related to both a restricted geographic domain and the wider international community. According to him, democracy, democratic institutions and agencies should be expanded into what he called 'the cosmopolitan model of democracy' (Held 1993: 39).

Archibugi (1998: 219) defines cosmopolitan democracy as the project of developing democracy at the level of nations, states and global processes and considers the EU the first international organization to have begun to develop a cosmopolitan model. It might seem too ambitious to consider critical globalism as a process actually being realized considering the negative examples of globalization that we have witnessed, and the nation state is still a powerful actor. Instead, critical globalism here could be seen as a process of transformation which should be encouraged. There are indeed optimistic views of the EU which can be considered in parallel with these ideas on a cosmopolitan model of democracy and critical globalism. Habermas (2001) underlines the fact that EU integration in politics is not as developed as economic integration.

He adds however, it may be late, but political integration is possible. According to him, the solution is a European Constitution which transfers some of the powers currently held by nation states to Brussels (2001). Both Habermas and Jospin (quoted in Çelebi 2002: 20) argue that, even though the EU works within the global market economy and global capitalism, it still has important potential to transform this system to global 'social market economy' and stresses that globalized capitalism can only be transformed into a post-nation social market economy by global scale regulations. For Çelebi (2002), the EU could be transformed even more. Social movements and the EU institutions contribute to constitute the European pubic sphere as a constituent element of European democracy and hence transform Europe. In Turkish context, these discussions could have the potential to move forward the limited debates on globalization. As Isik (1995) states, there are two main views of globalization in Turkey. One supports market economy and Turkey's inclusion within it without question while the other equates the state with public and completely scorns globalization as the 'new world order'. In this article, neither of these polarizing views which support either the state or the market will be followed. Rather than aligning itself with either of these camps in order to argue for or against the merits of either globalization or the EU, this article will investigate both the positive and negative effects (including potential effects) of the EU for Turkish communication policy.

The EU and democratization

EU communication policies do not regulate media content in detail, as mentioned above. Partly for this reason, and partly because of the other market-oriented dynamics discussed, the EU does not directly contribute pluralism in the media through its communication policies. However, EU policies are not limited to media policies; on the contrary, the EU has influence on politics more broadly in Turkey, which in turn affects media policies. The EU in general with its 'culture and tradition of law' (Çelebi 2002: 49), in accordance with the European Human Rights Convention, the European Union Basic Rights Charter, the EU Copenhagen Criteria and Amsterdam Treaty, has a democratizing effect on political culture and communication in Turkey through the legal changes made in order to become a member of the EU.

There are some views which are sceptical of these democratic developments 'for the sake of EU membership'. These ideas mostly propounded by Euro-sceptics ignore the fact that similar demands for democratization are shared by large sections of society, and fail to consider that democracy can be complemented by 'external dynamics' as well as 'internal' ones, and that international democracy can complement democracy (Connoly 1995). Following the enactment of the first and second series of laws aiming at Turkey's harmonization with the EU, there have been many advances in freedom of thought, expression and organization (Ilkiz 2003). The law numbered 4771, enacted on 3 August 2002 in accordance with the third set of harmonizing legislation is one of the most important steps in terms of achieving the Copenhagen criteria (Ilkiz 2003: 59).

The abolition of capital punishment is one of the developments least expected by both Turkey and the European Union. Besides that, there have been more developments in 'strengthening the legal guarantees of freedom of thought and expression' in accordance with the European Human Rights Convention (Ilkiz 2003: 60). Furthermore, the prohibition of Kurdish broadcasting has been ended by the lifting on the ban on broadcasting in different languages and dialects. As Timisi (2005) argues, this was a big challenge to the definition of national identity as previously constituted in official discourse.

Van Cuilenburg and McQuail (2003), consider the current trend in Europe to be the development of independent national regulatory authorities which enhance the benefits of the media in the public sphere. Pekman (2002) underlines that the EU, in its report or Turkey, expressed the necessity of strengthening the independent radio-TV authorities in Turkey. An attempt at harmonization in this regard in the future may also increase the autonomy of RTÜK and cause it to work more efficiently towards guaranteeing the pluralism which is threatened by both the state and the market.

The Europe-wide organization of labour, media professionals, activists, different excluded social groups and the strenghtening of their connections with the EU may also contribute to the development of democracy and democratic communication. The EU has started to take a role, at least in terms of gender inequality, by including women in policies related to the information society. The problems facing women in the use of and access to information technology have been discussed in EU summits, commission meetings and action plans and the positive outcome of this has started to become visible in European countries through public Internet access points and free training programmes aiming to enhance knowledge and access. 'All these policies may guide developments and be put into effect in Turkey', states Binark (2003) and she argues that these policies produce egalitarian solutions (at least in terms of gender) in the face of the polarization increased by neo-liberalism. There are also some EU-supported projects which can be evaluated in this context. An example not directly related to the media, but which can be considered a democratizing project with the potential to decrease gender inequality, is a training programme put into effect in 2000–01 by Ka-Der (an NGO which aims to support women in politics) and KASAUM (a centre for women's studies at Ankara University) with the support of the EU. The programme trained participants to direct training programmes for women who are interested in politics in accordance with the aims of Ka-Der to increase the participation of women, to implement positive action plans directed at gender equality. 80 active members from twelve cities joined the programme. KASAUM prepared six pamphlets and a video as training resources. 40 teams reached 4,000 women by the end of the programme.

Another project called Patikalardan Yollara (From Paths to Roads) was initiated in 2004 with the support of the European Commission and implemented by the feminist organisation Uçan Süpürge (Flying Broom) in 2004. The project, conducted in seven cities in seven regions in Turkey, aimed to increase dialogue and cooperation between local women's organizations, Uçan Süpürge's local women journalists and local government, and to contribute to the development of civil society in Turkey.

The same organization, Flying Broom, also made a series of live radio programmes, Kadın 2004 Radyo Programı (Women 2004 Radio Program) for TRT Radio 1 with the support of the European Union during 2004. A broad range of issues (such as local government and women, women's human rights and marital law, disabled women, women and the media, violence against women, international women's organizations and refugee women) were addressed in the programmes.[3]

Besides these, the BIA network (Independent Media Network), established in 1997 with EU support to produce and distribute local news, can be considered as an example. BIA created a network among local media organizations and a common news pool which disseminates the news through its website. BIA also formed a legal unit which aims to help local media organizations.

Thus, while NGOs work in a more free environment as an extension of legal changes in accordance with the EU accession process, the EU also supports these NGOs through training programmes. One very recent example is a project supported by the European Commission to develop civil society. The Civil Society Support Team was formed in 2002 and provided training programmes to hundreds of NGOs in different cities in Turkey until the end of 2004. NGOs which are trained by the team are also able to apply to the EU for financial support to implement their projects. One of the components of the programme, the Local Civil Initiatives, aims to decrease the gap between citizens and the state by promoting citizenship in all regions in Turkey. Some general topics of projects funded in 2003–04 include: human rights; struggle against violence and the exploitation of women and children; constituting a network for collective action by women and homosexuals; developing the social and economic status of women; empowering blind people; developing solutions for working children in the southeastern Anatolia region and improving the situation of prisoners.[4]

The EU, market mechanisms and 'cultural difference'

EU membership, which has been on the agenda since the 1950s, has become one of the most prominent issues in political culture in Turkey, especially since candidacy was approved in 1999. EU candidacy has become a rhetorical device in the society and has been used to create consensus and legitimacy on a number of fronts.[5] During the enactment of the law which brought changes in radio and television policy in 2002, the EU membership was thus used by both supporters and critics. Those who supported the law, mainly the Doğan media group and the owners of the large media organizations, editors, columnists, and the majority of the MPs, argued that 'If Turkey wants to be a member of the EU, this law has to be enacted'. The second group, 'Islamists' both inside and outside Parliament and some 'leftists' stressed that 'If this law is enacted, Turkey should forget about being a member'. The EU Turkey diplomat Karen Fogg argued that 'the law contradicts the EU's criteria for a fully functioning democracy which Turkey must embrace before starting accession talks'. EU diplomats also stated that the law would set back Turkey's bid to be a member of the EU since it tightens freedom of expression (Boulton 2002). The EU also mentioned their worries on concentration. When we look at the law, it can be seen that these evaluations are not wrong. The law allowed media owners to bid for government tenders and to purchase stock in the market; changing the limits on ownership to a 20 per cent stake and bringing a new understanding which limits ownership on the basis of audience share. There is no doubt that this will be harmful in terms of both content and structure. However, if we take into account the fact that the European Commission also suggested the same audience share model to European countries in order to limit ownership and the EU adopted a more liberal policy approach, it becomes more difficult to understand EU diplomats' criticism. EU diplomats employ a discourse of preconceptions concerning Turkey, based on the dichotomy of 'democratic Europe' versus 'non-democratic Turkey'. However, they do not question the position of the EU itself on these issues. While they criticize Turkey not being able to harmonize with EU policies, they consider the EU as a completed democracy project. They seem as if they were unaware of the fact that the market-oriented understanding adopted by Turkey has been adopted in the EU as well. In fact, despite some partial attempts, EU communication policies are not sufficient to guarantee pluralism and struggle with concentration, as mentioned above.

Basaran (2003) shows how telecommunication policies were manipulated, the sector had to be privatized and inequalities increased mainly as a result of the external dynamics including the influence of the IMF, World Bank and the EU and the penetration of market forces globally. The EU Commission's reports on Turkey in 2002 and 2003 suggested that Turkey should continue to implement the policies supported by IMF and World Bank, considering these as positive developments for the stability of Turkish economy and emphasizing that the privatization process should be advanced even further. This also shows the close relationship between the EU, World Bank and IMF and indicates that the EU is concerned about economic activities as well as political ones.

There are other concerns related to the EU's effect on the Turkish communication environment. Will these EU policies lead to an increase in the power of national media giants at the expense of small- and medium-sized companies? Will the principle of free distribution lead to the entry of big European companies into the national market and therefore reduce the power of national industry? Or, will these policies allow major European companies to dominate Turkish industry which 'does not have a chance to compete with the European giants', as Tuncel argues (Tuncel 1994: 82)? The answer to all of these questions depends on the negotiation process between Turkish nation state, the EU and the other actors.

If we return to the issue of EU bureaucrats criticizing Turkey in preconceived terms without considering negative tendencies in the EU at all, a possible interpretation is that the EU's cultural pluralism may not be broad enough to include a country the majority of whose citizens are Muslim. Despite arguments that it is not currently possible to talk about a common European culture (Schlesinger 1997; Morley and Robins 1997), it is very often heard especially from the right wing that Turkish culture cannot be included within European culture.[6] Kalipso Nikolaydis and Gilles Bertrand (2003: 10) argue as a reply to views opposing Turkey's European membership that Turkey's admission into the EU should be supported not for the sake of Turks but for the sake of Europe. The main question, according to them is not what Turkey is, but instead what Europe is: 'This discussion has shown us that Turkey is a mirror of us...a mirror which reflects what we are and what we want to be as the EU'.

As the time for membership comes closer anti-Turkish discourse may be strengthened in the EU and this may be aggravated by anti-EU forces[7] in Turkey and lead to more isolationist[8] or nationalist[9] reactions. In fact, the majority of 'lay people' in Turkey support EU membership, but at the same time they hold the view that 'The EU never accepts us' or 'EU membership is impossible in a few years'.[10]

One reaction to the 'anti-Turkish forces' can be seen in the stories of the success of Turks in Europe.

In recent years, besides the economic and political comparisons between Turkey and the EU, a cultural dimension has been added to the discussions. All the success stories (the Turkish football team's success in the 2002 World Cup; athlete Süreyya Ayhan's return with a gold medallion from the Europe Athletism Championship, director Nuri Bilgi Ceylan's two prizes won at the Cannes Film Festival, the award received by novelist Orhan Pamuk in Dublin and the others in fashion, beauty contests, etc.) have received considerable media coverage. The latest example was that Turkey's victory in the Eurovision Song Contest in 2003. For many years Turkey participated in the contest but was placed near the bottom of the voting. Most people watched the contests on TV every year on TRT by 1990 at which time there were still no commercial channels, so there was not much chance of 'zapping'. The following day, people would talk about and explain the results with the resentful sense that Europeans would not vote for Turks for political and cultural reasons. Finally, after the award was won, the Turkish media welcomed the result with great joy and stated that this result would provide a big boost in morale for Turkey on the way to the EU and a good response to the criticism that Turks are not culturally European.[11] These are important in terms of exemplifying the everyday life experience and mood of public in Turkey.

Since large populations of Turkish immigrants live in many European countries (mainly in Germany) and since this constitutes one of the sources of the image of Turkey and Turkishness in Europeans' minds, the Turkish diaspora should also be taken into account in these discussions of Turkish and European cultures. It is quite inadequate to think that both 'mainland' Turkish culture and diasporic Turkish culture are homogeneous in trying to differentiate them from European culture. Ayse Çaglar (2000), in an article on German Turks, reveals that it has taken almost 30 years to change the view of Turks from 'guest workers' to 'German-Turks', a 'hyphenated' and 'hybrid' expression. She traces the history of the Turkish diaspora starting from the 1960s when 'guest workers' had limited civil and political rights to the mid-1970s when Turkish immigrants were, both in official and academic discourse, seen in relation to their traditional culture. After the 1970s when the number of Turks increased, some shifts occurred as reflected in the use of terms such as 'Turkish immigrants' and 'the Turkish minority', but again the identities began to be conceived oppositionally in terms of 'traditional Turks' and 'modern Germans'. The situation of Turks was described pathologically as an 'identity crisis' and disorientation between two cultures. Starting in the 1980s Turks started to reject these definitions, and instead of negativity, the multiplicity of cultures has started to be emphasized.[12]

Research into Turkish diasporic identities in relation to the media also shows that binary dualisms such as European and Turkish culture are not meaningful in 'real' life. Binark's conclusion (2001: 86), in her study on Danish Turks through listeners' participation in c (community) radio programme, is a warning against simplifications about cultural identities:

> The radio program addresses their listeners with the identity of 'Danish-Turk'; their country is Denmark, their social identity is European and 'sub-identity' is, almost as a 'colour' Turk/ey origined. The positioning of 'Danish-Turk' is not homogeneous and singular; gender, religious belief and sects, different personal histories as a result of different immigration experiences, differences in cultural and social capital, all make this hyphenated positioning of identities heterogeneous.

Conclusion

This article, which aims to evaluate the effects of the EU on Turkey's media policies, argues that the EU has a positive effect on the democratization of Turkey which is in the process of joining the EU. The adaptation process has helped to reduce the power of the post-1980 military coup's legacy, and to lessen state-centred understanding at least in the legal regulations. It is obvious that the democratization of politics also affects the media. There have been improvements in freedom of thought and expression, organization, the protection of human rights and the reduction in gender inequality. The EU, in the future, may even help to increase the level of autonomy of media professionals by helping to place trade unions and the protection of rights on the agenda.

This article does not deny, on the other hand, that legal changes do not mean that democracy is finally achieved since laws are important but not everything in political culture. Thus, there is a need to overcome the existing contradictions and dualisms in the legal structure as well as a need to internalize these regulations. Besides lifting legal obstacles, the positive role of the EU in providing some support for the NGOs through training programmes and financial support of civil society projects is recognized. The EU also contributes to the Turkish media industry, mainly cinema, by leading to an increase in production and distribution of films through the support of the Council of Europe. As Ulusay (2003) explains, Turkish cinema which was not so international in terms of film export and co-productions, has started to be more internationalized through the support of Eurimages. However, while Turkish cinema mainly uses Eurimages support for the art films of young directors under Category 1, it is not able to use support given for high budgets films which have 'market potential', under Category 2. This also shows how EU policies have a dual structure and how Turkey is affected by that.

The EU's media policies have been criticized for being more market-oriented, for not being able to protect public service broadcasting and pluralism against concentration and commercialism. Market-oriented policies are not something that has arrived newly along with the EU to Turkey; these policies have been intensively applied in Turkey especially since the post-1980 military coup. This does not mean, of course, that the EU's policies will not have any effect on Turkey. On the contrary, EU policies in general, with their dual structure (democratic in terms of reducing the power of the state in politics, but not sufficient in terms of limiting market forces) may have a negative effect on the democratization of the public sphere in Turkey where the attempts to reduce the power of the state in politics are confronted by more resistance from those who consider these developments as an 'imposition' or 'conditon', while increasing market forces are less criticized and economic integration is more eagerly wanted. However, one thing which should not be forgotten is that the EU has no homogenous structure on the contrary to the reports of the mainstream Turkish media which cover the EU mostly when there are developments related to Turkey, and represent 'the EU view' without elaborating on the details of which group or party holds this view.[13]

Besides not being homogeneous, the EU is not a completed project; different actors and their struggles may make changes in the EU. As earlier work shows (Gencel Bek and Kevin 2005) communication policy has been shaped through conflict, compromise or consultation between a variety of interests including those of business, governance and citizens at both national and European levels. Even though currently the former has more influence than citizens, the hegemonic process continues. It is not likely at this point that the EU is capable of bringing about a more equal and fair society in Turkey on the basis of the distribution of wealth as it has positively contributed to the democratic transformation of the country in terms of freedom of expression, but this too is a potential which could be mobilized by demands at the level of the nation state, the EU, Europe and on a global scale. Since there is little research made on the relationship between the communication policies in the EU and Turkey, this article should be read as a preliminary argumentative article which aims to start a debate and lead to more developed research.

Notes

1. In fact, what these researchers discuss is not the EU's starting the deregulation process, but more the EU's speeding up that process.
2. The plan firstly aimed at the maximization of socio-economic benefits through advocating social and economic policies which would improve the economic position of low income groups. Secondly, it suggested adding the principle of universality of communication to legal regulation and directing these services towards low income goups, rural areas and immigrants. Besides TUENA, commissions constituted according to the Eighth Development Plan, similarly, included egalitarian suggestions on the issues of equal opportunuties, cheap access to Internet connection for schools and libraries where low income groups make use of these services. However, these issues were excised from the law during discussions in the Parliament. Also, as a result of the agreement made with WTO, foreign actors were permitted in the telecommunication sector. TUENA's plan has still not been applied (Geray 2002: 147–55).
3. For more information, see http://www.ucansupurge.org.
4. For details, see http://www.stgp.org.
5. For details, see Mine Gencel Bek, 'Communicating Capitalism: A Study of the Contemporary Turkish Press', unpublished Ph.D Dissertation, Loughborough University, 1999.
6. The ex-President of France, Valery Giscard d'Estaing argued in an interview with journalists that Turkish membership would be the end of the EU warning against the tendency to discuss European matters with people from a foreign culture (*Hürriyet*, 8 November 2002).
7. In Turkey almost nobody admits to being opposed to the EU membership. However, we can talk about a 'hidden' opposition or resistance as seen in expressions of 'making concessions to the EU', 'losing our national pride'. The army whose central place in Turkish politics is decreasing as a result of the EU adaptation process sometimes makes conflicting statements about EU membership. While the MGK (National Security Council) Secretary Tuncer Kılınç talked about the existence of different options for Turkey, in terms of international connections, such as Russia and Iran (*Radikal*, 9 March 2002), General Yasar Büyükanıt stated that the army considers EU membership as part of the civilization process as foreseen by Atatürk (*Hürriyet*, 30 May 2003). It is possible to say that the army in general continues to harbour some reservations on the issues of reduction of their authority, the Cyprus problem and Kurdish broadcasting.

   A petition signed by mostly private sector organizations in 2002 addressed both Ankara and Brusseles saying 'yes to the EU' (*Radikal*, 6 June 2002), and was followed by another petition one day later. The later petititon which was drawn up by mainly 'nationalist' left and right expressed worries about membership around the themes of independency, the Republic and national pride.
8. According to a questionnaire conducted by Galatasaray University with 1,500 people, 41 per cent of respondents replied 'Europeans view us as barbarians' to the question of 'How do Europeans perceive

Turks?' There were also other negative responses, such as Europeans view Turks as 'uneducated/ignorant' (27 per cent) and 'extremely religious' (22 per cent) (*Yeni Binyıl*, 23 July 2000).

9. Reactions against the NGO, Reporters sans Frontiers, for placing the photograph of General Hüseyin Kıvrıkoglu, the list of people who threaten freedom of expression in the world, on the floor of a train station in Paris (*Star*, 10 May 2002) and against Karen Fogg, EU envoy who it was claimed sent email messages expressing opposition to the President of Turkey, can be cited as examples of existing nationalist emotions (*Hürriyet*, 8 May 2002).

10. According to an opinion poll published in the newspaper Milliyet in 2000, 68.7 per cent support Turkey joining the EU, while 9.9 per cent are opposed to EU membership (*Milliyet*, 21 September 2000). According to Eurobarometer's poll in 2001, the rate of support is 77 per cent. However, respondents are of the opinion that Turkey will not be able to enter the EU soon (according to 56 per cent, membership will not be attained before 2008, for 19 per cent not before 2020) (*Radikal*, 19 March 2002). Moreover, INRA (International Research Associates) and Bilesim International polls indicate that 38.4 per cent of Turks believe that Turkey will never be accepted into the EU mainly because of economic underdevelopment and Muslim identity (*Yeni Binyıl*, 7 June 2000).

11. There were some who explained the victory as a result of Turkey's gaining sympathy from the European public after 'making concessions in Cyprus', and not sending Turkish troops to Iraq to support the United States. Also, some argued that the language of the songs being English, and the fact that the video took place in hamam (Turkish bath) reinforcing orientalist views of Turkey were worrying in terms of the representation of national identity (for example, Erdal Bilaller, 'Sözün Dogrusu', *Star*, 24 April 2003).

12. Çaglar still criticizes multicultural identity politics and argues that even expressing and theorizing identities as 'hyphenated' is not a solution since that can ignore space and time, prioritize nationality and ethnicity over other identities, exclude other ways of belonging and create the illusion that all German-Turks had the same problems and aspirations (Çaglar 2000). Kaya also similarly criticizes the way in which multiculturalism describes minority cultures as an unchanging whole, focuses only at the levels of culture and ethnicity and ignores the economic and political inequalities. According to Kaya (1999), the ideology of multiculturalism serves to exclude these groups as an extension of neo-right policies.

13. This representation (especially when some critical/anti-Turkish membership ideas of one European or EU diplomat are expressed as 'the EU' view) also may increase the popular opinion that 'the EU is against us, and whatever we do, will not change this', leading to a positioning of 'us' and 'them' (Gencel Bek 2001).

References

Archibugi, D. (1998), 'Principles of Cosmopolitan Democracy', in D.Archibugi, D. Held, M. Köhler (eds), *Re-imagining Political Community*. Cambridge: Polity, pp. 198–228.

Basaran, F. (2003), 'Telekomünikasyon Politikaları: Avrupa Birlisi ve Türkiye', in Mine Gencel Bek (ed.), *Küresellesme, Ietisim Endüstrileri ve Kimlikler, Avrupa Birlisi ve Türkiye'de Ietisim Politikaları*. Ankara: Ümit, pp. 65–104.

Binark, M. (2001), 'Kadının Sesi Radyo Programı ve Kimligi Konumlandırma Stratejisi', *Toplumbilim*, 14, pp. 75–89.

Binark, M. (2003), '"Avrupa Modeli Enformasyon Toplumu" Politikası ve Kadınların Bilgisayar ve Interneti Kullanmaları', in Mine Gencel Bek (ed.), *Küresellesme, Ietisim Endüstrileri ve Kimlikler, Avrupa Birligi ve Türkiye'de Ietisim Politikaları.* Ankara: Ümit, pp. 135–64.

Boulton, L. (2002), 'Turkey Seeks to Push through Controversial Media Bill', *Financial Times*, 24 April.

Boyer, R. and Drache, D. (eds) (1996), *States Against Markets.* London and New York: Routledge.

Castells, M. (1998), *End of Millenium.* Oxford: Blackwell.

Çaglar, A. (2000), 'Tire'li Kimlikler: Teori ve Yönteme Iliskin Bazı Arayıslar', *Toplum ve Bilim*, 84, pp. 129–49.

Çaplı, B. (2001), *Televizyon ve Siyasal Sistem.* Ankara: Imge.

Çelebi, A. (2002), *Avrupa: Halkların Siyasal Birlisi.* Istanbul: Metis.

Connoly, W. (1995), *Kimlik ve Farklılık.* Istanbul: Ayrıntı.

Deutsch, W. K. (1981), 'The Crisis of the State', *Government and Opposition*, 16: 3, pp. 331–43.

Galperin, H. (1999), 'Cultural Industries Policy in Regional Trade Agreements: The Cases of NAFTA, the European Union and MERCOSUR', *Media, Culture and Society*, 21, pp. 627–48.

Gencel Bek, M. (2001), 'Media and the Representation of the European Union', *Culture and Communication*, 4: 2, pp. 121–46.

Gencel Bek, M. (ed.) (2003), *Küresellesme, Iletisim Endüstrileri ve Kimlikler, Avrupa Birligi ve Türkiye'de Iletisim Politikaları.* Ankara: Ümit.

Gencel Bek, M. and Kevin, D. (eds) (2005), *Communication Policies in the European Union and Turkey: Market Regulation, Access and Diversity.* Ankara: Ankara University.

Geray, H. (2002), *Iletisim ve Teknoloji, Uluslararası Birikim Düzeninde Yeni Medya Politikaları.* Ankara: Ütopya.

Habermas, J. (2001), 'Avrupa Topluluğu Neden Anayasal Bir Çerçeveye Gereksinim Duyuyor?', *Cogito*, 26, pp. 69–84.

Held, D. (1993), 'Democracy: from City-States to a Cosmopolitan Order?', in David Held (ed.) *Prospects for Democracy.* Cambridge: Polity Press, pp. 13–52.

Hills, J. and Michalis, M. (2000), 'Restructuring Regulation: Technological Convergence and European Telecommunications and Broadcasting Markets', *Review of International Political Economy*, 7: 3, pp. 434–64.

Hirst, P. and Thompson, G. (1995), 'Globalisation and the Future of the Nation State', *Economy and Society*, 24: 3, pp. 408–42.

Hoffmann Riem, W. (1992), 'Trends in the Development of Broadcasting Law in Western Europe', *European Journal of Communication*, 7, pp. 147–71.

Ilkiz, F. (2003), 'Yakın Tarihimizde Iktidarların Basına Yaklasımı', in Dolan Tılıç (ed.), *Türkiye'de Gazetecilik.* Ankara: ÇGD, pp. 37–63.

Iosifidis, P. (2002), 'Digital Convergence: Challenges for European Regulation', *Javnost*, 9: 3, pp. 27–48.

Isik, O. (1995), 'Globalleme Süreci ve Kentin/Kentliligin Degisen Anlamları', *Birikim*, 68, pp. 98–105.

Kaitatzi-Whitlock, S. (1996), 'Pluralism and Media Concentration in Europe, Media Policy as Industrial Policy', *European Journal of Communication*, 11: 4, pp. 453–83.

Kaya, A. (1999), 'Türk Diyasporasında Etnik Stratejiler ve çok-KÜLT-ürlülük Ideolo isi: Berlin Türkleri', *Toplum ve Bilim*, 82, pp. 23–57.

Kaya, R. (1985), *Kitle Iletisim Sistemleri.* Ankara: Teori.

Kejanlioglu, B., Adaklı, G. and Çelenk, S. (2001), 'Yayıncılıkta Düzenleyici Kurullar ve RTÜK', in Beybin Kejanlıoğlu, Sevilay Çelenk and Gülseren Adaklı (eds), *Medya Politikaları*. Ankara: Imge, pp. 93–144.

Krasner, D. S. (1994), 'International Political Economy: Abiding Discord', *Review of International Political Economy*, 1: 1, pp. 13–19.

Morley, D. and Robins, K. (1997), *Kimlik Mekanları, Küresel Medya, Elektronik Ortamlar ve Küresel Sınırlar*. Istanbul: Ayrıntı.

Murdock, G. and Golding, P. (2001), 'Common Markets: Corporate Ambitions and Communication Trends in the UK and Europe', *The Journal of Media Economics*, 12: 2, pp. 117–32.

Mutlu, E. (1999), *Televizyon ve Toplum*. Ankara: TRT.

Naranen, P. (2002), 'European Digital Television: Future Regulatory Dilemmas', *Javnost*, 9: 4, pp. 19–34.

Nikolaydis, K. and Gilles, B. (2003), 'Avrupa Için Türklere Evet', *Radikal*, 13 May, p. 10.

Nordenstreng, K. (2001), 'Epilogue', in Nancy Morris and Silvio Waisbord (eds), *Media and Globalization, Why the State Matters*. Lanham, Boulder, New York, Colorado: Rowman and Littlefield, pp. 155–60.

Pekman, C. (2002), 'Audiovisual Policy on the Way to the EU: The Turkish Case', in Peter G. Xuereb (ed.), *Euro-Mediterranean Integration: The Mediterranean's European Challenge*, vol. 3. European Documentation and Research Centre, University of Malta, pp. 346–63.

Pieterse, N. J. (1996), 'Development of Development Theory: Towards Critical Globalism', *Review of International Political Economy*, 13: 4, pp. 541–64.

Piven, F. F. (1995), 'Is it Global Economics or Neo-Laissez-Faire?', *New Left Review*, 213, pp. 107–14.

Schlesinger, P. (1997), 'From Cultural Defence to Political Culture: Media, Politics and Collective Identity in the European Union', *Media, Culture and Society*, 19, pp. 369–91.

Semetko, H. A. (2000), 'Europeanised Politics – European Integration and Political Communication', *West European Politics*, 23: 4, pp. 121–41.

Servaes, J. (1992), '"Europe 1992": The Audiovisual Challenge', *Gazette*, 49: 1–2, pp. 75–97.

Spa, M. and Lopez, B. (1995), 'The Regions: An Unsolved Problem in European Audio-visual Policy', in Miquel de Moragas Spa and Carmelo Garitaonandia (eds), Decentralization in the Global Era, pp. 215–29. Eastleigh: John Libbey.

Splichal, S. (1999), *Public Opinion, Developments and Controversies in the Twentieth Century*. Lanham, Boulder, New York, Oxford: Rowman and Littlefield.

Timisi, N. (2005), 'Cultural Identities in Media Policies: Turkey in the EU Accession Process', in Mine Gencel Bek and Deirdre Kevin (eds), Communication Policies in the European Union and Turkey: Market Regulation, Access and Diversity. Ankara: Ankara University, pp. 445–92.

Tuncel, H. (1994), 'Medya Politikalarında Dönüşüm: Avrupa Toplulugu ve Türkiye'. Unpublished MA Dissertation. Ankara: Ankara Üniversitesi Sosyal Bilimler Enstitüsü Radyo-Televizyon Sinema Anabilim Dali.

Ulusay, N. (2003), 'Avrupa Merkezli Görsel-sitsel Kuruluslar ve Türk Sineması', in Mine Gencel Bek (ed.), *Küresellesme, Iletisim Endüstrileri ve Kimlikler, Avrupa Birlisi ve Türkiye'de Iletisim Politikaları*. Ankara: Ümit, pp. 59–96.

Van Cuilenburg, J. and McQuail, D. (2003), 'Media Policy Paradigm Shifts', *European Journal of Communication*, 18: 2, pp. 181–208.

Venturelli, S. (1993), 'The Imagined Transnational Public Sphere in the European Community's Broadcast Philosophy: Implications for Democracy', *European Journal of Communication*, 8, pp. 491–518.

Ward, D. (2001), 'The Democratic Deficit and the European Union Communcation Policy', Javnost, 8: 1, pp. 75–94.

Ward, D. (2005), 'Television Pluralism and Diversity: An Outline of the European Commission's Competition Policy and the Role of the member states Maintaining Media Pluralism', in Mine Gencel Bek and Deirdre Kevin (eds), Communication Policies in the European Union and Turkey: Market Regulation, Access and Diversity. Ankara: Ankara University, pp. 215–45.

19

RE-CONCEPTUALIZING LEGITIMACY: THE ROLE OF COMMUNICATION RIGHTS IN THE DEMOCRATIZATION OF THE EUROPEAN UNION[1]

Julia Hoffmann

Abstract

The supranational architecture and the indirect legitimation of decision-making of the European Union have posed challenges to traditional conceptions of democracy that warrant normative re-thinking of its core assumptions and, consequently, the notion of citizenship itself. A deliberative approach to European democracy has sought to contribute to this debate. It is argued here that in order to democratize the Union, it will be mandatory to supplement the ongoing legal constitutionalism with political constitutionalism that emphasizes the opportunities of active participation of European citizens in constituting themselves in an ongoing process of disagreement, dialogue and compromise. In this logic then, communication rights not only remain fundamental human rights, but gain additional relevance as new citizenship rights in evolving models of supranational democratic legitimacy. Far-reaching implications for policy-making are the consequence of such a rights-based conception of Union citizenship.

Keywords
communication policy, legitimacy, deliberation, communication rights, European citizenship, democracy

Introduction
Latest since the backlashes of the ratification process of the 1992 Maastricht Treaty[2] (Treaty of the European Union, TEU), it has become clear that the benevolent attitude of citizens in

European member states towards European integration can no longer be presupposed. What has been commonly referred to as the 'permissive consensus' seems not to have endured the long practiced elite-driven integration from above – intergovernmentalist decision-making in the tradition of classical bargaining diplomacy is no longer sustainable for or compatible with the nature of the European polity. It has become evident that it will be crucial to focus once more on the essence of what the European Union aspires to become in political, social and moral terms and to re-state and possibly renegotiate its underlying logic.

The supra-national nature of the European polity is simultaneously challenging traditional conceptions of democracy, legitimacy and citizenship that cannot be simply supplanted from the national level to the supra-national. The project of further integration thus forces scholars, policy-makers as well as its citizens at large to re-think the core assumptions of democracy in an era of accelerating globalization and regional integration. While integration theory has become a thriving research area and keeps bringing forward interesting approaches to understanding the processes of integration, the fundamental question of the moral validity of its implications is of utmost relevance especially at this point of the Union's development. Below, deliberative democratic approaches to alleviating the legitimacy deficit of the European Union and the role that communication rights play in those approaches will be elaborated. Subsequently, the underlying notion of European citizenship and its policy implications will be set out to serve as the basis for analysing the recent White Paper for a European Communication Policy.

The democratic deficit – a problem of legitimacy

The current supra-national architecture of the European Communities goes far beyond being a regulatory entity with merely economic tasks to facilitate the well-functioning of a market. The process that has gradually enhanced the powers and competences of what has become the European Union was partly instigated by external pressures,[3] partly consciously encouraged by governing elites and partly driven by institutional actors such as the European Court of Justice, whose case law has triggered a largely unforeseen and independent development of Treaty provisions. What has become clear by now is that the indirect legitimation of the EU – which may have been viable in the early stages of the EC, when an instrumental logic may have warranted a purely outcome-based legitimation (as conceptualized by Scharpf 1999) – is neither theoretically sufficient nor realistically sustainable anymore. Indeed, the experiences of the ratification of the 1992 Maastricht Treaty and more recently of the shelved ambitions to give the EU a formal constitutional Treaty have once more emphasized a fundamental need that has not been properly addressed. The introduction of the notion of European citizenship in the Maastricht Treaty and the inclusion of a Charter of Fundamental Rights in the Lisbon Treaty mirrors the realization that the EU needs some basic tenets of legitimacy. Still, addressing its democratic deficit is neither a matter of terminology nor of purely institutional reform to tackle its formal shortcomings.

Accordingly, the standard version of the democratic deficit as it is discussed in political sciences usually includes (a) the lack of European political parties, (b) the weakness of the only directly elected representatives' body, the European Parliament, and (c) a power bias favoring executive institutions in the EU on the list of sources of the deficit (Follesdal and Hix 2002: 4). The diffusion of power in its multi-level governance structure has sparked further worries about its lack of accountability and transparency while the large amount of autonomy that some actors have assumed in giving shape to integration weakens legal certainty and constitutional control mechanisms.

One of the most fundamental characteristics of a democratic polity is the civic capacity to exercise political authority. Traditionally, this authority is exercised through periodical voting for representatives. The supposed direct feedback link between voters and political actors as a basic assumption of liberal democracy has, however, already been realized to be problematic in many modern nation states, and is certainly untenable at the supra-national level. The lack of a pan-European public sphere that could fulfill the functions of transparency and responsiveness by scrutinizing EU policy-making and providing a more comprehensive communicative platform for public opinion formation is another facet of the procedural shortcomings. In sum, the issue of legitimacy of decision-making in a social collective that has been addressed at the nation-state level by means of representative democratic procedures has been brought to the forefront of political moral thinking again by the process of European integration.

The recipe that has already come under pressure within modern nation states is surely not applicable without modifications to the supra-national level, leaving Europe with the task of translating common intuitions about legitimacy – such as giving a voice to all affected in the decision-making process – into effective procedures and institutions.

The deliberative approach to European democracy

Partly in reply to the above mentioned challenges and approaches to the democratic quality of European integration, deliberative[4] theorists have set out to construe an alternative normative framework to sustain democratic values on the supra-national level. While deliberative democratic criticism has been applied to point out weaknesses in national democracies, those points of criticism are even more obvious and possibly more urgent on the supra-national level. What Robert Dahl (1989) has famously termed the 'third transformation'[5] of democracy that broadens the boundaries of democracies to include an ever larger polity in the face of globalization, is quite precisely what the EU is facing. The 'deliberative turn' that has been discernible in contemporary democratic theorizing (Dryzek 2000:1) has equally affected thinking about the EU's further integration process and the options available for its democratization.

Theories of supra-national democracy that place communication processes at the centre stage of attention tend to address procedural as well as substantial aspects of the deficit by means of processes of deliberation. They are seen as a means to supplement and enhance[6] the imperfect nature of democratic procedures to award political authority to citizens while at the same time providing a binding element that could compensate for a lack of a shared identity, thus facilitating the development of the congregation of European citizens into a full-fledged polity.[7] It should be made explicit at this point that the high formal demands that are often made for communicative processes to count as 'deliberation' may not be possible to meet on a mass scale and thus not be the aim of what has been termed deliberative supra-nationalism. As Young (2000) points out, for example restricting acceptable modes of speech to orderly, rational and eloquent reason giving may itself work as a powerful mechanism of exclusion of views. Also Eriksen has more recently argued, that it may be necessary to move away from the idea of consensus as the only legitimate outcome of deliberation and realize that indeed, 'working agreements' could be understood as something between a 'communicatively achieved consensus and a strategically bargained compromise to fill in the lacuna left open by the established discourse-theoretical typology' (2006: 5).

European citizenship and political authority

Federalize their wallets and their hearts and minds will follow (James Madison).

Much like Madison and Jean Monnet did, functionalist scholars[8] of today believe that the mere fact of intensifying (economic) integration will eventually have to take the peoples of Europe on a natural progression of shared solidarity, turning them into European citizens on the way. The assumed spill-over effects, however, have proven to be insufficient and the Union is left in need of sounder democratic foundations. Undertakings such as the foundation of monetary union would have required genuinely democratic economic governance, whereas Amsterdam failed to install this and instead deemed a college of fifteen finance ministers a sufficient match for the power of a central bank (Mancini 1998: 31). Even more disappointing, however, may have been the lack of commitment to enrich the sparse catalogue of rights that comes with Union citizenship.[9]

Even though the substitution in the text of 'European peoples' by 'European citizens' has already had (presumably unexpected) legal consequences,[10] the notion of citizenship will have to be filled with yet more substance, if it is to live up to the democratic aspirations of the EU.

In the modern liberal conception of democratic legitimacy, which is the foundation of most European states, more than free elections and majority rule is already required from political systems. State power is restrained by claims of individual citizenship rights and the concept of constitutionalism becomes a central feature of democracy (Stein 2001: 493). Bellamy (2001: 15) further distinguishes juridical from political constitutionalism. The former includes the rule of law, protection of basic rights and the separation of powers between institutions. The latter centres around the 'constitutive role of citizenship' which emphasizes the active role citizens play in constituting themselves in an ongoing process of disagreement, dialogue and compromise. In a more substantial view on democracy then – in which the communicative opportunities of citizens are at the centre stage of attention – the present day state of affairs in the EU does not satisfy the requirements of full-fledged democratic polity.

The meaning of citizenship thus becomes of prominent importance for thinking about how a European democracy could come about and implies a rights-perspective that goes beyond mere negative, protective rights against state interference to include positive rights of inclusion and participation that may demand obligations to act rather than merely to refrain on the side of public authority. Those rights are then not only an additional requirement to formally democratic decision-making procedures but instead their very enabling conditions. Instead of focusing on the existence of a predefined 'community of values' or uniform identity as a precondition for democracy as many sceptics of supranational democracy do (see *inter alia* Graf Kielmansegg 1996; Grimm 1995), in a deliberative logic the binding element of supranational citizenship must be found in the self-constituting opportunities it provides.

Advocates of participatory and deliberative models of democracy thus search for alternative means of translating the claim on authority of 'the people' into mechanisms to ensure responsiveness and accountability of representatives. While it is put forward that the paramount challenge to democracy is to be freed from 'interest formations that exclude others (and, thereby, create permanent inequalities)' (Bennett and Entman 2001: 3), rights are put forward in deliberative models of democracy as basic logic of justice that could provide for European constitutionalism (Eriksen and Fossum 2004). Many theorists of deliberative democracy at least implicitly assume the primary locus of deliberation to be institutions such as courts or the legislature,[11] while those that emphasize discourse ethics, locate deliberative practices primarily in civil society (Young 2000: 167).

Following Young in her argument, theorizing the concept of the public sphere in a complete framework of communicative democracy then mandates two adjustments to the typical understanding of deliberative democracy: 1) deliberative democratic processes in complex mass society are not necessarily face-to-face,[12] nor centred or unified, but rather dispersed and mediated, while 2) public communication covers more modes of communication than merely making claims or giving reasons, but includes such forms as art, culture and protest (ibid.). Thus, communication as a way to enter into the realm of political authority includes, but is not limited to, the introduction of deliberative processes within political decision-making fora or relatively small-scale attempts to create more direct feedback channels between citizens and EU institutions (such as Internet fora). Eventually, however, a public sphere that can sustain the high requirements of deliberative supranationalism must also include mass-mediated communication processes as an arena for communicative action.

In order to reach the full democratic potential of a polity, 'civic competence' is a mandatory feature of citizenship: the institutional capacity of citizens to enter into the realm of political authority on a socially equal basis with a view to sustaining a vital public sphere[13] (Chryssochoou 2001: 13). The central entitlement of citizenship then becomes the capability that membership of a community awards to actually change and renegotiate its very terms and conditions.[14] The model of deliberative democracy can accordingly be conceptualized as a 'framework of social and institutional conditions that facilitate the expression of citizens' concerns and ensures the responsiveness of political power', thereby 'intrinsically enhancing the legitimacy of government or governance' (Jakubowicz 2004: 5). Legitimacy of political procedures is thus no longer sought exclusively in the formal aggregation of preferences through voting, but encompasses much deeper citizen participation, while conceptualizing the citizen essentially as a holder of rights (Eriksen and Fossum 2004). The 'general accessibility of a deliberative process whose structure grounds an expectation of rationally acceptable results' subsequently becomes the prime source of legitimacy of democratic procedures (Habermas 2001b: 110).

Prominently, Erik O. Eriksen and his colleagues (see *inter alia* Eriksen 1999; Eriksen and Neyer 2003; Eriksen and Fossum 2004; Eriksen 2005) have contributed extensive writings that build forth on such an understanding of legitimacy to progressively formulate a comprehensive normative framework for deliberative practices in the European Union. The capacity to engage in communicative action here becomes a central tool for the exercise of political authority of a citizenship whose power to influence decision-makers by means of voting is not sufficient to satisfy the requirements of democracy. They thereby emphasize a communicative rationality of integration that can sustain a democratic polity of scale and great heterogeneity without compromising basic rights and freedoms for the sake of efficiency. This may indicate a certain degree of convergence between a European commitment to democracy and the protection of human rights, which here become a fundamental *prerequisite* for democracy to function instead of merely an addition.

In sum, deliberative legitimation of the EU policy-making process would have to be a combination of deliberative institutions and communicative power vested in European citizens through (1) communicative links that connect civil society actors and individual citizens with the levels of decision-making and with each other, and (2) communication processes in a mass-mediated public sphere. In both cases, it is essential that there be a more or less direct, identifiable relation between decision-making and prior deliberation. While it is practically impossible to require consensus on each issue before decisions can be taken, reference to prior deliberation is seen as a means to increase their legitimacy. Communication as such then becomes a fundamental civic competence.

Communication rights as citizenship rights

Obviously, for deliberation to deliver all the assumed benefits for a democratic, constructive polity, certain conditions would have to be met in order to facilitate full and equal participation. This subsequently requires a normative approach to policy-making. In this context, human rights instruments such as the European Convention on the Protection of Human Rights and Fundamental Freedoms are an obvious choice, since they emanate from common traditions. At the same time documents such as the Charter of Fundamental Rights of the European Union[15] illustrate the recognition of the fundamental importance of enshrining a number of basic rights into the constitutional edifice of Europe. Communication rights more specifically can be defined as those human rights – codified in international and regional human rights instruments – that pertain to standards of performance with regard to the provision of information and the functioning of communication processes in society (Hamelink and Hoffmann, 2004).[16]

While in liberal theories on representative democracy, freedom of expression and assembly are recognized as fundamental prerequisites to enable the emergence of a public sphere and thus democratic will-formation, deliberative theories – especially those that stress the importance of reciprocal granting of rights as a rationale for integration – command, but mostly only implicitly acknowledge, an even more central and far-reaching role of rights pertaining to communication processes. To come closer to the ideal of deliberative democracy, communication rights become part of the minimum, procedural requirements of democracy to work effectively. They are then not merely an external restriction to the exercise of authority to protect the private sphere of individuals from state interference, but are conceptually internalized in the democratic process and thus ought to be regarded as essential elements of political citizenship.

While liberal democracy presupposes communication rights such as freedom of expression and association, deliberative democracy attaches a more direct link between those modes of communication and decision-making. Those rights are thus not merely an enabling condition for public will-formation, but essential tools in the hand of citizens to enter into the realm of political power, assuming vital functions of accountability, justification and responsiveness of political actors, making communication a civic competence. The concept of deliberative democracy then ultimately requires more than mere non-restriction of the freedom of speech and goes further to imply the facilitation of communicative processes that include the rights to access to information, to be properly informed and ultimately the 'right to be heard'.[17] Even more, it requires for those rights to be put into the context of a forum where all perspectives converge and to which every European citizen has access. Subsequently, in democratic theories that emphasize deliberative opportunities of citizens as a source of legitimacy, communication rights ought to be especially emphasized among other rights in newly emerging supra-national governance modes and as such possibly added jointly to the catalogue of rights that are attached as entitlements of European citizenship.

Who communicates where?

One of the attempts of the European Commission to increase the quantity and quality of communication with European citizens has been the so-called Civil Dialogue.[18] In essence, the Civil Dialogue is intended to structure the participation of civil society in the Union's decision-making procedures. Through regular processes of consultation and discussion, the Commission opens its doors for those sectors of civil society potentially affected by its prospective actions, so they have a chance to have their opinions taken into account while those actions are still being developed. This constant dialogue is regulated through a set of minimum standards to be applied during the consultations to ensure participation, openness, accountability, effectiveness and coherence.[19] Following the adoption of these general principles, the Commission has concentrated on spreading a public consultation culture. However, there remain a number of issues that limit the application of those principles in the process.[20]

Following the analysis by Alonso Vizcaino (unpublished), the outcome has been that the reality of Brussels today could be depicted as a select group of actors, some of them with privileged access to the mechanisms of decision-making, who are working in an environment that does not offer unified criteria to measure their validity as counterparts of the Commission. So, while the Civil Dialogue is probably the closest that the European policy-making has ever gotten to the notion of open public deliberation described above, some of its constituent elements as well as the way the procedure has been implemented since its creation still places it far from the deliberative conception of a European public sphere. At its best, it offers an opportunity for the public to have their voice heard prior to voting, but it is still a narrow channel of communication where European citizens can merely react, while there continues to be no forum where decision-making procedures can be publicly scrutinized and discussed among citizens on a large scale.

Can there be a European public sphere?

Authors such as Dieter Grimm, Philip Schlesinger and Fritz Scharpf are generally sceptical towards the practical possibility of anything resembling a European public sphere emerging at all and thus regard a short-term democratization of the European Union to be impossible. Two main arguments re-surface in their works that seem to indicate that a European public sphere must be a pointless endeavour. Firstly, the large variety of languages and subsequent variety of frames of meaning are seen as a major obstacle for a pan-European public sphere (van de Steeg 2001). Secondly, there is the 'no demos' claim, which denies the existence of a European polity, based on a common identity and values, which in turn is regarded as a prerequisite for the feasibility of a European public sphere. This in turn makes democratic legitimacy depend on a variety of pre-political social variables such as social homogeneity or a commonly shared identity and sense of belonging, without which the social component of legitimacy seems unthinkable.

Thus, from a communitarian perspective, democracy comes to mean substantially more than merely a certain procedure to ascertain 'rule by the people' that can theoretically be installed to govern the relations within any congregation of individuals. It requires that this congregation already – before the political process can legitimately result in commonly binding decisions – has to consider itself a 'people'.

For example, Grimm (1995) sees true self-determination as dependent on the existence of a demos (since there is no European demos, there can be no democracy) – while Scharpf (1999) maintains that democratic self-government is dependent upon a high degree of cultural homogeneity. The two strands of argument both lead to the seemingly inevitable conclusion that 'the public sphere is delimited by the state's borders' (van de Steeg 2002: 505). This conclusion may however be based on the overly simplistic assumption that a European public sphere will have to be comparable to and look much like the national public spheres.[21]

As van de Steeg (2002) argues, all the above stated critical arguments can easily be applied to the nation-state setting. Those problems, however, do not seem to be considered as an insurmountable obstacle for the emergence of a public sphere under conditions of national plurality. Furthermore, it should not be forgotten, that the nation-state is a rather recent product of long historical, sometimes painful developments. As Habermas points out, it would be false to confuse a 'nation of citizens...with a community of fate shaped by common descent, language and history' – such a misconception would underestimate the 'voluntaristic character of a civic nation, the collective identity of which exists neither independent of nor prior to the democratic process from which it springs' (2001: 15). Furthermore, as Weiler argues (1999: 238), the principled precondition of homogeneity of ethno-cultural polities as tribe-like entities is caught up in an overly limited vision of *Volk* and *Staat*, which generally precludes any possibility of an international system of democratic participation to emerge, and thus the democratization of the European Union.[22]

This would lead to the rather fatalistic conclusion that there is no breaking the vicious circle and thus no chance for democratization of the European Union. Such a claim could then easily lead to a self-fulfilling prophecy and inaction since both deficits cause each other (Eder and Trenz 2004). Concluding, the academic discourse on the issue may significantly benefit if Risse's proposition to depart from the fixation on dichotomies (either *there is* or *there is not* a European public sphere) was to be taken over (2002: 1). More recently, there seems to be a growing consensus that a European public sphere may have to be understood as a process of growing Europeanization of national public spheres where the media play a capital role as active agents (see *inter alia* Trenz 2004; Downey & Koenig 2006).

Policy implications and the White Paper approach

When moving on to consider the implications of a deliberative approach and a broad understanding of the relevance of communication rights for their realization, it becomes clear that there is not only a duty of authorities to refrain from interference, but to ensure the effective exercise of those rights, protect them from interference by other citizens or private entities and promote their exercise through long-term policy (e.g. by actively engaging in increasing the knowledge base of citizens to realize their right to be properly informed). European citizenship remains a shallow buzz-word so long as the citizens that make up the Union continue to be largely apathetic and ignorant about European decision-making structures and their content.

Further, the promotion of a transnational European public sphere becomes of pivotal importance, so that mass media would have to be recognized more explicitly in their democratizing potential rather than their economic relevance.[23] When evaluating European-wide initiatives after the ill-fated experiment to set up a pan-European broadcaster in the 1980s, it seems that European institutions have become reluctant to actively regulate to that aim and seem complacent to leave the task of building transnational communicative spaces to the private sector[24] (Ward 2004: vii).

The White Paper in context

Talk of the 'democratic deficit' has been on the agenda even before the recent drawback of the ratification process. Accordingly, as a follow-up to the Laeken Declaration in 2001, a sequence of EU documents sought to 're-connect' with the citizen and to give back 'ownership' of the integration process to its constituency. Prominently, the White Paper on European Governance (2001) triggered much controversy and discussion on the future path of European democracy. After the referenda in France and the Netherlands that temporarily halted the process of ratification of the Treaty establishing a Constitution for Europe, a further series of three documents specifically relating to communication processes has been issued as a contribution to the 'period of reflection': the Action Plan to Improve Communicating Europe by the Commission (July 2005), the so-called Plan D for Democracy, Dialogue and Debate (October 2005) and, most recently, the White Paper on a European Communication Policy (February 2006). The latter will be subject of the below analysis.

What citizenship implies

Essentially, the approach to citizenship that has been put forward above embodies the bottom-up character of a rights-focused process of European integration. However, it also implies a top-down element including tasks for actors such as the Commission and the Member State governments to install the necessary institutions for the effective exercise of those rights.[25] In the White Paper the citizens' right to information and freedom of expression are clearly recognized in their relation to democracy. However, while stressing the need for communicating *with* and not *to* citizens as well as the lack of communication among citizens, the corresponding rights that would cover these processes are not included. The White Paper mirrors the realization of communication as a two-way process (Commission of the European Communities 2006: 7), emphasizes the need to listen (as already stated in the Action Plan) and even goes another step further to introduce a 'citizens' right to communicate' (though limited to the meaning of multi-lingualism, realizing the right of the citizen to having their institutions talk and listen to them in their own language).

In its conclusion, the White Paper states the citizens' rights to information, expression and 'to be heard' (ibid.: 13). Rather than specifying the implications of those rights for policy- and law-making, however, the White Paper suffices with reference to more general principles such as inclusiveness, diversity and participation that are put forward as guidelines for future policy (ibid.: 5). While these are worthy and largely undisputed principles, it remains an unfortunate fact that there are already countless declarations and documents to be found in which the commitment to many laudable principles can easily be found throughout the levels of European authority, while it remains the lack of enforcement mechanisms that often leaves them toothless in the end. In addition, the White Paper follows an unfortunate tradition of prior EU documents[26] when it names, but does not give content to those principles.

In sum, a rights-perspective on citizenship of the European Union is clearly discernible, while at the same time, those rights remain narrow and undefined. The introduction of a 'right to be heard', even if seemingly *en passant* constitutes a broadening of the understanding of communication in respect to earlier Commission documents, but its undoubtedly far-reaching implications are left implicit.

The aims of 'communicating Europe'

Facing the problem of the future of a European Constitution, the EU found itself at a crossroad. Despite a long history of attempts to inform the public, reach out to citizens and 'citizenship'-rhetoric incessantly repeated over years, the fact that a large amount of citizens remains politically inactive concerning the Union, bases their opinions on unfounded beliefs and is ill-informed may be tempting EU decision-makers to rely on strategic political communication that aims at 'emotional resonance' and persuasion rather than going down the rocky road of empowering citizens and enabling them to engage in the process through deliberation and thus eventually create a 'deeper' form of supranational democracy.

Having taken a 'period of reflection' after the referenda and having put out the White Paper it was finally decided by European leaders to 'move on' with a Treaty that has been stripped of its 'nationhood' symbolism but essentially barely changed. It is now more than doubtful whether any of the European citizens other than the Irish will get to take part in what was supposed to be Europe's constitutional moment.

However, when communication is understood as a way of empowering citizens who are not able to impact decision-making sufficiently via traditional means of voting and who lack the intermediary of a common public sphere, 'communicating Europe' becomes an essentially political activity, where democracy is at stake and 'selling' the idea of enlargement or specific policies can not be a legitimate, strategic aim. After all, the European Union is not a 'branded product' that has to be advertised and sold to citizens, but aspires to be a pluralistic democratic enterprise, which ought to be a product of its citizens' will to build a community beyond the nation state which 'citizens may decide *not* to like, even if they are properly informed' (Kurpas et al. 2004: 3, my italics).

Instead of advertising the added value of existing EU policies or campaigning to gain the benevolence of citizens before accession referenda, the aim of communication then ought to be stimulating deliberations about the very content and nature of integration, its underlying logic and aims. This means not presupposing any *finalité* of the process and considering options that may not be tabled in current discourse, which may result in a fundamental redefinition of what the EU should be.

While in Plan D 'explaining the added value of EU policies' could still be found throughout the document, the White Paper seems to have moved beyond the idea that promoting the integrationist movement ought to be the aim of communication.[27] The discourse of 'explaining' has been largely substituted by that of 'listening', whereas the proposals remain largely familiar from prior public relations efforts to create a shared 'toolbox' and fall short of providing inspiration for viable ways to implement the shift from explaining to listening.

The means chosen

It is the question if at all, and if so how, the envisaged citizen empowerment can be achieved at all in the context of such heterogeneity and scale as in the European Union. The White Paper chiefly relies on opinion polls and the Internet as tools to reach out to its citizens. Getting to know more about the attitude of European citizens would certainly be helpful, but can by no means replace genuine communication. The prime feedback channel for the consultation process relating to the White Paper as well as for more general debate on Europe remains the Internet. Making efficient use of available new media is most certainly to be applauded, relying on them to facilitate inclusive and diverse communication; however, is a known mistake. Just some months earlier, the ministers of 34 European countries endorsed the Riga Ministerial Declaration[28] setting out targets to tackle the problem of 'e-Inclusion', though their perception of the need for action seems to have emanated out of a more economic rationale. A lack of affordability, access, skills and motivation is keeping between 30 per cent and 40 per cent (50 per cent according to some estimates) of Europeans from taking advantage of the Internet. Not only is the internet not reaching all Europeans, it also leaves behind those who are more vulnerable to social and political exclusion in the first place.[29]

So while the special Internet site, which had been developed for Plan D, received thousands of contributions, Commissioner Wallström pointed out at a European Parliament debate that 80–90 per cent of those had been posted by young men.[30] Other than that, in 2006, the Commission launched the so-called 'Spring Day Europe' initiative as a tool to generate dialogue on European policies and even its own YouTube channel (EUtube). Those means put together, however, can hardly be seen as sufficient to establish the ambitious aim of the Commission to build a European public sphere that could sustain deliberation horizontally and vertically. More recent initiatives include the establishment of a network of radio stations (April 2008) and proposals of a network of TV stations, as the press release[31] explains, in order to help develop a European public sphere and to empower citizens by giving them access to information (Commission of the European Communities 2008). This latter initiative may be seen as an alternative to another initial idea contained in the White Paper that has met with fierce criticism.

Giving 'Europe' a voice?
An earlier version of the White Paper included proposals to convert Europe by Satellite into a European news agency to enhance media coverage of the European policy-making process. However, this proposal was met with such severe opposition that it had to be dropped in the final version. Even though, during the presentation of the White Paper to the press, Commissioner Wallström saw herself faced with a continuous stream of questions on the Commission's intentions underlying the wish to set up such a service. Clearly, suspicions and concerns about European propaganda efforts are shared by many journalists and other observers and have not been countered convincingly as yet.

So, whereas the noble intentions of the White Paper seem to have gotten caught up in 'just anger' and suspicion of propaganda on the side of professional journalism, the factual reality and aims of strategic communication efforts as exemplified in various pre-accession campaigns in the new member states remain outside the debate.

Concluding remarks on the White Paper: Between a rock and a hard thing
When it comes to the notion of empowering European citizens, there is another, related challenge, which is also similar to problems facing most modern nation states, but even more severely present at the supra-national level: there is a worsening degree of political apathy and mal-information among citizens about the EU that amounts to a civic deficit that makes any attempt to improve democracy through purely institutional reform seem utterly futile. This cannot

be simply blamed on unfavourable or lacking media coverage and will not be solved by producing better media material, coaching politicians and educating journalists, but will have to include a broader effort in civic education, which presupposes the political will of member states to implement. Indeed, the White Paper's proposals mirror this, but have no alternative but to leave this task to the member states.

More generally, one may wonder why the White Paper pays so little attention to other governance-related initiatives with which it shares a number of common elements and certainly common problems. The issue at stake is on the one hand so elementary and implies such a large area of policy that warrants a concerted efforts beyond the reach of one DG[32] – indeed beyond the reach of any EU institution – it seems almost like an indication of hubris, if not strong idealism, to issue such a document under the auspices of just one Commissioner. There is a related legal issue that must not be ignored in this context: according to its legal service, the Commission has the right (mind you: not the duty) to inform EU citizens about its activities as a result of its institutional prerogatives (Kurpas et al. 2006: 2). However, such a right is a far cry from a clear mandate to devise a more general policy that comprises all aspects of communication, while at the same time key areas such as civic education and media policy largely remain an exclusive competence of member states.

Conclusion

The gradual process of European integration, undemocratically initiated and driven since by elites, has only relatively recently been recognized as a development that is seriously calling into question the basic assumptions of liberal representative democracy in the face of the increasing impact of supranational law-making. The European Union is thus facing the paradox of presenting its citizens with many *faits accomplis* while at the same time claiming to count democracy to its core values and aims.

The 'permissive consensus' of its citizens that had benevolently supported – and thus indirectly given legitimacy to – the European project thus far has clearly reached its limits and political apathy (as mirrored in steadily declining turn-out to EP elections) and distrust have substituted complacency. The setback in the ratification process of the Constitution has made this clear once more: when finally being consulted on a major issue *after* most important decisions on the general course and aim of integration had already been taken without them behind closed doors,[33] Dutch and French citizens have clearly brought the message home.

Even if one wants to see the Lisbon Treaty as a bare pragmatic necessity to keep the Union function after enlargement, the challenge remains to find ways to effectively democratize the existing structures and thus give the emotional and intellectual ownership of Europe back to its constituent elements: its citizens. If Europe is not to compromise its moral aspirations, this challenge will mean overcoming the limited national vision on democratic processes that has become second nature to scholars, politicians and citizens alike and to re-state the normative principles on which future models ought to be based. These principles will then have to translate into modes of supranational governance that can approximate its underlying ideals.

The deliberative approach to these challenges, and its implications for the notion of citizenship, has been briefly set out above. Traces of the deliberative logic can be clearly found in the recent White Paper on a European Communication Policy and its approach to communication, whereas it is proclaimed here that translating the underlying principles into practice is not only a matter of human rights and democratic legitimacy, but also an ambitious task that goes beyond the realm of power of one Directorate General or even the Commission as a whole.

Legitimizing European policy-making ultimately remains a fundamentally moral issue, not a question of technical problem-solving. The essential function of communication rights of citizens then is to recognize everyone's fundamental entitlement to be taken into account during decision-making processes that affect her or his life and to take part in the philosophical exercise of defining a European vision on the 'good life'.

Notes

1. I would like to express my greatest gratitude to Jose M. Alonso Vizcaino for his inspiring contributions to this paper and, above all, his patience. Also, I would like to warmly thank Prof. Cees Hamelink for his valuable comments and for once more taking the time. As usual, all errors remain mine exclusively.
2. The series of lost referenda was then started with the Treaty's rejection by Danish voters.
3. Such as the breakdown of the Bretton Woods system and globalizing tendencies more generally that make collective action necessary.
4. While there are a great variety of perspectives on this concept, most draw on the Habermasian conception of communicative justice as the cornerstone of democratic legitimacy. Deliberation then must be seen as a process of communication that must fulfill a number of criteria concerning the quality of arguments used as well as concerning its formal nature (inclusion of all who are affected by a certain decision into the prior deliberation and the requirement that no point of view be a priori excluded from deliberations are examples of those criteria).
5. The first transformation refers to the undemocratic city-state starting in the fifth century BC, the second phase concerns the democratization of the nation state in the wake of the French and American Revolutions.
6. It is important to note here that arguing for the introduction of deliberative elements is not to say that representation could or ought to be replaced by them.
7. In order to warrant referring to a political community as 'polity', Walker (2001) identifies two important aspects: (1) a degree of autonomous political authority vested in the community as well as (2) what has been referred to as a 'feeling of belongingness' (Weiler 1999) or 'civic we-ness' (Chroyssochoou 2001). While the former is largely a matter of enabling the effective participation of citizens in the political decision-making processes of the EU (which in itself poses rather complex questions of feasibility), the latter facet touches on a more socio-psychological aspect of political community which includes matters of commonly shared identity, values and historical experience.
8. Abromeit (2003) in fact would put most deliberative theorists into this category, since she takes them to believe that the progressive introduction of deliberative processes will eventually lead to the alleviation of the democratic deficit.
9. The notion was legally introduced into the quasi-constitutional structure of the EU by the 1992 Maastricht Treaty.

10. See cases such as C-209/03 *Bidar* [2005] ECR I-2119, Case C-184/99 *Grzelczyk* [2001] ECR I-6193, and Case C-148/02 *Garcia Avello* [2003] ECR, I-11613. Here, the European Court of Justice has repeatedly emphasized 'that Union citizenship is destined to be the fundamental status of nationals of the member states, enabling those who find themselves in the same situation to enjoy the same treatment in law irrespective of their nationality, subject to such exceptions as are expressly provided for'.

11. See for example Gutman and Thompson (2002); Chalmers (2003).

12. As they have been understood in models such as Fishkin's deliberative polling.

13. The underlying normative assumption is that there is no way of *a priori* knowing, which is the best or morally sound way of conducting politics. It is rather a means of ensuring that people with not only a plurality of interests and opinions, but also with a plurality of values can find a way to peacefully co-exist, incessantly renegotiating the commonly binding rules and underlying values that govern public life, while the opinions of all members must principally be respected and represented.

14. While some deliberative theorists such as Habermas originally departed from the assumption that there was such a thing as a universal principle or common good underlying the processes of self-government, Bellamy (among others) emphasizes that in his conception, there is no such assumption and that the political process is better understood as a continuous process of identity formation and a joint construction of interests and positions that is potentially never ending.

15. The Charter should be understood to be – at least partly – a reaction to national constitutional judges' hesitations to fully accept the supremacy of EC law without sufficient guarantees of equivalent fundamental rights protection (especially the German Constitutional Court has made this point in its 'Solange'-decisions; see judgment of 29 May 1974, *Internationale Handelsgesellschaft mbH v. Einfuhr – und Vorratsstelle für Getreide und Futtermittel* (*Solange I*), 2 BVL 52/71; judgment of 22 October 1986, *Wünsche Handelsgesellschaft* (*Solange II*), 2 BVL 197/83).

16. Already in 1969 Jean D'Arcy proposed the addition of a human 'right to communicate' as a consequence of the newly available menas of communication by menas of broadcast satellites. In the years of debate that followed, UNESCO came to be the forum of one of the great show-downs at the Cold War front when the US and the UK quit their membership in the aftermath of the McBride Commission (1980). The World Summit of the Information Society in 2003/2005 has given renewed impetus to the debate (Mansell & Nordenstrang, 2007).

   As Bovens (2002) more recently elaborates concerning the modern nation-state, technological changes and the new possibilities they bring concerning the provision of information to citizens may in fact imply certain new 'information rights' and an increased responsibility of public authority to actively use them. .

17. The envisioned dialogical way of communicating is dependent on the capability and willingness of others to listen and take seriously what is being said. So, if understood as a moral claim to have one's perspective included in public communication and to be taken into serious consideration, such a 'right' is a logical consequence of some forms of argumentation concerning democracy. It should be clear, however, that this 'right' should not be taken to mean a proper legal claim, let alone a claim on 'getting one's way'.

   In the end, the right to be heard refers to a deeper cultural change that is assumed to be inherent in a proper implementation of deliberative democracy. This, however, is the realm of psychology and culture rather than law. The latter can merely be concerned with protecting and possibly enhancing everyone's opportunities to speak out and to have everyone potentially get access to public communication and vote; not with forcing anyone to listen.

18. The Civil Dialogue refers to a number of consultations such as the Dialogue with Business, Dialogue with Citizens, European Round Table of Democracy and others (see Obradovic and Alonso Vizcaino, 2006: 1051). In the draft EU Constitution, it was referred to as 'Participatory Democracy' in Article I-47: (1) The institutions shall, by appropriate means, give citizens and representative associations the opportunity to make known and publicly exchange their views in all areas of Union action. (2) The institutions shall maintain an open, transparent and regular dialogue with representative associations and civil society. (3) The Commission shall carry out broad consultations with parties concerned in order to ensure that the Union's actions are coherent and transparent.

19. However, it is interesting that since the moment the principles and standards for consultation were formalized in a Communication from 2002 [Communication from the Commission: 'Towards a Reinforced Culture of Consultation and Dialogue – General Principles and Minimum Standards for Consultation of Interested Parties by the Commission' COM(2002) 704 Final, 11.12.2002], the Commission has kept on identifying itself and the other European institutions as the main bearers of the responsibilities entailed by the document. It will be necessary to wait for more recent developments coming from the Commission, such as the 'Initiative on Transparency' promoted by the anti-fraud commissioner Siim Kallas or the recommendations for a code of conduct for non-profit organizations to see a more resolute request for openness, participation and accountability from other actors.

20. The first one is related to the very outset of the process: it is for the institutions of the EU to decide when and on what issue a consultation has to be launched, thus bringing up again a potential problem of legitimacy, since non-institutional actors lack the power to turn the policy-making machine on.

21. The early work of Habermas has frequently been criticized for a similar logical error, when he idealized the national polity as a single national public sphere (Schlesinger 1999: 265).

22. Also, it would be false to overestimate the stability and functionality of any theoretical national public sphere.. Within national boundaries a large variety of heterogeneous discourses coexist, since national public spheres are not dominated by one newspaper or one television channel, either, and it may be doubted whether a common language makes people talk about the same things in regions as different as Andalusia and Basque or Bavaria and Saxony.

23. In the years following the Television without Frontiers Directive, the policy focus seems to have shifted from the principal 'concern for information freedom for the citizen to participate in the political system, into freedom of the consumer to make market choices', whilst deregulation of communication was argued to be essential for economic growth (Sarikakis 2002: 82).

   The so-called Bangemann Report of 1994 is to be placed into the context of this discourse, as it advocates the inseparability of economic growth, liberalization and deregulation, especially when it comes to the (tele)communication sector (Commission of the European Communities 1994). In the period of increased liberalization and de-regulation, the focus of European communication policy has thus experienced a change in priorities, as it seems, away from the active promotion of citizen rights and freedoms with state intervention for the public good towards the protection of private interests (Sarikakis 2002: 83). For a forceful argument for a participative public space and analysis of prevalent logic of instrumental liberalism applied to information policy within the EU see also Venturelli (1998).

24. The creation of a pan-European communicative space was trusted subsequently to the commercial sector which can already be noted in the 1984 Green Paper called Television without Frontiers, which preceded the 1989 Directive, where any role for public service broadcasters to play in the emergence of a pan-European audio-visual space was 'conspicuous by its absence' (Ward 2004: 49). Rather, the European Parliament's focus shifted to the rather commercial concern of quota regulations intended to protect and support the European markets from the United States threat.

25. Much in accordance with the principle of 'positive obligations' as developed for example in case law of the European Court of Human Rights.

26. Such as the above-mentioned Communication entailing the principles to underpin the procedure of Civil Dialogue.

27. The change in names from the initial title of the White Paper on a European 'communication strategy' to 'communication policy' may indicate a deeper than merely nominal development, while the DG continues to be called Institutional Relations and Communication Strategy and its website continued to talk of the EU's new 'Communication Strategy' for some months after the publication of the White Paper (http://ec.europa.eu/commission_barroso/wallstrom/index_en.htm).

28. See Memo/06/237, Brussel, 12 June 2006, http://europa.eu/rapid/pressReleasesAction.do? reference=MEMO/06/237&format=HTML&aged=0&language=EN&guiLanguage=fr.

29. While only 10 per cent of people over the age of 65 use the Internet (whereas 79 per cent of Europeans aged eighteen to 24 and 63 per cent of Europeans aged twelve to seventeen), the groups most at risk of exclusion are the unemployed and those with a low education. Internet usage figures are also lower amongst women and in rural areas. Also within Europe there is a digital gap: on average, Central and Eastern European countries lag behind Western Europe in all measures of Internet access (see: http://www.cdt.org/international/ceeaccess/charts.shtml#13).

30. http://www.euractiv.com/en/constitution/future-eu-conference-involvement-civil-society needed/ article-156073.

31. http://europa.eu/rapid/pressReleasesAction.do?reference=IP/08/640&format=HTML&aged= 0&anguage=EN&guiLanguage=en.

32. Recognizing the role of those rights in bringing about modes of democracy that could face the challenges of supranationalism and enforcing them has far-reaching implications for policy-making. It comprises a wide range of areas covering media regulation as well as information and communication policy in the widest sense. Inter alia, control mechanisms of media concentration at EU level would need to be re-examined, the vulnerability of Public Service Broadcasting to claims of commercial competitors ex Article 87 EC on the prohibition of state aid would have to be scrutinized, the regime of access to information held by EU institutions would have to be strengthened and effective feedback mechanisms between citizens and decision-making institutions would have to be created. Locating the relevant actors in the complex structure within the multi-layered governance system that makes up the European Union, however, is a tedious task since competences are often shared between local, national, international and supranational entities while some others are too closely tied to the idea of national sovereignty to be within the realm of EU policy-making. The relevant fields of action further cut across diverse areas such as media concentration, the protection of journalistic sources or privacy regulation, all subject to diverging governance structures that involve all levels.

33. Especially French voters seem to have been motivated by concerns about the neo-liberal nature of the system that the Constitution would have codified (Commission of the European Communities 2006b: 2).

References

Abromeit, H. (2003), 'Möglichkeiten und Ausgestaltung einer europäischen Demokratie', in A. Klein, R. Koopmans, H. -J. Trenz, C. Lahusen, and D. Rucht (eds), Bürgerschaft, Öffentlichkeit und Demokratie in Europa. Opladen: Leske and Budrich, pp. 31–53.

Alonso Vizcaino, J. M. (unpublished), Just Good Intentions: the Limits of Participatory Democracy to Comply with the Principles of European Governance. University of Amsterdam.

Bellamy, R. (2001), 'The "Right to Have Rights": Citizenship Practice and the Political Constitution of the European Union'. At http://www.one-europe.ac.uk/pdf/w25bellamy.pdf. Accessed 3 October 2007.

Bovens, M. (2002), 'Information Rights: Citizenship in the Information Society', The Journal of Political Philosophy, 10: 3, pp. 317–41.

Chalmers, D. (2003), 'The Reconstitution of European Public Spheres', European Law Journal, 9: 2, pp. 127–89.

Chryssochoou, D. N. (2001), 'Towards a Civic Conception of the European Polity', ESCR, 'One Europe or Several?' Programme. Working Paper 33/01. Sussex European Institute.

Commission of the European Communities (2001), European Governance: a White Paper. COM(2001) 428 final. Brussels, 25 July.

Commission of the European Communities (2005d), The Commission's Contribution to the Period of Reflection and Beyond: Plan D for Democracy, Dialogue and Debate. COM(2005) 494 final. Brussels, 13 October.

Commission of the European Communities (2006a), White Paper on a European Communication Policy. COM(2006) 35 final. Brussels, 1 February.

Commission of the European Communities (2006b), Communication from the Commission to the European Council: The Period of Reflection and Plan D. COM(2006) 212 Provisional Version. Brussels, 10 May.

Commisson of the European Communities (2008). Communication to the Commission: Communicating Europe through Audio-visual Media. SEC(2998)506/2. Brussels, 24 April.

D'Arcy, J. (1969), 'Direct broadcast satellites and the right to communicate', EBU Review, 118, pp. 14–18.

Downey, J. and Koenig, T. (2006), 'Is There a European Public Sphere? The Berlusconi-Schulz Case', European Journal of Communication, 21: 2, pp. 165–87.

Dryzek, J. (2000), Deliberative Democracy and Beyond: Liberals, Critics, Contestations. Oxford: University Press.

Eder, K. and Trenz, H. J. (2004), 'The Democratizing Dynamics of a European Public Sphere: Towards a Theory of Democratic Functionalism', European Journal of Social Theory, 7: 1, pp. 5–25.

Eriksen, E. (1999), 'The Question of Deliberative Supranationalism in the EU', ARENA Working Papers, WP 99/4. At http://www.arena.uio.no/publications/wp99_4.htm. Accessed November 13 2006.

Eriksen, E. O. and Neyer, J. (2003), 'Introduction: Deliberative Supranationalism in the EU', in E. O. Eriksen, J. Christian and J. Neyer (eds), European Governance, Deliberation and the Quest for Democratisation. ARENA REPORT 2/03. ARENA/EUI: Oslo/Florence, pp. 1–22.

Eriksen, E. O. and Fossum, J. E. (2004), 'Europe in Search of Legitimacy: Strategies of Legitimation Assessed', International Political Science Review, 25: 4, pp. 435–59.

Eriksen, E. O. (ed.) (2005), Making the European Polity. Reflexive Integration in the EU. New York: Routledge.

Eriksen, E. O. (2006), 'Deliberation and the Problem of Democratic Legitimacy in the EU: Are Working Agreements the Most that can be Expected?' At http://www.arena.uio.no/publications/working-papers2006/papers/wp06_08.xml. Accessed October 15 2006.

Follesdal, A. and Hix, S. (2002), 'Why There is a Democratic Deficit in the EU: A Response to Majone and Moravcsik', *European Governance Papers*. At http://www.connex-network.org/eurogov. Accessed September 12 2006.

Grimm, D. (1995), 'Does Europe Need a Constitution?', *European Law Journal*, 1: 3, pp. 282–302.

Gutmann, A. and Thompson, D. (2002), 'Deliberative Democracy Beyond Process', *Journal of Political Philosophy*, 10: 2, pp. 153–74.

Habermas, J. (2001a), 'Why Europe Needs a Constitution', *New Left Review*, 11, pp. 5–26.

Habermas, J. (2001b), *The Postnational Constellation: Political Essays*. Cambridge: Polity, in association with Blackwell Publishers.

Hamelink, C. J. and Hoffmann, J. (2004, unpublished), *Assessing the Status Quo on Communication Rights*. Preliminary report. Amsterdam: University of Amsterdam.

Jakubowicz, K. (2004, unpublished), *Media Governance Structures in Europe*.

Kielmansegg, P. Graf (1996), 'Integration und Demokratie'. In M. Jachtenfuchs and B. Kohler-Koch (eds), *Europäische Integration*. Opladen: Leske and Budrich, pp. 47–71.

Kurpas, S., Meyer, C. and Gialoglou, K. (2004), *After the European Elections, Before the Constitution Referenda. Can the EU Communicate Better?* At http://shop.ceps.eu/BookDetail.php?item_id=1140. Accessed October 3 2007.

Kurpas, S., Brüggemann, M. and Meyer, C. (2006), *The Commission White Paper on Communication: Mapping a Way to a European Public Sphere*. At http://shop.ceps.be/downfree.php?item_id=1328. Accessed October 3 2007.

Mancini, P. (1998), 'Europe: The Case for Statehood. European Law Journal', 4: 1, pp. 29–42.

Mansell, R. & Nordenstreng, K. (2007), 'Great Media and Communication Debates: WSIS and the MacBride Report', Information Technologies and International Development, 3: 4, 15–36.

Obradovic, D. and Alonso Vizcaino, J. (2006), 'Good Governance Requirements Concerning the Participation of Interest Groups in EU Consultations', *Common Market Law Review*, 43, pp. 1049–85.

Risse, T. (2002), 'How Do We Know a European Public Sphere When We See One? Theoretical Clarifications and Empirical Indicators'. Paper prepared for the IDNET Workshop 'Europeanization and the Public Sphere'. European University Institute, Florence, February 20–22 2002.

Sarikakis, K. (2002), 'Supranational Governance and the Shifting Paradigm in Communications Policy-making: The Case of the European Parliament', in M. Raboy (ed.), *Global Media Policy in the New Millenium*. Luton: University of Luton Press, pp. 77–92.

Scharpf, F. (1999), 'Demokratieprobleme in der europäischen Mehrebenenpolitik', In W. Merkel and A. Busch (eds) (1999), *Demokratie in Ost und West*. Frankfurt aM: Suhrkamp, pp. 672–94.

Schlesinger, P. R. (1999), 'Changing Spaces of Political Communication: The Case of the European Union', *Political Communication*, 16, pp. 263–79.

Steeg, M. van de (2001), 'Rethinking the Conditions for a Public Sphere in the European Union', *European Journal of Social Theory*, 5: 4, pp. 499–519.

Stein, E. (2001), 'International Integration and Democracy: No Love at First Sight', *American Journal of International Law*, 95: 3, pp. 489–534.

Trenz, H. J. (2004), 'Media Coverage on European Governance: Exploring the European Public Sphere in National Quality Newspapers', *European Journal of Communication*, 19: 3, pp. 291–319.

Venturelli, S. (1998), *Liberalizing the European Media: Politics, Regulation, and the Public Sphere*. Oxford: Clarendon Press.

Walker, N. (2001), 'The White Paper in Constitutional Context'. At http://www.jeanmonnetprogram.org/papers/01/011001.html. Accessed October 3 2007.

Ward, D. (2004), *The European Union Democratic Deficit and the Public Sphere: an Evaluation of EU Media Policy*. Amsterdam: IOS Press.

Weiler, J. H. H. (1999), *The Constitution of Europe: 'Do the New Clothes Have an Emperor?' and Other Essays on European Integration*. Cambridge: Cambridge University Press.

Young, I. M. (2000), *Inclusion and Democracy*. Oxford: University Press.